Monograph Series on Modern and Contemporary Chinese Education
中国近现代教育文存系列丛书

Selected Works of Li Lianfang on Education

Li Lianfang

Translated by Yang Xinyao

Selected Works of Li Lianfang on Education
Author: Li Lianfang
Translator: Yang Xinyao
Language: English
Word Count (for space of all pages): 504 Thousand words
Publisher: Chicago Academic Press
Number of Pages: 596
ISBN: 978-1-965890-70-7

Publishing	Chicago Academic Press 5923 N Artesian Ave Chicago IL 60659
Email	contact@chicagoacademicpress.com
Website	http://chicagoacademicpress.com/
Book Size	6X9 inches
First Edition	October, 2025

Personal Profile

Yang Xinyao, Master of Arts in English Language and Literature, Associate Professor, Distinguished Teacher of Liaoning Province, Teaching Expert of Shenyang City, and Lead Instructor of a Provincial First-Class Undergraduate Course. Her research focuses on college English teaching and corpus-based translation studies. She has presided over six industry-collaborative and government-funded research projects in translation, as well as more than ten other provincial-level research projects. She has published over thirty academic papers and contributed to the development of national and provincial-level exemplary courses. She co-compiled the digital textbooks Energy and Power Engineering English: Viewing, Listening & Speaking and Energy and Power Engineering English: Reading and Writing. With years of part-time translation experience, she has substantial practical expertise in translation.

Contents

1925

1930

1931

1932

The Relationship Between China's Geography and the World

Now, among all the countries in the world, there are only a little more than fifty that can be titled as "powers." All those who are slightly stronger are eyeing covetously and craving eagerly, plotting to subjugate our country. Onlookers, when speaking openly about the current situation, all say, "China will perish, China will perish." Alas! In the 20th-century world, will the color of our country's map really change as expected by other nations? That is still far from certain. Even if the people of our country are lingering on the verge of extinction, like India and Egypt, with no patriotism or power to resist, can the spheres of influence of various countries really maintain their designated boundaries? I am afraid no one dares to draw a definite conclusion. Think deeply, when a pack of tigers devours meat, they will inevitably turn on each other. If they are equally matched, they will compete to choose the fattest and most delicious meat to devour; if their strength is uneven, the stronger ones will subdue the weaker ones and seize their spoils. Judging from today's situation and imagining the future changes, only if our country stands on its own feet can we possibly preserve peace in the 20th century. If things go on like this forever, with our country declining day by day and month by month, it may either be annexed by stronger powers or divided up by various countries. In either case, it will surely cause the heads and flesh and blood of all races in the world to be shattered amid the influences of European and American powers, leading to extremely fierce and cruel competitions. A pull on one hair can still affect the whole body, let alone the fact that our country's position is inherently closely related to the entire world.

Only Russia resolutely adopts despotic means to pursue imperialism without the slightest compromise. Standing dominant in the north, it shares borders with our country on three sides and takes advantage of the situation to march southward, like water pouring down from a high roof. It expands its territories and boundaries without the risk of interference from other countries, yet it also seeks to get its share of the Central Plains, which is the focus of universal attention, for gaining control of the Central Plains would be enough to dominate all powers and conquer the whole world. Therefore, it spares no effort in managing its dealings with the East. Let us not dwell on the past; just ask: what is the reason behind the fact that the Siberian railway has drained the nation's wealth without any concern? The Chinese Eastern Railway has also been completed in succession; the Beijing-Hankou Railway is secretly being hindered by it. In case of war, its dispatched troops can arrive on schedule. In the West, both Tibet and Xinjiang are completely under its influence. The vast land of China will soon be mostly within the reach of its military power. Even if Britain, Germany, and other countries occupy territorial rights, I fear they will be too far away to contend with Russia for supremacy on the mainland.

Then, can Japan be free from the fear that "when the lips are gone, the teeth will feel cold"? The territorial separation is but a mere strip of water. Both dwelling in Asia and belonging to the yellow race, among the numerous ethnic groups and countries, since they have successively been subordinated to the white people if China never achieves independence one day. Though Japan rose later to become a power, it has powerful Russia as its northern neighbor. The Korean Peninsula, within the reach of its influence, and Manchuria, occupied by Russia, are geographically intertwined. The world is ever-changing, and power is the only measure. As for the Liaodong Peninsula, which Russia had already occupied, Japan could still force it to withdraw; what about Korea, which is a joint protectorate? Its newly acquired territory of Taiwan in the south is separated from the Philippines, which the United States forcibly subjugated, only by the Bashi Channel. Now, the Nicaragua Canal has been resolved to be opened by the Americans, which has revolutionized the Pacific navigation routes. Commentators compare it to the Siberian Railway. China is at the center of competition in the Pacific. Those ambitious "fair-haired foreigners" are flocking eastward through this route, and Japan is actually bearing the brunt. When China is not yet partitioned, the storm it is buffeted by still shows a tendency to plummet. After China is partitioned, for a small island country in the Far East to long maintain the reputation of being of the same continent and race, it is extremely dangerous.

England comes next to Japan. Now, England and Russia are two powers that cannot prevail simultaneously; the strength of these two countries is entirely determined by the rights they hold in China. Moreover, China's survival or demise has an especially profound impact on England. For now, let us set aside the fact that England advocates commerce and that China's partition by various countries would hinder its interests in the "open door" policy. Let us compare the policies the two countries have recently implemented toward China. The rights to the railway from Shanhaiguan to Niuzhuang, which had already been seized by the British, were entirely handed over to Russia. Not to mention that when Russia occupied Lvshun and Dalian, England's protests and disputes were merely empty words. The Beijing-Hankou Railway, guaranteed by Belgium, is also controlled by Russia. If there is trouble in the Central Plains in the future, Russia can send its powerful troops directly to Hankou and occupy the heart of China. Even though England holds influence over the area north of the Yangtze River, it cannot rest easy. Furthermore, England's troubles are not merely confined to the scope of its holdings in China; it is particularly worried about the impact on its colony of India. The regions adjacent to India, such as Afghanistan and Baluchistan, are under British influence, and its policy of containing Russia can still be carried out as it wishes. However, along China's western borders, Russian territory is approaching day by day. If the southeastern regions of the Pamirs fall into Russia's hands, the entire northern border of India will be under the surveillance of Russian troops. Moreover, France, allied with Russia, could also launch an attack from Siam. As for the Indian natives, they have recently voiced many grievances and are not reliable for defense. Oh, England! Can it really not feel fear?

Both Germany and France have direct relations with China. The Yellow River region is an area where Germany operates. Guangdong, Guangxi, and Yunnan are areas where France operates. France adheres unswervingly to the policy of allying with Russia, aiming to hinder the progress of the British on the opposite side. Although Germany has a strong desire to act quickly to pursue its interests, because its country is close to Russia, it gets somewhat closer to Britain and Japan in dealing with China. It is an inevitable trend that one gains while the other loses. Therefore, for every inch of land that China loses, all the countries that occupy territories have vital stakes. Whether to preserve (the existing situation) or to carve up (China) is all determined by carefully considering their own country's position.

As a newly established state, the United States suddenly surged forward in the tide of national imperialism, focusing all its efforts on the Pacific Ocean. In one move, it annexed Hawaii; in another, it took over the Philippine Islands. With its foundational bases firmly established, it then sought to build the Nicaragua Canal to connect the maritime routes of the two oceans. It also encouraged Pacific navigation, established Pacific undersea telegraph lines, and prepared to compete with the powerful states of Western Europe for commercial influence in the East during the 20th century. Thus, the situation of the "Open Door" policy has transformed into one where colonial territorial expansion has become its actual implemented strategy. Since the United States has not designated any specific region in

China as its spheres of influence, it is inevitable that it will intrude into the spheres of influence of other powers to interfere with their rights and interests.

As for the countries bordering Russia—such as Turkey, Austria, Hungary, and the states of the Balkan Peninsula—all stand in the path of Russia's southward advance, their peril imminent by the day. Since Russia shifted the strength, it had once deployed in its western ventures to East Asia, the anxiety and fear of these states have undoubtedly diminished by countless folds. Yet no sooner had their border defense efforts eased than they turned their gaze eastward to the continent, watching as the powerful states eyed it covetously as if holding a map to carve it up. That insatiable Russia, with no remaining targets elsewhere and its old ambitions unforgotten, can it refrain from staging a comeback to fulfill its former aspirations? I fear that once alarms from the East spread like wind, these states will live in such dread that each day feels like their last.

In addition, among the various countries within Europe, some have newly emerged as independent states, some are in decline, and some are under the protection of others. All of them are managing their internal affairs and expanding their armaments to adapt to the rise of powerful and aggressive ethnic groups on the same continent, which is expanding outward. Suddenly, there is a country with the world's foremost natural resources, offering itself as a feast of delicacies. The major powers are so preoccupied with seizing it that they have no time for other pursuits. Moreover, bound by the concept of continental solidarity, they are reluctant to erode the mainland at first, for fear of weakening their own strength. Thus, these (weaker European) states have been able to take advantage of this gap to diligently govern themselves and plan for independence. However, with their foundations still unsteady, how can they withstand the onslaught of storms? If China were true to be carved up, with its branches and leaves already stripped away, the destruction would soon reach its roots. Looking eastward, the survival or demise of these (Asian) states would inevitably evoke a sense of uncertainty about their own future among all countries.

What is most alarming and terrifying, causing anxiety that danger may strike at any moment, is none other than the situation of Asian countries. It goes without saying that Siberia, Central Asia, and the Caucasus have already been taken by Russia; India and Burma by Britain; Annam by France; the Malay Peninsula under British rule; the Greater Sunda Islands under Dutch rule; the Borneo Islands as a joint British-Dutch territory; and the Philippine Islands under American rule. As for the so-called independent states—such as Korea, Siam, and Persia—how have they managed to survive to this day? It is because they border China. When the great powers began to expand their influence in China, they initially sought to occupy a foothold in the neighboring regions to consolidate their power. For the countries situated in between, with no clear dominance among the powers, the one that gained an early advantage prevailed, leading to inevitable mutual checks and balances to prevent any single power from monopolizing the interests. This mutual restraint exists solely for the purpose of expanding their influence in China. If China can no longer preserve its sovereignty, these three countries will either be occupied entirely by one power or partitioned among several. The vast Asian continent accounts for one-third of the world's total area and is home to half of the global population. Our China has long stood at the center of this continent, being its master for thousands of years. Yet now, not only can we not aid the crises of our fellow Asian states, but our own country is also lingering on the verge of collapse like a candle flickering in the wind, waiting to be fettered by the white powers. Looking at the map, I yearn to rally the passionate and valiant men of our continent, to rise up resolutely, and to save this lingering fate from total destruction.

Such is the situation of the Asian countries and the European countries, unable to assist each other amid these circumstances. The states bordering Russia are already struggling to look after themselves. The relations between the United States, Germany, and France amount to no more than vying for power and interests over territories; they harbor no regard or compassion for our country. Only Japan and Britain share deeply intertwined interests, for when the bond of mutual relevance runs deep, the strength of mutual support is bound to be great. Japan spares no effort in defending Korea, and Britain does the same for Turkey, devoting the full strength of their states to these endeavors. How much more intense, then, must their sense of urgency be when faced with the impact of events in our country, which strikes like the noonday sun or echoes like thunder? If they merely hide behind the name of "preserving" China to seize immediate gains, can this truly benefit the broader situation? I know not what policies the diplomats of these two states have formulated toward Qing China.

However, a state that seeks to stand by relying on others can never dominate the world; one that hopes for aid from others can never be saved from peril and ruin. Greece regained its independence by relying on the support of Britain, Russia, and France, yet its national power remained weak in the end. The United States broke away from Britain because every person possessed an ethos of independence, and now it has become a world power. Our country has such vast land, such a large population, and such abundant resources—with capable people to govern it, it could even unify the entire globe. Yet, the whole state remains muddled, sitting idle and waiting to be carved up like meat. The eighteen provinces have all been turned into colonial lands of white people; among the 400 million compatriots, many still linger in a dark and dismal cloud, gazing up at a sun and moon that seem to have lost their light. Alas, my anxiety knows no bounds! Without the rise of a powerful figure to inspire and revitalize the state, can we ever wash away the servility ingrained over thousands of years and stand alongside other civilized countries in the new world? I wish to plunge into the great oceans, surge up the tides of 19th-century Europe, pour them into the Yangtze River, let them flow through the Han and Mian Rivers, converge with the Five Lakes, then spread their ripples southward into the waters of Fujian, Zhejiang, Guangdong, and Guangxi, and northward into the estuary of the Grand Canal, crashing into the Yellow River basin—sweeping away all the filth upon our land, leaving behind a pure and clean territory as a homeland for the descendants of the Yellow Emperor. Are there countrymen willing to ride my waves and follow my current? Then take a draught from the Yangtze's flow!

Published in *Hubei Students' Circle*, Issue 1, January 1903.

The Relationship Between Geography and National Character

Unfolding the geographical records of the five continents, one observes that ethnic groups differ in their conditions, appearances, customs, languages, and preferences. In terms of the world as a whole, each continent is distinct from another; within each continent, each country is different from another. Even those who live in the same country and belong to the same ethnicity, if they reside in the north and south respectively, some may be strong and valiant, while others may be weak and effeminate, showing an extreme divergence. If this is not the influence of geography, what else could be the cause? However, from the perspective of geographers, the factors related to geography are not limited to one aspect.

The reasons related to terrain are as follows: initially, the people of mountainous countries, living amid vast deserts and connected high plateaus, with rolling hills and no thoroughfares for communication, make their homes in tents and move in pursuit of water and grass, engaging exclusively in plunder. From ancient times to the present, they have not yet advanced beyond the first stage of human evolution. As for those who are forced by powerful ethnic groups to abandon their lands and become like "raw barbarians (Sheng and Fan)" or "Miao and Liao" peoples, hiding in deep mountains and daring not to come out, gathering in caves and inhaling malarial vapors, they develop cruel natures. All these peoples cling to the unenlightened ways of ancient times and are unworthy of being discussed in terms of evolution. As for countries situated on the earth, surrounded by towering mountains, with slightly scarce natural resources and little human communication, the ethnic groups living their nurture qualities of simplicity, frugality, and endurance, yet tend toward narrow-mindedness. If there are exceptions, it must be because the influences they receive do not stem from a fixed type of terrain. Japan, as an insular country, has fostered in its people a strong habit of self-isolation, yet an ability to absorb foreign cultures, deep patriotism, but no capacity to embrace global structures. Switzerland, a state formed by attached plains, sees its eastern part inhabited by Teutonic peoples, whose temperament is full of forbearance, while its western part is home to Latin peoples, whose constructions tend toward luxury. In summary, those living in mountains are often ignorant of current affairs. Hence, the strategic locations of Ba and Shu (ancient names of Sichuan) have often been occupied by people from other regions to dominate the world, yet the local people are steadfast and daring to take responsibility. It is why the scholars of Hengyang and Hunan have become the heroes of the state.

Second, the people of the plain countries. There is no prosperous ethnic group or great cause in the world that does not arise from a vast and extensive geographical environment, though there are slight differences among them. For those attached to the mainland, I can cite examples from plain countries in Asia. From the horizon where the sun rises to where it sets, and from the mountain peaks where the moon emerges to where it dips, the wilderness stretches endlessly in all directions. The people are born here, grow up here, and die without interacting with outsiders. For this reason, they harbor the delusion of thinking themselves superior to all others and cling to the ignorant custom of adhering rigidly to ancient ways. Their communities are fragmented, the concept of ethnicity fades away, and they uphold the principle of universal harmony while lacking a deep sense of national consciousness. Thus, when conflicts arise, they are not with foreign races but among compatriots. Those who are not of their kind then take advantage of their weaknesses and loopholes to occupy their land. This is why China has repeatedly suffered humiliation at the hands of the Five Barbarians and the Tartars. As for those adjacent to the sea, I can refer to the plain countries in Europe. With winding harbors, scattered islands, and interlaced mountains and valleys, they are convenient for foreign trade and communication externally, and suitable for decentralized self-governance internally. The geographical environment they occupy is also relatively vast, so the people nurtured here are naturally open-minded. Moreover, shaped by the surging ocean currents, they have forged a lively, noble, independent, and unyielding European ethos. Their states always cherish hopes as boundless as the sea and tides, with an especially strong inclination for adventure. The calm and steady are inspired to become brave and resolute—this is why the Germans were able to unite in alliance and establish themselves. The enterprising are driven to act without regard for their own safety—this is why the French were able to sacrifice their blood and lives to purchase civil rights for the world. The plains inhabited by the Russians are even more extensive, so their nature is calm, resolute, profound, and vast, beyond comprehension. The great undertakings they have built remain unrivaled in the world.

Third, the people of island countries. Take those South Seas archipelagoes, for example. Formed by volcanoes and corals, they are scattered in fragments, too small to establish independent countries. The indigenous people there have been increasingly confined to preserving their species. I heard from explorers a few years ago that only one elderly woman remained—such cases are not worth discussing. What we should talk about are continental islands like Great Britain and Japan. Both stand out as archipelagic states in the sea, not connected to other landmasses. In this world, those with unique conditions will surely achieve unique results. Hence, the people of these two states are deeply committed to preserving their species and are passionately patriotic; they can remain unified without fragmentation, and their ethos of upholding justice and daring to sacrifice is renowned worldwide. Both are not too far from the mainland, and their geographical conditions are complete enough to stand firm like small continents. Constantly nurtured by ocean currents, they easily absorb cultures, then develop and elevate them. A clear proof is that Britain was the first in the world to create a constitution, and Japan was the first in Asia to bring a ray of light to political systems. However, those built on relatively narrow foundations are bound to have limited structures. Japanese elites have often worried about their people's inability to shake off their "island-dweller mentality." The British, though dominant in the world, adhere to a conservative philosophy—could this also be an influence of their geographical environment?

The reasons related to climate are as follows: In the torrid zone, products are abundant, and the materials needed by people are easy to collect. The clothes they wear do not need to be warm and thick, and the houses they live in do does not need to be solid. Those who find it too easy to make a living often struggle to develop their enterprising ethos, and their nature tends to be lazy. In frigid zones, all things are not prosperous. People spend the whole year working hard, barely enough to support their lives, and have no time for learning, so their nature tends to be dull and uncouth. In temperate zones, the cold and heat are balanced. People must take action to have food and clothing, so their nature is diligent, quick-witted, and brave. For all the inherent qualities of human beings, there is none that is not endowed by nature. The difference in climate actually holds the key to the deviation of character. By observing the traces of world evolution from this perspective, we can see that although both are land-attached plain countries, Siberia, due to its barrenness and cold, is not suitable for the growth of its people, and stupidity and stubbornness have become common customs. Although the knowledge of the Chinese people is not yet comprehensive, and they are still under the yoke of autocratic rule up to now, they organized a country thousands of years ago and nurtured civilization for the world. Generally speaking, if people developed early, they must have been blessed by nature. Egypt, India, Babylon, and other places, together with China, are all cradles of civilization, located in warm regions. It can be seen that the climate has a great influence on people. Among the sea-attached plain countries, France, with the most pleasant climate in Europe, mild cold and heat, and moderate rainfall, which is sufficient to nourish products, has fostered the habit of luxury and beauty among its people. Germany has a slightly colder climate, so its people are hardworking and enduring, not rigid about rituals, not fussy about goods. They are meticulous in doing things, which is incomparable to the impetuosity of the French. Moreover, Africa is surrounded by the sea on all sides, but it is called the "Dark Continent." The people there are cruel and mean, and they quarrel with each other. The whole continent is subordinate to the white race, and the indigenous people lie under them as slaves and cattle, killing each other until they perish. Europe is just a peninsula, but why, regardless of the size of the country, do all people have patriotism and unity, so that people of other races cannot conquer them? It is because the climate in Europe is mild, and it is easier for people to compete with natural forces. Although the cold in Northern Europe is strong, it is affected by the Atlantic Gulf Stream, so it is much milder than other regions at the same latitude. Most of Africa is located in tropical arid areas, which cannot support a good state. This is a natural trend.

What has been said above is a summary of the general aspects. Now, let's focus on the most significant elements that are part of the Earth and also related to humanity. To start with, rivers. There is no country in the world whose national development has not been aided by the functions of rivers. Regardless of the production and reproduction of people or the advancement of knowledge, they all take place along the banks of rivers. Even customs and human sentiments often vary with the local water and soil. Take our country as an example. The Yellow River in the north has turbid water, which cannot be used for washing, and there is always the worry of floods. The people there are mostly not neat or elegant, but they have a strong and bold ethos. The tragic songs of Yan and Zhao, and the farewells by the Yi River, are the representatives of their character. The Yangtze River in the south has clear and refreshing water, and the land is rich in scenic spots. The people there have a free and easy mind, a delicate nature, are full of ideals but lack practicality, thus forming a long-standing habit of being gentle and weak. Hand in hand on the river bridge, seeing off guests at the riverside, with the spring tides and autumn waves, their emotions interact with these scenes. Alas! Such famous rivers in our country, for thousands of years, have only produced materials for poems and paintings.

Last, volcanoes and earthquakes. For ethnicities where reason stagnates, although it is due to the weakness of human power, they are indeed largely hindered by natural phenomena. Even great rivers, high mountains, and vast deserts are enough to make those living among them feel terrified by the strangeness of such phenomena. How much more terrifying must the impact of volcanoes and earthquakes be on people's minds? This is particularly intense in Japan. Even in small villages with only a few households, people all worship incense and prostrate themselves before animal-shaped idols. Their so-called shrines, with towering ornamental pillars, often stretch for several miles. Although the trend of civilization has been introduced in succession in recent times, most people from the lower classes cannot break free from the old superstitions. For they always have the image of a volcanic or earthquake disaster hanging in their imagination and thus have to place their sincere prayers in such worship. The three countries of Italy, Spain, and Portugal are located in southern Europe, where there are more volcanoes and earthquakes. Their people are the most superstitious, and the power of the church is also strong. By analogy, the strong religious devotion of people is directly related to geography. There are other complex reasons, which are not easy to enumerate one by one, so we shall pass over them.

Published in *Hubei Students' Circle*[1], Issue 3, March 1903.

---

1 *Hubei Students' Circle* (also known as *Han Sheng* [Voice of the Han People]) was founded in Tokyo, Japan, in January 1903 by progressive Hubei students studying in Japan, including Liu Chengyu, Zhang Jixu, and Li Buqing (Li Lianfang). "It was one of the earliest-established and most influential revolutionary periodicals among the students studying abroad" and "the revolutionary periodical named after a province during the Xinhai period." (Ding Shouhe: *Introduction to Periodicals of the Xinhai Revolution Period*, Volume 1, People's Publishing House, 1982) Li Lianfang served as the chief editor of the "Geography Column" in this periodical. —Translator's note

Preface to *Lectures for Normal Schools*[2]

In the summer of the Renyin Year (1902), we went to Japan to study at a crash course for normal education, where we examined the general outline of their national education system and teaching methods. After eight months of study, we compiled the lectures we had attended and had them printed. In our humble hope, we aim to make this work a starting point (arrow shot, meaning pioneer) for education in our country, so that all who are interested in this field, by holding this book, may feel as if they were visiting schools in various countries, listening to the remarks of educators, and moving and conversing with them. Furthermore, we hope that those with aspirations in education, upon seeing this book, will collectively take education as their own responsibility, revitalize schools, cultivate citizens, and enable our state to compete with countries in Europe, America, and Japan. However, we must clarify. The principles of education are both profound and encompassing. Even educators who have researched them for over a decade still struggle to master them completely, so how can a hasty study of a few months allow us to fathom their depths? Moreover, our stay in Japan was short, and we did not fully understand the language. Relying on interpreters to conduct our studies inevitably led to misunderstandings. In addition, notes taken in haste resulted in the loss of 20-30% of the content, and when we occasionally supplemented them with materials from other books, we often worried about straying from the original meaning.

---

2 This book, consisting of four volumes, was jointly compiled and published in Tokyo in March 1903 by Hubei normal school students studying in Japan, including Huang Xing and Li Buqing (Li Lianfang). Its contents cover 15 categories: principles of education, outline of legal system, primary school education system, primary school teaching methods, educational systems of Germany, France, Britain and the United States, national pedagogy, types and systems of schools, normal schools, middle schools, outline of economics, outline of geography, outline of physics and chemistry, physiology and hygiene, extracurricular lectures, and visit notes. Due to its rich content, being compiled by Chinese people themselves, and having a great influence, its preface is selected here for readers' understanding. —Translator’s note

Furthermore, since the compilation was done by multiple people, there were inconsistencies in content and structure. Half of the terms used are borrowed from Japanese without time to translate their meanings. Given these shortcomings, it is undeniable that this book is far from perfect, and we feel regretful about it. Then, can this book be sufficient for practical use if we proceed with it? Education varies according to a country's national conditions and folk customs in its implementation. The educational system of the United States does not have to be the same as that of Britain, nor does Germany's have to mirror France's. It would be especially hard for a wise person to believe that adopting Japan's system rigidly in China would proceed without the slightest hindrance. Nevertheless, education in our country is only just taking its initial steps. We are like travelers walking at night without a candle or blind people without a guide. Under such circumstances, we have no choice but to learn from others to facilitate and guide the development of education. Japan is a country in the sharing continent and script, and its national conditions and folk customs are relatively close to ours. Drawing on the established educational practices of Japan for reference will be of some benefit to education in our country. The future of the school may perhaps derive a tiny benefit from it! Now that the printer has completed the work, I have therefore written these few words at the beginning of the book, first of all, to present them to the gentlemen who are concerned with education.

Recorded by Hubei Normal Students Studying in Japan on the 20th Day of the Second Lunar Month in the Guimao Year of the Guangxu Reign

General Theory of Teaching Methods for Various Subjects

1. The Essential Principles of Teaching

The function of education is mainly to develop an individual's physical and mental abilities and cultivate excellent citizens. In terms of its implementation, it is generally divided into three items: teaching, training, and nurturing. To elaborate: teaching is to impart knowledge and skills; training is to cultivate sentiments and will, so as to form good habits; nurturing is to care for the body and improve health. However, these three functions are interrelated, and the scope of teaching is the widest. If one does not demonstrate essential knowledge and skills through teaching or imparts them but with improper methods, the learners will not understand the ways of self-cultivation. Even if training and nurturing are applied alone, they will surely conflict and not integrate with each other. This is why teaching methods are of great importance.

Primary education is the starting point of a person's education. It is of the greatest significance and yet the most difficult to implement. Article 1 of the Regulations on Primary Schools issued by China's Ministry of Education states: "The aim of primary education is to pay attention to the physical and mental development of children, lay the foundation for national morality, and impart the knowledge and skills necessary for life." The reference to "developing physical and mental abilities" embodies the meaning of nurturing; "laying the foundation for national morality" embodies the meaning of training; and "imparting necessary knowledge and skills" embodies the meaning of teaching. Moreover, the emphasis on "paying attention to children" in relation to physical and mental development, "laying the foundation" in relation to national morality, and "being necessary for life" in relation to knowledge and skills are all based on the fundamental purpose of education. They represent a policy for guiding primary school education, formulated by considering the actual situation of children and the realities of being a citizen and making appropriate adjustments based on specific circumstances. The teaching methods compiled here are intended to elaborate on the implications of this policy. What this compilation discusses is solely teaching methods. However, we must first study what the purpose of teaching actually is. Regarding the interrelationship between teaching, training, and nurturing, is it that training and nurturing are only carried out outside of teaching as supplements, or can teaching itself contain the functions of training and nurturing? The view advocated here is that the latter is also feasible. For example, in moral education, we demonstrate practical application; in Chinese language classes, after explaining the text, we often take the words and deeds related to character contained therein to explore children's insights—this is embodied training in teaching. Similarly, selecting materials that are not excessive and explaining them in accordance with natural principles—this is embodying nurturing in teaching. Next, we must study: is the purpose of teaching merely to impart knowledge and skills, and is that all it can achieve? In terms of form, imparting knowledge and skills is indeed a function of teaching, but in terms of its essence, teaching must pay attention to the development of children's physical and mental abilities and lay the foundation for national morality. This is what is meant by teaching often relies on training and nurturing to supplement its functions. Therefore, in the implementation of teaching, to achieve its purpose, the first question is: what kind of materials should be taught? The second question is: what methods should be used to teach them? Let us first discuss this from its fundamental purpose.

One view holds that education should focus on imparting knowledge, arguing that those receiving education must acquire and become proficient in the necessary knowledge and skills regarding personal character and civic obligations so that they can establish themselves in society and lead an independent life in the future. This is known as substantialism. Another view emphasizes the cultivation of mental faculties, asserting that education should promote the mental development of learners, sharpen their perception, refine their observation, clarify their memory, balance their emotions, and elevate their aspirations. In this way, learners can apply what they gain from teaching to practical situations. This is referred to as formalism.

An overemphasis on substantialism leads one to value only extensive knowledge, disregarding whether children's minds can absorb it. It is like presenting a medley of fine dishes—overindulgence will inevitably cause stagnation. An overemphasis on formalism, on the other hand, ignores the nature and quantity of teaching materials, focusing solely on teaching methods and their impact on learners' minds. This results in either hollow content or a hodgepodge of trivialities. It is comparable to choosing food merely for its digestibility; if it lacks sufficient nutritional value, it will never serve the purpose of nourishing life. Both approaches have their strengths and weaknesses, and they should complement each other in a balanced way. On one hand, we should adopt substantialism to select appropriate teaching materials; on the other hand, we should embrace formalism to refine teaching methods. Additionally, we must arouse interest in knowledge acquisition, ensuring that concepts remain etched in learners' minds without fading. Only then can the goal of teaching be achieved.

2. Teaching Materials

To achieve the goal of teaching, one must rely on materials. Generally, this involves three aspects: selection, arrangement, and connection. These are discussed separately as follows:

2.1 Selection of teaching materials

Materials for primary school textbooks must be those that are truly suitable for primary school teaching before they can be adopted. There are three criteria for this: (1) They should be knowledge necessary for life; (2) They should be appropriate for moral cultivation and civic education; (3) They should be compatible with the level of children's physical and mental development.

Once the criteria are established, the method for selecting materials should be based on the things surrounding human life. Here are the points that require attention: to begin with, as the world evolves, things in society are becoming increasingly complex. Therefore, the selection of materials must adapt to the development of culture. Second, since individuals differ in their localities, life circumstances, and occupations, education must be tailored to each person, and there must be special orientations in teaching. Moreover, the Ministry of Education has announced its educational tenet: "Emphasize moral education, supplemented by pragmatic education and military-civilian education, and further complete education through aesthetic education." This statement of tenet is also something that those selecting materials should pay attention to.

Before the 19th century, educators across Europe engaged in extensive discussions on the issue of school curricula. Today, the subjects have become increasingly refined. Japan has drawn on the strengths of various countries, and our country has adopted such practices. The Regulations on Primary Schools stipulate that the subjects for lower primary education include Moral Education, Chinese, Arithmetic, Handicrafts, Drawing, Singing, and Physical Education. Female students have an additional Needlework course. For upper primary education, additional subjects are added, such as National History, Geography, Science, Agriculture or

Commerce, and English or another foreign language. These are the subjects that teachers must follow.

Regarding the content of each subject, according to the research of recent educators, primary schools should emphasize object teaching, and textbooks are almost unnecessary. However, given that teaching techniques in our country are underdeveloped, the use of new-style textbooks is indeed a preliminary step toward improving teaching. Therefore, the selection of materials for textbooks deserves in-depth discussion. It is true that most schools adopt textbooks approved by the Ministry of Education for teaching, which seems to leave teachers with little room for research on the selection of teaching materials. Nevertheless, due to differences in local conditions, variations in students' family occupations, and the imperfection of textbooks available in the market, there are quite a few instances where teachers need to add, delete, or revise content during actual teaching. For this reason, it is essential to fully understand each of the criteria for selecting materials listed above.

2.2 Arrangement of Teaching Materials

There are various methods for arranging teaching materials. The best approach is to integrate both linear progression and spiral recurrence approaches. However, it is necessary to appropriately allocate the materials based on their inherent nature, the developmental level of children, and the teaching hours of each school year to achieve suitability. The related items roughly include three types: to start with, the curriculum schedule; second, the detailed teaching syllabus; third, the timetable.

The allocation of each subject in lower and upper primary schools to each school year, along with the stipulation of the teaching level for each subject and the weekly teaching hours, is called the curriculum schedule.

The primary school curriculum schedule formulated by the Ministry of Education is now recorded at the end of this volume for easy reference.

Breaking down the annual proficiency levels as per the curriculum schedule, the teaching materials for each subject are first allocated to each school year, then to each semester, and further to each week—this is called the detailed teaching syllabus. When formulating the detailed teaching syllabus, the following points should be noted:

(1)Based on the curriculum schedule and textbooks, select items in accordance with the criteria for choosing teaching materials;

(2)It should be adapted to the organization of classes, local conditions, and the characteristics of boys and girls;

(3)Follow the inherent order of the materials;

(4)Pay attention to the connection with other subjects and the coherence between the previous and subsequent content within the same subject;

(5)The selected teaching materials should correspond to the seasons;

(6)Determine the amount of teaching time according to the difficulty level of the materials;

(7)Allow time for review during each section and vacation periods;

(8)Revise it every year based on practical experience.

The allocation of weekly teaching hours for each subject to individual days is called a timetable. The following points should be noted when setting a timetable:

(1)Core subjects and those that require intense mental effort should be taught when students are mentally alert; during periods of fatigue, subjects that involve physical activity or bring joy to the mood should be arranged.

(2)Subjects demanding mental effort and those that do not should be interleaved in the schedule.

(3)The same subject or subjects of similar types should not be taught consecutively for multiple periods.

(4)The class hours for each subject should be appropriately distributed across the calendar days with intervals between them.

2.3 Connection of Teaching Materials

The method of connecting teaching materials lies in following the inherent order of each subject, identifying points of connection without undermining their independence so that the knowledge acquired by children is systematic and well-organized. Furthermore, it enables children to sort out old concepts from the knowledge they have already gained, understand newly acquired knowledge, and form a central synthesis method, which is not far from being a forced integration. For example, science and arithmetic, history and geography, each has a close relationship; the teaching materials of Chinese include various aspects and are actually connected with all subjects; as for the Moral Education course, it takes advantage of the convenience of teaching various subjects, selects appropriate opportunities to cultivate children's moods, and yet remains the core of all subjects.

In implementing this method, two points should be noted: 1. Follow the inherent order of each subject, ensuring their progression is gradual and mutually connected so that during teaching, the relationship between previous and subsequent content is clearly understood. 2. Record the connection between different subjects in the detailed teaching syllabus to facilitate practical application.

3. Teaching Methods

Even if the teaching materials are excellent, if the teaching methods are inappropriate and fail to enable learners to comprehend them one by one, the goal of teaching will ultimately never be achieved. Now, the matters that should be addressed regarding methods are recorded as follows:

3.1 Teaching Segment

Based on the principle of the natural activity of children's minds, the sequence in which teaching materials are presented is called the "teaching segment." The framework of teaching segments was initially established through Herbart's theories, and his disciples further developed these ideas, with Rein achieving their full elaboration. This refers to the so-called five-stage teaching method: preparation, presentation, comparison, generalization, and application. Subsequently, through the experience of practical educators, various new formats were developed for the convenience of teaching. However, despite differences in form, the general framework remained unchanged. Regarding the formats prevalent in China in recent years, some merged the two stages of comparison and generalization into the presentation stage, calling it the three-stage teaching method; others extracted the item of "indicating objectives" from the preparation stage and explicitly highlighted it at the beginning of the lesson. Adopting the latest format, we divide it into four stages: preparation, presentation, practice, and organization, among which presentation and preparation are of primary importance. This teaching segment has been researched accurately both in practice and theory and is universally applicable to both knowledge-based and skill-based teaching materials without exception.

3.1.1 Preparation

The purpose of preparation is to arouse children's receptivity, organize their old concepts, and guide them towards new knowledge. The main teaching form in this stage is question and answer. The matters to be studied in this stage are as follows:

(1)Indicating Objectives

The indication of objectives should be simple, clear, and easy to comprehend. The methods of indication can be verbal explanation, display on a board, or demonstration with teaching aids. For the convenience of teaching, the indication can be done either at the beginning of the preparation stage or at the end of it.

(2)Reviewing the taught content

In this review stage, mere recitation should be avoided; instead, questions and answers must be used to arouse students' memories.

(3)Arousing existing knowledge

Existing knowledge may refer to commonly seen things or intuitive perceptions of the natural world.

3.1.2 Presentation

The purpose of a presentation is to impart new things, with the primary goal of enabling children to clearly comprehend them. Its methods vary according to the nature of the teaching materials: sometimes by showing real objects or standards, sometimes by demonstrating model observations, sometimes by delivering sequential lectures, and sometimes by providing step-by-step explanations. Above all, it is crucial to arouse the self-directed learning motivation of the learners. If the teaching materials can be divided into several sections, learners must be guided to focus their attention and achieve a thorough understanding of each section. Then, they can gradually move on to other sections and finally integrate all sections into a coherent whole. If the presentation is done properly, the assimilation of knowledge, as well as the cultivation of will and sentiments, can all achieve effective results. Hence, presentation is regarded as the core part of teaching.

3.1.3 Practice

The purpose of practice is to enable children to truly grasp knowledge and, primarily, to develop the ability to apply it. The methods vary according to the nature of the teaching materials: sometimes having them recount what has been taught, sometimes having them practice by imitating the demonstrated models, or posing problems for them to solve.

3.1.4 Arrangement

The purpose of an organization is to restore children's physical and mental calm after they have experienced intense focus through comprehending the teaching content. Its methods also vary according to the nature of the teaching materials. The points to be noted are as follows:

(1)Reading and explaining textbooks

Have students read the textbooks, understand the key points of each section and chapter so that the teaching content can be integrated.

(2)Study of Teaching Content

Depending on the nature of the teaching materials, one may use question-and-answer methods, create diagrams or charts, or take notes on the key points.

(3)Refinement of Teaching Content

After repeated practice, further, organize and polish it. This is most applicable to skill-based teaching materials; however, it can also be used in such aspects of Chinese language teaching as reading aloud, model reading, and correction.

The four stages of preparation, presentation, practice, and organization are originally based on Herbart's five-stage teaching method. However, slight adjustments and expansions have been made to their application after the presentation stage, making them most suitable for practical use. Nevertheless, during teaching, due to the varying nature of teaching materials and the differing moods of children, it is essential to adapt flexibly according to circumstances rather than rigidly adhering to fixed formats. A common flaw in China in recent years is that when compiling lesson plans if a subject adopts the five-stage method, every lesson from the first to the last in the textbook strictly follows the five-stage format; similarly, if a subject uses the three-stage method, all lessons adhere to that rigidly. Compilers ignore practical needs, and teachers merely go through the motions according to the plans, which obscures the true meaning of teaching. It should be understood that the sequence of teaching stages is a principle to be followed in teaching, not an immutable formula for lesson plans. For the convenience of teaching, it is acceptable to merge the practice stage into the presentation stage and use only three stages: preparation, presentation, and organization. Alternatively, one could integrate the organization stage into the presentation and practice stages, using only two stages: preparation and presentation. Furthermore, if the teaching materials for one lesson can be divided into several class periods, the materials within a single period, if subdivided into smaller sections, can each apply the stage-based methods as appropriate. Truly understanding the essence of these stages and applying them skillfully depends on the individual teacher—this is not something that can be grasped by those with only superficial understanding.

Carrying out teaching in accordance with the sequence of teaching stages, if not planned in advance, will inevitably lead to confusion and impropriety at the time of instruction. This is why lesson plans are important. There are two types of lesson plans: detailed plans and outline plans. Detailed plans are suitable for student teachers during their practical training, while outline plans are used in regular teaching. After all, during teaching, it is difficult to predetermine the teacher's questions and the students' answers. If one seeks excessive detail and completeness, such plans often cannot be implemented in practice. Therefore, the lesson plans used in daily teaching only record the materials in each teaching stage and the order in which these materials are presented. As for elaboration and expansion, they are to be carried out flexibly according to the circumstances at the time.

3.2 Teaching Methods

Teaching methods are the ways to convey teaching materials, i.e., the external manifestations of the teacher's initiation and the students' reception. Generally, they are divided into two categories: indoctrination and inspiration. There are five types of indoctrination methods: demonstration, modeling, lecture, explanation, and interpretation; there are two types of inspiration methods: questioning and task-setting. They are recorded as follows:

3.2.1 Demonstration Method

Showing real objects, specimens, models, pictures, etc., or conducting experiments to enable learners to observe their phenomena is called demonstration. This method is applicable to all subjects, but it is mainly used in science. The points to be noted when using this method are as follows:

(1)When having learners observe, they should proceed from simple to complex, so that they can observe in detail.

(2)It is necessary to point out the observation points so that learners can focus on the parts necessary for teaching.

(3)During observation, it is essential to carefully examine the learners' motives, ask questions in a sequential manner, provide supplementary explanations for unclear points, and correct their mistakes.

(4)Adding explanations during observation can be done simultaneously for simple things; for slightly more complex ones, explanations should be given after the observation.

3.2.2 Modeling Method

When a teacher demonstrates a model for learners to imitate, it is called modeling. This method is mainly used in subjects such as painting, singing, tailoring, and gymnastics; it is also applicable to calligraphy practice and pronunciation methods in Chinese language teaching. The points to be noted when using this method are as follows:

(1)The model demonstrated by the teacher should be completely clear, extremely skillful, and flexible, so as to enhance the learners' interest in imitating.

(2)When demonstrating, the key points should be explained first, and during the explanation, learners should not be asked to imitate at the same time.

(3)Learners should be allowed to practice repeatedly until they reach a proficient level.

3.2.3 Lecture Method

The lecture method employs vivid conversations to make children feel as if they are witnessing or experiencing things hand, thereby stimulating their imagination. The ways to present phenomena include: 1. metaphor; 2. realistic description; 3. mimicry; 4. personification; 5. exaggeration; 6. exclamation; 7. interrupted narration and continuous narration. This method is commonly used in the presentation stage of various subjects, and is particularly suitable for moral education and history. However, if teachers overuse it, learners will often remain in a passive position and lose their initiative. The points to be noted when using this method are as follows:

(1)Educational language should be clear and precise, and the cadence, pitch, and speed of the voice should be appropriately regulated.

(2)Real objects, specimens, pictures, and other materials should be utilized, or key points should be written on a board, to draw special attention from learners.

(3)The content of the lecture should be divided into segments. For each segment, important points should be highlighted and reiterated as appropriate, ensuring that learners achieve a clear understanding.

(4)Questions should be interspersed during the lecture, or inquiries should be posed at the end of each segment, to remind learners to pay attention.

3.2.4 Explanatory Method

The explanatory method uses logical reasoning to present facts, thereby stimulating learners' thinking. It is most applicable to teaching materials related to concepts and principles and is mainly used in arithmetic, science, moral education, and rhetoric. The points to be noted when using this method are as follows:

(1) Explanation should primarily use the inductive method. If children still fail to understand, the deductive method can be used to prove the conclusion. However, for older children, the deductive method can be used directly.

(2) It is necessary to rely on questions and answers. Based on the results of the questions and answers, the teacher can then make a decision in a few words.

3.2.5 Interpretation Method

The interpretation method aims to enable learners to read texts and understand their meanings. These meanings are divided into two types: form and substance. The form includes distinctions between speech, characters, and articles; the substance varies in interest across different subjects. The interpretation of meanings varies according to children's levels and the nature of teaching materials. Its application methods are as follows: in the beginning, translating into other languages; second, intuitive indication; third, showing characteristics; fourth, comparing and proving with other languages; fifth, enumerating included things; sixth, showing usage examples. This method is most applicable to graphic and textual materials. The points to be noted when using this method are as follows:

(1) Regarding the order of interpretation, when the characters, words, or articles are complex and difficult, or when the reading comprehension ability is weak, learners should first be enabled to grasp the substance, and then move on to the characters, words, and articles. If the goal is to cultivate their reading ability, they should follow the order of reading the characters, words, and articles while also being guided to understand their substance.

(2) Before and after interpretation, children should be asked to recite and practice the characters, words, or articles several times, so that they can understand them more easily and acquire solid knowledge.

3.2.6 Questioning Method

The questioning method is used to arouse children's initiative and is applicable to all subjects, being the most valuable among various teaching methods. During teaching hours, this method should be used in the following situations: to begin with, when arousing children's attention; second, when evoking children's existing knowledge; third, when forming concepts and discovering laws; fourth, when consolidating knowledge and honing skills; fifth, when organizing teaching content; sixth, when examining teaching effectiveness. However, the way of questioning should not be such that it wastes time and energy without achieving practical results. The points to be noted when using this method are as follows:

(1) Questions should preferably be completion questions, i.e., presenting part of the content first and asking learners to complete the rest (for example, "Where is the capital of China?"). Yes-or-no questions (such as "Is Beijing the capital of China?") and alternative questions (such as "Is water a solid or a liquid?") leave no room for learners to think and are not suitable for setting as questions. However, this method can be used occasionally when asking about difficult-to-understand things, preparing for proving something, or only asking underachieving students to answer.

(2) The scope of a question should be clear and accurate. One question should be limited to one answer and must not contain multiple meanings.

(3) The language used in questioning should be simple and clear. Both unnecessary words and insufficient expressions must be avoided.

(4) In terms of the tone of questioning, the tone should be stronger for the key points that need to be asked about.

(5) Questions should be adapted to the intellectual level of the learners; they should not be too difficult nor too easy.

(6) It is advisable to ask the whole class first and then designate one student to answer. Difficult questions should be asked to top students, and easy ones to underachievers. The observation should be thorough, and the distribution appropriate.

The questioning method is intended to arouse children's initiative, so there must also be appropriate handling of children's responses. The points to note are as follows:

(1)Responses should be made in a loud voice so that the entire class can hear them;

(2) If a response is unclear in wording, incomplete in meaning, mixed with redundant words, or involves irrelevant matters, it should be corrected;

(3) Regardless of whether a response is correct or not, one must not reprimand the child, as this would dampen their enthusiasm;

(4) One should not be satisfied merely because one or two students can answer; instead, it is necessary to check whether the entire class has understood;

(5) When a student gives a response, it is important to determine if they truly understand. If there is doubt that the answer was a lucky guess, one may either ask for the reasoning again, have them cite specific examples, or rephrase the question in a different form;

(6) The evaluation and correction of responses can be done either by the teacher themselves or by having the children assess each other;

(7) If a response is completely wrong or a student is entirely unable to answer, it is necessary to examine whether the cause lies with the teacher or the student. If the cause is with the teacher, it must be because the question was too difficult or unclear, in which case the question should be revised and rephrased. If the cause is with the student, those who are inattentive

should be roused, those who are timid should be encouraged, and those who are slow should be guided.

3.2.7 Task-Setting Method

The task-setting method is one in which the teacher poses questions and has the learners work out the answers by themselves. Like the questioning method, it arouses children's initiative, with the whole class practicing uniformly as its main form and individual inspection as its purpose. This method can be used in all teaching activities, but it is most suitable for arithmetic and Chinese composition. The points to be noted when using this method are as follows:

(1) When setting tasks, teachers should examine the practice system of each teaching material, pose questions in a sequential manner, neither skipping levels nor leaving gaps.

(2) While children are practicing, teachers should patrol around the children's seats, paying attention to each one, and provide appropriate guidance to underachieving students.

(3) The evaluation and correction of answers should follow the same principles as in the questioning method.

(4) When checking answers, merits should be praised, and shortcomings should be corrected.

3.3 Review

The effect of review is not only to enable the acquired knowledge to be firmly remembered, but also to cultivate the habit of self-study. However, purely mechanical review is prone to causing weariness. It is necessary to make children observe various aspects of teaching materials, various teaching methods, so that they can connect with what they have already learned and generate new meanings. There are two ways to use it: one is to use it before teaching new content, and the other is to set aside special time to review what has been learned. The methods are as follows:

For use before teaching new content, there are two methods. First, at the beginning of the teaching period, have students review the previous lesson or lessons related to the current one. Second, at the beginning of the teaching period, have students preview the content of the current lesson based on what they already know.

For review during specific times, there are four methods. First, at the end of each segment, allocate an appropriate amount of time for review. Second, set aside several periods within a week for reviewing previous lessons. Third, at the end of a semester or school year, arrange a certain amount of time to review all the lessons learned. Fourth, identify key points and have students review them at home outside of regular class hours.

Excerpted from Li Buqing (Lianfang): *New Methods of Teaching Various Subjects*, published by Zhonghua Book Company in early June 1914.

Should pragmatism be adopted in today's school education?[3]

During the late Qing Dynasty, I put forward some suggestions on pragmatic education. Nowadays, those advocating education have raised the issue of pragmatism and are collecting opinions. I hereby express my absolute approval. I will discuss it in the following sections: 1. On the trend of pragmatic education; 2. On pragmatism; 3. On why school education should adopt pragmatism; 4. Opinions on those who criticize pragmatism.

1.On the Trend of Pragmatic Education

When people engage in learning, they should focus on practicality. The fundamental purpose of education is to cultivate practical individuals. In times when collective wisdom was undeveloped, what people learned might have followed trends rather than addressing the essential needs of life. Even as the world progressed gradually, science remained underdeveloped. Although school education aimed to enlighten people with knowledge, it was not entirely suitable for practical use. It is this kind of practical learning that, along with the advancement of the world and in response to the needs of life, has gradually evolved to perfection.

Education in ancient Europe took practicality as its goal. For example, in Sparta of Greece, the practice of martial arts, writing, and arithmetic was mainly aimed at meeting daily needs, so the cultivated individuals were suitable for the practical use of the Spartan state. Moreover, the Sophists of that time focused on the intellectual aspect, intending to make all skills conducive to personal life. Although their doctrines were somewhat

3 This article won the prize in the "New Research on Pragmatic Education" prize essay contest organized by the editorial office of *Education Magazine*, and was included as the article in the magazine's supplementary issue "Special Issue on Pragmatism." — Translator's note

speculative and extravagant, it is universally acknowledged by educators that they initiated the application of knowledge to practice. Roman education emphasized practicality exclusively. When adopting Greek culture, only grammar and rhetoric among the subjects attracted scholars' attention. Additionally, since cultivated learning should be suitable for specific professions, schools were closely connected with the practical world. European education first took this path starting from Rome. However, what was called practical learning at that time seems far from impressive from today's perspective.

Education in the Middle Ages was dominated by the church. Although it managed to transcend social classes, the excessive prevalence of superstitions made the cultivation of people incompatible with the life of the present world. As industry and commerce gradually developed, municipal schools emerged, which were quite inclined towards vocational education. Even though their teaching methods were not suited to practical needs, their role in inspiring research on modern industrial education is something we must not forget.

Since the Reformation, the guiding principle of education has advocated humanitarianism. Although its proponents focused exclusively on internal cultivation, they sought to embrace all forms of learning and, based on the principle of "utilizing resources to enrich life," manifest the glory of God. This thus paved the way for the development of science. Even the Jesuits of the Catholic Church, adapting to the times, shifted their emphasis to substantive content. However, education at that time remained far removed from practical reality.

From that point onward, science advanced increasingly. Due to research into material substances, practical science, and scholarship became the prevailing trend of the times. Moreover, a group of educators emerged prominently during this period: Francis Bacon founded empirical logic, establishing experiment and observation as the criteria for acquiring knowledge; Comenius conducted fundamental research on teaching and created the natural theory of education; John Locke developed the theory of sensationalism. Consequently, the idea of object teaching was highly praised by scholars. Thus, education after the 17th century aimed to inspire individuals' rationality and cultivate their ability to apply knowledge. As a result, the selection of teaching materials grew ever closer to practical needs. It not only focused on the pursuit of knowledge but also drew people's attention to the realities of human life. For this reason, the fundamental planning of education shifted toward individualism, and driven by concerns about individual development, the trend in education leaned toward utilitarianism. This is why pragmatic education flourished day by day.

After entering the 19th century, greater emphasis was placed on the substantial content of education. All disciplines became increasingly refined; meanwhile, in line with the progress of the times and adjusted to local conditions, they were appropriately modified and balanced to achieve proper proportions. Through Pestalozzi's experiments on teaching methods, object teaching became prevalent worldwide, and even management and training began to align with the ways of dealing with people and matters in daily life. Up to the present day, the concept of social education has gradually flourished, and the implementation of education is entirely based on practical scopes. Some conduct segmented research on industrial education, while others discuss life education as a whole. Thus, practical materials and methods have increasingly provided us with resources for examination. However, looking at the current situation, elementary education tends to emphasize the practical-science orientation, while higher education has not yet broken away from the form of humanism.

From this perspective, European education only began to have practical value after the development of science. The emphasis on practicality originated from individualism and ultimately focused on social issues. The advocacy of individualism, on the one hand, stemmed from the development of psychological teaching, which necessitated research on individual personalities; on the other hand, it arose from the advancement of national education, which must fully address the way people should be. At that time, the proponents argued that by implementing education based on this principle, everyone could be cultivated into a useful person. Initially, this was not based on the fundamental proposition of national livelihood. As for the recent discussions on education by scholars, although they have argued from the perspective of livelihood, they have supplemented and corrected the flaws of previous doctrines based on earlier principles. All selected teaching materials and implemented moral education are oriented toward practicality, enabling individuals to contribute to society, each being self-reliant without conflicting with one another. This is what is called social education.

2. On Pragmatism

The essence of emphasizing practicality in education has been fully elaborated above. However, to specifically put forward "practicality" as a term and establish it as an educational doctrine, a systematic theory cannot be formed without a dedicated treatise. A detailed discussion cannot be conducted here, but if we want people in our country to understand what pragmatism is, the following issues are the ones we urgently need to discuss.

Looking at the various theories on pragmatism published in *Education Magazine* (Volume 5, Issue 7)[4], Mr. Huang said: Since people cannot abandon their families or sever ties with society, education should cultivate

4 The time was October 1913. In this issue, Huang Yanpei (1878-1965)'s *A Discussion on Adopting Pragmatism in School Education* and Zhuang Yu (1876-1938)'s *Adopting Pragmatism* were published, which aroused considerable repercussions in the educational circle. — Translator's note

them to possess the ability to be independent in family and social life and to appropriately interact with others. Mr. Ying said: What is pragmatism? It is simply that the education children receive at school should be suitable for the needs of social life. These provide an unclear explanation of pragmatism, but if we want to further discuss it, we must note that the scope of practicality is very broad. How should we guide its orientation? This is what Pernath meant by "toward which direction education should proceed," and what Rein meant by "it is necessary to clearly indicate the content of cultivating the mind." For example, what is the foothold of "needs of life", "ability to be independent", and "appropriate interaction"? From which aspects should we cultivate the qualities of "being suitable for life", "possessing abilities", and "being able to interact"? For now, instead of exploring the extent of various theories to put forward supplementary arguments, we will focus on fundamentally studying the definition of practicality.

In approaching this research, the question we must ask is: although the theories of modern educators all converge on practicality, their fundamental footholds differ. Is the pragmatism we now adopt impartial among these various theories? If so, we must reconcile them by selecting only their valid points for adoption—namely, from moralism, we take what aligns with practice; from naturalism, what suits understanding; from humanism, what broadens knowledge and insight; from utilitarianism, what contributes to happiness; from realism, what promotes "utilization for livelihood improvement." These are integrated into a single goal of pragmatic education, akin to the proverbial practice of "testing all options and choosing the best." However, if we arrange them hastily and combine them arbitrarily without establishing a definite order or clarifying the primary-secondary relationships, can this truly constitute a coherent goal? This is what Rein rejected and what scholars engaged in scientific research have failed to acknowledge.

Once the foothold of practicality is properly established, another issue that must be addressed first is whether what we advocate now is purely material-oriented. The development of pragmatic education is indeed rooted in the results of material research, yet the true essence of practicality does not lie in exclusively emphasizing material things while neglecting the spiritual aspect. In the primitive stage of human life, people were only concerned with issues of food, clothing, and shelter. But today, with frequent social interactions and the widespread advancement of collective wisdom, one cannot survive without morality, knowledge, and skills that meet the needs of the times. Therefore, the so-called pragmatism means that the materials and methods used in moral education, intellectual education, and physical education are all tailored to the practical needs of the present world. It is by no means purely material-oriented, and this reason is quite clear. The reason for emphasizing material things is that, in the reform of textual education, material objects are necessary as resources to enrich the content of teaching materials. Moreover, the improvement of teaching methods requires object teaching to enable children to understand things clearly and easily. If emphasizing material things is considered a loss of spiritual activity, such education would be nothing but mechanical, let alone practical.

The tendency toward materialism is merely a superficial observation. If we argue from the fundamentals, then is the foothold of practicality individual-oriented or state-oriented? Educational nationalism, as a purely political form of education, was once practiced in Sparta. Taking this as a standard, anything inconsistent with the state's demands would be completely eliminated or ignored. In the extreme, this would leave no room for individual free activity, which is fundamentally incompatible with the true essence of practicality. Hence, there is good reason why, despite the prevalence of national education in Europe, educational policies do not solely adopt nationalism. Educational individualism aims to enlighten people on how to be human; educational socialism seeks to cultivate individuals fit for a sound society. Though their methods of cultivation differ, they converge on the same truth. What we must examine is this: in the early 18th century, educational individualism, while establishing principles for education based on empirical reasoning, aimed merely to allow the natural development of human instincts, not to fully address practical needs. It was not until Herbert Spencer advocated utilitarianism, asserting that education should guide individual life, that practicality became established as the sole goal of education. Even Herbart, who argued that education should begin with forging a strong will, ultimately tied it to the sphere of life. This individualist doctrine remains prevalent to this day. The orthodox tradition of social education originated with Pestalozzi, focusing on communal life. Today, this idea has flourished, with the new education movement advancing by leaps and bounds. However, its proponents are divided: the philosophical-sociological school, as advocated by Natorp, conflates pure ideals with practical ones, seeking to encompass all education within will education, emphasizing moral training to the exclusion of all else; the religious-sociological school, as advocated by Willmann, rejects social egoism, focusing instead on cultivating inner virtue, developing natural abilities, and sustaining life's future needs. Such ideas, leaning toward spiritualism, remain unproven in their practical applicability. It was Durkheim who identified the promotion of happiness as education's purpose, bringing ideal cultivation closer to practical needs. Bergmann further argued, based on practical research, that societal life cannot prioritize individual happiness alone but must center on human activity, defining education's goal as fostering children's vitality to fulfill life's tasks. Most modern advocates of social education follow this view, shaping educational trends by observing real life. Thus, recent European education increasingly leans toward social orientation, though individualism retains significant influence. Both doctrines warrant study. Whether practicality should be rooted in society or the individual depends on analyzing China's realities through theory and fact—a question that cannot be elaborated here.

The foothold of practicality, whether individual-oriented or social-oriented, can be adopted as one wish. However, another question arises: should the method of education start from the objective perspective or the subjective perspective? From the perspective of individualism: Comenius, for instance, based education on observing external things and natural functions, taking objectivity as the principle. Rousseau argued that the development of our minds follows a certain order and should be nurtured in accordance with the laws of nature, which is a subjective principle. Herbart regarded morality as the highest goal, starting from the study of subjective will. Spencer first explained human life appropriately and made the function of will correspond to it, starting from the study of objective facts. As for Pestalozzi, his educational purpose—enabling everyone to support themselves—was the same as Spencer's; his advocacy of object teaching was consistent with Comenius' view. However, his cultivation method, which focused on developing human nature, started from the subjective perspective, differing from the two aforementioned scholars. From the perspective of socialism: Durkheim emphasized subjective emotions, taking the happiness of individuals and the whole as the ultimate goal of education; Bergmann valued objective activities, considering the ultimate goal of education to be that human activities can promote social progress. Nowadays, since Bergmann's theory is regarded as orthodox by social school, there is almost no objection to starting education from the objective perspective. Although the educational doctrines advocated in modern times all lead to practicality, they reach the realm of practicality through other doctrines rather than setting practicality as the direct goal. Therefore, when discussing individualism and socialism specifically, their starting methods indeed differ between objective and subjective. If practicality is taken as the standard, it is advisable to start from the objective perspective regardless of whether one adopts the individual-oriented or social-oriented approach. Why? The essence of practicality lies in the needs of life, which are nothing but practical morality, practical knowledge, and skills. Even the understanding acquired in teaching is derived from various senses, with traceable signs. If we start from the subjective perspective, we will be holding ideals divorced from reality, which will inevitably run counter to practical needs.

It might be argued that the above issues have little to do with the practice of education. Some may say, "We simply adopt pragmatism as our doctrine; in education, we merely need to ensure that all teaching materials and methods conform to practical needs, without concerning ourselves with whether they are individual-oriented or social-oriented, objective or subjective." However, the scope of practicality is extremely broad, and educators hold differing perspectives based on their varied observations. As a result, it becomes difficult to establish consistent standards for selecting materials and applying methods. It is easy to talk in vague terms, but implementation brings countless difficulties; general discussions may seem to agree, yet in-depth inquiries reveal a multitude of divergences. If we follow such arguments to their extreme, we might end up with a situation like ancient education, where rhetoric was deemed practical, or where studying classics and practicing stereotyped writing for imperial examinations was considered "practical" because it could lead to official careers. Even if that is not the case, superficial new scholars, with their half-baked understanding, might pile up bits of mechanical knowledge and cram them into students' minds, thereby misleading our promising youth.

What is called “practical education” would, in the end, drift further away from the true essence of practicality. Is this not a cause for concern? Regardless of the doctrine adopted, education must aim to cultivate an “ideal person,” shaping learners into such a model. Without a clear standard, how can we foster this ideal person? A disorganized education can never achieve this goal. This is why I have raised the above issues, to discuss them one by one with those who endorse pragmatism.

With the foothold of pragmatism established, let us compare it with various modern educational theories. Among the theories similar to pragmatism, terms such as “practicalism”, “lifeism”, and “activism” found in Japanese works mostly originate from the trend of social education. They also reflect the insight that the essence of industrial education cannot be universally applied, thus giving rise to various issues. To start with, in terms of terminology: The term “activity” has an overly broad meaning. All human behaviors are expressions of activity, but merely referring to “activity” cannot determine whether it is good or evil, true or false, beautiful or ugly. Since it lacks the inherent nature of truth, goodness, and beauty, it cannot be established as an educational doctrine. The term “actuality” lacks specific content; simply mentioning “actuality” provides no essential standard. Although the term “life” has meaning, its form easily gives those who seek comfort an excuse. Unlike these, the meaning of “pragmatism” includes the function of life and embodies perfect content, encapsulating all the capabilities of education in these two characters. As for industrial education, it is insufficient to encompass the scope of education. Real-science doctrine cannot fulfill all the functions of education; even the utilitarianism prevalent in the 18th century, which leaned toward egoism, is not suitable for today’s society. Only pragmatism, advancing with the progress of the times, responding to the needs of life, and guiding its orientation, can truly be said to be universally applicable and without flaws.

There is another point to be made: education can be observed from two perspectives: one is the substantive aspect, and the other is the formal aspect. The former can be called material, and the latter methodological. The perfection of pragmatism, viewed from the substantive aspect, means that in teaching, there is no bias toward material things, and in training, there is no bias toward emotions. From the formal aspect, it means that when imparting knowledge and skills, students do not feel troubled by the difficulties; instead, interest is aroused, and all learning can be applied to practical situations. However, these are just their distinctive features. As for its fundamental purpose, it lies in the ability to apply knowledge to real things and situations, enabling those receiving education to enhance their knowledge on the one hand and develop their individual characteristics on the other. If anyone practices this doctrine, I am certain that each school will achieve practical results corresponding to its own context, and each student will gain practical benefits suited to themselves. The effects will be visible in no time.

3. School Education Should Adopt Pragmatism

The fundamental issues of a state are tied to education. To formulate a guiding principle for a country's education and drive its advancement, one must both respond to global trends externally and examine the state's actual conditions internally. As the global trend in education is increasingly moving toward pragmatism, observing our country in light of this trend and exploring its history and current situation leads us to recognize that pragmatism is indeed an urgent priority. Let us elaborate on this.

3.1 Modern European civilization originated from the development of science. In our country, since the collapse of the ancient school education system, rulers have adopted a policy of keeping the people ignorant. Those who passed the imperial examinations specialized in poetry, fu (a prose-poem form), and stereotyped essays. This practice has prevailed for thousands of years, to the extent that people have almost forgotten what true learning is. With the influx of Western trends, Chinese people have gradually gained a vague understanding of practical sciences. However, despite more than a decade of educational development, we have merely borrowed Western knowledge without understanding the essence of practicality. As a result, those educated in schools, at the lower level, lack the ability to be self-reliant, and at the higher level, lack the ability to apply their knowledge. If we do not address this now, our industry and commerce will never thrive, and how can we survive in the world? This is the first reason, from the perspective of academic development, why we should adopt pragmatism.

3.2 The progress of education in various countries starts with educational reform. Our country has long been biased toward textual education. There have been those who claim to be erudite scholars, proficient in classics and skilled in literary composition, yet unable to recognize daily utensils or understand the format of ordinary documents. As the saying goes, "Scholars are the most useless," which indeed points to this phenomenon. Since the abolition of the imperial examination system, the content of schools seems to have changed slightly. However, the method of object teaching has not been studied, and not all things are taught through practical experience. Thus, although rote memorization has been abandoned, new knowledge cannot be fully absorbed, and students gain no real insights, which is no different from the past. The subjects in newly established schools are indeed based on foreign models, and there must be one or two useful textbooks. Yet, while foreigners use them to cultivate capable talents, our country shows no signs of progress. Could this be due to the failure to improve teaching methods? This is the second reason, from the perspective of teaching methods, why we should adopt pragmatism.

3.3 Generally, the establishment of a state must be based on its inherent characteristics, and it is the duty of education to develop these characteristics. The order and chaos of successive dynasties in our country have always been linked to the rise and fall of academic research. Therefore, despite repeated changes, the foundation of the state remains unshakable because the profound meanings of Confucian ethics are deeply imprinted in people's hearts. Once aroused, people can rise up to resist the rampant trends. This is the national essence that must be preserved. Although the world is increasingly evolving, and some articles of traditional morality may need to be selected or rejected, the emphasis on practical implementation remains unchanged through the ages. Rein said: Ethics clarifies the purpose of human life, from which the purpose of education can be determined. The relationship between education and ethics is so close, and practical education takes practice as its duty. To develop the inherent characteristics of the state, we cannot seek it elsewhere. This is the third reason, from the perspective of preserving national essence, why we should adopt pragmatism.

3.4 Our country is vast in territory and rich in resources, known as the first in the world. However, minerals are left in the ground without being mined, and forests are left in the mountains without being cultivated. Even the profits from silk and tea, which were once the main exports, are now declining day by day. On the other hand, the number of imported industrial products is increasing, leading to the decline of commerce and the poverty of the people, which is worsening day by day. With such abundant resources, why is the people's livelihood so difficult? If our people do not want to survive in the world, it is fine; but if they do, everyone must dedicate themselves to practical sciences, be able to utilize natural resources, and engage in appropriate occupations, so that the foundation of the state will not be shaken. However, this cannot be achieved without cultivating such abilities in schools. This is the fourth reason, from the perspective of developing national strength, why we should adopt pragmatism.

3.5 In a republican country, citizens stand on an equal footing. However, only when everyone has a certain occupation can politics be free from chaos; only when everyone has appropriate knowledge can laws be free from obstacles. In our country, the imperial system has just collapsed, the will of the people is extremely weak, and ambitious people manipulate them. If we do not cultivate the foundation, chaos will never end. To safeguard the republic, if we do not guide the people's life orientation through practical education and bring them into the orbit of order, the danger of collapse will be imminent. This is the fifth reason, from the perspective of maintaining the national system, why we should adopt pragmatism.

3.6 After the great French Revolution, people's minds were unstable. The rulers advocated industrial education as a way to relieve the situation, and its effects were remarkable. In our country's era of autocracy, suppression was prevalent, scholars lost their duties, and people lost their occupations. When suppression reached its peak, it led to extreme chaos. In the late Qing Dynasty, due to poor governance, the country fell apart. After the revolution, orders collapsed. The government has no way to reconcile, and the people have the desire to act recklessly, which is even more serious than in France. The root cause of the chaos lies in the difficulty of making a living. If this chaos continues, we will all perish together. This is the sixth reason, from the perspective of remedying people's minds, why we should adopt pragmatism.

Considering these six reasons, it is abundantly clear that education should adopt pragmatism. Not only can general education, when guided by this principle, cultivate well-rounded citizens; vocational education can also use it to produce much-needed technical skills. Even specialized and higher education, by applying this doctrine, can meet the needs of the times. Based on the current situation of our country, priorities can be determined, and decisions on adoption or rejection can be made by carefully weighing various factors. As for achieving in-depth learning and complete discipline development, that can be expected decades later when the country is highly developed. For the current education in our country, adopting pragmatism is truly a fundamental and sensible approach.

4. Views on Criticisms of Pragmatism

The main thrust of the criticisms from opponents of pragmatism is that it neglects the spiritual while emphasizing the material. However, as I have argued earlier, pragmatism is not purely material-oriented. The claim that the more one acquires material knowledge, the more one strays from national morality is utterly unfounded. National morality evolves alongside knowledge. When comparing the concept of morality among barbarians with that among civilized people, which is more complete? The evolution of humanity is indeed rooted in the development of material civilization, as evidenced by numerous historical facts. Let us take Japan as a case in point. Japanese education, in terms of material development, was not yet highly advanced; it is only in the past decade or so that education has leaned slightly toward material aspects. If we examine Japanese educational history, we can ask: Has the morality of the Japanese people—their way of conduct and sincerity in patriotism—progressed and become more widespread today compared to the early Meiji period? If, as critics claim, material knowledge is a medium for eroding morality, then all sciences should be abandoned, and we must revert to the old Four Books and Five Classics to achieve our goals. Would this not mean that school education worldwide has gone drastically astray? Even if this is not the original intent of the critics, their logic implies that we must follow religious figures in exalting faith to lure people's conscience, or Confucianism in focusing solely on inner reflection to inspire innate goodness. But let us ask: Can ordinary people, without developing the ability to make a living, be urged to become sages and worthies? Factually, this is impossible—I am certain of it. An overemphasis on material things is indeed inappropriate, but so is an overemphasis on the spiritual. It may be argued that promoting morality can rectify today's troubled minds, yet there is no established standard for which aspects of old ethics should be preserved and which of new ethics should be adopted. To put such a doctrine into practice, ethics must first be defined; otherwise, education cannot proceed. If we adopt pragmatism, not only will practical knowledge not be neglected, but moral standards can also be based on practicality. Thus, the significance of pragmatism is closely intertwined with the essence of morality.

The relative proponents advocate that national education and talent education should advance along separate paths, arguing that pragmatism may be inappropriate for talent education. In terms of their distinctive features, higher education and general education do have different purposes; however, their fundamental aim in cultivation is none other than to foster the same kind of personality, so adopting the same doctrine is indeed inappropriate. Moreover, given the current situation of our country—with strained financial resources and underdeveloped scholarship—not only should we plan for national education in advance, but talent education is even more urgently needed. To cultivate talents for today, we must weigh priorities, determine the principles for selection and rejection, and strive for practical application. How urgent and important is the pragmatism we now adopt? There is no need to cite the fact that in contemporary European education, elementary education advocates realism while higher education upholds humanism, and without examining their historical traditions, use this to cast doubt on the feasibility of pragmatism. As for the arguments of the proponents, some of their assertions are also incorrect, but I shall not discuss them here.

When I had finished drafting this article and was about to submit it, I happened to read a magazine where a certain Mr. X argued that pragmatism should take "life" as its standard. As I have previously discussed, the scope of pragmatism is broad, and determining how to guide its principles requires careful consideration. While Mr. X and I do share common ground in studying the content of pragmatism, I have some reservations about taking "life" as the standard. The term "life education" carries significant value in recent translations of Western works and Japanese writings. The pragmatism advocated here is indeed derived from life education. However, the reason for not adopting "lifeism" as the term is not only that the form of the word "life" is less comprehensive than "pragmatism," but also that its meaning is less precise and relevant. This can be seen from my arguments. Mr. X states: "Education for humans is education for life; learning for humans is learning for life." European educators have indeed made similar points. Those who advocate this view are mostly reacting to the hypocrisy of conventional education, thus proposing this idea as a correction. Although recent discussions on education have focused on life issues, when defining education—whether from a social or individual perspective—the core remains cultivating the perfect way of being human. It is acceptable to say that one cannot be fully human without adapting to life, but it is incorrect to claim that merely being able to live constitutes the perfect way of being human. If we divide human life into spiritual and physical aspects, and formally define "life" as preserving the physical body, then the reproduction of animals is also a function of life—yet we cannot say that life is exclusive to humans. To claim that "education is for life" and "learning is for life" leads to contradictions: some well-educated people may meet untimely deaths, while some uneducated people may survive in ignorance. How, then, can ordinary people who do not understand noble life comprehend the idea that "learning leads to survival, while not learning leads to extinction"? Fundamentally, those who sacrifice their lives for virtue abandon physical life to preserve spiritual life—this precisely fulfills the purpose of "education for life." This shows that the meaning of "life" is broad, and methods of cultivation cannot be reduced to simplistic explanations. How, then, can a "life standard" adequately define the function of pragmatism? I understand that the concept of "life" here refers to survival of the fittest in an evolving world: adapt or perish. By definition, pragmatism excludes anything unsuited to the present age. Rather than adopting a "life standard" requiring such elaborate explanations, "pragmatism" itself is more concise and clearer in meaning. Furthermore, Mr. X provides little discussion on why higher education (beyond general education) must adhere to a "life standard." It is also questionable whether all learning in higher education is related to "life." This is why some critics hold opposing views, as seen in contemporary European education: elementary education emphasizes realism, while higher education retains elements of humanism. Mr. X also argues: "The scope of life varies in breadth, and pragmatism must be pursued according to time and place." But if life is the standard for pragmatism, yet pragmatism is determined by the varying scope of life across time and place, then pragmatism becomes the standard for life—a contradiction that becomes clear when examined logically. I suspect that opponents and critics may mistakenly equate pragmatism with recent theories of life education, seeing no difference between them. Hence, this discussion: if "life" is taken as the standard, counterarguments become difficult. I append this clarification here.

Published in the "Pragmatism Issues" special supplement of *Education Magazine*, Volume 6, July 1914.

Introduction to the History of Education

Section 1 The Main Idea of the History of Education

The history of education is an account of how past education has undergone changes and developments over time to reach its current state. The evolution of all things has causes and effects that can be traced. Education is the foundation of a state and the source of all cultures. Although the education systems of European countries originated from ancient Greece and Rome, China had already advanced into a cultural era at that time. Most of the countries now called "powerful states" were still in a state of ignorance back then. Over the past few hundred years, education has flourished in Europe, to the extent that there are almost no illiterate people in these countries, and the knowledge imparted is all practically applicable. Driven by this trend, even Japan, our eastern neighbor, which once learned from China, now advocates Europeanization to strengthen its state. As a country with an earlier-developed civilization, China, however, lags behind other states in terms of people's wisdom and morality. This is not a result of a short period but has deep-rooted causes. Nevertheless, the educational ethos of ancient times is still worthy of being recorded. By reviewing the education systems around the world and examining the traces of their changes and developments, we can find models for improving today's education. This is why the history of education is compiled and written.

Section 2 The Essentials of the History of Education

To determine the essential facts of education, one must first clarify the scope of the history of education. To begin with, the history of education is different from the history of civilization. The history of civilization examines the origins and development of all cultural relics, institutions, and regulations of an era. The history of education, however, is defined solely by the influences exerted by education. Second, the history of education differs from the history of educational theory. The history of educational theory explores theories and methods from an academic perspective and traces their evolutionary trajectory. The history of education takes this as part of its materials but does not focus on how specialized skills are cultivated; its purpose is to enable educators to understand the strategies of guidance. Based on these distinctions, the essential facts of the history of education are as follows.

2.1 Social Trends

The trends of education in various countries are constantly influenced by their national political climates and customs. Therefore, the implementation of education either looks outward to the world and avoids being confined to parochialism or fails to examine the country's own situation and falls into rash advancement. To adapt measures to the times, it is particularly important to learn from the accumulated ills of society and formulate policies in response to the needs of the times. For example, Confucius taught loyalty and filial piety, and Mencius strictly distinguished between righteousness and profit, both aiming to uphold the moral values of their time. This is why those engaged in education should observe social trends.

2.2 Educational Systems

The unification of education in a country must be based on the formulation of an educational system. Without a fixed educational system, even the most perfect education cannot be expected to be implemented nationwide. This is why many countries adopt a compulsory system for national education. However, once the educational system is promulgated, due to the varying circumstances in different regions, the methods of implementation need not be identical. Different political views may lead to different approaches to education, but they can ultimately achieve the same goal through different paths. Therefore, it is necessary to explore the reasons behind educational laws and regulations, the status of school facilities, the adoption of textbooks, and so on.

2.3 Theories and Undertakings of Educators

All those who can establish new theories and accomplish new undertakings must possess appropriate attainments. When they first initiate their efforts, with their effects not yet evident, they may inevitably encounter criticism from the whole world. Only by maintaining an unyielding ethos can they make their theories flourish. The new education we enjoy today is none other than the spiritual heritage of educators throughout history. Therefore, regarding the theories of various educators—whether they elaborate on academic principles or summarize experiences—all those that are sufficient to influence an era must be thoroughly understood. As for those who dedicated their lives to educational undertakings and can serve as an inspiration to future generations, their stories must also be recorded.

Section 3 The Benefits of Studying the History of Education

The main ideas and essential facts of the history of education have been stated as above. It is evident that those engaged in studying education should research the history of education. The benefits of such research are listed as follows.

3.1 It enables us to understand the actual effects of education

It is a well-known fact that the tendencies of a state are shaped by education. However, without examining it through history, we cannot truly grasp its practical effects. In the Han Dynasty, the emphasis on Confucian classics led to the prosperity of Confucianism; in the Tang Dynasty, the focus on imperial examinations made scholars accustomed to stereotyped writing. In Europe, the Reformation spurred the development of science. Where educational advocacy lies, academic changes follow suit, and the popular mood and customs of a time also evolve with the tide. This is why those who read history are deeply aware that educational policies must not be implemented erroneously.

3.2 It helps clarify the trends of education

In ancient times, when collective wisdom was undeveloped and livelihoods were simple, education focused on textual learning, and those receiving education were mostly from the middle and upper classes. As communication became frequent, collective wisdom advanced, and competition for livelihoods intensified, practicality became essential for application, and universal education became necessary for survival. Thus, practical education and national education emerged simultaneously in modern times. Those who followed this trend prospered, while those who opposed it declined. Reading the world history of education allows us to grasp this general picture.

3.3 It enhances knowledge of education

Educational theories and methods emerge as truths only after extensive research by numerous people. Studying the history of education allows us to inherit the spiritual legacy of past generations and apply it. Moreover, objective facts can greatly supplement subjective research. Observing the successes and failures of ancient people, as well as the true nature of how social affairs either hinder or assist education, serves as a mirror for self-reflection.

3.4 It cultivates the character required for education

To engage in practical education, one needs not only educational knowledge but, more importantly, the character befitting an educator. There is no better way to cultivate such character than by taking ancient sages as models. Reading the biography of Wang Anshi can inspire one to be calm and profound; studying the works of Zhu Xi can encourage one to pursue learning. Hence, Mencius, by privately following Confucius' teachings, continued the Confucian tradition; Pestalozzi, after reading Rousseau's works, developed the resolve to dedicate himself to education. As the Book of Songs says, "The high mountain inspires awe; the noble path urges emulation." Admiration leads to inspiration, and inspiration leads to diligence, as if ancient sages were brought to life in the same room.

Section 4 The Purpose of This Compilation

To synthesize the educational theories of the East and the West, and to compile the historical records spanning thousands of years, one must engage in specialized research to grasp their true essence. Now, if we intend to outline the key points in a short volume, guide the national education of today, and provide reference for primary normal schools, it is essential to have a clear orientation to ensure practical application. Therefore, I put forward several principles here for research purposes.

4.1 Emphasis on the Modern Period

The compilation of history is generally divided into three periods: ancient, medieval, and modern. Tracing the origins, ancient history is indeed not to be overlooked, but modern education is truly the trend of today's education and is particularly closely linked to formulating policies for improving future education. Europe's national education began to take shape only 200 years ago. China's education, influenced by Buddhism during the medieval period, underwent a drastic transformation. In recent times, with the influx of Western learning, there has been a slight opportunity for reform; moreover, due to the convenience of sharing a written script with Japan, China has been greatly influenced by it. To ensure that the trends of new education and China's traditional education merge seamlessly, enabling the people to discard their conservative habits without incurring the criticism of blindly following foreign ways, attention must be paid to the history of modern education.

4.2 Emphasis on Reference to National Conditions

Prussia, after suffering a recent defeat, vigorously implemented national education and thus avenged the humiliation inflicted by France. France, seeing the large number of vagrants after the Revolution, focused on industrial education and thus stabilized the restless public sentiment. All such measures, adapted to the times, have been implemented by various countries with clearly evident effects. Looking back at our country: how does our national situation compare to that of Prussia during the period of French occupation? How does our social mood compare to that of France during the Revolution? As the Book of Songs says, "The stone from another mountain can be used to polish jade." If we wish to obtain such a polishing stone, how can we fail to seek a remedy that addresses our specific illness?

4.3 Emphasis on Research for Primary Normal Schools

The way of education is profound and extensive; the politics and scholarship of a nation can all be traced to their origins here. Those studying the history of education should, on the one hand, grasp its overall framework and, on the other hand, seek insights based on what learners are accustomed to. Most of China's ancient educators spoke of educating adults. In contrast, every educator in Europe over the past century began with primary education. This point of difference lies at the core of education. Primary normal schools are intended to train teachers for primary schools; primary education is the foundation of education and, indeed, the foundation of the state. By focusing on this, understanding the changes and developments in global education, one can clearly recognize one's own responsibilities.

Excerpted from Li Buqing (Lianfang): *A New System of the History of Education* [5], first published by Zhonghua Book Company in early May 1915.

5 The book is divided into four chapters: *Introduction*, *Education in Our Country Before the Maritime Ban*, *The Trend of New Global Education*, *Education in the Late Qing Dynasty*, and *The Educational System of the Republic of China*. By March 1922, it had reached its 13th printing. The review comment from the Ministry of Education stated: "This book narrates the rise and fall of education in China and foreign countries, as well as the similarities and differences in academic studies, mostly using comparative arguments. Moreover, it comprehensively covers the discussions of recent years, showing elaborate craftsmanship..." (*Chinese Educational Circle*, December 1916)

The Responsibilities of Students at School

1. Regarding the Rules at School

A school having rules is like a country having laws. They are established for the entire school, not for any individual; they are set up to maintain order among students, not to flaunt the school's authority. For us, regarding the rules, first of all, we should regard them as a public constraint. Violating the rules means going against public will. Second, they should be taken as a standard for cultivating habits. No matter how one's will is expressed, it must follow a certain scope to avoid overstepping boundaries. As habits become second nature, in future social interactions, one will naturally abide by the country's laws and social conventions. Third, adherence to rules should not rely on coercion. Laws exist to make up for the deficiencies of morality. If we practice morality earnestly, we can freely act within the bounds of laws even without the need for legal constraints. If one abides by the rules only out of fear of punishment, or refrains from breaking them only because of external interference, then the foundation of morality is unstable. Even if one manages to follow the rules by luck, their will is not firm and will eventually collapse. Understanding these three points, one will know how to encourage oneself. Once becoming a teacher, one will have grasped more than half of the way to train children.

2. Regarding the People at School

2.1 Towards Teachers and Elders

A student's moral growth and academic progress depend entirely on the guidance of teachers and elders, who take on the educational role in place of parents. Teachers rejoice when they see us diligent and quick-witted and strive to guide and encourage us when we are dull or lazy. Such is the dedication and sincere affection with which teachers treat students—

their hearts are weary from effort, and their feelings are especially earnest. When students reflect on this, it is only reasonable to respect, love, and obey their teachers. With respect comes no contempt; with love comes no resistance; with obedience comes sincere faith in what is learned and respect for teachers' instructions. Understanding that one should respect, love, and obey teachers also teaches educators the way to inspire such reverence, affection, and compliance.

2.2 Towards Schoolmates

Regardless of differences in intelligence (whether sharp or dull), ability (whether strong or weak), or circumstances (whether wealthy or poor), all schoolmates should be treated with equal affection and without prejudice. One must not bully or envy others, as this would undermine the bonds of harmony. School is a microcosm of social life. If one cannot transcend petty biases among classmates, how can they navigate a complex society without deceit or conflict in the future? Those in charge of student management should pay special attention to this.

2.3 Towards Visiting Educational Officials and Guests

Visitors who are educational officials or members of educational organizations should be received with proper courtesy. Such courtesy should follow the instructions of the school administration: excessive arrogance breeds conceit, while excessive deference borders on flattery—neither is appropriate. For visiting parents, siblings, or relatives of classmates, courtesy should be guided by clear roles and boundaries. Confusing roles lead to misplaced intimacy; ignoring boundaries leads to inappropriate affection. For example, guiding parents into restricted areas of the school violates these boundaries.

2.4 Towards School Staff

In general, students should handle school chores themselves. Only when students are too busy or unable to do so should school staff assist. Though their work may seem humble, school staff have their own responsibilities and must not be looked down upon. Scolding or humiliating them is especially inappropriate.

3. Regarding the Objects at School

3.1 Understand Property Rights

One has the right to use things that belong to oneself; one has no right to use things that do not belong to oneself. Even if something is not exclusively owned by oneself or others but is for public use, it should be preserved for public benefit. Mistakenly exercising rights—whether abandoning one's own rights or infringing on others' rights—is not a proper way to handle property. This principle is particularly important to understand in society, and schools are where such understanding begins. Let us categorize things as follows: one's own property, others' property, and public property.

One's own property: One should cherish and preserve it; others bear no responsibility for it. Carelessly defiling or damaging it, or allowing others to take it without inspection, is inappropriate—even if it harms no one else, it damages one's own property.

Others' property: One cannot use it arbitrarily, let alone damage it. In the past, Zilu aspired to share his car and fur with others until they wore out, without regret—but this applied only to things he owned. One cannot cite this as a precedent for using what belongs to others.

Public property: Since it is for public use, no single person can appropriate it. Everyone, including oneself, must have the intention to preserve and cherish it. It must not be used privately or shirked as the responsibility of someone else. For example, the flowers and trees planted in the school, as well as the stored books, specimens, and equipment—all students in the school are responsible for preserving and cherishing them. One cannot mindlessly waste or willfully damage them, claiming, "This has nothing to do with me."

3.2 Value Material Resources

All things produced to meet human needs have their corresponding value. Wanton waste not only harms financial resources but also constitutes a severe squandering of natural gifts. Therefore, one should set limits on school supplies and all necessities related to clothing, food, and shelter, maintaining the fine tradition of frugality.

4. Regarding the Responsibilities

Humans are of the same kind as me, and we indeed have responsibilities to fulfill towards them. As for all things in the world, although they cannot be compared to humans, if they come into our sight, we cannot say they have nothing to do with us. Extending the heart of loving those of the same kind to other species, we must have compassion for other animals. Birds, beasts, insects, and fish all have life. Those that are used by humans should certainly be treated with compassion; even those that cannot be used by humans, if they are not harmful to humans, should not be killed or harmed. However, loving creatures is not like the Buddhist precept of abstaining from meat.

The Book of Rites says, "Do not kill living beings without reason," and *Mencius* also said, "A virtuous person keeps away from the kitchen." This is specifically to nurture one's compassion. If we rely on things to nourish our bodies, it is naturally something that cannot be prohibited. As for eliminating harmful creatures, it does not conflict with the compassion for creatures at all. Just as in the case where "when beasts became increasingly oppressive to people, the mountains and marshes were set on fire" (a reference to ancient stories of taming nature), people still praise such efforts to this day.

Those that harm people should be eliminated; those that do no harm to people must be protected with greater responsibility. This applies to animals, needless to say. As for plants, if their resources are sufficient to benefit human practical use, or their forms are sufficient to provide people with enjoyment, we should cultivate them to ensure their growth. In Yueling (the lunar calendar guide in ancient China), it is stipulated that in the first month of spring, logging trees is prohibited, nests must not be destroyed, infant insects, unborn creatures, and young birds must not be killed, and eggs must not be smashed. All these are ways to fulfill the responsibility of protection.

Not only that, we should especially make use of all things to promote the civilization of society. For example, raising chickens and silkworms must follow proper methods; hides, horns, teeth, and furs should each be put to their respective uses. Similarly, the raw materials of plants, the properties of inanimate objects, and natural phenomena—all of these should have their natural powers harnessed to serve the needs of human life.

Another point that deserves attention is cherishing public property. Cherishing public property means not only refraining from damaging it but also treasuring and protecting it. Among public properties, the most important are ancient artifacts, which embody the spiritual essence of a state's civilization. For instance, historical sites and scenic spots can inspire people's admiration, while broken steles and ancient relics can facilitate research and verification. We should collectively protect such items to prevent them from decaying. Ancient inscriptions on metal and stone, as well as legacies of virtuous predecessors that are carefully preserved, should be stored in libraries, museums, and similar institutions to be shared with those who appreciate them, rather than being regarded merely as private treasures. It is contrary to the purpose of preserving national essence to wait for a good price and sell them to foreigners, which no patriot should do.

Excerpted from Li Buqing (Lianfang): *Lectures on Practical Self-Cultivation*, first published by Zhonghua Book Company in early December 1915.

Opinions on Preparing for and Establishing Vocational Supplementary Education

The true meaning of industrial supplementary education has been somewhat elaborated in recent translated books. Its organizational methods and theories are detailed in survey reports. In our country, the initiative and management of such education have already taken shape, but with numerous aspects to consider and the need to adapt to national conditions, how should we decide what to adopt or discard to achieve appropriateness? To start with, we should avoid the imperfect or erroneous practices that other countries have experienced in their developmental processes. Second, we should adopt the best methods and policies regarding the latest trends in supplementary education that are recognized by other states. Third, we must respond to China's specific circumstances, uphold the true essence of supplementary education, and provide appropriate supplementary education in various fields without rigidly adhering to the forms of implementation used in other countries. For situations similar to those in other countries, we should adopt their latest successful cases; for those unique to our country, we should also consider the circumstances to ensure that appropriate supplementary education is provided. Based on these three principles, I present the following opinions. Though the language is concise, the meaning is rich. Selecting and implementing them may prove beneficial. However, these views are based on the current situation, and readers should view them with discernment.

To begin with, set up supplementary schools in cities. In national capitals, provincial capitals, and major commercial ports, the local educational administrative authorities should make overall plans for the entire city, establish multiple schools in appropriate locations respectively, and set up one or several fully-fledged schools in the most convenient places.

The finest industrial and specialized schools should, based on the academic standards of their own institutions, consider the circumstances, and where results can be more easily seen, establish appropriate supplementary schools as affiliates. They may also set up various levels lower than the standards of their own schools. Additionally, due to local needs, even if certain subjects are not offered by their own schools, they may make appropriate arrangements to establish relevant supplementary programs.

The finest primary and secondary schools may, in light of local conditions and within the scope of their capabilities, establish appropriate supplementary schools as affiliates, with a focus on offering relevant vocational courses.

Public factories, companies, etc., should, through the joint efforts of this ministry and the Ministry of Agriculture and Commerce, be encouraged to establish their own supplementary schools to educate their employees. Alternatively, they may be allowed to raise funds on their own and entrust nearby appropriate schools to provide supplementary education on their behalf. In addition, for arsenals and shipyards under the jurisdiction of the Ministry of the Army and Navy, railways and China Merchants Steam Navigation Company under the jurisdiction of the Ministry of Communications, etc., this ministry should also collaborate with the respective ministries to make arrangements for establishing supplementary schools for employees such as those working on steamships and railways. The operation methods shall be the same as those for public factories and companies.

Private factories, companies, and shops that employ several hundred workers should, in collaboration with the Ministry of Agriculture and Commerce, be advised and persuaded to establish supplementary schools. The measures for doing so shall be the same as those for public factories and companies.

The curriculum arrangement and academic standards of industrial supplementary schools primarily focus on two groups: graduates of elementary schools and workers, both of whom should be given priority for admission. However, the establishment of such schools aims to enable all aspiring learners to receive appropriate supplementary education. In practice, there are often exceptions: courses are offered for elementary school graduates when they enroll; courses are provided for workers when eligible workers attend; and classes are arranged for other types of students when they come to study. Although the supplementary education programs for elementary school graduates are more common and do not solely focus on specialized vocational teaching, there are still suitable elective courses available for different learners. Therefore, the school regulations should not be limited to one aspect, so that students can choose according to their own convenience. It is a common practice that worker supplementary courses are attached to industrial schools, and supplementary courses for elementary school graduates are affiliated with primary schools. Nevertheless, when local needs arise, industrial schools may, based on specific circumstances, also offer supplementary courses for elementary school graduates, and primary schools may provide supplementary courses for workers. Thus, the regulations must be adjusted in accordance with local conditions and changing circumstances to avoid obstacles. The measures proposed in the conference of industrial school principals only set two types of regulations without allowing for flexibility, so this special explanation is added.

For supplementary schools that offer a greater number of subjects or grade levels, full-time teachers should be appointed.

For schools that offer industrial/vocational courses, instructors who are truly capable of teaching practical subjects should be hired.

For older individuals who have not received school education, except those whose life experience is equivalent to the academic ability of educated people and thus can be assigned to appropriate grades, special arrangements must be made for those at lower levels. Simplified textbooks should be compiled separately for the two subjects of Chinese and arithmetic. Each supplementary school may set up special classes, choose appropriate times for teaching according to local conditions, and allow them to choose courses freely, so as to help them acquire appropriate knowledge and fulfill the original purpose of providing supplementary education.

There are three methods to expand supplementary courses:

1. They are not limited to primary schools; all higher specialized schools and secondary schools may also attach them.

2. For those offering supplementary courses, the number of students is not restricted to those preparing for admission to the school itself, and students may choose to study one or several subjects.

3. Individuals with expertise in a general subject are permitted to establish their own supplementary courses—either offering a single subject independently or collaborating with others of similar expertise to offer multiple subjects—whichever is convenient.

The first two methods facilitate learning, while the latter allows for the inclusion of specialists from both traditional and modern fields, enabling them to contribute to society. Moreover, it provides a distinct path for traditional scholars to teach according to their strengths, thereby reducing the number of private tutors who inappropriately act as substitutes for formal schools or first infiltrate educational institutions without corresponding qualification.

The above two items may seem unrelated to industrial supplementary education, but in a broader sense, supplementary courses and industrial supplementary education both fall under the category of supplementary education, so they are mentioned here for convenience. Moreover, when other countries implement supplementary education, it is aimed at those who have received an incomplete education. For those who have not received a complete education, efforts should still be made to provide supplementary education, enabling them to gradually achieve a complete education. Taking a step back, for those who have not received any education at all, if we can find ways to provide them with supplementary education so that they can acquire some level of education, isn't this something that those engaged in supplementary education should regard as even more essential?

The academic year system and the subject system can be adopted either in combination or separately, whichever is convenient. However, within the academic year system, students should be allowed to choose elective courses. For the academic year system that includes industrial/vocational programs, the scope of subjects should be centered around a specific vocational discipline. The distribution of various subjects must be closely related to this core discipline, should not be overly broad, and the number of subjects should not be excessive.

In the subject system, there is no need to specify compulsory subjects. One may choose to specialize in just Chinese, just arithmetic, or take multiple subjects concurrently, whichever is convenient. However, for those taking multiple subjects, the class times of the chosen subjects must not conflict. It should be specifically noted here that the proposal from the

Conference of Industrial School Principals, regarding the adoption of the subject system, still requires that Chinese and arithmetic be taught alongside vocational subjects.

While the subject system indeed allows students to choose one or several subjects freely, the arrangement of subjects must be such that they are divided into individual courses yet grouped into distinct categories. This enables those choosing courses to study several related courses within a category, thereby acquiring a systematic body of knowledge in that field. Furthermore, to provide clear guidance for learners, in addition to the school regulations, subjects must be categorized and compiled with explanatory notes. Alternatively, under the provisions for diploma issuance, it should be specified that upon completing certain subjects, students will be awarded a graduation diploma in the corresponding field of study. This ensures that students taking multiple subjects or continuing their studies can clearly identify which subjects are interrelated.

For schools that adopt both the academic year system and the subject system, the two systems must be interconnected. For any identical subjects, students from both systems may attend classes in combined groups and can progress between the systems. For example, those who have completed the general courses under the academic year system may take courses under the subject system; moreover, the basic subjects in the subject system can serve as the foundation for the intermediate courses in the academic year system. All the details of teaching and the arrangement of class hours must be perfectly coordinated without any discrepancies.

For elective courses under both the subject system and the academic year system, when a student takes multiple courses in the same semester, the levels of these courses need not be equivalent. For instance, a student studying Chinese at Level A may also take Arithmetic at Level B; or a student taking Chinese of the first semester at a certain level may concurrently study Arithmetic of the second semester at that same level.

Recruiting students should be done by offering courses as circumstances in the locality permit, and there is no need for all subjects to hold entrance examinations at the same time. In case of special situations, if the academic ability of the applicants is deemed appropriate, they may be allowed to enroll in the middle of a semester or in the next semester.

For elective courses under both the subject system and the academic year system, the required academic qualifications for admission should be specified separately under each course. When recruiting students, only the academic level specified for each course shall be considered to determine whether applicants who wish to enroll in a particular course are truly capable of following the lectures at that course's level. Their general academic ability may be disregarded entirely.

The various subjects under the academic year system and the subject system may be added or removed as needed according to local conditions. Those not previously offered may be added; those already offered may be abolished, or those that have been suspended may be reintroduced.

For a school or a local area that offers several levels from elementary to advanced, the progression between each level must be coherent to facilitate appropriate advancement. Additionally, when multiple schools are established in a single area, their offerings should align with local needs and the preferences of applicants, and there should be no overemphasis on certain subjects. Efforts should be made to avoid redundancy or gaps in course offerings. Moreover, the locations of these separately established schools must be evenly distributed to ensure that students can attend school conveniently.

For the same subject or course, multiple levels from elementary to advanced may be established. In addition, if there are many applicants for a particular subject or course, it may be divided into several groups.

If there are not many students in several grades, or if it is convenient to combine several grades into one group, single-class teaching shall be adopted.

For a school that offers multiple disciplines, arrangements should be made based on specific circumstances: some subjects may be taught in separate grades or groups, while others may be taught by combining several grades or groups. Generally, industrial/vocational subjects are better taught in separate classes, and general subjects may be combined for convenience. When industrial/vocational subjects are taught in combined classes, they must be of the same type.

Schools established specifically for graduates of elementary schools or for women may offer full-day or half-day teaching. However, for elementary school graduates, whether they are attending industrial or commercial supplementary courses, or if the schools also admit older students, evening teaching may be arranged for convenience according to local conditions.

The study period for the subject system should be within one year; the study period for the academic year system shall be determined based on the types of disciplines and local conditions.

For evening teaching sessions, the most appropriate arrangement is twice or three times a week, with two hours per session. However, adjustments (in terms of frequency or duration) may be made according to local conditions.

The educational seasons may involve teaching throughout the year, or teaching in certain seasons during leisure periods; alternatively, teaching may be conducted multiple times intermittently within a year or a semester, or teaching may be carried out in a year excluding the busiest days and times. All these arrangements can be made as convenient.

It is acceptable to divide the academic year into either three semesters or two semesters, whichever is convenient. Additionally, the start of the semester may be set at an appropriate time based on local conditions, and is not limited to the period specified by the ministry regulations.

For evening classes, when there are practical training sessions, they must be arranged at appropriate times and conducted during the daytime.

Schools shall clearly indicate their types. For example, those established for women, or primary schools with two types of supplementary courses attached, may be called industrial supplementary schools (however, two types of supplementary courses may also be called industrial and commercial supplementary schools or agricultural and commercial supplementary schools). This is to allow adjustments and changes to the school's content without being restricted by the indicated name. They may also be designated in a narrow sense, such as sewing supplementary schools or English supplementary schools. This provision is put forward in accordance with Article 50 of the Industrial School Regulations.

The circumstances of industry and commerce are extremely complex. For those planning to establish relevant institutions in cities, they must first conduct a detailed investigation into the types of industries and commerce as well as the status of occupations. Special attention should be paid to the prevalence of the apprentice system in workshops and shops, so as to set up schools and formulate courses in line with actual conditions. It is particularly essential to carry out special classification based on apprentices' occupations and provide appropriate supplementary education accordingly.

Local public organizations, such as chambers of commerce, trade associations, education associations, agricultural associations, labor unions, autonomous institutions, and other various groups, must make efforts to communicate and collaborate in their endeavors.

The cost-saving measures for supplementary schools refer to the borrowing of school buildings and equipment. However, appropriate funds should still be allocated for teachers' salaries and teaching supplies.

A notification book should be kept, detailing the times of class start, class end, and absences, and this information should be communicated to the students' parents, employers, or guarantors.

Recorded in Li Buqing (Lianfang) and Lu Xiaozhi [6]: *Summary of Investigations into Japanese Industrial Supplementary Education* [7], published by Commercial Press in early September 1918.

---

6 Lu Xiaozhi (courtesy name Renfu), a native of Aowu, Shaanxi Province, was a graduate of agricultural studies in Japan with the title of "Ju Ren" (a successful candidate in the imperial examination at the provincial level). In the late Qing Dynasty, he served as a principal secretary in the Industrial Department of the Ministry of Education and a confidential senior clerk in the General Affairs Department. In the early years of the Republic of China, he successively held positions as secretary, section chief, and director of the Department of Specialized Education in the Ministry of Education. After 1919, he served as Director of Education in Hubei and Henan provinces, director of the Editing and Reviewing Section of the Ministry of Education, among other posts. At the time [of writing], he was an editor and reviewer of the Ministry of Education. — Translator's note

7 This book mainly covers the history, current situation, management, training, incentives, external connections of Japanese industrial supplementary education, as well as supplementary education for industry, commerce, agriculture, and women. The text [herein] is taken from its *Appendix*. — Translator's note

Reply to Mr. Lu Guiliang's Letter Questioning the Proposal of Separating Arts and Sciences

In a letter published in the *Current Affairs News* on the 29th of last month, Mr. Lu Guiliang, a member of the Secondary School Conference, wrote *Reply to the Proposal of Separating Arts and Sciences*. Regarding the points I questioned, he did not offer the slightest instructive explanation. Instead, he picked out a single phrase from my text that is irrelevant to the main argument and launched a discussion on it, which is far from the original intention of the questioner. I hereby refute each of his responses one by one—not out of a fondness for argument.

Mr. Lu claims that all the points I questioned had already been debated and resolved at the conference. Unfortunately, I was not present at the meeting initially and thus am unaware of the proceedings. Yet, as I published the previous article and Mr. Lu has earnestly responded with a letter for discussion, he might as well take the trouble to cite the arguments from the conference debates and address each of my questions directly. This would allow those who were not at the meeting but share my views to obtain a proper explanation. However, he has brushed the matter aside lightly, not uttering a single word in response to the points I questioned, which only deepens the confusion of the one who raised the questions.

Mr. Lu claims that the current system has the drawback of mandatory enforcement, while the resolved conditions leave room for flexibility and adaptability everywhere. What he refers to as "flexibility and adaptability" is cited from one or two of the stipulated measures, such as: provinces and regions that are unable to make immediate changes may proceed in due order; schools with grades that have not completed a full academic year may formulate appropriate methods; grades that have completed a full academic year may follow the existing regulations, and so on. A careful analysis of these provisions shows that on the surface, they are measures for phased implementation, but in reality, they are preparations for mandatory enforcement. For what is mentioned here only allows for differences in the timing of implementation, not flexibility or adaptability in the middle school regulations themselves. Mr. Lu, sharing my view in criticizing the uniformity of the current system, has nevertheless formulated a division between arts and sciences with an improperly defined and unclear boundary, along with fixed main courses and general courses. He intends to make those with inconsistent educational perspectives and varying local conditions implement this uniform proposal of separating arts and sciences one by one. This means that what he once criticized as the uniformity of the current system, he now follows in its footsteps without considering whether others will criticize it. This is where I cannot agree with Mr. Lu. My position is neither to absolutely preserve the current system nor to absolutely oppose the separation of arts and sciences. It is just that as the world progresses and knowledge advances, educational issues become increasingly complex. The methods and content of a type of school need not be entirely uniform to keep up with social trends. As long as the school is managed by competent people, abandoning the current system is not inappropriate; adhering to the current system is also acceptable; and adopting a divided system does not necessarily mean that separating arts and sciences is the only proper way. Therefore, the "flexibility and adaptability" I advocate lies in the stipulation of the school system, enabling educators to give full play to their sound ideals and experience in management, training, teaching, and curriculum design, and to formulate appropriate methods. It is not sufficient, as Mr. Lu does, to rely on a fixed separation of arts and sciences and a kind of phased implementation method.

Mr. Lu said that the amount of general courses should be increased or decreased, and they are not optional courses, and you should understand this meaning. In the previous article, I pointed out that in the original proposal, the practical track excluded Chinese from general courses, and I was worried that reducing the class hours for Chinese would lead to even worse results than the current situation. This clearly revealed the meaning of increasing or decreasing the amount of general courses. I never confused them with optional courses. Mr. Lu did not argue on the issue of whether Chinese should be a general course in the practical track, but only mentioned that the terms "general courses" and "optional courses" are different. This is really not understanding the meaning behind it.

The latter two paragraphs of Mr. Lu's remarks are quite lengthy, but their main points can be summarized into two: initially, a proposal decided by a general assembly admits no objections from individuals outside the assembly; second, a proposal resolved by middle school principals admits no objections from those who are not currently running middle schools. The conclusion he arrives at is that those who resolved the proposal to separate arts and sciences are qualified and learned, so their words must be without error, and others have no right to object. When discussing matters and clarifying principles, one should only argue over what is right and wrong. The distinction between right and wrong does not depend on who utters the words. If we set aside right and wrong, how can an individual's opinion stand against the authority of a resolved proposal? Instead of debating the merits of the points I questioned, Mr. Lu merely insists that an individual's opinion should not override a resolved proposal—how excessively anxious he is! Moreover, regarding the first point: the authority of an educational conference over the Ministry of Education is not the same as the authority of a national assembly over the government. Even a proposal put forward by a national assembly cannot force the government to implement it exactly as proposed. The resolution by Mr. Lu and others to separate arts and sciences is nothing more than a proposal. The Ministry of Education inherently retains the discretion to decide how to implement the original proposal. Even if the original proposal were to be implemented, reforming the school system is a matter of immense importance. Academically and practically, anyone should be entitled to express their views and discuss how the proposal should be revised for reference. As for whether the authorities will fully adopt the resolved proposal in the future or also incorporate opinions from other quarters, it depends entirely on whether the authorities possess sound and fair judgment. Individuals outside the assembly have no right to interfere, and even the members of the conference cannot constrain them. Because someone raised a mild objection, Mr. Lu declared that at the conferences of civilized states, no individual opinion can override a resolution. Does this mean that once a matter is resolved, others are not allowed to voice opposition? Do the conferences of civilized nations really have such arbitrary and biased practices?

Let us further address the second point. Those who are engaged in middle school education are naturally the most familiar with the flaws and problems in middle schools. However, those involved in middle school education are not limited to the members of the conference, nor are they exclusively current middle school staff. Their knowledge of these flaws is also confined to the schools they have personally worked in or inspected, and they do not necessarily understand all schools. Educational undertakings involve extremely complex issues. Even in the educational systems of civilized countries today, which have been meticulously studied by countless schools of educators, there are still dissenting opinions regarding their implementation. Mr. Lu and others, through a conference of several dozen people, hastily claim that their propositions are satisfactory and appropriate. When anyone voices even a slight objection, they denounce such opinions as being put forward by those not currently engaged in middle school education, dismissing them as irresponsible and groundless in practice. In the current state of education in our country, the problem lies precisely in the scarcity of people who truly study education, leading to widespread indifference toward educational issues. Those who can put forward valuable opinions are not necessarily irresponsible or detached from practice. Conversely, those who merely echo others' views, even if they hold current positions, are not necessarily responsible or pragmatic. Moreover, the reform of the school system, though focusing on one specific aspect, is interconnected with numerous other issues. How the middle school system should be revised is not a matter that concerns only middle schools themselves. The authorities of the Ministry of Education should certainly adopt the views from the middle school conference, but they must also incorporate opinions from other relevant quarters. If, as Mr. Lu claims, discussions from outside the conference or from those not currently running middle schools are inadmissible, then the middle school system would be determined solely by the middle school conference. By extension, the primary school system would be determined solely by the primary school conference, and the specialized education system solely by the specialized education conference, with no coordination between different sectors. If the resolutions fail to align or contain conflicting views in terms of systemic coherence, how can we reach a unified and correct conclusion? A clear example is the current conference: middle schools advocate separating arts and sciences, while specialized institutions advocate merging liberal arts and sciences. In my previous article, I referred to the proposal to separate arts and sciences as being based on the ideals and experiences of a segment of people. The wording may have been inappropriate, but it is irrelevant to the main argument. Moreover, describing it as "a segment" cannot be considered an erroneous statement. The proposal to separate arts and sciences, having been voted through the conference, was certainly supported by a majority—perhaps even unanimously—in the middle school conference. However, from the perspective of the entire education community, this proposal is indeed a suggestion from a segment of people. Not only were there dissenting voices within the middle school conference, but principals of specialized institutions related to middle schools also raised many questions during joint meetings, and a large portion of the broader education community also opposed the proposal. It is thus reasonable to say that this proposal is shaped by the ideals and experiences of a segment of people. Mr. Lu also claims that most of the participants in this conference are graduates of universities in Europe, America, or Japan, with accumulated experience ranging from over ten years to as few as five or six years. However, there are many others with the same qualifications outside the conference. Whether all overseas graduates truly have profound insights into education, or whether those with years of experience are all grounded in academic rigor, is not for me to judge. He also mentions middle school tracking, citing the outstanding achievements of schools such as Nankai, Pudong, Nanyang, Minli, and various normal schools in Jiangsu Province as evidence of the benefits of tracked education. However, I have never argued that middle schools should not adopt tracking; I merely object to forcing the entire state to adopt a single model of separating arts and sciences. Furthermore, we must ask: were the achievements of the aforementioned schools all attained after the implementation of tracking? And is the inadequacy of middle schools in our country entirely due to flaws in the school system? These are questions that deserve our deep reflection.

Furthermore, one should not be dogmatic in educational perspectives; truth becomes clear through mutual debate and criticism. If Mr. Lu does not regard my words as an insult, I hope he will generously offer his guidance on the doubts and refutations I have raised. Even if we engage in hundreds or thousands of exchanges, I will be happy to discuss them with him.

Buqing (Li Buqing) writes.

Published in the "Xuedeng" (Academic Light) supplement of Shanghai's *Current Affairs News*, December 10, 1918.

Reply to Mr. Tong Fei on the System of Separating Arts and Sciences in Middle Schools

In the *Current Affairs News* of the 18th of this month, there is an article by Mr. Tong Fei entitled *A Letter to Mr. Lu on the Discussion of the Separation of Arts and Sciences in Middle Schools*. It seems that Mr. Tong has no objections to the methods I proposed in my previous letter, so there is essentially no need for me to add further comments. However, in order to defend the methods and explanations of the proposal to separate arts and sciences, Mr. Tong has rashly made arbitrary remarks about my previous letter. I cannot acquiesce in this, so I venture to elaborate further. My intention is to clarify the true meaning, not to argue over opinions.

The first of these arbitrary assertions is that my opinion aims to retain the name of the existing system while surreptitiously introducing the substance of a tracked system. Regarding the current system, I have never said it cannot be revised, as I made clear in my two previous articles. My opposition to the separation of arts and sciences rests on two points: originally, middle school education is general education. According to educational principles, it should not adopt a tracked system. Even if courses are divided into primary and secondary categories, this merely reflects differences in emphasis and detail for the convenience of study; the overall academic standards should remain roughly comparable. This differs from the allocation of courses in specialized education and should not be termed a "tracked system." Second, in today's age of science, the separation of arts and sciences is flawed because the literary track cannot stand independently in opposition to the practical track. Mr. Cai Yuanpei has elaborated on this point in great detail and precision. Since all of you have heard his lectures, there is no need for me to repeat them. These are objections to the form of the proposal to separate arts and sciences. As for my fundamental opposition, it aligns with your own criticism of the uniformity of the current system: I do not wish to force the entire state to follow the proposals of a few individuals, which would lead to numerous obstacles. Thus, the methods I have proposed are broad enough to accommodate both the advocacy of tracked systems and other viewpoints—fundamentally different from your proposal to impose a uniform regulation. This is by no means a case of retaining the name while secretly implementing a tracked system.

The second arbitrary assertion is that in my previous text, the refutations I put forward have refuted themselves, and the doubts I raised were never truly doubts. Mr. Lu did not utter a single word in response to the doubts and refutations in my previous text, which was already insufficient to resolve the questioner's doubts. Mr. Tong goes a step further, actually asserting that the refutations have refuted themselves and the doubts were never real doubts. Mr. Lu is not me, so how could he know that I had no doubts? Without pointing out the contradictory points in my previous text, what basis is there for claiming that the refutations refuted themselves? Mr. Tong's intention to end the dispute is kind, but such a way of ending the dispute is far from fair.

The third arbitrary assumption is that the difference between my approach and the proposed plan lies in the allocation of hours and time for each subject: one advocates that such allocation be determined by the school itself, while the other insists it be set by the Ministry. However, the proposed plan advocates for a uniform regulation of separating arts and sciences. My proposition, on the other hand, is that each school should allocate primary and secondary courses according to its specific circumstances, and even be allowed to add vocational courses, enabling those running the schools to formulate appropriate methods based on their sound ideals and experience—avoiding the rigidity of a fixed separation of arts and sciences and the flaw of "cutting one's foot to fit the shoe." This represents a fundamental difference in institutional perspectives. It is inappropriate to overlook this fundamental divergence and focus merely on phrases in the text, reducing the difference to whether the curriculum is set by the Ministry or by the school itself. Moreover, since the system is not rigidly confined to a fixed form, the advocated methods will naturally vary with time and place. The Ministry cannot possibly anticipate and regulate every detail in advance; it is more appropriate for schools to first determine the curriculum themselves and then submit it to the Ministry for review and approval. The reason why I did not elaborate on this in my previous article is that, according to established practice, matters such as school establishment, class expansion, and staff changes are all reported to the Ministry for approval and registration. It goes without saying that special curriculum regulations would also require such reporting. The Ministry, in overseeing schools nationwide, should naturally formulate appropriate standards to decide on approval or rejection, rather than allowing schools to act arbitrarily without oversight. As Mr. Tong mentioned regarding graduation curricula and their alignment with further education, these can be directly discussed and decided upon by middle schools in consultation with universities and specialized institutions.

Published in the "Xuedeng" (Academic Light) supplement of *Current Affairs News*, December 28, 1918.

A Discussion on the System of Middle Schools

The school system in our country is largely modeled on the Japanese system. In the late Qing Dynasty, the idea of separating arts and sciences in middle schools gradually gained momentum. Consequently, the Ministry of Education adopted the form of the German system, combined with the understanding of scholars steeped in traditional learning, to arrange the curriculum. However, when various provinces proceeded to restructure their schools, they mostly failed to grasp the true essence of education. Coupled with various practical difficulties in implementation, the outcome became increasingly unsatisfactory. After the founding of the Republic of China, drawing lessons from past failures, the Ministry of Education formulated a new middle school system, which still followed the Japanese system implemented a few years earlier. Over the years, those in the middle school sector, through their experience, have struggled with the heavy curriculum load. Moreover, the uniformity of the system was criticized for its lack of flexibility. As more and more scholars studied in the United States, they witnessed the smooth implementation of tracked and elective courses in American middle schools. They vigorously advocated adopting this model as the basis for reforming middle schools in our country. Last year, the Ministry of Education convened a middle school conference, where members proposed the separation of arts and sciences. The proposal was endorsed by the majority of members and submitted to the ministry. Fundamentally, this proposal differed from the revisions made in the late Qing Dynasty. Nevertheless, the original plan still suffered from the drawbacks of a uniform system and an overloaded curriculum. Additionally, there were many who advocated preserving the old system, leading to numerous objections. At that time, I took the trouble to raise some criticisms of the original proposal. Furthermore, I put forward flexible suggestions that balanced educational theory and reality. Later, the Jiangsu

Provincial Education Association presented my views to the ministry. After several meetings held by the ministry, these suggestions were finally implemented, as seen in the Instruction No. 177 issued on April 28, 1919 (It should be noted that according to the regulations on middle school subjects stipulated in the Ministry's Middle School Order, the aim is to provide a complete general education. Since their implementation, observations on the operation across various regions have revealed that the current subjects are somewhat overly burdensome. Meanwhile, the trend of development necessitates the addition of other subjects. To adapt to the times and ensure smooth implementation, the ministry has carefully deliberated and formulated flexible measures. Henceforth, all existing middle schools in various provinces may, in accordance with local specific conditions, appropriately adjust the subjects listed in Article 1 of the Implementation Rules for Middle Schools, and may also modify the number of class hours specified by the ministry. However, any adjustment to subjects must be accompanied by detailed justifications from the school and can only be implemented after obtaining approval from the ministry, to ensure solemnity). The main idea of this instruction was based on my views. Regrettably, it was issued as a separate document without revising the relevant laws and regulations. Moreover, no further measures were taken to promote the flexible measures, and there has been no news of other reforms. This is indeed a matter for regret.

Now, in discussing the middle school system, in my opinion, there are three major issues that should be addressed .

At the beginning, middle schools constitute a part of the school system. What needs to be studied here is whether changing one part will affect other interconnected parts, and whether there are issues with the nature of the system's structure. Beneath middle schools in our country are higher primary schools and national schools. Primary education operates as a separate system, independent of middle schools. If a tracked system were to be implemented from the first year [of middle school], newly enrolled students—who are unfamiliar with their teachers—would face challenges in appropriately allocating or selecting subjects. This is the first point. (In countries with a parallel education system, students in preparatory schools are groomed to enter middle schools. While children's abilities and personalities are not fully developed in early years, making it difficult to fully discern their potential, the close integration of primary and middle education allows for a general understanding through years of observation. Those entering middle school without attending preparatory schools are relatively few.) Second, if middle school education were extended to five years, could higher primary education be shortened to two years? Conversely, if higher primary education were improved, would it be unnecessary to extend middle school years? (From the perspective of practical life applications, extending school years would be beneficial; yet from the standpoint of national economic conditions, such an extension would be inconvenient. A major reason for the poor performance of middle schools in recent years—aside from issues with teaching materials and methods—is the lack of qualified specialized teachers in local primary schools, leaving students inadequately prepared. As a result, many middle schools have established a one-year preparatory course, making their nominal four-year program effectively five years.) Third, graduates of national schools cannot directly enter middle schools. Under the existing system, higher primary schools share general subjects with middle schools. Should they be separated to achieve the benefits of "circular teaching," or merged for the convenience of "progressive teaching"? (In countries with longer compulsory education, students proceed directly from national primary schools to middle schools. Where higher primary schools still exist, they are makeshift arrangements tailored to local conditions, not the standard model.) Above middle schools are specialized schools and universities. First, if middle school education were extended to five years, should the preparatory courses in specialized and higher institutions be appropriately abolished? Second, if middle schools adopted a tracked system, should the preparatory courses in specialized and higher institutions be revised? (The purpose of preparatory courses in specialized and higher institutions is to supplement previous learning and prepare students for specialized studies. If middle school standards were not raised, adding a year of study only to require further supplementation would waste time. Conversely, if middle schools adopted tracking, would their nature align with that of preparatory courses? If so, preparatory courses should be abolished—and if abolished, would the duration of undergraduate programs need to be extended?) Operating alongside middle schools are normal schools and vocational schools. Secondary education is divided into three types—middle, normal, and vocational—each with distinct characteristics. Educators establish appropriate schools based on local needs and their own capabilities; students choose schools based on their circumstances and aspirations. Meanwhile, normal and vocational schools can provide supplementary education for middle school students (current or graduated). This differs fundamentally from the American system, where middle schools are not rigidly divided into three types and can be either separated or integrated. Reforming our middle school system by entirely adopting the American model thus raises questions: Should the parallel systems of normal and vocational schools also be revised? Or are middle schools unrelated to these two types, allowing for independent reform? Given current realities, a parallel primary education system is ill-suited for a democratic state. Compulsory education cannot be extended due to resource constraints, and higher primary schools remain necessary due to specific local conditions. Normal and vocational schools, already well-established, also need to coexist due to practical considerations. Middle school years, constrained by national economic factors, cannot be easily extended.

Similarly, preparatory courses in specialized and higher institutions cannot be hastily abolished, as local middle schools are unlikely to improve overnight. Thus, while the current school system requires significant internal reforms, its overall structure remains largely unalterable. Only after determining the framework of the entire system can reforms to individual parts be grounded in a solid foundation. This is the first key issue in resolving middle school system reform.

Second, the current state of middle school education in our country. First, regarding funding issues. Education cannot be popularized, and there are not many students continuing to higher education. Coupled with the inability to expand school buildings, most middle schools across the country have only one class per academic year, and even those with two classes are still few in number. Moreover, facilities are simple and crude; instruments, specimens, and books are mostly insufficient for teaching purposes. Since the outbreak of wars, they have been repeatedly damaged, and even the original conditions have not been fully restored. Second, regarding talent issues. Although education has been promoted for decades, a sufficient number of suitable talents have not been cultivated. Among current school administrators and teachers, those in charge of liberal arts are mostly people from the imperial examination era, with outdated and absurd ideas, which are common everywhere. Those in charge of science either lack sufficient academic competence or are poor at teaching methods. As for skill-based subjects, there are especially few proficient teachers. These two issues are not only the reasons for the poor performance of middle schools but also create numerous obstacles to the implementation of a tracked system. Most of those advocating for system reform today point out the drawbacks of the previous middle school education: the curriculum is too heavy, easily exhausting students' mental energy; learning is not specialized enough, making it difficult to achieve practical utility; and the uniform learning model fails to develop students' strengths. These listed drawbacks are indeed as described. However, whether these drawbacks arise purely from the system itself remains to be considered. If we do not strive to increase funding, pay attention to cultivating talents, and improve teaching materials and methods, even a good system will ultimately fail to bring about improvement. The improvement of teaching materials is not only a problem for middle schools themselves; the curriculum of higher primary schools, which is connected to middle schools, should also be organized to ensure that each level is appropriate, interconnected, and not overly complicated. (Current textbooks mostly present a jumble of knowledge, arranged in a sequence that follows the scientific system but is inconsistent with educational methods. For subjects shared by higher primary schools and middle schools—such as Chinese, history, geography, science, and mathematics—the content of textbooks differs only in the amount of information and the depth of difficulty. The division of teaching content, in terms of quantity, level, and scope, lacks proper arrangement and is merely done arbitrarily by editors. If the Ministry of Education does not formulate appropriate plans, teaching efforts will be wasted, and time will be squandered without remedy.) No system is fixed forever; it must be adapted to the times and local conditions. Therefore, in educational approaches, on the one hand, we should respond to trends, and on the other hand, we must carefully consider national conditions. This is the second key issue in resolving middle school system reform.

Third, the purpose of middle school education. What needs to be studied here includes several critical questions: 1) The distinction between middle school education and secondary education. This should be examined based on facts, not merely the breadth or narrowness of terminological meanings. For example, in the American system, middle schools are not further divided into normal schools and vocational schools; their structures can be either separated or integrated, allowing middle school education to be regarded as secondary education. However, in our country, where middle schools, normal schools, and vocational schools operate in parallel, although all three fall under secondary education, each has distinct purposes. Middle schools occupy a central position in the school system, while normal schools and vocational schools can offer short-term courses for middle school graduates. Though they constitute a significant part of secondary education, middle schools cannot fully replace secondary education as a whole. 2) Should middle school education be classified as general education? Recently, advocates of the American system, observing its extensive use of tracked curricula—unlike our country's middle schools, which are structured around purely general subjects—have criticized the "outdated system" for its supposed mistake of adhering rigidly to middle schools as institutions of general education. Some even go so far as to argue that middle schools should not provide general education. Their reasoning, however, is not rooted in educational theory but merely cites the American system and similar models as evidence. They fail to investigate whether the American system truly lacks elements of general education, instead presenting various curricula as irrefutable proof. Given the superficial understanding of education among many in our country today, such arguments easily mislead new learners, making it imperative to clarify this issue. To elaborate: By definition, "general" in this context distinguishes from "advanced", not merely implying "comprehensive." To confirm this with established practices: The Ministry of Education's Bureau of General Education oversees not only primary and middle schools but also normal schools and vocational schools—both of which have tracked features—yet they are all classified under general education, as opposed to specialized schools under the Bureau of Specialized Education. Furthermore, Article 2 of the Vocational School Regulations states that Type A vocational schools provide "complete general vocational education," while Type B vocational schools offer "simplified general vocational education." Despite their diverse specialties and subjects, vocational schools are collectively described as "general," indicating that general knowledge and skills inherently include life necessities. This intent is clearly articulated in legal provisions. In terms of educational philosophy, "general education" is a term that, when referring to people, distinguishes from "special education" (e.g., education for the blind, deaf-mute, or disabled), denoting education that all should receive. When referring to subjects, it contrasts with "specialized education," meaning the general education everyone should acquire. Its content consists of basic knowledge and skills, conveyed through subjects—but subjects are tools of education, not its ultimate goal. The study of subjects in themselves, categorized by nature into systematic disciplines, belongs to academic research. The educational value of subjects lies in selecting those relevant to human life, enabling understanding of the world—that is the purpose of education. Thus, there are two principles educators should understand regarding methods to impart general knowledge and skills: first, this does not require a multitude of subjects; even centering on one or two subjects and integrating practical life skills can achieve the goal. General education aims to equip students with knowledge and skills for current life, not merely to mandate a set of general subjects. Second, there is no uniform standard for the scope or limits of such knowledge and skills. In society, people work in division and collaboration, each developing their strengths through education based on individual abilities and aspirations. One need not master all subjects equally to complete general education. However, regardless of their focus, middle school students—still young and academically immature—must acquire adequate foundational knowledge and skills. Therefore, tracked middle schools must not neglect core subjects. The question is whether these core subjects should be studied separately or integrated and taught flexibly, depending on the educator's arrangement. 3) Is middle school education preparatory education? "Preparatory" here carries two meanings: preparation for further studies and preparation for employment. These are fundamentally distinct. Theoretically, middle schools should not be mere preparatory institutions, but reality often contradicts this. Middle school graduates either pursue further education or enter the workforce, leading educators to increasingly lean toward a preparatory orientation due to perceived inadequacies in graduates.

Regarding preparation for further studies: Historically, many middle schools worldwide have served this function, particularly for students from affluent backgrounds with academic aspirations, shaping curricula accordingly. In our system, the separation of middle schools from normal and vocational schools makes them well-suited for academic preparation. Yet critical questions remain: Can all middle school graduates attend higher education? Do institutions of higher learning have the capacity to accommodate them all? Would academic preparatory curricula, aligned with specialized studies, leave non-advanced students with impractical knowledge? These challenges prevent such a model from achieving satisfactory results. Moreover, even "preparation" should emphasize essential general knowledge and skills, not prematurely adopt a specialized focus—narrow-mindedness is common among so-called specialists, often stemming from insufficient general education. Thus, stronger general education lays a better foundation for advanced specialized studies. Regarding preparation for employment: This arises from concerns about graduates' inability to contribute practically to society, amplified by trends in vocational education. Key questions here include: Should middle schools teach specialized vocational skills? How to tailor diverse vocations appropriately to students? Is graduates' incompetence solely due to general education? One need only observe the performance of specialized school graduates in society to doubt this. These questions undermine the case for vocational preparation as a primary goal. These two forms of preparation are mutually exclusive, creating trade-offs. Furthermore, middle school students—still adolescents with underdeveloped judgment—risk being channeled into narrow paths, leading to misguided life choices. This is particularly worrying. In summary, middle schools exist to provide complete general education. Their purpose is not to require mastery of all subjects but to impart practical knowledge and skills through appropriate curricula. Such knowledge and skills should foster holistic development to meet diverse life needs, rather than confining students to single skills or trades. While life paths vary, leading to slight differences in practical knowledge, a solid grasp of foundational subjects and alignment with life needs will equip students for both higher education and employment—with supplementary training for specific vocations, if needed (e.g., short-term courses in normal or vocational schools for graduates). Thus, implementing tracked curricula in middle schools should neither arrange subjects solely for preparatory purposes nor dismiss general subjects as useless. Instead, it should nurture students' strengths according to their abilities and aspirations during their formative years, enabling them to contribute to society and pursue advanced studies. This is the true purpose of complete general education. This is the third key issue in resolving middle school system reform.

Now that the three major issues have been resolved in advance, the purpose and direction for how middle schools in our country should be established and operated have become clear. Based on this purpose, I will further elaborate on the outline of the school system.

(1) The Issue of Subjects

There is an almost unanimous view in academic circles in both China and Japan that middle school subjects are overly burdensome. Yet from the perspective of learning, students struggle with the sheer volume; from the perspective of practical application, the curriculum is still deemed inadequate. According to Article 1 of the Implementation Rules for the Middle School Order, the subjects taught in middle schools are: Ethics, Chinese, Foreign Language, History, Geography, Mathematics, Natural Science, Physics, Chemistry, Law, Economics, Drawing, Handicrafts, Music, and Physical Education. Girls' middle schools add Home Economics, Gardening, and Sewing. These more than ten subjects are made compulsory for all students. With such a broad scope, the depth of learning inevitably suffers. Moreover, the curriculum requires students to take at least eleven subjects per academic year. Juggling so many subjects simultaneously leads to divided attention and neglect of some areas. Additionally, Chinese, Foreign Language, and Mathematics are given equal emphasis, each occupying the largest share of class hours. These three subjects, distinct in nature and each highly demanding, are expected to be mastered to the same standard. This is the primary reason why today's middle school students exhaust themselves mentally yet fail to achieve satisfactory results—a clear case of "excessive learning becoming a burden." Advocates of middle school education today generally acknowledge the merits of a tracked system. However, when discussing subjects, many argue that the current curriculum is insufficient to cultivate sound character or fulfill the goals of moral and national education. Some propose adding subjects like Sociology, Logic, and Philosophy. Admittedly, sound character cannot be fostered merely through classroom instruction, but transmitting such general knowledge via academic subjects remains crucial—hence the emphasis placed on this in education. Furthermore, the superficial, not-specialized coverage of all subjects offers little practical benefit, which explains the perception of "inadequacy for application." The solution to this issue will become clear in the discussion of the following two problems. The root cause of these flaws, however, lies in the rigid uniformity of the system, which allows no room for flexibility. The

Ministry has now permitted adjustments to middle school subjects and class hours, and while the old system has not been entirely abolished, tracked systems may be adopted—seemingly enabling flexible and effective implementation. That said, no guidelines for subject revisions have been provided, relevant regulations remain unamended, and the old curriculum timetables and standards persist. There is no way to determine whether subject standards can be adjusted or varied, creating obstacles to flexible implementation. This cannot yet be considered a fundamental reform.

(2) The Issue of Subject Content This involves several critical points: first, the organization of teaching materials in various subjects should break away from academic disciplinary structures. Instead, it should select topics closely related to practical life from nature and human affairs, exploring their truths and interconnections. (For example, history should focus on matters that cultivate young people's character, downplaying political relics; geography should emphasize topics related to human life, not just topographical symbols.) Even if subjects remain separate, such a unified approach to content selection ensures that breadth of coverage is balanced with practical utility, fostering meaningful connections between subjects. That said, nature and human affairs are vast, and there is no fixed standard for "practical life application." Content must adapt to social environments, carefully identify common knowledge essential to citizens, and further provide relevant practical knowledge based on young people's career tendencies. For instance, many middle schools teach "General Theory of Law" or "General Theory of Economics" in their Law and Economics courses, resembling old-style cataloging—this is a particularly grave mistake. Second, teaching materials should adapt to local conditions and include elements of specialized relevance. (For example, middle schools in agricultural regions should emphasize agriculture across subjects; those in commercial regions should highlight commerce.) This integrates general

education with locally needed practical knowledge: students bound for higher education will still have a solid foundation in core subjects, while those entering the workforce, though lacking specialized skills, will possess basic specialized knowledge. With short-term training in relevant institutions, they can quickly acquire applied skills. This eliminates the need for specialized vocational schools in certain areas while preparing mid-level vocational talent. (Current vocational schools suffer from poor facilities, a shortage of teachers, and empty reputations; the proposed approach separates knowledge and skills for more effective cultivation.) Third, Subject standards should abandon rigid uniformity. The ministry's allowance for adjusting subjects and class hours already accommodates tracked systems, and their implementation should now be prioritized. In a tracked system, the same subject in different tracks (e.g., Track A and Track B) will naturally have varying standards if their purposes differ. For example, mathematics in a liberal arts track, intended solely for daily use, requires only proficiency in arithmetic—algebra or trigonometry are unnecessary. This logic applies elsewhere. The ministry's flexible policies permit adjusting subjects and hours, but it remains unclear whether adjusted subjects should retain old standards. Reducing hours while demanding the same proficiency as before is impractical, even without empirical proof. Thus, tracked systems must determine content and standards based on needs, then allocate hours accordingly. Rigidly enforcing uniform standards under the guise of "flexibility" is obviously flawed; equally problematic is arbitrary, unregulated adjustments (a flaw in the original proposals of the Middle School Conference, the elective course timetables of Jiangsu provincial middle schools, and even Japan's widely praised Proposals for Improving Middle School Education by Zhang Wenduo). Additionally, subject content should adapt to the nature and needs of each track. To outline general curriculum standards: Ethics courses, which currently distribute moral duties across years without expanding content with age, contradict educational principles. Key ethical concepts and national moral characteristics should be taught throughout, not confined to the fourth year. Chinese courses covering "etymology," "grammar outlines," or "Chinese literary history" are overly complex and unnecessary. Grammar, in particular, is better taught through context. History courses, which currently split ancient, medieval, early modern, modern, East Asian, and Western history into rigid years, raise questions: Is such fragmentation necessary? Must the sequence be strictly chronological? Does uniform scheduling constrain teaching? Geography courses, which separate "basics" from "general theories" (physical and human geography), fail to clarify how these differ. Teaching physical and human geography in isolation from national or foreign geography overlooks their substantive relevance. Law (to cultivate civic knowledge) and Economics (to enhance human well-being), both tied to ethics, could be integrated into Ethics courses. For girls' schools, science courses (biology, physics, chemistry) should align with home economics—e.g., biology focusing on gardening, hygiene, and care; physics/chemistry on cooking, laundry, and household chemicals. These are general suggestions; specific content should be detailed by individual schools.

(3) The Issue of Subject Configuration This issue can be divided into several categories, largely distinguishing between the general curriculum system and the tracked curriculum system. The general curriculum system, such as the old system, still exists in some American middle schools. In my opinion, it can coexist harmoniously with the tracked system. Many critics denounce this system, but it is far from certain whether the malpractice they cite stem from poor subject content, ineffective teaching methods, improper arrangement, or inherent flaws in the system itself. However, since the development of individuality has proven its true value in education, the

adoption of the tracked system has become an inevitable trend. The tracked system falls into three types: fully compulsory, fully elective, and partially elective. The fully compulsory system, such as the separation of arts and sciences, features mostly the same subjects but with differences in class hours and difficulty levels. Compared to the general curriculum system, this model only offers slight advantages in terms of preparing for higher education; in terms of learning outcomes and employment ability, it yields results similar to the general system. The fully elective system, which allows students unrestricted freedom of choice, has not been fully implemented in any country. Given the current state of education in our state, this approach is not feasible and can be set aside for now. The partially elective system designates core subjects as compulsory and specialized subjects as elective. Elective subjects can be either restricted or unrestricted. Unrestricted electives allow students to choose any number of specialized courses within a specified time frame. Restricted electives fall into two sub-types: first, students may only choose courses from a specific category and must complete all courses in that category; second, students must take at least a certain number of courses from a specific category. When organizing such a tracked system, careful consideration must be given to determining the necessary core subjects and their content, as well as classifying specialized subjects based on demand. These details require continuous revision to ensure appropriateness. Two critical questions arise here: At what stage should electives begin? What proportion of credits should compulsory and elective subjects each account for? Regarding the first question, introducing electives in the first year would lead to numerous problems: 1) Students' personalities are not yet fully understood, making proper guidance impossible; 2) Young students lack sufficient knowledge across subjects to make informed choices; 3) Early tracking hinders general education and risks fostering narrow-mindedness. Educators argue that tracked learning should start at age 16, which, in our system, would mean beginning from the third year of middle school—a more appropriate approach. As for the second question, the provincial middle schools in Jiangsu Province have proposed that compulsory subjects account for two-thirds of credits and electives for one-third, with electives starting in the first year. If electives were instead introduced in the third year, the shorter duration would require more class hours per course, making it impractical to calculate credits uniformly across all years. In my view, from the third year onward, compulsory and elective subjects should each account for half of the credits. To ensure the success of this system, the Ministry of Education should establish a special research committee. This committee would, on the one hand, compile and translate detailed curricula and methods from tracked schools abroad, and on the other hand, draft various organizational plans for tracked schools. These materials should be published by the ministry, with all previous curriculum standards abolished, allowing middle school educators to refer to these guidelines without being constrained by rigid regulations. This would significantly aid educational progress, and it is the responsibility of the authorities to implement this promptly. Additionally, subjects should be arranged in a balanced, interleaved manner to avoid overloading students with too many courses simultaneously. For example, history and geography could be sequenced such that national history is taught after national geography, and world history after world geography. Similarly, biology could be taught before physics and chemistry. Such arrangements help reduce learning strain and unify knowledge concepts, which deserves careful attention.

As for the extension of school years, it is constrained by national economic conditions, while adjustments to time limits are permitted as appropriate; neither constitutes a major issue in terms of the system itself. If the fundamental issues are resolved, the rest can be settled without further elaboration.

Published in *Education Magazine*, Volume 12, Issue 9, September 1920.

Plan for Reorganizing Education in Henan Province

1. Plan for Affiliated Funds

1.1 Formulate Standards for Schools' Disposal of Funds

It has been examined that the educational funds of Henan Province are less than those of provinces such as Jiangsu and Zhili. However, when it comes to a single school, its regular funds are not inferior to those of schools of the same level in other provinces. Judging from the results, the academic level of graduates is quite inferior. The reason for this, upon investigation, is that the allocation of funds is not used to increase teachers' salaries and school equipment, but is mostly wasted on useless things. Therefore, to reorganize school funds, it is first necessary to set standards for their allocation.

The various existing drawbacks:

1.1.1 Teachers' salaries are too low

It has been found that the salaries of teachers in various secondary schools are generally no more than 40-50 yuan, with some as low as 20-30 yuan. Few teachers receive salaries equal to that of the principal, even though their academic qualifications and capabilities are no less than the principal's. Such a practice seriously defeats the purpose of recruiting talented personnel for schools. It is practically impossible to expect excellent teachers with the lowest possible salaries. This is the first issue that should be reformed.

1.1.2 Inappropriate allocation of teaching staff

It is reasonable for school teachers to be full-time employees. The allocation of subjects and teaching hours must also be appropriately balanced to achieve twice the result with half the effort. However, investigations show that many schools have an excessive number of teachers, mostly due to the employment of part-time staff or nepotism. When educational undertakings are used as a means of favoritism, corruption and neglect of duties are inevitable. This is the second issue that should be reformed.

1.1.3 Too many redundant staff

It has been found that each school generally appoints one supervisor for every two classes of students, and some even have two supervisors for three classes. In addition, there are positions such as accountants or general affairs officers (who also take on clerical roles), rent collectors, librarians, instrument managers, and lecture note managers, along with 3-4 or even 5-6 clerks. In reality, the work of three such staff members could easily be handled by one person. This is the third issue that should be reformed.

1.1.4 Excessive number of servants

Investigations reveal that each class in schools is allocated an average of about six servants, with some schools exceeding this number. This not only wastes money but also fosters a sense of arrogance and laziness among students. This is the fourth issue that should be reformed.

1.1.5 Inadequate facilities

This is identified as the most serious shortcoming in various schools. Most expenses in their reimbursement records are for non-essential items. Necessary facilities such as libraries, instrument rooms, physics and chemistry laboratories, botanical gardens, recreation rooms, and sports equipment are completely neglected. Even when funds are reported for books, they mostly cover textbooks used by students. Such a situation not only hinders students' academic progress but also prevents teachers and administrators from acquiring new knowledge. This is the fifth issue that should be reformed.

1.1.6 Redundant expenses should be cut

School reimbursement records show questionable expenditures: for example, payments for tea and water suggest the tea boiler operation is contracted out; expenses for coal amounting to dozens of yuan are incurred even when it is not winter; some small schools with few classes report monthly tea expenses of over ten yuan. Additionally, expenses for oil, candles, paper, printed materials, and miscellaneous items continue as usual during summer and winter vacations. The irregularities here are obvious at a glance. This is the sixth issue that should be reformed.

1.1.7 Formulating allocation standards

The purpose is to comprehensively review the expenditures of each school, ensure funds are spent based on actual needs, eliminate redundant staff and miscellaneous labor, and reallocate all savings to teachers' salaries and matters beneficial to practical education. In addition to the Education Department setting tentative standards for various expenditures, reviewing school budgets and accounts, and formulating regulations on salary grades for teaching and administrative staff, the following allocation methods are proposed. (Omitted)

1.2 Establish a School Fund Review Committee

In Henan's academic circles, attacks on school principals are mostly triggered by issues related to funds, and the same goes for the seeking of official positions. Whether such problems truly lie with the principals themselves, or with corrupt practices among accountants, general affairs staff, or others, cannot be generalized. To clarify the truth, it is essential to ensure that all uses of funds are correctly determined in advance and clearly presented afterward. Moreover, there must be appropriate inspection methods and an independent organizational structure for oversight. Only in this way can virtuous personnel in these positions vindicate themselves, while unworthy ones are prevented from embezzling funds. The proposal to establish a School Fund Review Committee is thus a plan to address this issue. Not only will it enable proper auditing of fund disbursements to eliminate inaccuracies and omissions, but it will also make everyone aware that the allocation of school funds is not the sole responsibility of the principal. All teaching and administrative staff share this responsibility, and no one can manipulate funds for personal gain. With such transparency, suspicions can be dispelled, and trust can be fostered, thereby curbing the trend of unwarranted attacks. The regulations are as follows. (Omitted)

2. Plan for Assessment

2.1 Strictly formulate the appointment procedures

Teachers in various schools shall still be employed by the principals. However, when employing teachers, specialized schools must submit the matter to the director of the Education Department, who shall then submit it to the Ministry of Education for approval. Provincial secondary schools must submit it to the Education Department for approval. County schools must submit it to the county magistrate, who shall then submit it to the Education Department for approval. The procedures for dismissal shall be the same.

According to the regulations of the Ministry of Education, teachers are to be employed by school principals, a measure intended to rectify the malpractice of appointment by educational offices during the former Qing Dynasty. Yet where there are advantages, drawbacks follow. Among the fragmented educational factions in Henan Province, the abuse of this system to appoint cronies and monopolize schools is particularly severe. However, abruptly reverting to the old system would not only conflict with the ministry's regulations but also risk improper personnel allocation, as the Education Department may lack full knowledge of all educators across the province. Such a move could exacerbate rather than ease factional strife, concentrating hiring power in the hands of the department and prompting educators to scramble for favor there, thereby fueling more school disturbances. Currently, there is a lack of proper oversight over principals' hiring practices, leading to extreme abuses: when a new principal takes office, incumbent teachers often coerce them into renewing contracts, while job seekers pressure them to dismiss existing staff. Even cliques collude to secure a principal's position as a pretext for mutual advancement; some schools even secretly rehire individuals who have repeatedly been removed from their posts. These are recurring phenomena in Henan. To address this, we propose a modified approach: the power to propose hires remains with principals, while the authority to approve or reject such proposals rests with the government. This way, nepotistic practices cannot be carried out arbitrarily, and the tendencies toward concealment and coercion can be somewhat curbed. All appointees must receive official approval before assuming their duties. In exceptional cases, temporary appointments may be made, provided that the reasons are clearly stated and submitted to the Education Department for review and decision.

2.2 Formulate Regulations on Salary Grades for Teaching and Administrative Staff in Provincial Schools

The living conditions of teaching and administrative staff in Henan Province have an impact on the future of education for three reasons. First, their salary grades are meager and insufficient to support their families. Second, the salary amounts are fixed; regardless of the length of service, or the quality of knowledge and ability, the payment is uniformly the same.

Third, the salary amounts of schools outside the provincial capital are vastly different from those of schools in the provincial capital. For these reasons, teachers only consider becoming administrators as a good plan, and those outside the province only regard being transferred to the province as a career advancement. They abandon the old and seek the new, perfunctorily maintaining the status quo. Due to the lack of an ethos of diligence and enthusiasm, they lose the interest in in-depth research. Treating schools as temporary lodgings and discarding teaching positions like worn-out shoes has actually become a major obstacle to the improvement of education. It is found that teaching and administrative staff in various countries in the East and West all have a system of annual merit-based salary increases. Now, following this idea, we have formulated 15 articles of regulations on salary grades and 2 tables, aiming to maintain their livelihoods, reward excellent staff, eliminate the drawback of inequality, and reassure those who have served for a long time. Nothing is more urgent than this. The formulated regulations are listed below. (Omitted)

2.3 Establish Procedures for Assessing Teaching and Administrative Staff

It has been the usual practice in the past to assess teachers based on inspectors' reports. When inspectors visit various schools, aside from investigating assigned cases item by item as required, their assessment of teaching and administrative staff never follows scientific norms or applies appropriate standards. They merely form specific evaluations based on abstract observations made in an extremely short period of time. Moreover, 80 to 90 percent of the items listed in the prescribed inspection forms could have been filled out by the schools themselves upon instruction, without the need for inspectors to compile and submit them. Inspectors write reports as a routine, and administrative agencies issue orders based on these reports as a routine. Instances of inaccuracies and arbitrariness in this process are often heard of. As a result, those who receive the orders handle them perfunctorily as a routine, and in some cases, the orders even become empty documents while operations remain unchanged. There are also cases where superiors and subordinates collude to cover up issues, solely aiming to avoid trouble. With such practices, it is extremely difficult to see effective implementation of assessments or promotion of school progress. To rectify these past drawbacks, specific measures are hereby formulated as follows. (Omitted)

2.4 Plan to Verify Teaching and Administrative Staff of Secondary Schools

The cultivation of academic ethos and the improvement of teaching curricula all depend on teaching and administrative staff. Among the teaching and administrative staff in Henan's schools, although there are no shortage of qualified individuals, the drawbacks lie in the fact that their academic competence and teaching methods are often crude and shallow. If they were to study diligently, they could undoubtedly perform their duties satisfactorily and with ease. However, perfunctoriness and shirking of responsibilities have become a common practice. After classes, few engage in further learning, resulting in a listless ethos in actual teaching. Those with shallow academic attainments, being incompetent in teaching, only seek to become principals or supervisors as a way to avoid teaching duties. Recently, incidents of students collectively dismissing teaching and administrative staff have occurred repeatedly. These are consequences of their own actions, and it is inappropriate to force the students to accept them. However, once this trend spreads, the dignity of teachers will decline. Gradually, even excellent teachers, affected by this, will resort to catering to others to gain acceptance. The increasing number of school disturbances has a long-standing origin. To seek a fundamental solution, we must still address the issue through the teaching and administrative staff themselves.

The solution should start with verification. Once the incompetent are removed, those who are negligent in their duties or have improper conduct can be dealt with accordingly, and excellent ones can also strive to excel. However, the regulations of the Ministry of Education stipulate that for teaching and administrative staff, only qualifications are considered. There is no differential treatment between new graduates and those who have served for a long time, despite the differences in their abilities. Without proper incentives and penalties, the education sector lacks vitality. If we conduct verification in accordance with the methods used for primary schools, which only involve testing those without appropriate qualifications, it will merely increase the number of people permitted to be teachers. It will not be able to assess whether the academic competence and teaching methods of all current teachers are truly competent for their positions, making the verification an unnecessary formality. Moreover, those who meet the qualifications specified in the ministry's regulations cannot have their qualifications revoked even if they are incompetent. Failing to screen those with qualifications would also be insufficient to show due prudence. Therefore, we should formulate a method of treatment, using verification to distinguish different levels, so that there can be appropriate screening of each staff member's abilities, without conflicting with the ministry's regulations. Furthermore, if verification is based solely on examinations, without the implication of promoting academic development, it will be difficult to inspire an ethos of research. Hereby, we propose measures that balance these purposes. In addition, a longer preparation period is specially allowed. Through the supervision of verification, teaching and administrative staff will be compelled to review their knowledge, study the subjects they teach, and compete in academic pursuits to seek exemption from examinations. Even those who are unqualified or idle will strive to study to meet the standards. In this way, academic progress can be expected invisibly.

The funds required for the first round of verification can be covered by the savings from the arrears owed to the Education Department by the Finance Department upon repayment, without the need for additional funds to be raised separately.

2.5 For the time being, graduates of schools above the higher primary school level shall be examined by personnel dispatched by the Education Department; for entrance examinations of provincial schools above the secondary level, personnel dispatched by the Education Department shall also be sent to supervise the examinations.

It has been the usual practice in Henan that for students entering or graduating from various schools, examination papers are submitted to the Education Department for review and approval or rejection, which seems to be a cautious approach. However, whether the examinations are conducted seriously, whether there are falsifications in the papers, and whether graduates have practical experience—all these cannot be truly verified merely through reports. Investigations into the performance of graduates in further studies and employment have shown extreme inadequacies. While it is true that progress can hardly be expected without improving daily teaching, the overindulgent admission of students and the practice of judging graduates solely by the length of their study period rather than their academic proficiency are also major contributing factors to this situation. To address this malpractice, supervision measures should be implemented. For all schools above the higher primary level holding graduation ceremonies, the Education Department shall dispatch personnel to conduct examinations. If students are indeed qualified for graduation, their graduation scores shall still be mainly based on their school performance. The Education Department will only conduct additional reviews for those cases where there is a significant discrepancy between the scores from the examination committee and the total scores of the school performance. In this way, the quality of performance will not be judged by a single day's performance; meanwhile, schools will be able to use this as a means of supervision on the one hand and verify the authenticity of results on the other. As for the entrance examinations for students entering schools above the secondary level, the Education Department will also dispatch personnel to supervise. The purposes are as follows: first, to ensure that students truly have the academic ability for further studies, thereby eliminating the malpractice of lax standards. Second, to ensure that certain schools genuinely admit students who are suitable for their programs, thereby eliminating the malpractice of inappropriate admissions. Third, to prevent teaching and administrative staff from showing favoritism toward students from specific regions or lowering admission standards when there are fewer applicants from certain areas, thereby eliminating the malpractices of unfairness and inequality. Some may suspect that such measures risk showing distrust in schools. However, it should be understood that administrative policies value adapting to the times; empty talk of lofty ideals is of no benefit to practical matters.

3. Plan for Teaching

3.1 Improve the teaching method of reciting from the textbook

It should be noted that although there are occasional commendable aspects in the teaching practices of schools in Henan, the majority still remain within the confines of textual teaching. What is referred to here as "textual teaching" is not a matter of teaching materials but of teaching methods. Not only do teachers of theoretical subjects merely pick out phrases and sentences from texts, but even those teaching physics, chemistry, and natural history go through the motions by adhering rigidly to the text. This malpractice is particularly severe compared to other provinces. To say nothing of the fact that useful sciences are reduced to empty talk on paper, the intermingling of explanations of words and phrases with elaborations on principles and phenomena in teaching easily confuses students' listening and makes them lose focus. An investigation into the causes reveals that teachers of practical subjects attribute it to a lack of instruments and specimens, while teachers of theoretical subjects blame it on students' poor proficiency in Chinese. As a result, initial-stage teaching progresses extremely slowly, and the prescribed curriculum can mostly not be completed on schedule. Newly appointed teachers, seeking to gain students' approval, invariably stick strictly to textbooks, explaining each sentence in detail. Thus, what both teachers and students regard as "diligent and meritorious efforts" are largely expended on the wording of textbooks. With such teaching methods, how can one expect students to apply what they have learned? To eliminate this malpractice, we must address its root causes. The factors mentioned above are indeed part of the problem, but there are two more fundamental causes of error: ly, the structure of commonly used textbooks is flawed, with text and principles/phenomena presented in a jumbled manner. In countries where spoken and written language are consistent, such compilation is not a major issue. However, in our country, the gap between spoken and written language is too wide; if teachers do not also teach the text itself, students will indeed struggle to fully comprehend. Secondly, teachers are accustomed to the textual teaching methods inherited over thousands of years. They do not study educational principles, nor do they know how to select teaching materials oriented toward practical application or use clever communication techniques to present principles. They merely adhere to old habits, considering it their duty to explain clearly. This is why the practice of teaching by reciting from textbooks is so prevalent, with no one realizing its great absurdity. To improve teaching, we must emphasize scientific research and downplay the significance of textual meanings; this is the fundamental reform needed. However, textbooks cannot be abolished overnight, and there are no suitable textbooks available for the time being. Considering the current situation, the only way is to temporarily require teachers to formulate outlines based on the textbooks they use. During actual lectures, they should adopt appropriate teaching methods (using both verbal explanation and demonstration) according to the nature of the teaching materials. Students, in addition to doing exercises, should focus on taking notes. Only in this way can we completely rid ourselves of the old practice of teaching by reciting from textbooks, and gradually enable students to apply their knowledge in practice. The points to note are as follows:

(1) Except for the two subjects of Chinese and foreign languages, textual teaching shall not be adopted.

(2) It has been found that currently used textbooks do not have a structure that only lists outlines. For any teaching conducted using textbooks, teachers shall extract key points and outline the contents of the original books. During teaching, they shall give lectures item by item based on these outlines, and students may refer to the original books while listening.

(3) Teachers may appropriately add or delete contents when extracting key points, outlining, or giving lectures based on the original books, but such additions or deletions shall not be excessive, so as not to inconvenience students' self-study.

(4) For teaching materials and exercises of practical subjects, adjustments may be made with consideration to practical application.

(5) For any subject, teaching must be interspersed with practice.

(6) For practical subjects, emphasis shall be placed on experiments and observations; for theoretical subjects, emphasis shall be placed on application-oriented exercises and research.

(7) Students shall take notes of key points during teaching.

(8) Textbooks compiled by teachers themselves shall only list outlines. If such books are adopted by various schools, reference books shall be compiled separately.

(9) For matters not covered herein, teachers may implement them at their discretion and may also present their opinions to the Education Department for consideration and implementation.

(10) At the beginning of each semester, teachers shall allocate the key contents of teaching materials according to the teaching hours of the subject. At the end of each month, they shall check whether the predetermined amount of teaching materials is roughly in line with the actual situation, so as to make timely adjustments without affecting the overall teaching progress.

3.2 Integrate examinations into teaching

The issue of examinations has now become a major point of contention. It is unnecessary to discuss the reasons for advocating or abolishing examinations; however, in the current actual situation, in schools that implement examinations, presetting the scope of examination questions has become a common malpractice. This only serves to grade students and provide convenience for teachers, but fails to reveal the true level of their academic performance. As for abolishing examinations, students generally welcome it. Although this idea arises from the motivation of new trends of thought, if implemented improperly, it will only benefit those who are not diligent in their studies and those with poor academic performance, with even more serious drawbacks. A major flaw in current teaching is that, except for English and mathematics, which have routine reading, explanation, and problem-solving exercises in each class, other subjects, such as history, geography, and theoretical disciplines, hardly have any appropriate exercises at all. Teachers usually regarded as excellent are merely those who explain clearly; they never delve into whether students can understand each item. The results evaluated through mid-term and final exams are also insufficient to prove students' gains in each class. If examinations are like this, it goes without saying what would happen if they were abolished. To ensure that students truly gain knowledge, their academic performance is authentic, and to avoid the drawbacks of previous examinations, a fundamental solution should not first focus on discussing whether to abolish examinations, but rather on checking the truth of students' comprehension and in-depth understanding in each class. The purpose is to enable students to express and apply what teachers have taught, and to check their ability to comprehend and delve into the knowledge. In this way, the assessment of students' usual performance can be based on this, without the need to conduct it at a specific time or in a specific form. After all, any method of assessing performance, in one way or another, falls into the trap of examinations. If education is implemented by checking whether teaching is effective, then the pursuit of students' true learning gains becomes the standard for assessing performance. By doing so, students will not feel much difficulty in temporary examinations, and even if examinations are abolished, they will not dare to be slack. This is the effect of "integrating examinations into teaching." It not only solves the problem of examinations but also lays the foundation for improving teaching. However, given the current ignorance of teachers and the laziness of students, both lacking an ethos of research, implementing this method rashly will definitely be considered a hardship. Nevertheless, if we adhere to the old ways without reform, education will decline day by day. It all depends on the awakening of the education community in Henan. The points to note are as follows:

(1) Within one hour of teaching, there must be a small amount of time for students to act independently or for interaction between teachers and students, ensuring that appropriate practice is carried out.

(2) At the end of a lesson or a topic, a summary must be made to enable students to conduct appropriate practice.

(3) Individual activities need not cover all students each time, but attention must be paid to implementing them in turns.

(4) There are various ways of inspection, such as conducting experiments, using question-and-answer sessions, setting topics for discussion, having students retell the content, or drawing charts. The practice should be carried out flexibly according to the nature of the teaching materials.

(5) During inspection, teachers should record particularly excellent or poor performances in a notebook respectively, with special emphasis on the assessment of individual characteristics. The symbols used for classification can be chosen at their convenience.

(6) Written answers should be inspected after class.

(7) The amount of teaching materials must be refined, precise, and applicable, so that teaching and practice correspond to each other; there should be no greed for excessive content. However, the topics and levels to be taught in each subject must be appropriately considered and determined in advance, and should not be arbitrarily omitted during teaching.

(8) At the end of each semester, all the inspections conducted regularly should be summarized to form the performance assessment.

(9) For matters not covered herein, teachers may implement them at their discretion and present their opinions to the Education Department for consideration and adoption.

3.3 Establish a Teaching Materials Research Association

It should be noted that teaching materials for the same subject must be more or less adjusted due to differences in the nature of schools and varying local conditions. Textbooks available in the market are characterized by disorganized content, improper arrangement, and a structure that is close to lecture notes, making them quite unsuitable for use. Moreover, there are few types of textbooks; those suitable for School Type A may not be suitable for School Type B, and those suitable for Locality A may not be suitable for Locality B. Without research and evaluation of teaching materials carried out independently by each province, no matter how much teaching methods are improved, proper results cannot be achieved. Furthermore, current educational trends are increasingly emphasizing practicality. If we allow popular textbooks, which are filled with trivial and vague knowledge, to serve as the standard for teaching implementation, what would become of school education? For the sake of reform, we propose the establishment of a Teaching Materials Research Association, with the following measures:

(1) First, for general subjects, the Education Department shall, for each subject, appoint special commissioners from among teachers of similar schools who are excellent in knowledge and experience, and also assign teachers with rich educational research experience to jointly organize a Teaching Materials Research Association.

(2) There is no fixed number of personnel appointed by the Education Department, and their term shall last until the teaching details are formulated.

(3) Discuss policies regarding subjects, time, quantity, level, etc., as well as the selection and arrangement of teaching materials according to the type of school.

(4) Based on the decisions made in the above discussions, the special commissioners in charge of each subject shall compile teaching details and introduce applicable and reference books by subject. However, the content and distribution order of teaching materials must break away from the perspective of a rigid scientific system.

(5) When compiling teaching details, each commissioner may, for the subject they are responsible for, raise questions at any time to seek opinions from teachers who teach the same subject in similar schools.

(6) After the compilation of teaching details is completed, the Education Department shall assign personnel by subject to review them before publishing them.

(7) After publication, all new students' teaching must be carried out in accordance with these details. For existing classes, appropriate adaptations shall also be made to gradually align them with the published teaching details.

(8) If teachers of various schools believe that it is necessary to adapt the published teaching details, they may present their opinions.

(9) The academic proficiency of students taking entrance examinations shall be assessed based on the published teaching details.

(10) The funds for the Teaching Materials Research Association shall be shared equally by all schools.

(11) All commissioners shall serve in an honorary capacity, but upon completion of the compilation, the Education Department shall submit a request for special rewards for them.

(12) If, after experimentation, the published teaching details are deemed to require revision, the Education Department shall handle the matter as appropriate.

(13) The research on specialized teaching materials shall be conducted in accordance with all the above provisions.

3.4 Establish Vacation Seminars

Educational scholarship advances with each passing day. What was once regarded as a new method may now have become a thing of the past; those who are now praised for their capabilities may, in a few years, be outperformed by others. Primary school teachers, with meager salaries and heavy workloads, have relatively limited energy for research. Moreover, being confined to remote areas, they rarely have the opportunity to observe and learn from others. To enhance their knowledge and learning, relying solely on their own research is not as effective as having higher-level local educational authorities promote it through various means, which can achieve widespread impact with greater force. Furthermore, having teachers with stronger academic abilities participate in seminars allows them to share their research findings with others. It is with this intention that we propose the establishment of vacation seminars. As for secondary school teaching and administrative staff, their capabilities are somewhat stronger than those of primary school teachers. Either inviting renowned scholars to give lectures to clarify doubts, or having colleagues share their insights and exchange knowledge, will be of great benefit to the advancement of scholarship.

Funds for the seminars for secondary school staff and administrative personnel have been included in the budget. As for the funds for primary school workshops, which are operated as an adjunct to provincial schools, an annual subsidy of 400 yuan is planned for each of the five locations, resulting in an annual expenditure of 2,000 yuan. It is proposed that this amount be included in the budget under the education funds for the 10th fiscal year.

3.5 Establish a teaching council for primary schools affiliated to normal schools

To improve primary school education, it is essential to enable teachers who have served or are currently serving to understand the methods of improvement, and to equip the teachers currently being trained with the knowledge and skills for such improvement. For the former, it is crucial to have models to learn from; for the latter, it is vital to have model practices. Primary schools affiliated to normal schools actually bear both responsibilities. Among the provincial normal schools (for both males and females) in Henan, only the first Normal School has relatively complete grades; the others fall short of this, with particularly shabby facilities and teaching. In addition to having already ordered the expansion of grades and earnest reorganization, we now propose the establishment of a Teaching Council as a starting point for improving teaching. The most important thing in improving teaching methods is the ethos of mutual research and mutual assistance. Without mutual research, one will be content with ignorance; without mutual assistance, one will easily become narrow-minded. Both ignorance and narrow-mindedness can hinder educational progress. To break through this obstacle, we should start by earnestly implementing the council system. This approach allows those with better abilities to benefit from observing and learning from others, thus moving toward greater perfection; those with slightly lower abilities can also draw lessons from others and gradually refine themselves. It is faintly heard that there are two objections to this:1) Scholars, due to long-standing habits, are quite reluctant to have others evaluate them. What is shameful is not knowing but refusing to seek knowledge, having faults but refusing to correct them, and even rejecting others' observation and learning. If one does not know but seeks knowledge, or has faults but can correct them, there is nothing to be ashamed of. 2) There is concern that exposing weaknesses through evaluation may affect one's position. In fact, if there are weaknesses, getting others' evaluations to help improve is precisely a way to maintain one's position. If one adheres stubbornly to old ways, they may even lose their position despite wanting to keep it.

Therefore, the establishment of this council is not only for improving primary school teaching but also a good remedy for teachers' ignorance and narrow-mindedness.

Published in *The Chinese Education Circle*, Vol. 10, Issues 11 and 12, May and June 1921; also in *Education Bulletin*, Vol. 8, Issues 6, 7 and 8, June, July and August 1921. It has been considerably abridged in this book.

Plan for the New-style National Schools

Introduction

During the two years I served as an educational inspector in Zhongzhou (Henan), I took charge of organizing compulsory education in the provincial capital. Aspiring to put into practice my long-cherished ideals of educational reform, I began with primary schools, aiming to cultivate the general public. To this end, I drafted a four-chapter plan for new-style national schools: 1. Curriculum, 2. Organization, 3. Facilities, 4. Teachers. The first chapter outlines the general principles and key points, while the latter three specify the implementation methods. The main purpose of this plan is to set the direction and path for newly established schools, thoroughly eliminating the drawbacks of old-style education—such as going against children's instincts and being impractical. Focused on practical implementation, it does not aim for exhaustive detail. I hope that this modest contribution can guide various efforts toward a common goal. If it thereby stimulates nationwide research on primary education and inspires the reform of secondary education, this work will have pioneered a new example. Aware of my own inadequacy and limited knowledge, my words may fail to fully convey my intentions. I earnestly request scholars and experts across the country to correct and improve it.

1. Curriculum

The division of subjects is for the convenience of arranging teaching materials, not for the purpose of education. However, it has led to a drawback: subjects have become isolated from one another, often emphasizing their own systems, which deviates from the purpose of education. As a result, teaching materials are mostly impractical, and teaching methods tend to be monotonous. The purpose of education is originally to cultivate children's physical and mental development, enabling each to develop in accordance with their instincts. In the old way of classifying subjects, there were no appropriate courses for cultivating children's abilities, and character training was even carried out outside of academic subjects. This is inconsistent with the original intention of establishing subjects. With such an arrangement, no matter how hard teachers work on research or adopt innovative methods, they will inevitably be confined by the scope of subjects and unable to fully achieve the goal of cultivation. Moreover, primary school children are young, and their learning approaches are quite different from those of adults. The arrangement of the curriculum should be based on the needs of life and in line with the natural development process of children. If we adopt separate subjects, even if we select appropriate teaching materials and try to connect them with each other, it would be putting the cart before the horse. This will reduce students' interest in learning, and it is indeed not easy to achieve good results. Therefore, reforming the curriculum is an extremely urgent issue for primary schools.

The curriculum of national schools is hereby divided into six categories, with a brief explanation of the purpose of each category as follows: 1) Games (including five items: etiquette drills, cultivation of senses, cultivation of intelligence, sports, and singing); 2) Observation (including two items: natural observation and social observation); 3) Work (including five items: drawing, handcraft, gardening, animal rearing, and cleaning/arranging); 4) Conversation; 5) Reading and Writing (including punctuation); 6) Arithmetic.

Now that the categories have been established, a brief explanation of their purposes is as follows.

The purpose of the game class is to observe the innocence of children in their playful activities, and to formulate learning courses using game formats based on their life needs and abilities. It is divided into five items:

1.1 Etiquette Drills. This shares the same purpose as the old-style "cultivation of virtue" courses, but when taught through textbooks, it often becomes a matter of abstract moralizing that fails to stir students' emotions. Worse still, it is treated as a subject similar to Chinese language studies. In contrast, this category adopts practical social scenarios as materials and presents them through concrete, performative rituals. For example, when practicing banquet etiquette, local customs are investigated, with unrefined or overly cumbersome elements removed, and universal etiquette may be moderately incorporated—all selected for their demonstrative value and practiced strictly according to the rituals. One student acts as the host, several as family elders or younger relatives, and the rest as guests. They first practice greeting guests, then serving tea, and finally seating arrangements. Details such as the order of seats, the placement and movement of cups, chopsticks, bowls, and plates, as well as the exchanges between hosts and guests, must all closely resemble real-life situations. If there are gender-specific etiquettes, these should be explained during the post-performance discussion. Though seemingly trivial, it is common to see adults in our country mishandle seating arrangements or tableware placement. If children practice such rituals at school from an early age, their proper conduct alone will earn them respect in society. Extending this to practices like celebrations, condolences, and meetings—where children collaborate on designing decorations and purchases—not only aligns with social life but also integrates language, crafts, drawing, and arithmetic into the drills, eliminating the monotony of traditional teaching. Unlike the old "virtue cultivation" method, which taught one ritual at a time with little engagement, this project-based approach makes learning effortless for children.

1.2 Sensory Cultivation. This plays a significant role in physical activities and hands-on work, though it is also implicitly present in other subjects. Here, it is treated as a dedicated category to specifically train vision, hearing, touch, etc. Drawing largely on Montessori methods, it aims to sharpen children's senses through practice, thereby realizing the educational value of sensory development. For instance, visual training may involve quickly distinguishing complex or subtle colors, or practicing long-distance vision. Auditory exercises could include identifying faint sounds, recognizing sound sources or distances with eyes closed. Tactile training might teach distinguishing textures (rough/smooth), hardness, weight, or temperature through touch, and even inferring objects by feel. These sensory drills can also be integrated into other subjects: visual skills through arithmetic estimation, auditory skills through musical rhythms, and so on—all depending on the teacher's ingenuity in application.

1.3 Intellectual Cultivation. This focuses not on testing but on fostering quick thinking, meticulous attention, and accurate perception. Materials such as error-detection tests, maze puzzles, cancellation exercises (from psychological tests), building block toys, and popular riddles are excellent teaching tools. However, items from Binet-Simon intelligence tests that serve only as assessment tools without educational value in cultivation need not be adopted. Other beneficial exercises include asking children to describe the distance from their home to school, the names and layouts of streets traveled, or the items and arrangements in school rooms based on their observations.

1.4 Physical Exercises. This aligns with the purpose of traditional gymnastics but emphasizes games, avoiding overly rigid routines or exercises unsuitable for young children. Dance games are particularly beneficial. Incorporating competitive activities related to academic tasks into exercises also adds interest.

1.5 Singing. This need not be a standalone subject but should be taught by teachers at appropriate times, integrated with other lessons, or performed during designated periods to lift children's ethoss. The goal is to let their moods resonate with the songs, free from feelings of drudgery.

Currently, most primary and secondary schools in Bian (Kaifeng) teach only single-tone numbered musical notation, even simplifying standard musical scores into this form, resulting in monotonous rhythms. Starting from the third grade, students should be taught standard notation directly. Initially, focus solely on symbol recognition without explaining musical theory; avoid overwhelming them with complex notations or scales early on, which would stifle interest by restricting their minds.

The purpose of the Observation class is to adhere to the principle of object teaching by designing learning courses based on the things necessary for life, taking into account timing, location, and opportunities. In a broad sense, "observation" here includes experimentation. It is divided into two categories: Natural and Social Observation.

Natural Observation is considered particularly important in primary school education. However, due to the difficulties urban schools face in natural research, greater emphasis is placed on Social Observation. Therefore, the Observation curriculum at Kaifeng Compulsory Schools should focus on social aspects, broadly categorized as follows: 1)Operations and conditions of industrial and commercial enterprises; 2) Status of the transportation industry; 3) Quality of goods; 4) Workflow in manufacturing plants; 5) Construction materials and processes; 6) Historical relics. Beyond supplementing learning materials for other subjects, the primary goal of this observation is to help students understand human labor and social living conditions. For Natural Observation, plant cultivation should emphasize experimentation. For example, students can observe the growth of identical seeds planted in pots with different soil types or fertilization methods, or track the sequential development from germination to maturity. Teachers may also take children to suburban fields for observation or use household plants as teaching materials. For animal studies, common local species or seasonal specimens are ideal. Catching insects like frogs, butterflies, dragonflies, and crickets for research can enhance interest. After analyzing their morphology, students should study habits and living conditions to cultivate empathy and kindness toward animals. Regarding natural phenomena, students should observe weather and seasonal changes in detail, make comparisons, and receive timely explanations. Tools like barometers and thermometers should be provided for measurements. The materials used in this course not only impart knowledge but also greatly assist in conversation, literacy, composition, and practical work. Simple physics and chemistry experiments, which effectively stimulate children's thinking and abilities while being highly engaging, should also be incorporated as appropriate.

The purpose of the work class is based on the principle of integrating learning into practical tasks, aiming to cultivate an ethos of diligence, perseverance, and love for work, as well as to develop creative abilities. The curriculum is divided into five items: in drawing, the drawbacks of the old method—focusing solely on copying models—should be avoided. Instead, children should be asked to sketch concrete objects, with an emphasis on simplicity in brushwork; bold, heavy lines are acceptable. Uncolored pictures can also be used for children to fill in colors: biological illustrations should be painted realistically, while work-related drawings allow for creative color matching. For crafts such as paper crafts, clay modeling, and bamboo/woodworking, children should be encouraged to make toys they enjoy, thereby practicing their skills. In short, drawing and handicrafts focus on fostering expressive abilities; during learning, children should be allowed to create freely according to their wishes, rather than being restricted to making identical works. For gardening, if there is no open space, potted plants can be used for cultivation and irrigation. Raising animals—such as chickens, ducks, fish, and birds—can also help children understand the living conditions of animals. In terms of cleaning and organizing, all tasks such as sweeping, dusting, and arranging the school premises should be done collaboratively with the children. They should also be encouraged to find ways to change the layout of the facilities from time to time, so that their ingenuity is exercised alongside physical labor. The surrounding areas outside the school must also be kept clean collectively to leave a good impression on the community. In addition, when craftsmen are hired for tasks like painting, varnishing, or pasting in the school, children can be taken to observe and study the process; a portion of the unfinished work can be appropriately assigned to the children to complete on their own.

The purpose of the conversation class is to capitalize on children's childhood fondness for fairy tales, selecting content that benefits the cultivation of their character and knowledge, as well as materials conducive to practicing language and writing, thereby formulating the learning curriculum. The types of conversations include stories, tales, fables, etc. In terms of material selection, apart from humor and morality, common sense conversations can also be appropriately used—these should be about concrete things that children can understand and find highly interesting. The content can be told by teachers, narrated interactively by children, or even reenacted through performances. Special emphasis is placed on mutual debate, as it can stimulate the desire to practice speaking. All language practice tasks related to the Chinese language subject are implemented in this class. However, its learning function, while embodying the educational value of both the "Moral Cultivation" and "Chinese Language" subjects, differs in purpose. Those subjects, confined to their own scopes, select fixed teaching materials, leading to a focus on acquiring subject-specific knowledge, which often fails to align with children's psychology. In contrast, this class purely examines children's interests and preferences, chooses lively and engaging materials, and through the cultivation of games, achieves the educational effects of academic subjects from both the material and practice aspects. Thus, it avoids the drawbacks of being dry and uninteresting, unlike the "Moral Cultivation" subject which overemphasizes morality, or the "Chinese Language" subject which overemphasizes formality.

The purpose of the reading and writing class is to develop children's abilities in recognizing characters, writing, composing essays, and reading through games and practical needs, based on the way young children learn language, thereby formulating the learning curriculum. In other classes, there are indeed occasional opportunities for practice, but since the focus is not on these abilities, it is impossible to systematically organize the Chinese language learning. Moreover, Chinese characters are complex and numerous; without appropriate practice, it is difficult to achieve a solid grasp. Therefore, a special curriculum must be designed for learning. Here are a few points based on relevant insights:

(1) Regarding the learning of national phonetic alphabets, in current actual teaching practices, there are several approaches. First, teach the national phonetic alphabets alone for two or three weeks, then start teaching Chinese characters while also instructing on phonetic notation. Second, compile textbooks using characters with phonetic components and teach them, only introducing Chinese characters after one year or half a year. Third, intersperse characters with phonetic components in the textbooks for teaching. The first approach is most widely implemented, but many critics denounce it as meaningless teaching that does not conform to principles. The second and third approaches are advocated by the new school of thought. I have very little research on this matter, but I find that the third teaching method, which alternates between Chinese characters and characters with phonetic components in the text, is quite similar in form to

Japanese textbooks. Moreover, it easily confuses children's concepts of character formation. In addition, when characters with phonetic components are not yet commonly used alongside Chinese characters, if the second or third teaching methods are hastily adopted in areas with a conservative atmosphere, it may further breed misunderstandings, even shaking the foundation of learning national phonetic alphabets. It is proposed to temporarily adopt the first teaching method to practice the articulatory organs. If taught properly, it can be used to correct pronunciation, and can also achieve some effect in cultivating the senses. As for the experimentation with other teaching methods, efforts should be made to gradually try them out.

(2) Regarding the learning of characters, teachers must, before teaching each character, find ways to make children feel the need to recognize that character—only then will it be effective. When teaching characters, textbooks should not be used at all. Instead, adhering to the principle of object teaching, teachers should select characters based on what children need and like at that moment: objects in the classroom, parts of the human body, weather phenomena, actions that can be performed, or descriptive words with clear imagery. Characters with simple strokes and easy-to-understand meanings should be taught along with explanations of their corresponding states. Gradually, characters related to observed things can be introduced. Even abstract words, if they are simple and of the most urgent need, can be appropriately presented based on immediate usage. Although what is learned at this stage consists only of words and phrases, lacking the appeal of literary texts, it aligns with the way children naturally acquire language—so children will not find learning tedious. Moreover, without wasting effort on practicing textbook passages, they can learn more characters; after one year of such practice, they will easily be able to read longer texts.

For disyllabic or polysyllabic content words (real words that form phrases), their pronunciation should first be read character by character, then as an entire phrase, followed by an explanation of their meaning. If a phrase cannot be interpreted by analyzing its individual characters—even when the phrase contains a mix of familiar and unfamiliar characters—it should be explained as a whole. One must not rigidly stick to interpreting single characters, as is the flawed practice of, for example, defining "pi" (in "pipa") as "a type of tree" or "dun" (in " Washington") as "a personal name."

For characters with multiple meanings, only the meaning relevant to the current lesson should be explained. For instance, if the text uses "kebo" (mean-spirited), one should not additionally mention the meaning of "shike" (moment/time). However, if a later-taught meaning is derived from a previously learned one and is easy to understand, it can be clarified. For example, after teaching "zhujie" (bamboo joints), when later teaching "jiecao" (moral integrity), one can explain the extended meaning.

The text should be in the colloquial style. When a character's meaning cannot be further paraphrased, its nature, context, or function should be explained. One must avoid the flawed practice of circular definitions such as "ku (cry) is just cry," "shuo (speak) is speaking," or "mai (wheat) is wheat."

When explaining a character's meaning, if its form has not significantly deviated from its original pictographic or ideographic structure, one should flexibly use the principles of Shuowen Jiezi (Explaining Simple and Analyzing Compound Characters) to elaborate. Phonetic compounds account for 80–90% of Chinese characters; except for a few cases with abbreviated phonetic components or drastic sound changes over time, one can use Shuowen's interpretive methods to link meaning through radicals and sound through phonetic elements. Associative compounds (huiyi), formed by combining two or more components, also follow logical patterns. Pictographs (xiangxing) and indicative characters (zhishi) that retain their original forms are similarly easy to explain. Interpreting meaning through form not only adds interest but also aids memory and comprehension.

New characters in a text should be taught as they appear in sentences, rather than adopting the flawed practice of teaching all new characters first before introducing the text—this separates characters from their context, making them isolated and uninteresting. Additionally, the pronunciation, meaning, and writing of each character should be practiced several times within its word or phrase before moving to the next. Avoid teaching too many new characters at once and mixing their practice (of sound, meaning, and writing). Focused attention deepens impression, ensures accurate understanding, and achieves more with less effort.

Repetition is especially crucial for character recognition. The common method of rote review is dull and ineffective; daily recitation, too, is vague and aimless. Instead, select previously learned difficult characters and newly acquired ones, and frequently use them in writing exercises. This embeds review naturally and allows one to determine the number of repetitions needed for long-term retention.

(3) The learning of grammar should be supported by separately compiled systematic grammar tables and a progressive grammar curriculum. Through reading and by means of exercises in composition, students can grasp grammatical usage. Guidance on the study and discussion of textbook passages should be provided opportunely as the lesson proceeds; it should not be confined to a fixed period of time dedicated solely to teaching grammar after the entire passage has been read.

(4) Punctuation marks play a considerable role in expressing the structure of sentences and the coherence of discourse. Understanding their

usage is highly beneficial for grasping the key points of grammar and correcting incomplete language habits. Guidance on punctuation should be provided promptly in relation to those used in the textbook passages.

(5) Points to note in reading and writing: When reading texts, one should conform to the natural rhythm of the spoken language. Both the old-style intonation used in reading classical Chinese and the prevalent bad habit in schools of reading one character at a time should be abolished. Special attention should be paid to the writing of characters. Because the Chinese (colloquial Chinese) is easier to read and explain than classical Chinese, many children can read and explain the texts they have learned but still cannot write them from memory. Therefore, it is essential to set aside specific time for character practice every week. However, it is more appropriate to practice writing characters that have already been learned. The purpose of the Arithmetic class is to design a learning curriculum based on children's intellectual development and the progression of arithmetic studies, through practical exercises tailored to the computational needs of daily life. Currently, there are three common flaws in arithmetic teaching: 1) Overemphasis on practicing symbols, which does not align with children's psychology. 2) Overreliance on textbook-based calculations, which fail to be applied in real-life situations. 3) Neglect of mental arithmetic practice, leading to incompetence in quick counting. To rectify the first two flaws, it is not enough to abolish textbooks; we must adopt realistic methods and appropriate teaching materials. Therefore, learning tools such as abacuses, various physical objects, rulers for measuring length, scales for weighing, containers for measuring volume (e.g., liters, bushels), geometric models, replicas of currency, bills, account books, and specimens must be prepared. When beginners learn to count, they must use physical objects and pictures to practice counting before recording numbers with symbols. It is particularly important to conduct various exercises in actual measurement,

visual estimation, and step-based measurement in appropriate settings. For example, when learning to calculate length, measure the length, height, and width of desks and chairs, the dimensions of blackboards, the area of classrooms and school yards, or students' heights using rulers or steps. For weight calculations, first weigh objects or students' weights with scales, then compare and compute; or assign problems using pre-weighed objects, then verify the results with scales. This not only practices calculation but also teaches the use of scales, which is especially useful for practical purposes. Progressing further, calculations related to tuition fees, school supplies, prices and discounts of daily necessities, currency exchange, and household income and expenses must be designed as scenarios that mirror real-life usage. Such "applied practice" ensures genuine utility and prevents children from struggling with theoretical speculation while remaining confused about fundamental principles. Explaining problems through written symbols requires prior understanding of mathematical logic and computational rules, which young children often fail to grasp. In contrast, counting with physical objects and practical scenarios allows children to comprehend mathematical logic, deduce rules, and obtain real verification through hands-on practice—clearly distinguishing ease from difficulty. Additionally, installing more blackboards on the walls (front, sides, and above) in the classroom facilitates competitive speed arithmetic, which is essential. Mental arithmetic practice should last only 2–3 minutes per session to avoid causing distress. For number practice, it is not sufficient to memorize only the multiplication table. Addition and subtraction within 100, including single-digit and tens-digit operations, should also be memorized through tables (e.g., 1+1=2, 1+2=3, etc.). Each set of ten numbers should be integrated into comprehensive exercises, repeated until proficiency is achieved. The multiplication table and abacus rhymes should follow this example, divided into small, sequential exercises so that each session involves memorizing only a few phrases, making repetition easier for mastery. Mental arithmetic drills for problem-solving should be conducted at the start of each class, using memorized tables, rhymes, simple computational rules, or relevant numerical conventions related to the current teaching content, practiced through question-and-answer sessions.

As suggested in the above opinions on the curriculum for various subjects, the primary principle is to avoid using textbooks. For reading and writing classes starting from the second grade, although teaching may involve text passages, current textbooks are still unsuitable. A syllabus should be formulated before each season, and detailed teaching materials and learning procedures should be specified before each week. Prior to finalizing these, teachers should, based on their strengths and interests, take charge of systematic research on specific subjects or topics within subjects, propose teaching materials and their organization, then collectively review, discuss, and consolidate them. At the end of each season and each week, joint meetings should be held to discuss the implementation of the curriculum. Although the above teaching materials and methods have been elaborated in detail, with frequent guidance on how to integrate and flexibly apply them, we must still guard against the risk of their gradual separation and overemphasis on the internal system of individual subjects. Therefore, when determining teaching content each week, more integrated project-based approaches should be adopted. In addition to holding celebratory events through project-based teaching for festivals or commemorative days, at least one small-scale recreational gathering should be held monthly, and one large-scale recreational gathering per season. These events serve as the best project-based teaching designs in the school and offer the optimal opportunities for integrating teaching across different subjects.

Within the daily scheduled study hours, apart from the content of each class, there should be a few minutes set aside for two types of training: 1) Inspection of cleanliness. Check whether children's faces, hands, fingers, clothes, and shoes are clean; whether daily items are messy, and ensure proper tidying up is done every day. 2) Training in tranquility. The purpose of this is not necessarily to urge self-reflection, but specifically to allow a little peace amid usual activities. It may involve training their hearing through quiet rest during games, or having them take a short nap after activities. Choose an appropriate time each day to let them close their eyes, hold their breath, and sit quietly for two to three minutes. With long-term practice, they will gradually enter a state of calm and develop the habit of tranquility. Some may doubt that this method is incompatible with children's psychology. However, Montessori has applied it effectively in training young children; from what I have seen, when national schools in our country follow this practice, children show no signs of discomfort. Moreover, it eases their physical activities to reduce excessive mental excitement, straightens their muscles and bones, and helps concentrate their minds—all of which have considerable value in both teaching and hygiene.

Hours allocated to each subject: Games account for 25%. Observation, and Reading & Writing each account for 20%. Arithmetic accounts for 15%. Work and Conversation each account for 10%. The specific allocation and adjustment of hours for sub-items within each subject, varying by nature or school year, shall be determined flexibly according to the progress of each semester during implementation.

Daily study hours total seven, with a reduction of one or two hours on Wednesdays and Saturdays. The last hour of each day is reserved for children's free activities at school. Study sessions are divided into approximately ten periods, following the aforementioned percentage allocation. With 60 minutes per hour, the weekly hours break down as follows: Games: 510 minutes; Observation, and Reading & Writing: 408 minutes each; Arithmetic: 306 minutes; Work and Conversation: 204 minutes each. Session duration is determined by subject nature: Reading &

Writing and Arithmetic sessions should each last around 40 minutes (approximately 10 sessions weekly for Writing, 8 for Arithmetic). Games, Observation, Work, and Conversation sessions should last around 20 or 40 minutes, averaging 30 minutes (approximately 14 weekly sessions for Games, 12 for Observation, and 7 each for Work and Conversation). Daily session scheduling roughly follows: 2 sessions each for Games and Observation; 3 combined sessions for Reading & Writing and Conversation; and at least 1 session each for Arithmetic and Work. This is a general framework, subject to flexibility in practice. For example, project-based teaching may require 5–6 or even over 10 sessions for a single unit, integrating multiple subjects—making it difficult to align with fixed allocations. In such cases, weekly curricula should be adjusted to supplement areas insufficiently addressed in the project. Additionally, room must be left for adapting materials to weather conditions or modifying time limits based on learning progress. Field observations, for instance, may require extended conversation practice or follow-up performances, making it impossible to rigidly fix daily subject timings. However, the following principles apply to scheduling: 1) Most sessions should involve integrated projects; even for separate subjects taught on the same day, materials must be interconnected. 2) Subjects should be alternated to avoid monotony. 3) No single session (except field observations) should exceed 2 hours.

Break times can be flexibly adjusted according to the length of the current study session and the nature of the lessons, and are not restricted by fixed rules of starting and ending classes after each lesson. Generally, after each lesson, there should be a short break of a few minutes. However, if consecutive lessons accumulate to more than two hours, a 20-minute break is necessary. Therefore, there should be one formal break in the middle of the lessons both in the morning and afternoon. Even during breaks, teachers should still take on the responsibility of supervision, because children's free activities during breaks can also be regarded as part of the curriculum. Under the current system, the teaching hours in national schools are generally three to four hours per day, with a maximum of no more than five hours. With seven hours set here, there is no need to worry about children getting fatigued. Why is that? The old-style curriculum could only discuss the content and teaching methods of subjects to cater to children's psychology. Therefore, from the perspective of children acquiring new knowledge, it is naturally appropriate to have about four hours of teaching. Moreover, the teaching materials were constrained by the inherent system of the subjects, making children prone to fatigue, hence the restriction of 45 minutes for one teaching session. As a result, in the compiled lessons, even if a lesson did not require 45 minutes of teaching, or if it was an isolated subject that was most interesting, there would be combined teaching of two subjects within one session. Adopting teaching materials from separate subjects and organizing them in a connected way is indeed valuable in education. However, if there is no connection in content but two subjects are taught together within one session, it is merely to fill the specified time and has nothing to do with the purpose of combining or separating subjects. The new-style curriculum, in terms of substantive cultivation, only seeks appropriate teaching materials based on children's own conditions and environment, as well as their needs and interests. In terms of formal cultivation, it specially uses game organization to exercise their instincts, without being constrained by explanatory words or the scope of subjects. Everything that comes into their sight and hearing can be teaching materials, and the way of learning must start from perception. Furthermore, the curriculum is divided into many items, which can be easily changed, avoiding the rigidity of lessons. Learning is counted by the number of sessions, and with more sessions, the time limit can be adjusted according to the nature of the lessons and the learning situation, without the drawback of uniform time. What is particularly important is that the learning of the curriculum corresponds to children's activities. The so-called curriculum and learning are nothing more than enabling children to engage in purposeful and regular activities. During their time at school, everything they do is a learning matter, and every event is a cultivation of the curriculum. Wherever teachers and children are, that is the place for learning, which is not limited to the classroom. All aspects of children's words, expressions, movements, and behaviors are under the supervision of teachers, and the appropriate cultivation given is the curriculum for children's learning, which is not limited to the teaching of certain fixed subjects for learning to be necessary. Not only are teaching and training not separated into two things, but there is also no distinction between in-class and out-of-class. The reason for stipulating the curriculum is just to show teachers the direction of cultivation in various aspects, so that they can implement educational functions on children's character and intelligence, and then the goals and rules of their activities can make progress day by day in an orderly manner. In this way, children's learning is completely different from the old-style learning that focuses on memory, consumes mental energy, is not suitable for application, makes children uninterested in the curriculum, and easily causes weariness. Therefore, even with more hours, it is not troublesome but beneficial. Moreover, the stipulation of teaching hours in the current system only considers avoiding fatigue, but it brings about many drawbacks. 1) Extracurricular review is either conducted at specific times arranged by the school or assigned as tasks for children to complete at home. In families that value academic performance and schools with rigorous management, this is regarded as a top priority. The flaw of the old system was that teaching was limited to scheduled class hours, resulting in incomplete mastery of what was learned—especially in Chinese language studies—making additional review essential. This was partly due to ineffective teaching methods, but more fundamentally, the heavy and tedious curriculum could not be fully mastered within limited class time.

Increasing teaching hours further would only make children more weary, leaving no easy solution. Practice must follow immediately after teaching to ensure effectiveness; otherwise, practice becomes aimless and meaningless. The structured curriculum does not require introducing new materials or adhering strictly to formal teaching formats in every session. Treating in-class teaching as “main lessons” and review as “extracurricular” violates the principles of education. Moreover, without proper guidance, home-based review often becomes empty rhetoric. This is one drawback. 2)Unregulated play outside school. A flaw of the old system was that children spent only half a day at school, with the rest of their time spent idling outside, exposed to harmful social influences. Such exposure could often jeopardize their morality and health, while the long hours wasted were also regrettable. This is why many parents criticized schools for being less restrictive than traditional private tutors: keeping children at school all day, they believed, would ease family worries. This is another drawback. With the increased daily hours stipulated here, the aforementioned flaws can be easily avoided. As for concerns about fatigue, they are unnecessary due to the fundamental reform of the curriculum, as previously explained.

2. Class Organization

A common flaw in today’s school education is that students with varying intellectual abilities are grouped together in the same class and taught the same content at the same pace. The progress is based on the standard of the majority of average students: the gifted are stifled in their talents, while the less capable struggle to keep up. This is even less effective than the old-style private tutoring, where each student studied different books at a pace suitable to their ability, making it easier to achieve tangible results. Thus, adopting group teaching and breaking away from the grade system have become the most crucial issues in education. However, given the current state of education in our country, breaking the grade system is more difficult to implement outside of metropolitan areas where schools can easily collaborate. In provincial capitals, where compulsory education is provided and there are a large number of students at the same level, and with dedicated personnel overseeing the matter, adjusting class groupings (combining or splitting them) will not be hindered. Moreover, provincial and county primary schools located in the same city can also be encouraged to collaborate. Therefore, the regulations for organizing classes are as follows:

(1) The first semester of the national school enrolls new students, with the maximum age not exceeding 9 years old, and enrolls at least 6 classes each time. Upon initial enrollment, psychological tests shall be used to assess children's intelligence and abilities. Based on their differences, they shall be divided into three groups: A, B, and C, with 2 classes in each group, and still receive the same teaching. Among different groups, observe the progress of children in each group; among classes in the same group, observe the teaching methods of teachers. The admission test method shall be formulated separately.

Each student shall enroll in the place where their group is located according to the determined differences. If, due to the family's distance, they need to enroll in a school closer to their home but there is no appropriate group, they may be admitted as appropriate; however, the teaching progress cannot be based on the student's ability.

(2) There is a promotion every six months. The original groups A, B, and C are merged, and the promotion standard is determined by the newly measured differences and the performance assessment differences. Those who are promoted are divided into groups A and B for teaching. After progressing to the end of the second academic year, different courses for each group shall be determined as appropriate according to the progress of their performance, and the study period of group A shall be shortened. The

method for assessing the performance of each course shall be formulated separately.

Although children are grouped according to the differences in their intelligence and abilities upon initial enrollment, the tests may not be accurate, and after the implementation of education, their development varies. Teachers must pay attention to assessing performance in daily life, record them separately. Before promotion, the Education Department shall send personnel, together with the special commissioners in charge of compulsory education, to conduct appropriate tests and verify their performance. The temporary test method shall be formulated separately.

(3) Enrollment is conducted in both spring and autumn, and the two are connected and progressing together. Students who repeat a grade are merged into the classes of the next season for grouping.

(4) Higher primary schools are closely related to national schools. For higher primary schools established in the provincial capital, the number of classes and methods must correspond to those of national schools. It is proposed to divide the higher primary school curriculum into two types: two-year and three-year. The two-year curriculum is for the top graduates of national schools. Promotion and grade repetition are also limited to half a year, and enrollment is conducted in both spring and autumn to facilitate connection and progress. The curriculum and organization shall be reformed separately with reference to the purpose of national schools.

If provincial and county higher primary schools adopt this system, students who are promoted without graduating from the new-style curriculum shall undergo a strict test using a newly formulated test method upon initial enrollment. For those who graduate from national schools and are eager to make a living, vocational schools equivalent to higher primary schools shall be established. Their methods are different from those of type

B industrial schools specified by the ministry, and their curriculum and organization are different from ordinary ones.

3. Equipment

Due to the financial constraints of the local area, it is impossible to implement all equipment in accordance with ideal standards. However, for outdated and inappropriate ones, as well as those indispensable for learning in the new-style curriculum, efforts must still be made to raise funds and set them up.

The school building is borrowed from a public office, but it must have at least one classroom, one workshop, one playroom, and an open space for 100 people to exercise. The layout of each room will be gradually improved and renovated. Specialized personnel in charge of equipment will inspect the needs from time to time and purchase and arrange them accordingly. The length and width of the site, as well as the length, width, and height of each room, must follow construction standards, with symbols marking the dimensions to facilitate children's practical measurement and verification.

Learning tools, such as those required in the curriculum description, must all be purchased and prepared.

The rostrum in the classroom should not be placed in the center; instead, it should be set up at a suitable location on the side of the upper part, with desks and chairs. Teachers' reference books and materials can all be placed on the desk, and no separate rest room is needed. The blackboard set above should be approximately equal to the width of the classroom; avoid using boards that can move up and down, and appropriately set up blackboards on the left and right sides as well. Except for the central part of the blackboard, the rest should be covered with light blue cloth curtains when not in use. In addition, several small blackboards should be made for teachers' preparation. Desks and chairs should not be painted black, and those that can rotate left and right are most preferable. Their dimensions must be appropriate, with heights roughly divided into three grades, so that children can sit in order, each fitting their own height. Moreover, as they grow taller year by year, only part of them need to be replaced, which can also save funds.

4. Teachers

The organization of new-style schools is implemented step by step based on theories. Whether it can achieve practical results depends entirely on the capabilities and enthusiasm of teachers. Therefore, the fundamental reform of education starts with the transformation of the curriculum and is determined by the implementation of teachers. The methods are briefly listed as follows:

(1) Selection of teachers: It is planned to select recent normal school graduates under the age of 25, with excellent academic performance and enthusiasm for educational research, to take up the positions.

(2) Allocation of teachers: Each school shall open at least two classes, with three teachers assigned to take charge of them collaboratively. Firstly, this facilitates learning from each other's strengths and dividing the teaching tasks. Secondly, it enables the exchange of knowledge from time to time. Thirdly, during class hours, one teacher can be assigned to prepare for temporary lessons or assist in organizing children's learning. However, the two classes must be in different groups to allow children to enroll nearby and to mutually verify the different progress and educational effects of children in different groups. As for sports and music, if teachers are insufficient in academic ability, several weekly lessons can be temporarily assigned to specialized teachers on a part-time basis.

(3) Training and supplementation of teachers' academic abilities: Regarding the organization and application of teaching material design as

well as the research on teaching methods, celebrities with profound knowledge and rich experience shall be regularly invited to provide guidance for several weeks. For subjects such as science, horticulture, and animal husbandry, several specialized teachers proficient in physics, chemistry, and agriculture from provincial secondary schools or above shall be hired as consultants; if primary school teachers have any unclear understanding when using teaching materials, they can put forward questions and ask for instructions. For games, sports, and music, people with rich research experience nearby shall be hired to teach several hours a week for supplementary lessons. The above-mentioned personnel shall be selected and hired by the Education Department, and the expenses shall be covered by the regular funds for compulsory education.

All the aforementioned plans, after being tested for a season or a school year, may be put forward for discussion if any doubts arise. However, such discussions must be based on scientific experimental insights. One must not raise doubts or modify the original plan simply because the implementation methods are improper.

Published in the Supplement to *Henan Education Bulletin*, Vol. 1, No. 1, October 1921; also in *Education Magazine*, Vol. 14, No. 1, January 1922.

Notice from the Director of Henan Education Department

To run a school, one must understand the current trends in education. From now on, those who come to this department seeking employment must have read Dewey's *Educational Philosophy*, Mill's *Education for Life*, Liao Shicheng's *Outline of Educational Psychology*, etc. They should first present their insights gained from these books before being interviewed. This is hereby announced.

Published in *Henan Education Bulletin*, Vol. 1, No. 21, August 1922.

Opinions on Vocational and Supplementary Education in the Draft of the New School System

- Doubts exist regarding the full-time vocational programs spanning the first, second, and third years of secondary education.

  The proportion of general subjects and vocational subjects should be determined based on their nature, duration, and objectives.

    For vocational programs divided by academic years, only the minimum and maximum durations need to be specified to allow flexible adjustment.

- Supplementary education should be stipulated as a component of compulsory education.

  The curriculum of supplementary education should be calculated by hours rather than years.

    Supplementary education should not be limited to working children.

- The scope of training programs for vocational educators should be expanded.

In general, I agree with the draft school system formulated by the current Provincial Education Federation. I quite wish to further elaborate on my own views, but due to the overly broad scope of my thoughts and my busy schedule, I have not been able to put them into words. Regarding the school system itself, I only hold slightly different opinions on the two plans concerning vocational education and supplementary education. Recently, the China Vocational Education Association has solicited opinions on the vocational education system and put forward four questions, which are largely related to what I intend to say. Taking advantage of the leisure during the winter vacation, I have drafted this article, hoping to discuss it with like-minded people and fulfill my personal responsibility of researching the school system.

1. Issues on the Organization of Vocational Programs in Secondary Education

The original plan divides vocational programs into three categories, which are discussed separately as follows:

(1) The original plan refers to the one-year, two-year, and three-year programs as "complete vocational programs." Is the meaning of "complete" appropriate here? It is found that the original plan, in contrast to the four-year and five-year vocational programs that combine general studies and the three-year vocational program that follows three years of general education, specifically intends to highlight that those longer-duration programs have a more comprehensive range of subjects. If viewed in terms of simplicity versus comprehensiveness, the "completeness" lies in those longer programs rather than these. Yet these are specially termed "complete vocational programs," which seems to imply that "complete" here means "purely vocational." It is true that the flaw in current industrial schools is that they randomly include many general subjects while lacking adequate training in the practical knowledge and skills required for industrial work. To rectify this, on one hand, efforts should be made in terms of equipment and teaching to ensure they can meet vocational needs; on the other hand, irrelevant general subjects should be eliminated, and the teaching materials of general subjects should be improved to make what is learned closely related to vocational life. For there are two types of capabilities that humans should possess in life: one is the moral knowledge and skills for ordinary life, which should be cultivated in general education; the other is the ability to engage in one's occupation, which should be developed by specialized

teachers. Moreover, much of this specialized cultivation—largely vocational skills—is achieved entirely within vocational programs. Part of it, namely vocational ethics, should be fostered through specific training in both vocational and general subjects. During the period of secondary education, if the basic general education is insufficient, abolishing all general subjects would not only hinder academic progress but also, even if technical skills are mastered, such mechanical proficiency would be insufficient to promote human well-being. Furthermore, there would be no need to establish schools to cultivate such skills. However, due to the varying circumstances of individuals, some who are eager to make a living have to be taught simple livelihood skills, such as in apprentice education. Although it is close to mechanical training, it is indeed more sophisticated than the old apprenticeship system; moreover, it does not completely abolish general education, but the shorter the duration, the fewer general subjects there are. We should know that the study of general subjects in vocational programs is purely for the purpose of applying them to vocational life. If they are unrelated to such life, there is no need to study them. This is not only true for vocational education; even in general education, if the teaching materials are irrelevant to life needs, they can be omitted. The boundary for reforming the flaws of traditional education is precisely based on this. It is not true that reducing general subjects can achieve the goal of vocational education. It is impossible to prove whether the "complete vocational programs" in the original plan refer to apprentice education, but interpreting "complete" as "purely vocational" is prone to misunderstanding. It may imply that general subjects are completely unrelated to occupations, and those engaged in occupations only need to apply mechanical skills. Although this aims to correct the flaws of the old system, the potential misunderstanding cannot be ignored. Furthermore, vocational programs, despite their different structures—due to the difficulty of their nature, the breadth of their scope, the length of their duration, or special circumstances—have no distinction between being "purely vocational" or not. It is really unclear what the term "complete" is intended to mean.

(2) Is the intention of the original plan—gradually reducing general subjects and increasing vocational subjects in the four-year and five-year vocational programs—appropriate? For longer-duration vocational programs, which have identified the necessity of combining general subjects, the reasons for such combination are nothing more than the following two: first, the subjects studied must be the basic disciplines for the occupation; second, to enhance general moral knowledge and skills. The former, based on the foundation of the vocational program studied, includes certain general subjects or parts of them, which must correspond to the nature of the vocational program. In addition, certain subjects or parts of them should be more advanced than those studied in general education, and one cannot proceed to study certain aspects of the vocational program without reaching a certain level of proficiency. Therefore, although they are general subjects, they can actually be regarded as a type of vocational subject. Such subjects are generally completed before vocational subjects. The latter pertains purely to general cultivation, but it also has considerable value in improving one's ability to cope with vocational life. Why? The tools that humans use in social life to enhance their status are, on one hand, specialized skills, and on the other, sufficient common sense. Without sufficient common sense, even with proficient skills, one can only qualify as a worker. Moreover, improving the effectiveness and pleasure of labor especially relies on general cultivation. Therefore, education researchers attach great importance to enhancing general moral knowledge and skills. Such subjects should be evenly distributed across each academic year for appropriate cultivation, and some of them should be completed before vocational subjects. Therefore, in terms of the curriculum structure, there

are naturally more general subjects than vocational subjects in the early years of study, and reducing the hours of general subjects will certainly increase the hours of vocational subjects. However, the sequence of arranging general subjects and vocational subjects depends on the teaching procedures, and the increase or decrease of subjects is determined by learning psychology and the distribution of total hours. Therefore, the arrangement and adjustment of various subjects are all based on the above two principles, rather than balancing the gradual increase of vocational subjects against the gradual decrease of general subjects. The number and proportion of general subjects should be determined according to the nature and duration of the vocational program, as well as the expected goals of the learners, and thus vary with different vocational programs. For example, the description in the original plan and the illustration in the diagram showing an equal division [of general and vocational subjects] are fundamentally wrong.

(3) The original plan divides vocational programs into five systems with duration of one, two, three, four, and five years. Is it appropriate to advance by year? The old system was most criticized by people for its uniformity; the new system, which specifies various duration, seems to have more room for flexibility. However, stipulating each year separately still inevitably gives a sense of rigidity. In my humble opinion, it is better to specify the minimum and maximum duration, allowing free adjustment within such limits, which seems more convenient for implementation.

2. Issues of Supplementary Schools

The original plan's explanation of the primary education stage states that supplementary schools should be established for elderly dropouts. The explanation of the secondary education stage indicates that supplementary schools are specifically set up for working children. Are the supplementary schools referred to in these two contexts one and the same or two different types? If they are considered two types, then the symbols “Ren” and “Gui” in the diagram indicate that they are specifically for working children. What exactly do the supplementary schools for elderly dropouts refer to? If they are regarded as one and the same, whether working children include elderly dropouts is a matter I will not delve into for now. I will only discuss the most obvious provisions.

(1) Is it appropriate for supplementary schools to be positioned above the six-year complete primary school? According to the original plan, primary school education lasts six years, divided into two stages, with four years of compulsory education. As stipulated, will the progress of supplementary courses be based on the six-year complete primary education or the four-year compulsory education? If based on the former, can students who have only received compulsory education achieve a comparable level to connect with the courses? If based on the latter, students who have completed the full six-year primary education will find the level incompatible. Therefore, supplementary schools should be stipulated to be built upon compulsory education; as the duration of compulsory education is extended, supplementary education should advance accordingly.

(2) Is it appropriate to limit supplementary schools to a level equivalent to two years of secondary education? This can be discussed in two aspects: 1) Level: The development of supplementary schools relies on the elective course system, which is widely practiced. Thus, more comprehensive supplementary schools are divided into three levels: advanced, intermediate, and general. For example, the supplementary schools attached to the Higher Technical School in Tokyo, Japan, have these three levels, while many others elsewhere have two levels, with the advanced level approaching professional education. This provides great convenience for those who cannot enter regular schools to obtain remedial education. Hence, it should not be limited to the level of two years of

secondary education. 2) Duration: Supplementary schools are established to allow those who cannot attend regular schools to study during their spare time from work—whether a few hours a week, on Sundays, or during seasonal breaks. In Japan, some rural supplementary schools have students studying continuously for eight or nine years. Therefore, the curriculum of supplementary schools should be calculated by cumulative hours rather than years. The two-year stipulation in the original plan is inconsistent with reality; cases where study hours are the same as regular schools are exceptions. My work Notes on Investigating Japanese Industrial Supplementary Education and the collected curricula and organizational details of German industrial supplementary schools elaborate on relevant examples and reasons, which were published by the Commercial Press. The original plan's division of supplementary schools into one-year and two-year programs suggests a lack of clarity regarding their purpose and organization.

(3) Is it appropriate to specifically establish supplementary schools for working children? The purpose of setting up supplementary schools lies in two aspects: 1) It implies extending primary education, enabling the state to achieve its goals for the capabilities of citizens that were not fully developed by primary education. 2) It allows those who cannot enter regular schools after compulsory education or who dropped out midway to study relevant subjects during work breaks based on their occupations and goals, for practical application, and to enhance the effectiveness and pleasure of their labor. This functions to supplement both general education and vocational education, addressing the limitations of regular schools. Thus, it differs from regular schools in ethos: regular schools have fixed age restrictions, while supplementary schools accept students regardless of age (in foreign countries, there are cases where grandparents and grandchildren attend classes together); regular schools have fixed schedules, while

supplementary schools can be attended every other day or week; regular schools require uniform academic levels in the same grade, while supplementary schools focus on the academic ability for specific subjects (even senior high school students can study the same subject as primary school children); regular schools calculate academic progress by semesters, with enrollment only at the start of the first semester, while supplementary schools divide subjects into segments with clear conclusions, allowing students to choose any segment. From the above, supplementary schools provide appropriate learning opportunities for those who cannot attend regular schools and lack certain knowledge or skills. They cater to both elderly dropouts and working children, depending on the perspective—both are inherent meanings of supplementary schools. Defining them solely as for elderly dropouts is too vague, while limiting them to working children is overly narrow. Supplementary education should primarily target those who cannot enter regular schools after compulsory education, regardless of whether they are still children. Even adults who have not received compulsory education should be allowed to attend if they have the academic ability to learn—there are many such people in China's industrial and commercial sectors. For those who have not received compulsory education, supplementary schools can offer appropriate levels of Chinese and arithmetic as elective courses within general subjects. It is also crucial to set up relevant vocational supplementary courses for workers currently receiving education. Supplementary subjects should focus on vocational relevance, with general cultivation as a supplement. By extension, even the supplementary courses specified in official regulations can be integrated into supplementary schools, provided that methods are adjusted. Adopting the ethos of the elective course system and applying it to education beyond secondary level would allow students who failed to enter higher education to identify and study the subjects they need to supplement. If all preparatory courses in schools are abolished and replaced by such supplementary education, it would eliminate drawbacks and double the benefits.

3. Issues of Vocational Preparation

We must first clarify the meaning of "preparation" before we can discuss the issue. The term "preparation" refers to anticipatory actions aimed at cultivating sufficient capabilities during this period. In other words, it is about equipping individuals with tools for practical application. However, the concept of "preparation for further education" easily leads to misunderstandings. The tools required for preparing to enter higher education are limited to what is necessary for admission. Once enrolled, the subsequent learning activities become preparation for the future, with a different orientation from the preparation undertaken before going to a higher school. Vocational preparation, by contrast, is distinct. The preparation in question encompasses all actions involved in engaging in a profession; its effectiveness depends entirely on whether the tools trained during preparation can be applied in practice. Its utility is not confined to a temporary phase, unlike preparation for further education. From this perspective, only vocational programs can truly fulfill the essence of vocational preparation. Yet, once a program is designated as a vocational course, it should not additionally bear the label of "vocational preparation." Does the "vocational preparation" mentioned in the original plan refer to preparation for studying a vocation or preparation for engaging in a vocation? If it is preparation for studying, one must ask: Will all children preparing for this necessarily enroll in vocational programs in the future? Given the wide range of vocational subjects and the diverse aspirations of students, a uniform form of preparation cannot possibly meet everyone's needs. Since the original plan abolishes other preparatory courses, this form of preparatory study—similar to pre-college programs—naturally becomes irrelevant. If it refers to preparation for engaging in a vocation, then according to its definition, separating “preparation” from “vocational programs” makes it unlikely to achieve the goal of preparing individuals for work. Presumably, the original plan proceeds from the following reasoning: Those who have only completed compulsory education are still too young and lack sufficient general education to immediately undertake vocational courses. This argument is valid from an educational standpoint, as evidenced by the experiences of running lower-level industrial schools in the past. At the same time, there is a need to provide basic livelihood education for those eager to earn a living. Thus, allocating part of the upper primary school curriculum to include vocational preparation is not without merit in intent. However, its ambiguous definition may confuse practitioners about its purpose. If “vocational preparation” is treated as separate from “vocational programs,” its content would inherently differ from vocational courses. Based on current educational practices, there are roughly two approaches to this: 1) Adding industrial subjects based on local conditions. Past results show this method has limited effectiveness, as the content taught is purely book-based knowledge, often misaligned with children’s psychology. Poor outcomes are not accidental. Rather than creating isolated, dry subjects, it would be better to center teaching materials around local contexts—e.g., emphasizing business/industrial content in commercial areas or agricultural content in rural areas. This way, children can acquire vocational knowledge while studying general subjects, fostering greater interest. Such a selection criterion is a general principle of education, applicable beyond vocational preparation; it should be clarified in explanatory notes or primary school regulations rather than being specially highlighted in diagrams.2) Using vocational cultivation methods. This involves emphasizing facilities for labor and creation, integrating children’s work with their playful instincts and connecting it to social life. Though not focused on vocational subjects, this approach aligns closely with the goals of vocational education. It can be applied as a guiding principle for cultivating students from lower primary to secondary education, reflecting the overarching aim of life education rather than narrow vocational preparation. Given this, vocational preparation cannot form an independent framework separate from vocational programs, nor is vocational cultivation limited to part of the upper primary school. It is also important to address how those who have only completed four years of compulsory education (rather than the full six-year primary education) can access livelihood education if vocational programs are placed after six-year primary school. This is precisely why I advocate for supplementary education to be positioned after compulsory education—as a remedy for this gap.

4. Issues of Training Vocational Educators

In the original plan, the training of vocational educators is attached to the vocational programs of senior high schools. According to the original plan, middle schools that are capable of concurrently running normal education (teacher training) for primary schools are allowed to do so, and workshops with appropriate durations may be established based on local needs. However, the training of vocational educators is limited to the vocational programs of senior high schools. It is indeed insightful to recognize that vocational education cannot be carried out without adequate facilities. Nevertheless, since vocational education is an urgent task, there is a large and pressing demand for such educators. A limited number of training institutions will be insufficient to meet the demand, and a lack of diverse training methods will result in educators who are not fully suitable for the roles.

In my humble opinion, if middle schools with sufficient capacity are allowed to concurrently run normal education, then normal schools with sufficient capacity should also be allowed to concurrently run programs for training vocational educators. Additionally, following the two-session system of the old regulations, workshop programs can be established to specifically enroll graduates of vocational programs with a duration of four years or more. Since there are no such graduates at present, graduates of Type A industrial schools can be temporarily recruited for these workshops to meet urgent needs. Furthermore, normal colleges of universities or higher normal schools can attach programs for training vocational educators or set up workshops, admitting graduates of senior vocational programs or those with equivalent academic qualifications. In the absence of such graduates currently, graduates of specialized industrial schools can be temporarily recruited.

Having concluded the discussion on these issues, I would like to further elaborate: Supplementary schools are the most convenient and effective method in vocational education. The difference between them and vocational programs, apart from the aforementioned reasons that distinguish them from regular schools, is that vocational programs are established for those who will engage in occupations in the future, focusing on training practical tools; supplementary schools are established for those currently engaged in occupations, aiming to enhance their ability to apply these tools and also extending primary education, though not solely for the purpose of continuing primary education. Moreover, vocational schools require relatively complete facilities, and the programs they offer must be sustainable and capable of continuous operation. Vocational-related programs in supplementary schools, however, do not need to be subject to such restrictions.

In the original plan, supplementary education is placed above vocational preparation, divided into two years, and listed separately from vocational programs on the left. Vocational programs are divided year by year, ranging from one to five years, with the four-year and five-year vocational programs shown in the diagram as having an equal division of general and vocational subjects. Based on the above reasons, I propose a revised diagram as follows:

In the diagram, the vocational programs have a minimum duration of one year and a maximum of five years, with flexible adjustment according to the nature of the offered programs, not restricted by annual progression, hence indicated by a diagonal line. Supplementary education is listed alongside vocational programs, with the left side indicating their connection to vocational education.

Opinions on Vocational and Supplementary Education in the Draft of the New School System

School System Charts

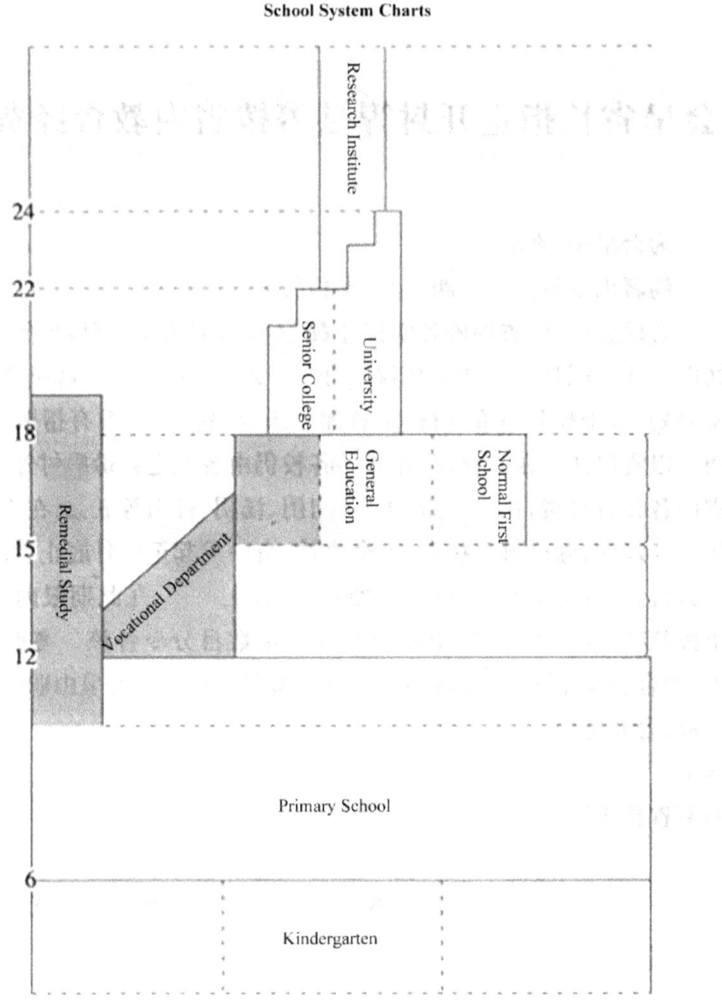

Published in Education and Vocation, Vol. 3, Issue 9, February 1922.

Joint Petition to the Provincial Governor Requesting Designation of Kaifeng and Other Counties to Allocate Provincial Educational Funds

For the matter of joint submission: Regarding the case received

Your Excellency's Office Instruction No. 1438 (Education Section) states: Approved...

We, the undersigned, hereby submit this joint report:

We have received Instruction No. 1438 (Education Section) from your esteemed office, which states: "The Provincial Assembly has advised that the failure to disburse funds to schools inside and outside the province on a monthly basis is hindering the operation of school affairs. You are hereby ordered to promptly consult with the Department of Education to conduct a thorough review and submit recommendations for decision." In compliance with this order, we have endeavored to formulate practical plans to maintain school operations and ensure their progress. However, due to the emptiness of the provincial treasury, it is truly difficult to meet these obligations. The only feasible way to secure additional funds is to allocate resources from counties outside the provincial capital. After careful deliberation, we have resolved the following. Schools outside the provincial capital shall continue to receive funding from their originally designated counties. For educational funds for institutions within the provincial capital, five counties—Kaifeng, Zhongmu, Heyin, Tangyin, and Lushan—are designated. From within their land tax revenues for the 11th year (1922), after deducting amounts already remitted, the remaining funds shall be allocated uniformly from January to the end of June. These counties shall remit the specified monthly amounts to our Education Department for onward distribution to the schools. During this period, no other funds shall be allocated from these counties to ensure accountability. The Department of Finance will determine the specific amounts and issue orders to the respective counties for compliance. We hereby submit this report for your review and request that you issue instructions to Kaifeng and other designated counties to follow these arrangements. Additionally, this report is drafted by the Department of Finance, as we jointly confirm.

Respectfully submitted to

Zhang Fengtai, Governor of Henan Province

Li Buqing, Director of Henan Provincial Department of Education,

Wang Guangdi, Director of Henan Provincial Department of Finance

March 15th, the 11th year of the Republic of China (1922)

Excerpted from *A Record of Henan's Educational Earmarked Funds*, published by the Henan Educational Funds and Properties Management Office in December 1934.

Discussion with Mr. Gong Peicheng on the Homeroom Teacher System in Middle Schools

I have recently read Mr. Gong's *Doubts and Research on the Homeroom Teacher System in Middle Schools* published in the fifth issue of the fourth volume of *New Education*. The research is extremely detailed, and I am deeply impressed. However, most of Mr. Gong's arguments are based on the facts that have gone astray in the implementation of this system, rather than the problems of the homeroom teacher system itself. Taking the liberty, I would first expound on the original proposal I advocate, and then discuss the doubts and research. I think this is also what Mr. Gong would be glad to hear. I also hope that those who are enthusiastic about researching middle school education will join in the discussion.

1. Supplementary Description of the Original Plan Proposal

My advocacy for the homeroom teacher system aims to rectify the flaws of the school supervisor system, as Mr. Gong has already noted. However, Mr. Gong has not yet addressed the specific implementation methods, so I will briefly supplement and outline them as follows:

The original plan states: "Gradually seek to abolish the school supervisor system and entrust training affairs to homeroom teachers." It also mentions: "It is difficult to select qualified homeroom teachers, and there is a fear that management may fall into laxity." This shows that the core purpose lies in abolishing the school supervisor position, not in considering the homeroom teacher system as omnipotent, nor in regarding the homeroom system as the sole method to reform middle schools. This indicates that the concern about talent shortages raised by Mr. Gong had already been anticipated.

The original plan further states: “To achieve the unification of management and teaching, emphasis should be placed on the moral education committee, and all school affairs shall be resolved and implemented by this committee.” It also specifies: “All teaching staff shall share the responsibility of joint management. Teachers who teach a particular grade shall provide guidance and correction regarding the individual characteristics and behaviors of that grade, and shall prepare records to be submitted to the moral education committee for review.” Although this was stated with reference to situations where school supervisors had not yet been fully abolished, in essence, the homeroom teacher system should operate in accordance with these principles. It can thus be seen that the emphasis is on integrating teaching, training, and management into a single approach, with all teaching staff sharing collective responsibility.

2. Discussion on Mr. Gong’s Doubts and Research

2.1 Discussion on Doubts about the Role of the Homeroom Teacher System

The following is divided into three parts based on the original text. The first part of the discussion expresses opinions on secondary education beyond the homeroom teacher system. Since discussing a matter requires clarifying all its related aspects to understand its ultimate purpose, readers are kindly requested not to avoid the wording verbose.

2.1.1 Mr. Gong argues that extracurricular management in middle schools is completely different from that in primary schools and does not require strict and trivial supervision.

Middle school students are older and have stronger self-governance abilities, so the management methods are naturally different from those in primary schools. However, in my opinion, secondary education and primary education should follow the same orientation. The so-called "same orientation" means:

First, teaching, training, and management should be integrated; training and management should not be regarded as separate from teaching. All teaching must contain the function of training so that teaching can be effective and achieve educational goals. What people perceive as "close to training" in certain matters is due to differences in the nature of teaching materials; what is perceived as "close to training" at certain times is due to differences in teaching procedures. The ineffectiveness of education in our country lies in the fact that the knowledge imparted is irrelevant to character cultivation and cannot be put into practice. The reason for this is that teaching is separated from training, and training is separated from teaching. As for management, school faculty and staff should handle matters appropriately in accordance with school regulations based on their respective duties and the circumstances at the time. This is a common responsibility of all faculty and staff and has no significant independent value in education. It is puzzling why the current situation in various schools often regards management as a responsibility outside of teachers' duties, and training is not integrated into teaching but instead considered a matter of management. Even educational theorists classify training under management rather than teaching. No wonder education is ineffective.

Second, except for rest, sleeping, and eating times, there should be no distinction between "in-class" and "extracurricular." The so-called "in-class" refers to the teaching hours stipulated by each school; "extracurricular" activities include self-study (with a fixed daily time), study groups, and supplementary lessons, whose times are specified as needed. This raises the following questions:

(1) Should students at school be given educational opportunities at all times and in all matters related to school life?

(2) Should extracurricular learning require appropriate guidance and assessment?

I believe that those who answer these two questions will not give negative responses. If these two questions are indeed beyond doubt, then there must be reasons to doubt the current teaching situation and curriculum arrangement in middle schools.

What doubts arise regarding the current teaching situation? Researchers studying fatigue issues today all agree that daily study time should not exceed six hours. However, this standard is based on the conventions of traditional teaching methods to determine the limit of mental fatigue. It fails to consider that, out of 24 hours a day, half the time remains after accounting for sleep, meals, and rest. Should our use of mental energy be tested through concentrating it into several consecutive hours following traditional teaching routines, or should it be distributed over more hours to measure daily mental capacity? Agricultural and industrial schools in other countries, which include practical training hours, and laborers often work seven to eight hours a day. If teaching methods are reformed, there is much room for discussion about extending study time.

Most middle schools in our country adopt a boarding system, separating teaching hours from self-study time. During teaching hours, educators focus solely on covering the scheduled content for each hour—do students truly gain understanding? Considering whether students grasp the material, can the prescribed curriculum be completed within the daily hours allocated? Moreover, can the suitability of the curriculum and students' learning fatigue be accurately measured using only traditional teaching conventions as the standard? These are questions we should reflect on. Furthermore, whether self-study time is scheduled outside teaching hours or integrated into them is more effective, yet this is rarely judged based on learning psychology.

What doubts arise regarding curriculum arrangement? Middle school curricula are divided and sequenced by subject, which cannot be entirely dismissed. However, many important parts of various subjects can be taught through students' daily activities and tasks, making academic knowledge practical. For example, legal knowledge can be taught through managing student councils as situations arise; accounting and interest calculation can be taught through running school stores. Learning for life greatly enhances teaching efficiency. Yet in most schools, teaching subjects and guiding practical affairs are treated as separate tasks—this is deeply puzzling to me. Additionally, curriculum integration merely involves one subject referencing others, which has limited educational value and is often theoretical rather than practical.

Recent advancements in project-based learning have become increasingly sophisticated. If key issues are proposed and explored through interdisciplinary study, students' interest in learning will undoubtedly increase. Unfortunately, middle schools rarely engage in such research. Without reforming teaching materials organization and seizing teaching opportunities, mere research into methods will ultimately be of little practical use.

Based on the above doubts and identified issues, I put forward the following propositions:

(1) Middle school courses can be divided into three parts.

(a) Courses for subject teaching. —— These are conducted during the traditional teaching hours. However, the curriculum organization and teaching procedures should be reformed.

(b) Courses for preview and review. —— These are carried out during the traditional self-study hours. Nevertheless, in the past, self-study often lacked purpose because teachers did not specify the scope, and the results could not be verified. To make self-study effective, teaching procedures should be reformed; roughly, 60-70% of the self-study time should be used for previewing teaching materials, and 30-40% for students to organize their learning insights.

(c) Courses for service and special research. —— Middle schools in our country generally adopt the boarding system, and it is appropriate to do so due to social conditions. Therefore, it is necessary to formulate detailed regulations for service and special research, and they should be regarded as formal courses. The ability for social life should be cultivated through the purposeful and regular life of the school.

(2) For teaching lessons, teachers should, one day before the class, specify the starting and ending points of the textbook content to be previewed, as well as the relevant parts of reference books; for practical and skill-based courses, they should also assign specific exercises to be prepared in advance. During the class, based on the designated preview content, teachers should conduct question-and-answer sessions and discussions in an orderly manner, and provide appropriate explanations and supplements in the process. After the discussion, they should summarize the key points concisely. Furthermore, they should guide students in in-depth exploration and practical exercises. In this way, the self-study conducted by students is purely for the purpose of the class, and the class time becomes a period when teachers guide students to solve problems or practice lessons, rather than focusing on teachers' non-stop lecturing and gesturing as the sole fulfillment of teaching responsibilities.

(3) When a teacher is assigned to teach a certain course for a specific period, they should calculate the number of hours required based on the amount of content that should be taught in the course. After taking on the teaching task, they should assess on a weekly and monthly basis whether students have mastered the taught content, and adjust the actual teaching

hours accordingly. They must not merely focus on whether the scheduled hours have been completed, regardless of whether students have truly mastered the material.

(4) For various subjects, except for content related to service matters, which should be taught separately in a way that corresponds to practical situations, it is particularly important to select key parts of each subject for more project-based teaching. This can be done by taking one subject as the core and integrating other subjects into it; this depends on teachers collaborating and discussing with each other from time to time.

(5) Various service activities and special research projects should be guided by faculty and staff according to their respective natures.

All the above-mentioned points apply the principles of primary school teaching. If we adhere to these ideas, I am confident that secondary education can be reformed.

2.1.2 Mr. Gong argues that in terms of assessing students' individual characteristics, the efficiency of assessment by a small number of homeroom teachers is not as great as that by all faculty and staff. This view is indeed correct. However, the establishment of homeroom teachers does not mean that other faculty members can neglect the assessment of individual characteristics. If, following the erroneous convention, training and management are regarded as the responsibilities of the principal and school supervisors alone, then having more homeroom teachers take charge of assessment will still be more efficient than having only a few principals and supervisors do so.

2.1.3 Mr. Gong holds that for integrating teaching materials, middle schools cannot find such all-capable talents to serve as homeroom teachers, and this is especially incompatible with the elective course system. In fact, the arrangement of teaching materials is the responsibility of the academic affairs committee, and homeroom teachers can also take part in this work. A homeroom teacher who can also take on academic affairs responsibilities is certainly an excellent one. However, regarding the integration of teaching materials for each grade, the academic affairs committee should first formulate an outline, and then teachers of various subjects in each grade should work out detailed items. Even if there were all-capable talents, it would be impossible to entrust this task to a single person. In middle schools implementing the elective course system, classes are complicated: some elective courses are for specialized study in a particular grade, while others are for general study across multiple grades. Only the divided parts of the courses, whose content and procedures are suitable for elective study, are selected, and whether the content is interconnected cannot be taken into account. Moreover, in the elective course system, grades are not divided but grouped, and it is appropriate for each group to have a director.

No matter how thorough management may be, it must never adopt an attitude of surveillance. Nor can there be effective education if teaching is separated from the function of training, or if teachers shirk their management responsibilities. Furthermore, in education below the secondary level, faculty and staff, in their interactions with students, are always responsible for guidance. They must not relax their responsibilities just because students have stronger self-governance abilities.

(I) believe that the role of the homeroom teacher system lies in selecting a particularly responsible person for each grade or group to coordinate and oversee the various plans, implementations, and assessments made by all teachers of that class. In well-equipped schools with many classes, subject directors should be appointed for each grade. The more detailed the division of labor, with a coordinator for each part, the easier it is to accomplish tasks. In less well-equipped schools where not all teachers are competent, having a responsible person for each grade will undoubtedly help promote reform.

2.2 Discussion on Doubts Regarding Students' Psychology

The classification of grades in middle schools, rooted in students' psychological development, is related to the presence or absence of homeroom teachers. When trends among students shift due to a homeroom teacher's words and actions, the outcomes are not entirely negative. However, a homeroom teacher's approach to moral education should align with the core principles set by the moral education committee, rather than being influenced by personal biases. As for the impact of an individual's words and actions: only those with exceptional abilities can inspire students. If such teachers exist, they would easily influence students even without holding the position of homeroom teacher. Regarding the mutual exploitation between homeroom teachers and students, or the emergence of attitudes like contempt or indulgence between students of one grade and another due to their lack of affiliation—if a school exhibits such phenomena, one can well imagine the incompetence of its principal, the poor quality of most teachers, and the degenerate academic atmosphere. Such a school is hardly worthy of discussing whether to establish a homeroom teacher system at all.

2.3 Discussion on Doubts Regarding the Qualifications of Directors

Mr. Gong argues that it is difficult to find individuals who are both academically excellent and proficient in administrative work, and that there will inevitably be a shortage of such talents if a considerable number of homeroom teachers are appointed. In my opinion, among the talents in Henan's education sector, apart from the lack of these two qualities, the most pressing issue is the scarcity of a sense of responsibility. If one is highly responsible, their academic knowledge can gradually become excellent through research, and their administrative skills can gradually become proficient through diligence. Therefore, the establishment of homeroom teacher positions can actually serve as a way to cultivate administrative talents. As for the ineffectiveness or failure of the current homeroom teacher system, from what I know, it is not entirely due to the academic incompetence or poor administrative abilities of homeroom teachers. The main reasons for such ineffectiveness and failure are roughly as follows: Some schools blindly follow the homeroom teacher systems of outstanding schools without examining the practical conditions for implementation and other related factors, and set up the system rashly. Others only aim to put up a new "signboard" for the school's administration without considering how to carry it out in practice. Principals often fear that if homeroom teachers gain students' trust, it will threaten their own status and personal interests, so they only grant homeroom teachers empty titles without entrusting them with real responsibilities. Homeroom teachers, on the other hand, seeing that principals handle affairs without transparency and have their own confidants involved in confidential matters, tend to avoid taking responsibilities to steer clear of suspicion. Furthermore, some people take the position of homeroom teacher because it comes with a higher salary, fewer teaching hours, and the privilege to control other teachers; in some cases, principals even use the position to place their own associates. In such situations, if there is a violation of political principles, the educational administrative authorities should have ways to supervise, urge correction, and rectify the issues.

2.4Discussion on Doubts Regarding School Affairs Management

The establishment of homeroom teacher positions may reduce the heavy workload of those solely responsible for academic and disciplinary affairs, but this is no reason to abolish the academic administration altogether. Individuals can take on concurrent roles, but institutional functions cannot be mutually substituted. The benefits of division of labor have long been an inviolable principle in management. The cohesive ethos of a school depends on how its affairs are handled, and will not be fragmented merely because responsibilities are divided. As for the concern that teachers taking on disciplinary and management duties alongside teaching may neglect one for the other, I have already clearly argued against separating teaching from discipline and management. Moreover, Mr. Gong himself advocates that all faculty should assess students, so why single out homeroom teachers for doubt? Some may argue that having both homeroom teachers and academic deans could lead to conflicting opinions. (Whether a secondary school should have an academic dean is a separate issue.) However, homeroom teachers and those in charge of academic affairs each have their own responsibilities and do not hinder one another. Accusations of redundancy are issues of personnel, not of the system itself. There is also the claim that with homeroom teachers in place, other teachers will disregard student affairs. But discipline should never be separated from teaching, and management is a shared responsibility of all teachers. The homeroom teacher's role is merely to consolidate and oversee the plans, implementation, and assessments for their grade, bearing heavier responsibilities than other teachers. If discipline and management were entirely entrusted to homeroom teachers alone, one might well ask: what would then be the ultimate purpose of teaching?

Regarding Mr. Gong's final observations on success and failure cases: I cannot believe that success is solely attributable to the effectiveness of the homeroom system, for a well-functioning school depends on more than just one form of organization. Nor can failure be blamed on the system itself, as the cases cited merely pursued the name or abused the title without genuinely fulfilling the responsibilities inherent to the homeroom system.

In conclusion, reforming middle schools is not limited to adopting the homeroom system as the sole method. Yet to claim that the homeroom system is absolutely inapplicable to middle schools, and to deny its potential for universal implementation based on the cited facts and reasoning, is something I find perplexing.

Published in *New Education*, Combined Issue of Vol. 5, Issues 1 & 2, August 1922;

Also published in *Henan Education Bulletin Supplement*, Vol. 1, Issue 5, 1922

Plan for the Implementation of Compulsory Education[8]

During the turbulent years of the Republic of China, education has stagnated. For years, provinces across the country have issued proclamations and promoted plans for establishing compulsory education, but in terms of actual implementation, only the Shanxi Provincial Government has made vigorous efforts. The number of primary schools and students in Shanxi has been increasing day by day compared with other provinces. The educational circle in Jiangsu has taken more responsibility; for example, according to the reports of the Compulsory Education Promotion Association, various counties there have made some efforts to formulate measures. Among the plans for compulsory education carried out in provincial capitals, the one by the Guangzhou Municipal Bureau of Education is the most comprehensive. As for the plans implemented at the local level, the one in Nantong County, Jiangsu Province, is the most complete. Even so, there are only some initial signs of progress in Jilin's provincial capital and Changchun Commercial Port. Beyond that, there is nothing worth mentioning.

To ensure that compulsory education can truly be popularized nationwide and that the education provided is truly effective, we must pay attention to the following three key points:

1) We should not merely rely on advocacy and supervision on paper. Nowadays, those in charge of compulsory education: the Ministry of Education issues orders to all provinces with empty words; education departments issue orders to all counties with empty words. The higher

8 This article is one of the two proposals submitted by Li Lianfang at the first annual conference of the China Education Improvement Society in 1922; the other is *Outline for Reforming the Educational Administrative Organization*. — Translator's note

authorities reproach the lower ones with empty words, and the lower ones deceive the higher ones with empty words. No one takes responsibility for whether the formulated measures are practical or whether they have been implemented in accordance with the measures. Even if there are some implementations, they are nothing more than tools to decorate the facade. Although we talk about running compulsory education every day, what good does it do in reality? This is the first point we should pay attention to.

2) We should seek solutions from the root, not just engage in trivial planning. Nowadays, the plans for establishing schools and raising funds either only cover a part, or are constrained by other aspects. Although much effort is exerted, the results are very meager. A little obstacle will cause them to waver, for there is no fundamental plan. This is the second point we should pay attention to.

3) We should not regard merely increasing the number of schools and students as the goal of achieving compulsory education. The popularization of education certainly lies in the increasing number of schools and students. However, if we only focus on the increase in numbers, we can instantly add countless schools by simply letting private tutors hang a school signboard. Compared with private schools, how much more effective is the primary education in various counties today in terms of the value of life? People only know how to establish schools but do not understand the true meaning of education. It is no wonder that schools in our country exist in name only. This is the third point we should pay attention to.

Based on these three principles, we will further seek solutions and describe them in the following order: first, the fund plan; second, the teacher plan; third, the school - establishment plan; fourth, the clarification of the fundamental law for promoting compulsory education. As for the curriculum design and courses, there have been many discussions, so we will not repeat them here. My work Plan for New - style National Schools and the letters discussing with scholars across the country may be discussed together.

1. Fund Plan

1.1 Fund Raising

This is a prerequisite question: should the burden be borne by the state, or by local authorities? If by local authorities, should it be borne by the province, or raised independently by the county? Looking at the established practices of other countries: under the new republican laws of Germany, the entire burden is borne by the state; in other countries, the responsibility is shared between provinces and localities, with the central government providing partial subsidies; some divide the responsibility among the central government, provincial governments, and localities in fixed proportions; others have the state cover teachers' salaries while localities handle the rest; in some cases, cities share the burden between the state and localities, while rural areas are fully supported by the state.

In our country, the state has not allocated special funds for this purpose. Although provincial governments have included it in their budgets, such allocations are mostly earmarked for compulsory education in provincial capitals, with no overall planning for counties. Counties rely on their own resources, limited to small miscellaneous levies. Moreover, since these depend on approval from centrally appointed financial officials, funds are difficult to raise. The state shirks its responsibility, while financial management is monopolized by certain parties. In one region, people may collectively petition for funding but fail to secure it; in another, a school may be established but halted due to lack of subsidies. Even increasing the number of schools is extremely difficult, let alone achieving universal education.

Therefore, to ensure the popularization of compulsory education, there is absolutely no hope of success without fundamentally resolving financial issues and clarifying responsibility for funding. Speaking of this, we cannot avoid addressing general fiscal problems. If this issue can be resolved, all other problems will be easily solved.

It is divided into three items: Establishing the foundation of funds; Planning and allocating special funds; Rectifying existing funds and properties.

1.1.1 Establishing the Foundation of Funds

I would like to present my propositions as follows:

First, delineate the fiscal revenues of the central government, provincial governments, and local authorities, and establish the independence of tax sources and the authority over tax collection. (The term "local authorities" here includes counties, cities, towns, municipalities, and townships. In other contexts, "local authorities" may refer to the combination of provinces and counties, or to cities, townships, municipalities, and towns below the county level; readers should distinguish between these usages.) China's finances have long suffered under autocratic rule, which monopolizes resources in the name of the state. Expenditures that should be borne by the state are instead imposed on localities; tax sources that should belong to localities are appropriated as state revenue. What are called "local taxes" consist only of surtaxes and exorbitant miscellaneous levies (some surtaxes even accrue to the state, such as the price increase on salt). There are no independent, stable local tax sources. Even local taxes are monopolized by officials appointed by the central government. Taxes that the people are willing to pay are obstructed by financial authorities and cannot be used for local undertakings. Local initiatives are stifled by financial constraints and cannot develop. When provincial assemblies were established in the late Qing Dynasty, many provinces debated the division between national and local taxes, but due to the constraints of the political system, a thorough division could not be achieved. In 1913–1914 (the 2nd–3rd years of the Republic), financial authorities set criteria for division: first, the allocation of financial burdens between the state and localities; second, the division of tax sources and collection powers between the state and localities. Budgets were formulated based on these criteria. However, at that time, President Yuan Shikai had just suppressed the Second Revolution and vigorously advocated centralization, so the division still favored the state. Even this was deemed insufficient by the authorities: in June 1914, the Ministry of Finance petitioned to abolish the distinction between national and local taxes, paving the way for the abuse of local tax revenues. In August 1916, after President Li Yuanhong took office, the State Council resolved to restore the budgetary system in place before June 1914, but this was never implemented. Moreover, some provinces divided their total revenue into shares, with certain proportions allocated to the state and others to localities, resulting in confused authority. When military governors began interfering in governance, the central government's monopoly policy was transferred to warlords, leaving both the central and local governments paralyzed. Furthermore, most of the original educational funds in counties were seized by corrupt magistrates and local bullies to fund military and police forces. As a result, local schools existed in name only in eight or nine out of ten cases. Therefore, clarifying revenue divisions is not only a crucial measure to streamline finances and consolidate the national foundation but also essential for the popularization of compulsory education.

Once the division is clarified, there are three benefits: at first, the central government, provinces, and local authorities can each manage and expand their respective revenue sources without being constrained by other parties. Second, each can allocate appropriate uses based on their revenue amounts, thereby assuming clear responsibility for their financial burdens. Third, each will have independent and stable tax sources, avoiding disputes over revenue. Regardless of whether the government adopts a federal system, a decentralized system, or a centralized system, referring to the systems of European and American countries, there is no doubt that tax sources must be divided. If a centralized system is adopted, the state will certainly control most tax sources, and thus the state should take responsibility for compulsory education. Its funds should either be fully provided by the state or mostly subsidized by the state, rather than merely relying on empty edicts to pressure provinces. If a decentralized or federal system is adopted, it is necessary to clarify which parts of the funding should be subsidized by the central government, which by provincial governments, and which borne by local authorities. Tax sources must be clearly delineated, with a certain proportion earmarked for compulsory education. There must be no arbitrary revenue and expenditure without standards, nor should officials shirk their responsibilities on flimsy pretexts. To clean up the foundation of governance and revitalize education, there is no other way but this.

The criteria for division, as proposed by various parties, are as follows:

(1) Provisions of the Hunan Provincial Constitution: Customs duties, salt taxes, tobacco and alcohol taxes, and stamp duties shall be classified as national taxes. Other types of taxes and levies may be levied by the provincial government in accordance with provincial laws. Counties may, within the scope not conflicting with provincial decrees, formulate county taxes, surtaxes attached to provincial taxes, and other public revenues to fund county autonomous affairs, subject to supervision by the provincial government. -class and second-class cities, under the supervision of the provincial government, may formulate various municipal taxes, including:

house tax, horse tax, tax on theaters and other entertainment venues, slaughter tax, tavern tax, surtaxes attached to provincial taxes, and other taxes approved by the government.

(2) Provisions of the Zhejiang Provincial Constitution: All taxes in the province are provincial revenues, levied by the provincial government in accordance with legal provisions. The burden on the national government shall not exceed 30% of the total provincial revenue. Various taxes originally owned by counties shall still be levied by the counties. Counties may, within the scope not conflicting with provincial laws, formulate county taxes, surtaxes attached to provincial taxes, and other public revenues. In addition to the original taxes and levies, special cities may formulate municipal taxes such as house taxes, land value increment taxes, luxury goods entry taxes, entertainment venue taxes, catering industry taxes, surtaxes attached to provincial taxes, other taxes approved by the provincial government, and other public revenues, provided that they do not conflict with provincial laws.

(3) Outline of the Jiangsu Provincial System: Salt taxes, customs duties, tobacco and alcohol taxes, and stamp duties shall be attributed to the central government; existing county taxes shall be attributed to each county; land taxes, commodity taxes, and existing miscellaneous taxes within the provincial scope shall all be included in provincial annual revenues.

(4) Ding Foyan advocated that: land taxes, deed taxes, brokerage taxes, pawnshop taxes, tobacco and alcohol taxes, slaughter taxes, fishery taxes, miscellaneous taxes, and revenues from various regular and miscellaneous taxes should all be provincial revenues. National taxes usually include stamp duties, transportation revenues, etc.; various national taxes may be formulated, and public funds from provinces may be collected.

(5) Tong Xinyi advocated that: customs duties, salt taxes, and alcohol taxes are national taxes; land value taxes, house taxes, business taxes, and other miscellaneous taxes are local taxes.

(6) Lan Gongwu advocated that: in addition to customs duties, salt taxes, tobacco and alcohol taxes, and stamp duties, which should be classified as national taxes, other taxes and levies are provincial taxes.

(7) Wang Zhengting advocated that: those belonging to the federal central government include post and telecommunications, customs, state-owned railways, salt taxes, tobacco and alcohol taxes, stamp duties, etc. Those belonging to the provincial government include land taxes, mines, roads, product taxes, and all profit-making undertakings owned by the province. Those belonging to cities and townships include land taxes, house taxes, business taxes, surtaxes, all licenses, taxes on profit-making undertakings, etc.

(8) Sun Zengda advocated that: salt taxes, customs duties, tobacco and alcohol taxes, stamp duties, income taxes, etc., are national taxes; land taxes, consolidated levies, silk cocoon levies, tea levies, mineral taxes, business taxes, house taxes, registration taxes, etc., are provincial taxes. His views on local taxes are the same as those stipulated in the Zhejiang Provincial Constitution.

Second, stipulate the proportion of administrative allocation from each of the three types of revenues (central, provincial, and local). Compulsory education funds should account for 5% of the total revenues of the central government and provincial governments. For local total revenues, excluding existing educational funds, compulsory education funds should account for one-third (the specified proportions should be proposed to increase in due course as finances are consolidated and education develops in the future).

Even if the three types of tax sources are divided, if the allocation proportions for each administrative sector are not determined, powerful entities or financial authorities in certain sectors may arbitrarily allocate funds. When revenues fluctuate, the drawbacks will be even more pronounced. The government will only strive to meet the funding demands of powerful entities, while neglecting the administrative undertakings that should be carried out and the responsibilities that should be fulfilled. As for local revenues, they should also be regulated separately to minimize disputes. The lesson from the late Qing Dynasty is clear: when local self-government was implemented back then, not a single project was accomplished, yet educational funds were repeatedly embezzled. It is stipulated in the Guangdong Constitution that educational funds must account for 20% of the total provincial revenue. The Hunan Provincial Constitution stipulates that annual educational funds must account for at least 10% of the province's total annual expenditures (implying potential increases) and that the educational fund must be at least 1%; this does not include compulsory education funds borne by local self-governing organizations. The Zhejiang Provincial Constitution stipulates that educational funds must account for at least 15% of the province's total annual expenditures and that the educational fund must be at least 2% (the "provincial total" here refers to the combined revenues of the central government and the province). One-third of the provincial educational funds should be earmarked annually to subsidize the funds for national schools across the province; in addition, the provincial government may compel county or municipal/township self-governing organizations to establish national schools using locally raised funds. All funds or properties originally allocated to education must not be diverted for other purposes. Overall, these stipulated proportions are already lower than those for educational funds in other countries. However, in China's annual budget proposals, the central Ministry of Education has never included funds for subsidizing provinces, nor have provincial education departments included budgets for subsidizing counties. Moreover, local revenues are entirely controlled by the government. It is no wonder that compulsory education has made little progress!

For the convenience of reference, here are a few examples of the general situation regarding fiscal division and compulsory education funding in European and American countries. It shows that in other countries, the more tax sources are allocated to the central government, the heavier its responsibility to support localities. Our government only seizes local revenues without undertaking local affairs—this is a wake-up call we must heed:

(1) In the United States, consumption taxes on beverages, tobacco, etc., and customs duties are national taxes; general property taxes, occupational license taxes, income taxes, stamp duties, inheritance taxes, etc., all belong to the states. Regarding compulsory education funds, there are different allocation methods: some states bear 40%, counties 50%, and localities 10%; some have states, counties, and localities each bear one-third; some have states bear one-fourth and localities three-fourths; some have states bear two-thirds and counties one-third; in the city of Chicago, the entire cost is borne by the city, with the state providing a 10% subsidy.

(2) In the United Kingdom, customs duties, excise taxes, income taxes, and land rents are central tax sources. Recently, it has been stipulated that compulsory education funds are shared equally between the state and local authorities.

(3) In France, taxes on land, houses, taxes on people and animals, and window taxes are central tax sources. For compulsory education funds, teachers' salaries are borne by the state, while other expenses are borne by localities.

The propositions mentioned above should be put forward as a special proposal. We should unite people from all sectors to make a concerted appeal to the government, the National Assembly, and the Financial Discussion Committee. The State Council should instruct the Ministry of Finance to collect relevant data, then appoint scholars with profound financial knowledge and select a number of financial administrators to hold meetings and jointly formulate a plan. The formulated plan shall be submitted to the National Assembly. Alternatively, it can be initiated by the National Assembly itself or proposed by the Financial Discussion Committee.

Each province, in accordance with the standards stipulated above, shall dispatch administrative heads of various departments to work out detailed measures and submit them to the provincial assembly. If there are slight differences of opinion on the central government's proposal, suggestions can also be made. However, since the education sector has relatively heavy responsibilities, more people should be sent to attend the meetings.

It is also found that the compulsory education funds raised by various provinces, such as in Shanxi where business donations, shop donations, and household donations are the main sources in towns, and mu (a unit of area) donations are the main source in rural areas; the special tax on goods and materials to be levied as discussed in Jiangsu; the additional tax on land taxes to be levied as discussed in Zhejiang, etc., are all in line with local tax sources and common to all localities. All provinces should first use these funds to prepare for compulsory education, and then make an overall plan after local self-government is established.

1.1.2 Planning and Allocating Special Funds

If the propositions mentioned earlier can be implemented, the earmarked taxes here should naturally be merged into the previous framework and determined in accordance with the principle of division. However, since the preparation for compulsory education is just starting, it is also an urgent national need for the government to designate special funds for subsidies or as educational funds, etc.

(1) Income Tax: The Ministry of Education has ordered that 20% of income tax be allocated to local educational expenses. Because the funds are earmarked, military and civil officials cannot misappropriate them. Financial administrators also cannot collect them to curry favor, so so far, it has mostly not been implemented. If the government resolutely enforces it, there should be no obstacles. If all the income tax is allocated to compulsory education expenses, after being implemented for a while, the revenue will surely increase. The authorities should be urged to handle this promptly and designate it for the purpose of establishing additional primary schools in local areas.

(2) Newly Increased Customs Duties: The State Council once sent a circular, allocating a certain percentage to educational expenses. Director Qin of Shandong proposed to use it specifically for running primary schools, and many provinces agreed. It is advisable to propose to the Ministry of Education to submit it to the State Council, so that this fund can be specifically used to subsidize provinces in establishing additional primary schools.

1.1.3Rectifying Existing Funds and Properties

(1) Sorting out sources of income (such as rents from school-owned land, interest from pawnshops, etc., which have many drawbacks).

(2) Strictly setting standards for allocation.

(3) Strictly formulating regulations for custody.

Items (1) and (2) should be handled by county magistrates and education promotion offices. They should specify the sources, approximate annual revenue, management status, and location and boundaries of properties one by one, compile detailed lists, and draft rectification plans and allocation methods, then report them to the education authorities for filing and review. For item (3), each province should formulate its own regulations. If officials or gentry misappropriate the funds again, they shall be severely punished.

1.2 Fund Allocation

Items to be disbursed by the central government: pension expenses; consolation expenses; central government subsidies.

Items to be disbursed by provincial governments: primary school teacher training expenses; provincial government subsidies; provincial government incentives; regular expenses for special primary schools; special workshop expenses; primary school inspection expenses.

Items to be disbursed by local authorities: salary expenses; start-up expenses; subsidies; incentives; workshop expenses; visit expenses; assistance expenses; inspection and guidance expenses.

The above allocation is determined by considering China's political system and financial situation, integrating the criteria of educational administration, and based on the proposition of dividing tax sources. If the collection of taxes still adopts a centralized system, an extreme federal system, or only divides national and local taxes without clarifying the authority over revenues between provincial governments and local authorities, or if the revenue division is made but tax sources remain largely confused, the allocation may not be appropriate. As for the annual amount of each disbursement, there can be hope for gradual increase only based on the progress of undertakings, the disarmament of troops, the consolidation of national taxes, and other such circumstances. Here is an explanation of each allocated item based on the division:

1.2.1 Expenses borne by the central government

Pension expenses and consolation expenses are paid from the national treasury in all countries. The central government subsidies shall, after the division of tax sources, determine the scope and annual amount of subsidies according to the amount of central revenue. In terms of feasible subsidies: 1) subsidies for annual merit-based salary increases; 2) subsidies for rewarding excellent teachers; 3) assistance for primary schools in border areas; (4) assistance for special needs in primary education.

1.2.2Expenses borne by the provincial government

Training expenses for primary education: Normal schools that train primary school teachers are mostly established with provincial funds in each province. County-owned normal schools are insufficient in financial resources and talents. For the sake of popularizing education, more funds will be needed for adding schools and grades in the future, and the provincial government should bear full responsibility for this.

Provincial government subsidies:1) subsidies for annual merit-based salary increases; 2) subsidies to make up for the insufficiency of county funds; 3) subsidies based on the number of school-age children in each county; 4) subsidies for the start-up and annual expenses of primary schools in poor areas; 5) subsidies for visit expenses, which must be designated by the Education Department; 6) subsidies for rural areas to jointly establish complete schools; 7) subsidies for special classes set up for gifted or underachieving students.

Provincial government incentive funds:1) incentives for excellent teachers; 2) incentives for excellent schools. The annual amount of both items shall be determined according to the revenue of the provincial government after the division of tax sources.

Regular expenses for special primary schools: Such primary schools should be well-equipped and well-organized, which requires more funds. They are established with provincial funds in places with convenient transportation, aiming to serve as models for other schools.

Special workshop expenses: Divided into two types: workshops for normal school teachers and workshops for primary school teachers.

Primary school inspection expenses: As education strives for popularization, the original inspectors are insufficient for deployment. It is necessary to send more people to guide various places, so this fund should be increased year by year.

1.2.3 Expenses borne by the local government

Salary Expenses: This includes the annual salaries of primary school teachers, seniority increments, and the salaries of personnel related to primary education.

Start-up Expenses: As the number of primary schools gradually increases, each new school or additional class requires a relatively large amount of temporary start-up funds. Therefore, a separate item should be established when education has not yet been popularized.

Subsidies: These refer to the subsidies that should be provided in addition to the various items listed in the provincial government subsidies.

Lecture Fees: Lectures are divided into two types: voluntary attendance and rotating supplementary classes.

Visitation Fees: Used for travel expenses for visits.

Assistance Fees: Established for poor children with excellent performance, providing supplies or additional allowances.

Inspection and Guidance Fees: This includes the fees for itinerant instructors in addition to school inspectors.

2. Teacher Training Plan

First, this plan aims to train teachers, and the number of teachers trained should correspond to the number of newly established primary schools. Second, it aims to improve the efficiency of those serving as primary school teachers, which implies urging them to make improvements. In implementation, there is no clear boundary between these two objectives; however, the implementation plan should conform to these purposes. What I am eager to elaborate on is that the poor quality and difficulty in promoting local education today are fundamentally due to the corruption and backwardness of normal education, and the short-term normal schools run by localities are particularly the source of this deterioration (there are some relatively good short-term normal schools run by localities, and some even have excellent talents, but these are exceptions). As a result, the content of primary schools is mostly no different from that of old-style private schools. To be fair, even provinces that have made the greatest efforts in compulsory education are probably not immune to this problem. Therefore, in managing compulsory education today, if we do not reorganize the existing primary schools, there will be many obstacles in the process; if we do not cultivate teachers and establish schools based on genuine educational concepts, funds will only be wasted. Rather than following the path of making do with shoddy work, setting up many nominal schools that damage social credibility, it is better to strive to ensure that the schools established can achieve the purpose of education. Additionally, by adopting methods of subsidies and rewards and implementing policies to regulate private schools as a remedy, we can ensure that both the name and reality are consistent. I believe that to implement this proposition and cultivate teachers, it should be directly handled by the Education Department, with funds fully borne by the provincial government. If localities truly have the necessity to set up (relevant institutions) and the financial capacity to manage them, it can be handled after consideration and approval by the Education Department. The following are the opinions based on the plan:

It is divided into eleven items: (1)Demarcating normal school districts; (2) Planning and establishing branch normal schools; (3) Defining the responsibilities of normal schools; (4) Reforming the curriculum of the regular normal school program; (5) Reorganizing affiliated primary schools; (6) Supplementing the academic knowledge of normal school teachers; (7) Reformulating measures for the workshop courses; (8) Promoting the measures for the second division; (9) Short-term workshops; (10) Introducing new books; (11) Compulsory supplementary studies.

2.1 Demarcating Normal School Districts

Based on an overall assessment of the province's geographical conditions and the development plan for primary education, school districts shall be divided, with each district governing several counties. A number of new schools shall be established in addition to the existing ones. Before the new schools are set up, a designated school shall temporarily govern a specific district.

2.2 Planning and Establishing Branch Normal Schools

(1) Specifically for women's normal education Female teachers are most suitable for primary schools. However, in all provinces, the number of women's normal schools is even smaller than that of men's. Establishing separate men's and women's normal schools in different locations would inconvenience students; adding women's normal programs to existing men's normal schools would strain financial resources; and co-educational normal schools, in the context of secondary education, have long been

controversial in both practice and theory. Therefore, establishing women's normal branches in districts where men's normal schools are located will help achieve gender equality in education while being economical in terms of both talent and funding. Similarly, existing women's normal schools may set up men's normal branches to avoid imbalance.

(2) Specifically for rural education Since rural areas account for the largest share of primary education, more teachers trained to adapt to rural life should be cultivated. Such branches shall be established in suitable rural areas.

(3) To meet local needs These branches may be established either by local request, to address temporary needs, or to increase the number of teachers as primary education expands. They are not limited to offering regular programs.

2.3 Defining the Responsibilities of Normal Schools

Currently, school administrators often consider their duties fulfilled merely by following regulations. However, normal education has a profound impact on the nation's future and is closely linked to local education. With clear district divisions, each school shall assume specific responsibilities, including formulating plans for graduates' employment, expanding branch schools and classes, dispatching staff to inspect primary schools in the district, improving primary school teachers' teaching methods and academic proficiency, and promoting local education development. Concrete implementation measures must be developed for each responsibility.

2.4 Reforming the Curriculum of the Regular Normal School Program

This issue is complex; the key reforms are as follows: Before the new educational system is implemented, normal schools shall abolish preparatory courses. The first three years (early stage) shall focus on general subjects and foundational education courses. In the last two years (advanced stage), students shall take specialized elective courses in addition to education courses. Internships shall begin in the first semester of the first year of the advanced stage, integrated with theoretical studies and conducted simultaneously. All teachers shall be those who have studied normal education or have long-term research experience in primary education. During the advanced stage, teachers shall guide students in discussing primary school teaching materials based on the subjects they teach.

2.5 Reorganizing Affiliated Primary Schools

Affiliated primary schools must meet the following criteria: 1)Sufficient capacity to facilitate student internships; 2) Both single-grade and multi-grade class structures; 3)Additional grades specifically for testing new systems and teaching methods, in addition to regular grades; 4)Comprehensive facilities; 5) A weekly joint critique meeting for all grades.

2.6 Supplementing the Academic Knowledge of Normal School Teachers

Higher normal schools shall offer supplementary courses (of less than one year) for current normal school teachers (including middle school teachers) in each province. Courses shall be optional, with teachers from each province attending on a rotating basis.

2.7 Reformulating Measures for the Workshop Courses

The current workshop system is highly inconvenient, as it groups students with varying academic levels and ages together, teaching them the same general subjects. Graduates of higher primary schools, with their limited academic proficiency, cannot 胜任 teaching roles even after short-term studies. The revised measures are as follows:

(1) For graduates of higher primary schools: A 3-year program. General subjects shall follow the early stage of the regular normal curriculum but with reduced difficulty or content. Education courses shall be increased in the second year, and internship hours shall be added in the second semester of the second year.

(2) For current primary school teachers: A 1-year program. Core education courses are compulsory; optional courses include general subjects (arithmetic, natural science, physics, chemistry, history, geography), skills, design-based teaching methods, Chinese teaching methods, and psychological testing. Students must take at least 2 optional courses and complete internships related to their chosen subjects.

(3) For private tutors who have passed qualification assessments: A 1-year program. The curriculum shall be based on the current 1-year workshop courses, adjusted according to local conditions and the tutors' proficiency levels. This program may be managed by counties themselves.

(4) For accelerated specialized teacher training: Open to graduates of regular normal programs, with a 1-year duration. Students may choose 2 subjects from 5 options: fine arts, crafts, music, physical education and games, and Chinese. In addition to their chosen subjects, they must take general teaching methodology.

2.8 Promoting the Measures for the Second Division

Currently, many middle school graduates who cannot pursue further education, as well as graduates of Type A vocational schools, remain unemployed; some even work as unqualified primary school teachers. By strictly defining qualifications for primary school teachers, offering preferential treatment to teachers, and expanding the "Second Division" in normal schools, more such graduates will enroll. The curriculum shall be revised in accordance with official regulations, referencing the second and fourth types of workshop courses outlined in Item (7), with special emphasis on education courses and internships.

2.9 Short-term Workshops

(1) Vacation workshops Duration: 20 to 50 days. The number and types of courses shall be determined as needed. Each normal school (including branches) must hold at least one such workshop annually.

(2) Mobile workshops Duration and courses shall be the same as above. These shall be organized by counties, which shall invite education experts to lecture at central locations in various townships. All teachers from public and private schools must attend. Lectures may be held every other day or for half a day to avoid conflicting with regular classes.

2.10 Introducing New Books

Each year, new books for primary school teachers shall be introduced in three categories: 1) General educational books; 2)Subject-specific teaching books; 3) Books specifically for private primary schools or traditional private tutors. Before normal school districts are formally divided, the Education Department shall issue a circular requiring the purchase and reading of these books.

2.11 Compulsory Supplementary Studies

Two groups of primary school teachers are particularly challenging to address: 1)Those with valid qualifications but insufficient academic proficiency;2) Those without valid qualifications but with potential for improvement. To facilitate their improvement, school inspectors shall conduct strict evaluations and arrange for them to attend relevant workshop courses (specifically the second and fourth types in Item 2.7 in phases.

Their positions shall be temporarily filled by county-appointed substitutes, and they shall resume their roles upon completing the supplementary studies. Each summer, inspectors shall submit a list of teachers requiring supplementary studies to the Education Department, which will assign them to normal schools and issue orders to the relevant counties for implementation.

3. Plan for School Establishment

Plan for School Establishment: Reorganize existing public primary schools; Ban private tutoring schools; Evaluate private primary schools; Promote compulsory education.

3.1 Reorganize existing public primary schools

For an existing public primary school to be necessary, it must meet one of the following criteria:

(1) It has a reliable regular fund and can run classes for four or more grades.

(2) It has appropriate school buildings and facilities.

(3) It currently has a large number of excellent teachers.

Reorganization measures for item (1): If a school lacks appropriate school buildings and facilities, it shall be required to raise temporary funds, with the province or county providing a corresponding subsidy; if it has no excellent teachers, it shall be reorganized immediately.

Reorganization measures for item (2): If the teachers are not excellent, the school shall be reorganized immediately; if the regular funds are insufficient, efforts shall be made to allocate funds.

Reorganization measures for item (3): If funds are insufficient, or the school buildings and facilities are inadequate, funds shall be allocated respectively to effectively maintain the school.

Therefore, the necessary conditions that a primary school should meet are briefly listed as follows:

(1) School buildings and facilities must be suitable for use. Each province must formulate appropriate regulations and publish documents related to these aspects for reference.

(2) Teachers' salaries must be paid appropriately, and school operating expenses must be allocated properly. Each province must formulate relevant regulations in this regard.

(3) The curriculum of primary schools should mainly conform to the first item of Article 13 of the current National School Regulations, and it is even better if new-style organizational methods can be adopted for reference.

(4) Teachers who have performed excellently in primary school teaching positions or who have recently graduated from normal school undergraduate programs are considered appropriate.

The total amount of existing educational funds shall be allocated for rectification in accordance with the criteria for the existence (of schools). In addition to disbursing other legitimate funds, if there is any remaining money, new primary schools can be established in places with appropriate school buildings or suitable locations in accordance with the above-mentioned necessary conditions. The newly added funds can also be used for school establishment.

3.2 Ban Private Schools

(1) The Education Department of each province shall order the county magistrate to work with the Education Promotion Office to conduct a detailed survey of all private tutoring schools in the county, report the results within a specified time limit, and after the report is submitted,

arrange for personnel to be dispatched to various counties on a scheduled date to assess the private tutors. The county magistrate shall, in accordance with the order, issue a notice in advance.

(2) All private tutors, except those who are normal school graduates or have passed the qualification examination, shall take the assessment test. After this examination, those who fail shall not be allowed to run private tutoring schools; otherwise, such schools shall be banned. Those who employ unqualified private tutors to run schools shall be punished.

(3) Private tutors who pass the examination and have a good command of Chinese and a basic knowledge of elementary arithmetic shall be rated as Grade A; those who have a good command of Chinese only shall be rated as Grade B.

(4) Private tutors who pass the examination with the highest scores in either Grade A or Grade B may serve as teachers in supplementary schools (supplementary schools are specified in the following four items).

(5) Students of private tutoring schools shall not have the right to transfer to other schools.

(6) For local private tutoring schools where the tutors are normal school graduates, have passed the qualification examination, or have passed the assessment, and whose facilities are in line with the nature of a school, after inspection by school inspectors, the better ones may be renamed private primary schools; the county government shall report to the Education Department for examination, verification and filing. Such private tutoring schools may also apply to the county government on their own initiative for inspection.

(7) Tutors who have passed the assessment, can read the introduced educational books, are recognized by school inspectors as having truly gained insights, and whose teaching methods are relatively good may apply

to the Education Department for approval to work as substitute primary school teachers. Those who graduate from and pass the tutor workshop courses shall be qualified to work as primary school teachers.

3.3 Evaluation of private primary schools

(1) Private primary schools are allowed to make flexible adjustments to the ministry regulations regarding their curriculum structure, allocation of teaching and administrative staff, and tuition fee collection. However, the subjects that can be omitted must be limited to those specified in Item 2 of Article 13 of the current National School Regulations.

(2) Except for teachers who are normal school graduates or have passed the qualification examination, teachers in private primary schools shall undergo the same assessment as private tutors. Those who fail the assessment shall still not be allowed to work as teachers in private primary schools.

(3) County magistrates shall instruct county school inspectors to conduct detailed investigations into local private primary schools (including mission schools). If a school fails to comply with the provisions in the preceding two items, those that have been registered shall be ordered to rectify within a specified time limit; those that have not been registered shall be immediately abolished.

(4) Private primary schools may receive public funds as subsidies and rewards. The specific measures shall be formulated by each county on its own and submitted to the Education Department for approval.

(5) Private primary schools that are deemed by school inspectors to meet the standards for the existence of public primary schools and the necessary conditions mentioned above may apply to the Education Department for approval to become substitute primary schools.

3.4 Promote compulsory education

3.4.1 Encouragement and Promotion Measures of subsidies and rewards shall be adopted to set an example and strive for expansion.

(A) Encouragement and promotion for local school establishment

(1) For localities that can raise funds for school buildings and start-up expenses on their own, appropriate annual subsidies shall be granted based on the scale of the planned school establishment.

(2) For localities that can raise annual operating funds on their own, appropriate start-up expenses shall be provided, and assistance shall be given in securing school buildings.

(3) Newly added county funds shall be allocated proportionally, requiring localities to raise a certain amount on their own with the county providing corresponding subsidies; however, specific regulations shall be made based on whether the location is urban or rural and the local level of affluence.

(4) For existing schools that add grades and can raise part of the funds locally, appropriate subsidies shall be granted.

(5) Special subsidies shall be given to townships that jointly establish schools with more classes, or to poor villages that jointly set up schools, provided they can raise appropriate funds.

(6) Subsidies shall be granted to urban areas where schools (either jointly or in nearby clusters) establish public classrooms for science, handcraft, home economics, etc., as well as children's libraries, with adequate funds raised.

For the above items, those who enthusiastically raise funds and achieve remarkable results shall be given appropriate rewards.

(B) Encouragement and promotion for private individuals in school establishment

In addition to following items (1), (2), and (3) under (A), rewards shall be granted in accordance with regulations.

(C) Encouragement and promotion for private primary schools

(1) After annual inspections by school inspectors, bonuses shall be awarded to outstanding teachers to encourage their academic efforts and improve teaching methods, thereby increasing the number of substitute primary schools.

(2) The addition of grades in substitute primary schools may be handled with reference to item (4) under (A), and they shall be allowed to form alliances as specified in item (6) under (A).

3.4.2 Compulsion The compulsion referred to here differs from the scope stipulated in educational laws and regulations. At the initial stage of compulsory education planning, instead of compelling the establishment of schools, people are compelled to attend school; instead of punishing those who fail to establish schools, those who fail to attend school are punished. This can be described as a complete reversal of priorities! It is often the case with us Chinese that when undertaking a task, we copy regulations without attending to practical realities. The measures of compulsion I advocate are as follows:

(A) Compulsion regarding the establishment of primary schools

(1) Gentry and directors shall be punished if cities, towns, and townships fail to establish at least a certain number of new schools each year.

(2) Presidents and directors of chambers of commerce shall be punished if areas with a chamber of commerce fail to establish at least a certain number of new schools each year.

(3) Village chiefs shall be punished if a village with more than 100 households fails to establish a primary school.

(4) County magistrates and directors of Education Promotion Offices shall be punished if their counties fail to establish at least a certain number of new primary schools each year.

(5) Educational commissioners or promoters responsible for specific regions shall be punished if they fail to establish at least a certain number of new schools each year.

The specific measures for the above items shall be formulated by each province.

(6) Provincial administrative chiefs shall be punished if their provinces fail to establish at least a certain number of new primary schools each year.

(B) Compulsion regarding supplementary education

The ministry regulations on supplementary schools are extremely vague and should be thoroughly revised. My work Notes on Investigating Japanese Industrial Supplementary Education can serve as a reference.

(1) All public institutions shall provide appropriate supplementary education for their staff, either independently or jointly; heads of institutions that fail to do so shall be punished.

(2) The navy and army shall provide appropriate supplementary education for their officers and soldiers at their respective stations. If, after a government order is issued, any officer or soldier who has served for more than one year still cannot recognize 300 or more characters, their superior officers shall be punished.

(3) Companies and factories owned by merchants that employ more than 100 people shall provide appropriate supplementary education for their employees; those that fail to do so shall be fined accordingly.

The regulations for the above items shall be formulated and promulgated by the respective ministries.

(4) Supplementary schools shall be attached to all areas with schools. Secondary schools and institutions of higher education may arrange for students in the third grade or above to take turns teaching in these supplementary schools.

3.4.3 Supplementation

(A) Regarding various skill subjects, each county may select and employ a number of specialized teachers for the most essential ones, who shall take turns going to schools lacking such talents to teach on a rotating basis.

(B) For the purpose of improving private tutoring schools and private primary schools, special instructors may be assigned to visit each school in rotation for guidance.

4. Clearly Define the Fundamental Law for Promoting Compulsory Education

It is divided into four items: Provisions belonging to the national constitution; Revise the regulations on the assessment of magistrates and local personnel; Issue laws and decrees on preferential treatment for teachers; Formulate regulations on dereliction of duty by teaching and administrative staff.

4.1 Provisions Belonging to the National Constitution

The national constitution should stipulate clauses regarding the duration of compulsory education and compulsory schooling. Recommendations should be submitted to the National Assembly, and educational circles across all provinces should be informed to make consistent requests.

Most constitutions of other countries have explicit provisions on the duration and compulsory nature of compulsory education. Recently established new governments have made even more detailed regulations. Compulsory education is the foundation of a state. As China is formulating its constitution, it should adopt the established practices of other countries and specifically include relevant clauses.

4.2 Revise the regulations on the assessment of magistrates' school-running performance and the assessment of local personnel engaged in promoting education, which were formulated by the Ministry of Education.

The Ministry of Education shall submit a request to the President for official promulgation by decree, and each province shall formulate separate regulations on its own.

Such assessments are not limited to compulsory education, but compulsory education actually accounts for the largest part of local affairs. In China, the assessment of officials has traditionally focused on suppressing bandits and managing finances, with no attention paid to education. Ordinary laws and decrees are treated as mere formalities. Therefore, the ministry's regulations on the assessment of magistrates are only empty texts without the same binding force as the Civil Servant Disciplinary Law. There are questionable points in their content: for example, the assessment of magistrates is conducted after they have been in office for one year; if they have been in office for less than a year, there are no appropriate rewards or punishments. The assessment items have no fixed standards, making it easy to evade responsibilities. Moreover, if provinces do not formulate separate regulations, it is difficult to ensure proper handling of priorities. The regulations on the assessment of local personnel engaged in promoting education do not include the educational staff in county governments or county school inspectors, and rewards and punishments are purely applied for by magistrates, which may be inappropriate. The entire text is too general, and it does not mention whether provinces can formulate separate regulations. All these urgently need to be revised.

4.3 Preferential Treatment for Teachers

Laws and decrees should be specially issued regarding matters such as pensions, bereavement allowances, seniority increments, and salary grades for rewarding excellent teachers.

Such measures are of great significance for encouraging teachers and promoting education, and are stipulated in various countries. In China, teachers have heavy workloads but low salaries, which are barely enough to support their families. Some even receive the same salary as they did more than ten years ago. Therefore, capable people often switch to other occupations out of necessity. To revitalize education, teachers must have adequate salaries to maintain their lives, and special preferential treatment to encourage their dedication. Thus, there should be appropriate regulations on pensions, bereavement allowances, seniority increments, and rewards for excellent teachers. As for teachers' salaries, since they cannot be unified across provinces, each province may formulate its own regulations.

4.4 Formulate Regulations on Dereliction of Duty by Teaching and Administrative Staff

The current underdevelopment of education is largely due to the dereliction of duty by teachers. While providing preferential treatment on the one hand, there must be disciplinary measures for those who neglect their duties on the other. The Ministry of Education shall formulate relevant regulations (not limited to primary school teachers).

In addition, matters such as surveying school-age children, demarcating school districts, and compulsory schooling are indeed part of compulsory education, but I believe they are not urgent priorities at present. Regardless of whether Shanxi Province has handled these matters properly, its provincial government has incorporated them into its overall administrative planning, which is indeed a crucial undertaking. However, in the plans formulated by other provinces, the first two matters are either fabricated or empty promises, and the third has not yet been regulated. When I first took charge of educational administration in Henan Province, I reviewed relevant records and documents from other provinces, and found that all of them emphasized these issues, yet I couldn't help but sigh at the abundance of empty paperwork. Now that this proposal is drafted, I have attached these remarks.

Published in *New Education*, Volume 5, Issue 3, October 1922.

A Discussion on Primary School Teaching Materials

This topic was put forward by members of the Hubei Winter Vacation Lecture Association. It was originally intended to be discussed in detail, but due to the rush of time, I will now only raise a few fundamental questions regarding how primary school teaching materials should be prepared.

1. The Relationship Between Teaching Material Organization and Teaching Methods

In the past, research on teaching methods focused more on formal aspects, often treating teaching methods as a tool to achieve educational goals. To prove this mistake, let's take a carver as an example: a carver uses different methods to engrave seals, ordinary wooden or stone utensils, and hard crystal stones. If one only knows the methods but uses the same knife for all, they will still fail. This shows that methods and tools are only related but cannot be confused as one. Therefore, the tool to achieve educational goals is "teaching materials," not teaching methods. Without tools, we cannot talk about methods of use. The problem with the traditional adherence to formal teaching methods lies in the failure to recognize that teaching methods emerge from teaching materials. John Dewey once said: "To understand the relationship between 'teaching materials' and 'teaching methods,' one must understand the distinction between 'what' and 'how.'" In my opinion, empty discussions about teaching methods are not as good as delving into the sequence of teaching materials; the so-called teaching methods are inherently contained within this sequence. However, discussions about teaching materials must also be based on learning psychology. Otherwise, even if we list many good teaching materials, we still cannot select or arrange them properly.

In the past, research on teaching materials purely determined selection criteria and arrangement sequences based on the materials themselves, which was just as wrong as discussing teaching methods in isolation from teaching materials. We need to understand that the sequence of teaching materials has two meanings: one is the sequence of teaching materials themselves, which is an issue inherent to the materials; the other is the sequence in which materials are taught, which is an issue of learning psychology. It is a fundamental mistake to apply the sequence of learning psychology entirely during teaching while completely ignoring it when organizing teaching materials. Let's use these two meanings to examine China's primary school textbooks. Regardless of whether the sequence of the materials themselves is properly organized, there is very little consideration of the sequence of learning psychology. Now, let's discuss China's primary school textbooks by dividing them into two categories:

(A) Textbooks that teach characters, such as textbooks for Chinese and Chinese literature. In terms of paying attention to the sequence of learning psychology, apart from the teacher's judgment on the difficulty level of the content, the focus is on the following aspects: (1) the number of new characters, (2) the length of sentences, (3) the complexity of character strokes, (4) the length of the text. Such a sequence is entirely formalistic. I am not saying that form can be ignored entirely, but this is not a fundamental issue. The fundamental lies in adhering to the principles of learning psychology. For solid memory, repetition is necessary, but repeating an entire lesson is uninteresting. To arouse interest, there must be various changes; to facilitate memory, review must be integrated into teaching. If these three methods are only applied during teaching, although there may be some effects, reading aloud will lack interest, and teaching will be laborious and time-consuming—with results that are far from natural. Textbook publishers, when organizing teaching materials, do not pay attention to fundamental issues. Therefore, the lower the grade, the shorter the text, the more meaningless it is, and the more it deviates from children's psychology!

(B) Textbooks that use characters to record teaching materials, such as textbooks for ethics, civics, history, geography, and science. Generally, the content of the teaching materials is mostly overshadowed by the descriptive text. During teaching, because it is necessary to explain characters incidentally, most of the efforts of both teachers and students are wasted on characters, thus abandoning the essence of the teaching materials. Teaching based on the organization of such textbooks makes it difficult to implement even the best teaching methods. Therefore, the revolution in textbooks is the foundation of the revolution in teaching methods.

Children's supplementary readers also suffer from the same drawbacks: works like *Children's World*, *New Method Story Readers*, *Little Friends, and Children's Educational Pictures* are quite popular among children; however, upon careful examination, despite the editors' diligent efforts, the benefits and effects that children gain are not very significant. Among these books, *Little Friends* and *New Method Story Readers*, with their descriptive texts, have some understanding of children's learning and are relatively valuable works; but because the editors focus on lower grades, the sentences are still unavoidably cumbersome. Moreover, with long narratives, lower-grade students cannot finish reading the full text, and higher-grade students, if they read too many, will easily become bored. *New Method Story Readers* combines stories with literature. If a few lessons are selected as literary readers for higher grades, they can still be used. However, if such texts are used entirely, the original nature of the content will be lost, and they will not be favored by higher-grade students. As for those who like to read such books, they are mostly lower-grade children, who focus on looking at the pictures or having older people tell them the stories from the books, without gaining a sense of initiative. Therefore, children's supplementary readers should also be compiled according to different grades to be suitable for use.

There is another common problem: much of the content in various textbooks is not suitable for many localities. Supplementary readers are mostly used as entire books. If teachers only select one or two texts from a supplementary reader and require children to purchase the entire book as a reader, it is both inconvenient and uneconomical. In my opinion, textbooks should use common teaching materials, but at least one-third of the class time should be reserved for adding local materials or temporarily needed teaching materials. For supplementary readers, we can follow the example of Children's Science Series: each volume focuses on one subject, published as a small booklet, allowing teachers to select and use them at any time. This way, purchasing them individually would be much more convenient.

Now, according to my views, I propose the following format for compiling readers:

1.1 Literary Readers

In the past, Chinese textbooks included content from history, geography, and science. Although today's literary readers still draw on such materials, their sole purpose is to teach language and cultivate an interest in literature.

For teaching characters in the first semester of the first grade, I am not in favor of using readers. Instead, during appropriate teaching moments—when children are learning about things—we should take the opportunity to help them recognize the written forms of single words and phrases. Additionally, when young students are learning characters, they should not be forced to write them. Taught this way, children will undoubtedly learn more characters. By the second semester, using readers to teach them will naturally make reading easier.

Teaching children characters through readers is most challenging in the first three years of primary school. If the texts contain too many sentences with numerous unfamiliar characters, they will be beyond the ability of young students. Conversely, if the sentences are too simple and lack strong interest, young children will not enjoy reading them. To avoid these issues, we must apply two principles of learning psychology: "repetition" and "variation." Even if there are many sentences, there should not be too many new characters; while the text repeats, the meanings should vary.

Examples of this approach can be found in several lessons published in Teacher's Friend and Little Friends. The Literary Reader recently published by Commercial Press also adopts this format. The Commercial Press's *National Language Reader* and Zhonghua Book Company's *National Language Reader* for the new educational system—each with one volume released—also emphasize character repetition, representing a significant improvement over earlier versions. However, they are not entirely thorough: (1) They focus too much on repeating single characters rather than sentences, failing to create textual variations through repetition. This not only weakens the depth of meaning but also misses the opportunity to integrate review into teaching. (2) Excessive changes in both content and form make them unsuitable for lower grades. Compared with these two, the Literary Reader seems superior. Nevertheless, it has its own shortcomings: (1) There are too many identical examples of repetitive patterns. (2) The previous volume did not sufficiently use minimal variations in content.

Given these issues, if we do not provide appropriate explanations of various patterns through inductive methods, readers will only recognize the benefits of repetition without understanding the variations in structure.

Below, I categorize and list several examples for reference in primary education:

1.1.1 Pattern of Repetitive Phrases

In such examples, each lesson is divided into several paragraphs, and each paragraph uses the same sentence pattern, with one or two characters possibly replaced. However, the same sentence pattern should be expressed in varied ways, so that readers do not feel a sense of repetition—that is the essence of this pattern. The following example is taken from the readers of Henan Compulsory Schools:

Big mouse, medium mouse, little mouse, went out to play together. They met a dog, and the dog talked to them.

The dog said to the big mouse, "Where are you going?" The big mouse said, "I'm going to visit Uncle Cat." The dog said, "You mustn't go." The dog said to the medium mouse, "Where are you going?" The medium mouse said, "I'm going to visit Uncle Cat." The dog said, "You mustn't go." The dog said to the little mouse, "Where are you going?" The little mouse said, "I'm going to visit Uncle Cat." The dog said, "You mustn't go." Big mouse, medium mouse, and little mouse, after hearing what the dog said, all didn't go to see the cat.

1.1.2 Pattern of Substance Replacement

In such examples, the form remains unchanged, but the substance is replaced. The replacements here are relatively more numerous. Let's explain them by categories:

Change of Subject—Only the subject is changed, while the rest of the sentences remain roughly the same. The text is from *Little Friends:*

Mimi! Xiao Hei, Xiao Hei, come quickly to eat fish. Little black cat, meow meow, walks over to eat the fish in the black basin. Mimi! Xiao Bai,

Xiao Bai, come quickly to eat fish. Little white cat, meow meow, walks over to eat the fish in the white basin. Mimi! Xiao Hua, Xiao Hua, come quickly to eat fish. Little tabby cat, meow meow, walks over to eat the fish in the flowerpot. After Xiao Hei finishes eating the fish, it watches Xiao Bai and Xiao Hua eating; after Xiao Hua finishes eating the fish, it looks at Xiao Hei, looks at Xiao Bai, and says loudly: "Wash faces, wash faces, everyone wash faces."

Change of Copulative Words The sentence structure remains the same, but the copulative words are varied. Such texts have been widely used in schools in Suzhou and Shanghai. The following example is taken from the readers of Henan Compulsory Primary Schools:

The ant was sweeping the floor at home and found three copper coins. The ant wanted to buy a watermelon, but then thought, "Watermelons have rinds," so he decided not to buy a watermelon.

The ant wanted to buy a peach, but then thought, "Peaches have pits," so he decided not to buy a peach. The ant wanted to buy fish, but then thought, "Fish have bones," so he decided not to buy fish. The ant wanted to buy clothes, and thought, "Clothes are good to wear. I'll buy a piece of clothing." The ant used the three copper coins to buy a red piece of clothing. When he put it on, he turned into a red ant.

Successive Replacement In such examples, the sentence structure of each paragraph remains unchanged, but the substituted content in the latter paragraph directly follows from what happens in the previous paragraph. The following example is taken from the readers of Henan Compulsory Primary Schools:

Three Mice: There is a big mouse, a medium-sized mouse, and a small mouse, living together in a small house. In the house, there are three beds: the big bed is for the big mouse to sleep in, the medium bed is for the medium-sized mouse to sleep in, and the small bed is for the small mouse to sleep in. To the left of the beds, there are three chairs: the big chair is for the big mouse to sit on, the medium chair is for the medium-sized mouse to sit on, and the small chair is for the small mouse to sit on. To the left of the chairs, there are three pieces of clothing: the big piece of clothing is for the big mouse to wear, the medium piece of clothing is for the medium-sized mouse to wear, and the small piece of clothing is for the small mouse to wear.

1.1.3 Cumulative Pattern

In such examples, the substance mentioned in the previous paragraph will reappear in the subsequent paragraph. The substances are added in succession in sequence, while the sentence structure remains unchanged. However, sentences can also be accumulated to form the text. The following text of the cumulative substance example has been used in various schools in Suzhou, Shanghai and Henan Compulsory Primary Schools:

A sparrow carried a bag of rice, but couldn't walk anymore, so it sat on the mouse's back. The mouse carried the sparrow, but couldn't walk anymore, so it sat on the hen's back. The hen carried the sparrow and the mouse, but couldn't walk anymore, so it sat on the yellow dog's back. The yellow dog carried the hen, the sparrow, and the mouse, but couldn't walk anymore, so it sat on the black donkey's back. The black donkey carried the yellow dog, the hen, the sparrow, and the mouse, but couldn't walk anymore, so it sat on the boat. The boat, which carried the black donkey, the yellow dog, the hen, the sparrow, and the mouse, stopped by the river and didn't move.

Sentence cumulative pattern, examples are as follows:

It's Grandmother's birthday. What should we give her? The eldest brother said, "What should I give? A mirror is the brightest. I'll go buy a mirror to give to Grandmother." The second brother said, "A mirror is the brightest, so you go buy a mirror. What should I give? Honey is the sweetest. I'll go buy honey to give to Grandmother." The youngest brother said, "Honey is the sweetest, so you go buy honey; a mirror is the brightest, so you go buy a mirror. What should I give? Little white flowers are the loveliest. I'll go pick little white flowers to give to Grandmother." Grandmother was delighted when she saw the gifts. She said, "The mirror bought by my eldest grandson is the brightest; the honey bought by my second grandson is the sweetest; the little white flowers picked by my youngest grandson are the loveliest."

1.1.4 Intricate Pattern

Examples of this kind involve alternating changes in both the content and form of sentences, while the words are repeated. Here is an example:

The younger brother sang, and the elder sister laughed. The younger brother said, "If you laugh, I won't sing." The elder sister said, "I won't laugh; you sing, you sing." The younger brother said, "I'll sing, and you listen; after I sing, you sing along with me." The elder sister said, "You sing, and I'll listen; after you sing, I'll sing along with you."

1.1.5 Circular Pattern

There are two examples of this kind. In the simple example, the sentence patterns are the same, but the substituted substances go back and forth, like a chain link.

Fingers clamp the palm; the palm wraps the fist; the fist presses against the fingers.

A complex example can be divided into two or three sections, with the sentence patterns of each section (both the preceding and the following ones) forming a consistent style within their own sections. The transformation of substances in the preceding section follows a progressive pattern, similar to the successive pattern. For the following section, the succession can either be in reverse order or continue in a progressive manner—there is no fixed rule. However, it must adopt methods to repeat the substances or sentences from the preceding section. The example is taken from the *Literary Reader* published by the Commercial Press:

Old Yellow Dog found a bag of rice. He ate half of it and left the rest at Cat's house. Cat ate half of the rice and left what was left at Mouse's house. Mouse ate half of that and left the remainder at Little Bird's house. Little Bird ate half of the rice and left what was left at Mantis's house. Mantis ate half of that and left the remainder at Cicada's house. Cicada took half of the rice in its mouth, leaving just one grain behind. Old Yellow Dog went to ask Cat for the rice. Cat said, "It's left at Mouse's house." Old Yellow Dog went to ask Mouse for the rice. Mouse said, "It's left at Little Bird's house." Old Yellow Dog went to ask Little Bird for the rice. Little Bird said, "It's left at Mantis's house." Old Yellow Dog went to ask Mantis for the rice. Mantis said, "It's left at Cicada's house." Old Yellow Dog went to ask Cicada for the rice. Cicada said, "The last grain was eaten by an ant." Old Yellow Dog said, "This is Cat's fault. I'll go bite Cat." Cat said, "This is Mouse's fault. I'll go catch Mouse." Mouse said, "This is Little Bird's fault. I'll go bite Little Bird." Little Bird said, "This is Mantis's fault. I'll go catch Mantis." Mantis said, "This is Cicada's fault. I'll go catch Cicada." Cicada had no way out and hid in the tree, crying!

The examples listed above amount to nine in total. When compiling textbooks, these examples can be used in combination. For instance, examples of quality conversion can be mixed with two or three other examples; examples involving repetition, quality conversion, accumulation, and complex structuring can also be combined in two or more ways. With diverse variations, numerous different patterns can be derived. Additionally, for students in the second grade or above, when compiling textbooks using the above examples, the content can be gradually expanded in volume while allowing slight adjustments to sentence structures. For beginners, the content can be even more simplified. All these depend on the compiler's judgment based on the students' proficiency levels.

For literary readers used in the first three grades, the organization of texts should primarily rely on transformation methods and repetitive sentence patterns. However, it is equally essential to include texts for practice. The structure of such practice texts should not resemble those in previous textbooks, which focused solely on reviewing familiar characters. Even if a lesson contains many new characters, it does not matter. Nevertheless, three criteria should be noted:

(1) The organization of sentences should include examples where replacing new characters is highly flexible. For instance, under the character "kan" (look) in a picture-related context, many words representing different things can be connected; however, for "pai qiu" (pat a ball), the character "pai" (pat) cannot be connected with many words representing different things.

(2) When replacing new characters in the original sentence, it is necessary that the original characters can be combined with many characters that have already been learned. For example, take the sentence "zhuo shang you shu" (There is a book on the table). If children are supposed to replace "shu" (book) with characters like "bi" (pen), "mo" (ink), "tu" (picture), "yan" (inkstone), etc., they must have been taught these characters beforehand. This way, they can practice grammar while reviewing the characters they have already learned. However, there is no

need to impose such restrictions on the characters that children combine on their own.

(3) Attention should be paid to the progression of arranged practice texts, considering the characters that have been taught in various courses and the natural development of children's intellectual abilities. Each text, though, should serve a grammatical purpose. Practical writing should be compiled separately and not included in literary readers. Instead, various forms of practical writing can be compiled into a collection and taught when appropriate, for teachers' reference. As for the wording of poems and new-style plays, some lessons can be selectively taught starting from the third grade.

Practice texts, as well as the wording of poems and plays, should be compiled into separate books. When editing such texts, they can be particularly rich in content, allowing teachers to choose freely and have children copy them to read. Currently, the nursery rhymes, children's poetry, and children's play books available in bookstores have limited materials, which are still insufficient for teachers' selection. Practice texts can be compiled by Chinese teachers themselves.

For literary readers used in the fifth and sixth grades, there is no need to adhere to the previous examples. Excellent works by famous writers can be selectively taught, but they should be simple and accessible.

1.2 Story Readers

Such readers serve two purposes: on the one hand, they are used for conversations and performances related to Chinese literature and art; on the other hand, they are used for narrative talks in subjects such as ethics, civics, hygiene, and history. To avoid the drawbacks of previous supplementary readers, in my opinion, they should be divided into three formats based on the proficiency levels of each school year.

1.2.1 Type A Story Readers

These are intended for -grade students or second-grade students in the first semester. The editing goal is to use illustrations to depict the progression of the story paragraph by paragraph, with brief explanatory text added below each illustration. This format is adopted because story talks for lower-grade students are delivered in a lecture style. During the lecture, it is difficult to keep children's attention focused, and it is extremely challenging to have them retell the story afterward. If they cannot retell it and the lecture is repeated, the original interest will be lost, and it will inevitably become a mechanical process of lecturing and retelling.

Based on past experience, teaching materials from subjects like ethics, civics, history, and hygiene are divided into paragraphs, and illustrations are used to depict their scenarios. For each paragraph, the illustrations arouse children's curiosity and prompt questions. Teachers should explain accordingly to help them understand the story content and teach the text notes below the illustrations. The interest in the illustrations and the story will spark an interest in recognizing the text below the illustrations; in turn, recognizing the text will stimulate an interest in associating it with the story events. Story illustrations like those in Little Friends (a children's magazine) have appropriate styles and structures. However, their story content is somewhat simplistic, lacks depth of meaning, and the text is slightly redundant. Here is an example for reference:

The story is adapted from *The Tumor Old Man with a Tumor* in Japanese national language readers.

Picture shape Annotated characters

(1)*The tumor old man resting on a rock in the mountains — The tumor old man.*

(2) The tumor old man watching a group of goblins dancing — Dancing.

(3) The old goblin gesturing to the little goblins — The old goblin.

(4) The little goblins seizing the tumor old man — The little goblins seize the man.

(5) The tumor old man seeing the old goblin and practicing boxing — Practicing boxing.

(6) The old goblin talking to the tumor old man and cutting off the tumor — Cutting off the tumor!

(7) The tumor old man talking to another thin tumor old man — Why is your tumor gone?

(8) The thin tumor old man practicing boxing among the goblins and getting an additional tumor — Another tumor has grown!

The example cited above has been used in trial teachings multiple times using this method, and the results are as follows:

(1) Each picture presented can arouse children's appropriate motivation for each paragraph and help them discover the actual content. Children can provide reasonable explanations and ask relevant questions about the facts in each paragraph, without relying solely on the teacher's lectures.

(2) Thanks to the effect mentioned in point (1), children receive deeply stimulating impressions. They gain a thorough and genuine understanding of the story's meaning, and find it easy to remember the narration of events accurately. They can grasp the entire story clearly without the need for repeated lectures.

(3) Because of the scenarios depicted in the pictures, children gain the ability and opportunity to make discoveries on their own. Therefore, beyond the inherent value of the story itself, their interest is doubled, enabling them to concentrate their attention without feeling bored.

1.2.2 Type B Story Readers

These are designed for second and third graders in primary school. They are largely similar to Type A, except that the sentences annotated below the pictures should be able to indicate the main point of each paragraph; or, if there are crucial sentences in the story, they should also be annotated under the pictures to allow children to read them repeatedly.

1.2.3 Type C Story Readers

These are intended for upper-grade primary school students and above, mainly focusing on narrating facts through text. Illustrations are used as supplements to enhance children's interest or to compensate for what the textual narration fails to convey. The narrative text should be particularly concise, but this conciseness differs from the so-called conciseness in ordinary styles of writing. The structure and sentence organization like those in Children's Plays are quite appropriate; however, their overall textual structure is different. Genres such as those in Chinese Stories and Children's Science Series, which are almost identical to novelistic language, are not suitable for readers. The key criteria to note are as follows:

(1) Divide the text into paragraphs according to the sequence of the story; do not use a single whole piece of text.

(2) The facts in each paragraph should describe the important parts.

① At the connections between paragraphs, redundant text can be omitted; the sequence of the preceding and following paragraphs should be clear, and there is no need to ensure the coherence of the rhetorical tone.

② Unimportant sentences and irrelevant facts can all be deleted

③ Facts that require students to think and meanings that are implied should not be explicitly stated. For example, in *The Story of the Greedy Dog*: ."*.. it saw a dog in the water holding meat in its mouth, not knowing it was its own reflection.*" The part "*not knowing it was its own reflection*" can be deleted. Another example: ."*.. the dog barked fiercely at the dog in the water, wanting to bite it; the other dog also bit back at it. The dog did not know the river was very deep, so it jumped down to fight, and then fell into the water...*" The part "*the dog barked fiercely at the dog in the water, wanting to bite it; the other dog also bit back at it. The dog did not know the river was very deep*" can be deleted. And in ."*.. fortunately, it was very close to the shore, and with all its strength, it finally managed to climb onto the shore; however, it was hoarse and exhausted, and its whole body was wet. When it looked for the meat it had placed aside, it had already been carried away by another dog!...*" All the text above "*the meat it had placed aside*" can be deleted... If the deleted text needs to show the scenes, they can be presented in separate paragraphs with pictures.

As for the progression of story materials, generally, -grade readers should focus mainly on stories about immortals, monsters, humans, animals, etc. For second and third grades, in addition to the aforementioned types, emphasis should be placed on adventure stories, fables, and the like. For fourth grade and above, besides the previous categories, priority should be given to realistic stories, legends, historical talks, etc. Jokes can also be included as appropriate.

It is most important that these three types of story readers are each printed as separate booklets for each story, making them convenient for purchase and use. However, the readers themselves should not contain the full text of the stories; instead, a separate compilation of complete texts should be made outside the readers. Such books will consist entirely of text without any illustrations, containing multiple stories in one volume, specifically for teachers' reference. The previous teaching guides can all be discarded.

1.3 General Knowledge Readers

These include subjects such as civics, hygiene, nature, history, and geography. The purpose of compiling textbooks around a single subject is to enable children to acquire general knowledge about things they cannot observe directly through such readers. Their format and methods are the same as those of story readers, but only two types—Type A and Type B—need to be compiled.

All the above-mentioned readers should be supplemented with illustrations, and the following criteria should be noted:

(1)Each lesson should be divided into segments and illustrated according to the sequence of the content.

(2) Each illustration should be able to present the important part of a segment of facts.

(3) The form of the illustrations should be simple, but the content should be rich—because the purpose of using illustrations is to show the sequence of facts, not to enhance artistic interest.

2. The Relationship Between Preset Teaching Materials and the Integration or Separation of Subjects

The subjects for primary schools stipulated by the Ministry of Education include Morality, Chinese, Arithmetic, Science, Drawing, Handcraft, Music, Gymnastics, Geography, History, and Home Economics. The curriculum of new-style primary schools differs from the subjects specified by the ministry, with approximately two differences:

(A) The range of subjects in any school is broader than that stipulated by the ministry. For example, Morality has been changed to Civics and Society; Gymnastics has been changed to Physical Education and Hygiene. These are typical examples.

(B) Regarding the expansion of children's general knowledge and practical abilities, subjects such as History, Geography, and Science were previously specifically established only in higher primary schools; in national primary schools, they were merely included in national language readers and taught incidentally through narrative texts. Now, even lower grades have specially designed courses for these subjects, which are taught separately.

Next, comparing the curricula of new-style primary schools across different regions, all schools offer subjects such as Arithmetic. For subjects like Civics, Geography, and History, their presence varies by school; however, despite differences in names, their content is inherently included in other subjects rather than being omitted entirely. For example, subjects like Commerce, Agriculture, Bookkeeping, Home Economics, and Sewing are added or omitted based on local conditions and the nature of the school. The Girl Scouts is a special organization and not a mandatory practice for all students. Gardening can be integrated into the Science curriculum. Some schools, such as the Affiliated Primary School of Beigao and the Model Primary School of Hubei Province, have established a special subject of "Local Studies." In fact, local knowledge serves as the foundation for teaching various subjects and thus does not require a separate course. The Model Primary School's approach of teaching Local Studies and Crafts as special subjects in the third grade, and Geography and History as special subjects in the fifth grade, is based on specific viewpoints—whether such an approach is appropriate, however, remains open to discussion.

Regarding the merging, splitting, addition, or reduction of subjects, each school has its own propositions, and even the names of subjects often differ. Nevertheless, despite variations in names, their content is generally similar. Even in terms of content, the division of courses across subjects may vary, but the overall curriculum is roughly consistent. Therefore, there is no need for uniform subject regulations across all schools. Similarly, dividing the curriculum by "unit-based subjects" is not suitable for new-style primary schools. In my view, however, researching teaching materials and arranging the curriculum are two separate matters. For the convenience of studying teaching materials separately, it is advisable to conduct research by subject. Moreover, aligning with the subjects stipulated by the Ministry and adapting them to unit-based disciplines facilitates research. It is only necessary to expand the scope beyond the ministry-stipulated subjects and supplement the teaching materials accordingly.

What I mean by researching teaching materials starting from unit-based subjects is that within a unit subject, it is easier to assess which content is essential and which can be simplified in terms of nature and quantity. When arranging the curriculum, however, it is crucial to evaluate the value of keeping various teaching materials independent or integrating them from three perspectives: the efficiency, interest, and practicality of learning.

The reason we oppose purely subject-based curriculum arrangements in primary schools is that in the past, subjects were isolated, often emphasizing their own internal systems. As a result, much of the teaching materials used were inconsistent with the educational goals, making instruction monotonous and inflexible, thus wasting time and effort. If we only focus on merging, adding, or reducing subjects without researching the individual teaching materials themselves, even the most up-to-date subjects will fail to eliminate the old problem of isolated disciplines.

The currently popular project-based learning method, which uses children's holistic and dynamic experiences as the basis for applying teaching materials, is theoretically irrefutable. However, if implemented improperly, it may even be less effective than the old fixed textbooks in ensuring steady progress. Conversely, we should not completely reject project-based learning and revert to the old curriculum arrangements simply because independent subjects retain the value of their own systems. The strength of project-based curricula lies in their freedom from rigid subject divisions while preserving the independent value of each subject. It would be dangerous to reform teaching methods by merely adopting the form of project-based learning and completely discarding traditional structures.

It is important to understand that reforming teaching methods requires identifying steps and plans within the learning process based on the entire body of teaching materials, and applying subject-specific methods accordingly. It does not mean organizing teaching materials and instruction using unit-subject methods. Guided by this principle, we should first establish a general framework, allowing teachers to gradually refine their practices and avoid going astray.

Therefore, my propositions are as follows. First, evaluate the value of keeping various teaching materials independent or integrating them; second, design the learning process based on the holistic nature of the teaching materials. This approach adopts the essence of project-based learning, progresses sequentially, and does not completely abandon the effectiveness of traditional subject divisions—it is not a compromise. Let me elaborate:

(A) The planning of large-unit designs can be divided into two categories, both of which can be predetermined by teachers before the semester begins.

a. With an event as the main body, determine the sequence for delivering teaching materials. Every school holds activities such as recreational evenings, sports meets, parent-teacher meetings, trips, visits, commemorations... in each semester. In the past, these events were mostly carried out without clear objectives. No corresponding plans were formulated based on specific goals, thus wasting the best opportunities to integrate learning materials. For such designs, all the teaching materials that can be taught in various subjects during that period can be incorporated according to the needs of the event, and delivered in accordance with the planned sequence. Such plans should be predetermined by a group of selected teachers. In advance, the person in charge of the event and students of the relevant grades should discuss, step by step, the tasks to be completed and the procedures to follow. During the event, the responsible teachers should take charge of guidance and organization respectively.

b. Identify key teaching materials from subjects and determine the learning sequence based on the holistic aspect of the materials.

① In nature studies, there are important natural products in each period. Select a key natural object, and conduct observations and experiments sequentially from the starting point to achieve the final result. However, the purpose of selection and the experimental procedures should enable students to acquire methods through this material, allowing them to infer or solve all problems related to the phenomena of similar natural products. This means choosing one thing to learn as the basis for learning other things; all designed teaching materials should follow this principle.

② For character cultivation, during a semester, there should always be several specific issues for cultivating students in a certain class. Whether through conversations or practical activities, there must be a focused goal. The issues targeted by the goal, whether it is correcting habits or developing new ones, must undergo repeated cultivation. If a habit has not yet become natural, training cannot stop; moreover, if a habit has not been formed, only the methods can be changed, not the goal. In the past, many subjects were taught each semester, but only whether students were proficient in reciting or performing was examined, which ultimately failed to achieve educational objectives.

③ School tasks, such as arranging flower beds and decorating rooms, can all be designed as projects.

④ For subjects like crafts and fine arts, creating larger works; for subjects like history and geography, collecting specific materials or conducting performances—these are also suitable for project-based learning. Such designs are generally a form of subject-specific teaching materials, but in the learning process, wherever there are connections with other subjects, or where reading, writing, and calculation can be integrated, opportunities for practice must be provided. This ensures that students can grasp the entire sequence of the teaching materials they are learning.

(B) Predetermined integration of teaching materials from various subjects

Before each semester, review the predetermined details of each subject, identify those with interrelationships, those whose learning sequences are not exclusive to a single subject, and either combine them into a unit lesson plan to be taught in stages or arrange them to be taught on the same day or week. There are many such related materials. Taking subjects alone as an example: the practices in morality education can be incorporated into performances in other subjects; moral knowledge can be taught in conjunction with social studies and civics. Except for specific time slots, Chinese language and literature skills—such as character recognition, writing, composition, and performance—can be practiced in other subjects whenever opportunities arise. The same applies to arithmetic. Fine arts and crafts, music and physical education can often be connected, with opportunities for practice even within other subjects. In the first and second grades, general knowledge from subjects such as morality, language arts, civics, social studies, nature, hygiene, history, and geography should be integrated into conversations or story readers for teaching.

The Commercial Press has compiled two types of connected teaching materials, but in terms of form:

a. The subjects involved in the connection are fixed, which easily leads to a mechanical form of connection.

b. The connection of teaching materials is merely based on the similarity in the nature of subjects, rather than integrating subjects according to the inherent relationships and progression of the teaching materials themselves. This does not align with children's holistic experiences.

In my humble opinion, teachers should study the relationships and learning processes of specific teaching materials, and integrate various subjects into the learning sequence of such materials. There are many such cases. If teachers compile lesson plans based on their research insights and collect them together, it will surely make significant contributions to the field of primary education. However, it should be clarified that my advocacy for connecting teaching materials is based on two principles: first, the connection should be observed from the perspective of individual teaching materials themselves, not merely by combining subjects based on their nature; second, the connection should be natural, with each part having its due value. It should not be a mere nominal connection. As long as the teaching materials themselves have important value and can arouse interest in learning, even teaching them independently is valuable.

With the above two principles, the proportion and time allocation of the selected teaching materials across various subjects cannot be fixed. However, selecting teaching materials in this way, adapting to needs, and adjusting monotonous teaching methods will certainly provide many opportunities to organize children's holistic and dynamic learning experiences. Beyond these two cases, when teaching materials are delivered through separate subjects, the drawback of isolation will naturally be avoided, and their inherent value will not be neglected.

c. Discussing and determining the progression of teaching materials:

Step 1: Prepare methods for collecting materials

① Collect summaries and detailed lists of teaching materials specified in various educators' discussions on textbook standards, textbook content, and other sources (the reference materials listed below are general and contained in entire books).

For textbook standards, references include: Chapters 16 and 17 of *Democracy and Education*, Chapter 4 of *Life Education, Journal of School System and Curriculum Research*, Chang Daozhi's *Research on Primary School Curricula*, and the original preface to *New Schools in Belgium*.

For textbook content, references include: Chapters 18, 19, and 20 of *Democracy and Education, New Schools in Belgium, Plan for New-style National Schools,* and previous editions of *Methods of Teaching Various Subjects*.

For summaries and detailed lists of teaching materials, my available materials include: *Curriculum Standards for Primary Schools under the New School System* by the Jiangsu Primary School Union, *Curriculum Standards by the China Education Improvement Society, Curriculum Guidelines of Shanggong Primary School, Curriculum Guidelines of Yuanyi Primary School* in the provincial capital of Henan, *Curriculum of the*

Affiliated Primary School of Beijing Normal University, Curriculum of the Affiliated Primary School of Wuhan Normal College, Model Primary School Curriculum, and Wu Yanyin's *Draft Curriculum for Primary and Junior High Schools.*

② Reflect on subjective experience: first, carefully review the reference materials mentioned in item ①. Then, cross-verify the textbooks I have used before or self-compiled curricula with the teaching experience and reference materials.

③ Investigate social needs: this should be conducted with clear purposes and standards after completing the first two items. Teachers can be divided into groups by subject or task to conduct appropriate investigations. Investigations can be divided into two types: general teaching materials and local teaching materials. For the purpose of investigation, Journal of Curriculum Research and Yu Ziyi's *New Curricula for Primary Schools* can be referenced. For investigation methods, Mr. Wang from *North Normal University's Report on the Factory Market Survey*, Gu Yinting's *Outline for Vocational Education Facilities* can be referenced. In addition, reports from provincial industrial promotion conferences, *Vocational Survey Reports* by the China Vocational Education Association, *Railway Scenic Spots* by the Ministry of Communications, and *Provincial Surveys* by the Ministry of Agriculture and Commerce are also useful references.

④ Test students' abilities. After the winter vacation, at the start of the new semester, primary schools in the provincial capital can join together to conduct a unified test on the teaching materials previously taught in each grade of primary schools (both elementary and higher levels) using the same questions for each academic year. The results will be compiled into statistics to serve as a reference for determining the minimum limits of detailed items for each subject.

Step 2: Formulate the outline

① Formulate the general outline

The general outline serves as the standard for the entire curriculum. It is necessary to first study the discussions of various scholars regarding standards and content mentioned in Step 1, Item ①, incorporate one's own insights, consider local conditions, and then formulate the outline. Primary schools should organize teaching material research associations, select individuals who are enthusiastic about research and have rich experience to draft the outline, distribute it to teachers of various subjects for comments, and then hold meetings to finalize it.

② Formulate subject-specific outlines

This requires first studying the reference materials related to the summaries and detailed lists of teaching materials mentioned in Step 1, Item ①. Based on the general outline, carefully examine the intrinsic value of teaching materials for each subject and formulate the outlines accordingly. The following points should be noted:

(1) The purpose and significance of each subject.

(2) The style and format for conducting each subject.

(3) The minimum requirements for each subject.

During the winter vacation, teachers of each subject can put forward their opinions separately, which will be compiled into a report. After the general outline is approved, discussions will be held on the general framework of each subject. Then, personnel will be appointed for each subject to draft the outlines. If there are slight differences of opinion on the content of each subject, several alternative methods can also be formulated for schools to choose from.

Step 3: Formulate detailed lists of teaching materials

This should be compiled independently by each school based on the subject-specific outlines and with reference to detailed lists from various sources. For those that have already been drafted, they can be revised after the start of the new semester based on the discussed outlines and the statistical results of the tests; for those not yet drafted, the same method as mentioned above shall apply.

Step 4: Establish a teaching materials review committee

Each school shall, based on the outlines and detailed lists, determine the amount of teaching materials to be allocated and the sequence of implementation before teaching sessions, either weekly, biweekly, or monthly; or report the results of the taught content, discuss matters requiring revision, and confirm the subsequent teaching materials to be covered.

Published in *New Education*, Vol. 6, No. 3, March 1923.

Solutions to Organizing Teaching Process

1. Teaching Process and Instructional Sequence、

Discussing teaching methods without examining the teaching process is like a boatman who only knows how to steer but is unaware of the waterline—such a person can never travel far.

The previously used instructional sequences were rigidly structured into formal stages, controlling facts through the process of thinking. This might be applicable in simple cases, but if we abandon the natural order of facts and the proper order in which facts should be studied, the result would be even worse than the boatman mentioned above, wouldn't it?

2. Teaching Process and Stages

Since the Herbartian school created the five-stage teaching method, dividing it into preparation, presentation, comparison, generalization, and application, those who have used this method have made minor adjustments, but the overall framework has remained largely unchanged.

In the past, when using the five-stage method, each unit of teaching material was divided into several stages: preparation, presentation, comparison, generalization, and application, with a predetermined number of minutes allocated to each stage. This led to the following drawbacks:

(1) It is difficult to align the actual teaching time with the predetermined lesson plan time. Either the lesson plan is completed with time remaining, or the lesson plan is not finished due to insufficient time. The drawback of the former is that it leads to pointless practice; the drawback of the latter is that it results in hasty and shoddy outcomes.

(2) Dividing the teaching into segments with strict boundaries tends to diminish the cohesive effectiveness of learning. For example, in the

preparation stage, all the teaching materials of the lesson are listed and questioned, leading to a jumble of ideas. When it comes to the presentation stage, because there is a disconnect in time from what was previously asked, it becomes hard for students to fully comprehend. The presentation stage takes a relatively long time, making it impossible to sort out and apply each item in a continuous manner. By the time of the generalization and application stage, students have forgotten much of what the teacher said earlier, rendering the presentation ineffective.

As for the five-stage method itself, the preparation stage is regarded as the most crucial teaching segment. However, its function lies in using the review of past experiences to connect with newly taught facts. Relying solely on fragmented connections, how can students form general concepts? If this is used to arouse motivation, it is merely a repetition of old facts; the so-called "arousing motivation" is nothing but a fantasy. Moreover, the rigid separation between each stage is particularly inconsistent with the actual process of thinking. From the perspective of actual thinking, when recalling old experiences, the examples cited often start with comparison. For intelligent children, once a comparison is made, implications immediately arise, which involves comprehensive concepts. Or when they further investigate other matters to support these implications, this in turn involves application-related issues. All these can occur before the preparation and presentation stages are completed and before accurate explanations are given. If one rigidly adheres to the teaching stages, such fixed steps will actually block the progress of children's thinking development. If not, what is the point of such a rigid format?

The five-stage method is not without considerable value for the acquisition of knowledge; however, we should pay attention to the following points: 1) Each teaching stage should be merged or omitted according to the nature of the teaching materials. 2) It is advisable to apply this method to a single item within a unit of teaching materials and conduct teaching in a connected and sequential manner.

Most of the above arguments are drawn from my works written in the first year (1912) and the seventh year (1918) of the Republic of China.

3. Deduction and Induction

3.1 Issues of induction to be discussed in the five-stage method

The currently prevalent inductive heuristic teaching method, with all its key details, is derived from Herbartian theories. Its flaw lies in overemphasizing form while neglecting the coherence of concepts. Moreover, the presented materials tend to be oversimplified, failing to demonstrate students' creative abilities. This has led to a backlash against the once-dominant five-stage method. Dewey wisely remarked: "This merely represents the teacher's organization of materials, not the path followed by students." Induction constitutes only one aspect of the thinking process; the other aspect is deduction. For instance, the application stage in the five-stage method already incorporates deductive functions, albeit without clearly defining the processes of deduction and verification. In reality, thinking proceeds naturally, making it difficult to strictly distinguish between induction and deduction. Their manifestation in teaching methods depends on whether hints arise alongside the problem: in deduction, hints are inherent in the problem itself; in induction, hints need to be identified and explained. Even when a problem exists, induction requires gathering facts to formulate hypotheses. Once a hypothesis is discovered, the rigid boundary between deduction and induction dissolves. Whether hints stem from collected facts, are derived from existing experience, are new or old, they hold equal significance, regardless of their nature or the level of understanding involved. Thus, any discussion of induction must simultaneously consider deduction.

3.2 Issues of deduction to be discussed in the Dalton Plan

Modern psychology has proven that thinking begins with general concepts, which are then analyzed into independent elements to form universal truths. The traditional inductive teaching method, passed down through generations, actually violates this psychological principle. The Dalton Plan's specification of course outlines is seen by some as a rebellion against old teaching methods and an emphasis on deduction. If this approach emerged as a reaction to outdated methods, there is little disagreement. The flaws of current heuristic methods—using fragmented questions to motivate knowledge acquisition—stem precisely from overvaluing inductive forms. In terms of methodological form, current practices often start with abstract knowledge when researching problems, which inherently involves deductive processes. A notable example is the common teaching of mathematics, which forces abstract thinking before concrete explanations are provided. Furthermore, gathering materials in induction, while formulating hypotheses, inherently contains elements of general concepts, albeit more ambiguously. Additionally, the introductory guides in the Dalton Plan serve the same purpose as the "statement of objectives" in old methods, and solving problems through gathering materials still relies on induction. Clearly, distinguishing methods purely by form is pointless.

3.3 The "expanded concept" in project-based learning

This differs from the "general concepts" emphasized in the Dalton Plan. Knowledge acquired must be applicable to solving similar problems, gradually expanding the chain of core ideas and enabling the continuous reconstruction of experience. In the developmental sequence of thinking, deduction and induction interact, with deduction always grounded in concrete explanations. Applying induction and deduction in this way is more aligned with purpose than merely supplementing the five-stage method with deductive forms or acknowledging deduction within induction. However, focusing solely on form over function is problematic. Dewey, the pioneer of project-based learning, outlined teaching steps as: specific facts first, then concepts and reasoning, and finally applying results to specific facts—progressing from induction to deduction. Ironically, this sequence mirrors the five-stage Herbartian method. Why, then, do they differ fundamentally in purpose? Because the five-stage method subordinates thinking to knowledge acquisition, while project-based learning subordinates knowledge acquisition to the development of thinking. Understanding this is crucial for teaching. Literature cannot always rely on induction or deduction, nor can lower grades. Sometimes, only one method is needed: for example, teaching rice cultivation using induction to derive growth principles, then applying those principles deductively to teach wheat cultivation—a most efficient approach.

4. Discussions on Various Revised Teaching Sequences

4.1 Revised Herbartian Teaching Sequences

(1) Three-stage model: Divided into three stages—preparation, presentation, and organization or application. It incorporates comparison, generalization, and application, with adjustments made to their inclusion or exclusion. This model was quite prevalent before the early years of the Republic of China (1912–1949).

(2) Teaching sequence of the Jiangsu Primary School Teaching Method Discussion Association: Divided into preview, practice, organization, and application, with sub-items under each stage. This model was revised in response to the trend of student autonomy. After 1914, it was widely adopted in lesson plans of normal schools, teaching method books published by various presses, and regulations issued by educational authorities.

Both models are still used in some places today, largely adhering to the structure of the five-stage method. Most of the flaws of the five-stage method persist in them, and thus they are rarely favored by contemporary scholars specializing in teaching methods.

(3) Dewey's merging of the five stages into three: 1) Recognition of specific facts; 2) Rational generalization; 3) Application and verification. This is only found in his theoretical discussions.

4.2 Project-based Teaching Sequence

It is roughly divided into three stages: objective, planning, and result, with teachers and students each undertaking appropriate tasks in each stage. Recently, many teaching method books published by presses have adopted this model.

In terms of form, it first demonstrates the role of teacher-student collaboration; second, it avoids the rigid logical constraints of the five-stage model. In terms of applied theory, the project-based approach argues that teaching sequences should be flexibly adapted to time, place, individuals, and materials. Compared to the Herbartian emphasis on inductive heuristic teaching, which confines all courses within the five-stage framework, this approach is more practical in application.

4.3 Doubts about Formalized Steps

If the aforementioned models are merely used as points that teachers must consider when preparing lessons, any model can be effective. However, when they rigidly prescribe the actual teaching process, they tend to disrupt the natural development of students' thinking. The key doubts are as follows:

(1) Categorized regulations are still not fully suitable for unit-based teaching: In the five-stage method, adjustments were once made by

separating knowledge and skills into different stages—for example, knowledge subjects culminating in application, and skill subjects in organization. Recently, some have formulated teaching sequence guidelines by classifying learning functions into heuristics, practice, review, appreciation, etc. In project-based learning, teaching procedures are defined separately for creation, verification, appreciation, and habit formation. In fact, no subject belongs exclusively to a single category, nor can a unit of teaching material be entirely governed by one category. For practical purposes, we divide them into multiple categories, but even after classification, we cannot rigidly apply a specific teaching sequence to a specific type of material. Thus, categorized regulations cannot serve as a clear pathway for actual teaching.

(2) They easily lead teachers to fragmented and vague preparation: The stages are fixed yet empty of practical use. Enforcing inflexible forms to handle diverse teaching materials is like "cutting one's feet to fit the shoes"—problems are inevitable. It is common to see student teachers drafting lesson plans by haphazardly extracting materials and questions from textbooks to fit fixed stages. Each stage may seem appropriate in isolation, but when taught sequentially, students only gain fragmented knowledge. What they can comprehend is simplistic, and when materials are more substantial, they fail to reach proper conclusions. Even in project-based learning, while fragmentation is avoided, the flaw of vagueness remains the same.

Nevertheless, if there are no norms to guide the teaching process and control learning, teachers' preparation and actual teaching will be disorganized, resulting in even greater drawbacks than rigid formalism. For effective knowledge transmission, teachers must not only master the materials but also align them with the cultivation of thinking. To achieve this alignment, formalized steps and methods are necessary—and this forms the basis of my argument.

5. The teaching process formulated and expounded by me

5.1 Fundamental Issues in Teaching

5.1.1Textbooks must be reorganized

Following the original sequence of textbooks as the actual teaching sequence is a major reason why predetermined processes fail to adapt to reality. We should understand that: (1)Except for literary readers, no subject should involve excerpting phrases and wasting time on textual research. (2) Reciting textbooks mechanically, without substance, cannot enable students to acquire valuable knowledge. (3) Learning procedures must be flexible according to circumstances and cannot be rigidly bound by logical order. Therefore, when using textbooks: (1)Adjustments or modifications to content and quantity should be made based on local conditions, time, and students' circumstances. (2) The sequence of teaching materials should be outlined in advance according to how the materials will be studied, but this outline can still be revised during actual teaching.

5.1.2 The problem-solving method should be adopted

Regarding the problem-solving method, we must clarify the following:

(1) It differs from heuristic questioning. Heuristic teaching includes two types of questions: those before instruction (to facilitate knowledge acquisition) and those after (to assess acquired knowledge). Neither, however, leads to systematic knowledge through problem-solving. Drawbacks of this form include: 1) Using verbal questions as the sole method to arouse motivation, which has become a rigid routine at the start of lessons. 2) Enforcing rigid rules for questions (e.g., multiple-choice formats, prohibiting two answers to one question), which only facilitate

memory testing and fail to truly inspire thinking. Despite claims that such methods stimulate reasoning, limiting responses to verbal answers renders "stimulating thinking" an empty phrase. Heuristic questioning does have some value in teaching, but we must distinguish two functions of questions: 1) Supplementary to teaching: Fragmented questions aimed at recalling existing experiences (as used in heuristics). 2) Solving overall or partial doubts: Systematic, holistic questions that use existing experiences as a means to seek knowledge (the focus of our discussion here). This distinction has been overlooked in traditional teaching methods.

(2) The problem-solving method shares the same function as project-based learning. Common questions often merely prompt repetitive restatements of facts. Due to their prevalence, people mistakenly limit the role of questions to what is described in heuristic methods, confining their form within heuristic boundaries. This obscures the fact that a project is essentially a type of problem. While such questions (aligned with project-based learning) may also take the form of inquiries, their answers must form integrated knowledge with the value of resolving doubts. Recognizing the importance of problem-solving while being trapped in heuristic questioning methods reflects an incomplete understanding.

5.2 The Teaching Process

5.2.1 Structuring units around problems

Each unit of teaching material must form a major problem. Teachers may either organize a unit around a problem or frame an existing unit as a problem, depending on circumstances. This major problem includes numerous minor problems (using "major" and "minor" rather than "general" and "specific" to avoid misunderstandings). The sequence of these minor problems constitutes the teaching process. Solutions—whether from existing books or experiments (including practical exercises and hands-on work)—proceed under the teacher's guidance. Principles and methods are derived through solving problems, and only when valuable knowledge is acquired is the problem resolved. A comprehensive conclusion to the major problem emerges once all minor problems are thoroughly understood, as each minor problem derives from the major one. (Note: Independent things cannot logically be grouped into a single entity; even if arbitrarily combined, they retain separate functions. Nor can an integrated entity be divided into entirely independent parts—divisions, if made, must have interdependent relationships. Each part, defined by distinct attributes or relationships, deserves specific attention.) A unit of teaching material, as a problem, is inherently an integrated entity. Dividing it into minor problems facilitates study, but only if the interdependence of parts is understood—preventing fragmentation or isolation. Hence, we use derivation rather than analysis, emphasizing hierarchical connection and expansion. Whether addressing factual or reasoning problems, content must form a holistic part of the major problem, with interrelated propositions to sustain learning interest. The purpose of this structure is as follows:

(1) It is different from the marginal headings in old books. Those headings aim to mark out the outline and arouse attention, while the purpose here focuses on hinting, through which conclusions can be drawn.

(2) It is different from the formal teaching stages. The latter is stereotyped: teachers only record the matters to be taught in each stage based on the fixed teaching materials that have already been organized. Here, however, the methods to solve problems are sought according to the hints of the problems regarding the matters that should be studied at that time. Even if all materials are contained in textbooks, it is up to students to organize them independently and make selections or omissions as appropriate. Moreover, each problem is derived from reality. By examining a certain problem, one can know what learning matters should be included

in it. It is not like the formal teaching stages, which are empty and have no use in guiding learning at all.

(3) It is different from the propositions in the heuristic method. In addition to the reasons mentioned above, the formulation of each problem in sections cannot be done without understanding the entire unit of teaching materials. It is not like the heuristic method, where one can ask random and fragmented questions within the scope of the formal teaching stages.

5.2.2 Within each minor problem, key points to note, items to practice, criteria for free selection, reference books, and things to observe must be appended.

All methods of assigning tasks in the Dalton Plan can be applied here. As for heuristic questioning, it can only be used within the context of guiding research for the current problem. However, the explanations of work details in the Dalton Plan still need revisions.

(1) The work details include two items: topics and questions. Regarding the explanation of questions, the scope indicated only pertains to matters and fails to clarify the formal domain that questions should occupy, inevitably repeating the flaws of the heuristic method. The questions customarily used in heuristics can only be raised at any time during direct instruction. When applied to students' independent research, such questions allow for effortless excerpting without critical thinking, leading to uniform answers for everyone, which is far from sufficient to reveal students' ability for independent research. Moreover, these fragmented questions prevent students from integrating materials into a systematic structure. In my observation, students following the Dalton Plan today work according to outlines, similar to how they used to answer exam questions in the past. Is such learning any better than the rote memorization of the old days? In my opinion, the "topic" should be a weekly general topic, i.e., the major problem I discussed earlier, while "questions" should correspond to the minor problems I mentioned. However, the Dalton Plan uses a week as the

unit, with topics centered on a unit of teaching materials; sometimes a week may require multiple topics, sometimes one topic, and sometimes a single topic may span several weeks—this should be determined based on the teaching materials and students' circumstances.

(2) The various tasks listed under the questions in the work details must be assigned according to the essential tasks required for each question, to demonstrate that tasks and questions are inseparable. Although discussions on the Dalton Plan mention their interrelationship, they fail to explain this point thoroughly.

5.2.3 Principles for formulating questions

Recent updated lesson plans adopt the project-based approach, and although the form of teaching stages has been reformed, the design of questions still follows the old heuristic model. The Dalton Plan's use of questions, while different from heuristics, also lacks distinctive characteristics, as previously discussed. Based on the above reasons, the principles for formulating questions are as follows:

(1) Questions must contain hints that help solve difficulties.

(2) Questions must form independent parts while being interconnected, such that the progression of these questions leads to systematic knowledge.

(3) The answers required by questions must prompt the respondent to think critically, select materials based on their own insights, and seek solutions.

(4) Questions must arouse children's interest in research based on their existing experiences or current observations.

(5) The connection between preceding and subsequent questions must sustain students' interest in continuous learning.

Published in *Elementary Education*, Vol. 2, No. 2, June 1924.

Issues Concerning Primary Education Funding

A primary school consists of two levels: lower primary and upper primary, with the lower primary being a national school. According to the general practices of education worldwide, national schools are for compulsory education. As stipulated in the "Primary School Regulations" of the first year of the Republic of China (1912), the former (lower primary schools) were established by towns, townships, and villages, while the latter (upper primary schools) were established by counties. In other countries, compulsory education covers the entire primary school education. In China, primary education is divided into lower and upper levels. This division was mostly due to the framers of the school system considering the country's insufficient financial resources, so they separated the lower primary level in the hope of making compulsory education easier to implement. In reality, in China's situation, the idea of compulsory education has only been a nominal rule; moreover, since the implementation of the new system, the upper primary level only lasts for two years, and it is more convenient to set them up in a combined manner. Thus, the division between lower and upper primary levels is no longer in line with reality. Now, we should only consider the local financial capacity and the need for establishing schools; as for the regulations on which authority should establish them, they are quite meaningless.

Regarding primary education funds in various countries: For example, according to the new republican laws in Germany, they are all borne by the state. In other cases, the funds are shared by provinces and localities with some subsidies from the central government; or the central government, provincial governments, and localities each bear a certain proportion; or teachers' salaries are borne by the state, and the rest is covered by localities; or in cities, the funds are shared by the state and localities, while in rural areas, they are borne by the state. Now, when discussing primary school funds, should they be borne by the state or by local authorities? If it is to be borne by local authorities, should it be borne by provinces or raised by counties themselves? However, for these preliminary issues, first, we should divide the fiscal revenues of the central government, provincial governments, and local authorities, and clarify the independence of tax sources and the authority to collect taxes. Second, we should stipulate the proportion of expenditures for various administrative departments from the revenues of the central government, provinces, and localities to establish the foundation of primary school funds. I have elaborated on this fundamental proposition in my "Plan for the Implementation of Compulsory Education", and readers can refer to it. What is discussed here is that, while we should work together to advance this fundamental proposition, our current efforts cannot wait solely for the realization of this fundamental proposition. Therefore, assessing local conditions, striving to consolidate and expand primary school funds, and ensuring they are highly economical and efficient are urgent priorities. Let's discuss them separately:

1. What is the way to consolidate it?

First of all, the issue of educational fund independence

Recently, there have been strong calls for the independence of educational funds, and its benefits need not be discussed here. However, merely advocating for independence still entails many difficulties. Even if earmarked funds are designated, government agencies cannot exercise the right to allocate them and shirk their responsibility to supervise and urge collection. They may even secretly embezzle or borrow the funds under pretexts. The situation of educational funds in Henan Province is a prominent example. This is undoubtedly caused by poor governance, but if those in charge of education have the right to participate in the appointment of personnel in the collection agencies or the right to audit revenues, the manipulation and control by government agencies could be somewhat curbed. Since the collected funds are exclusively for education, or a certain proportion is used for education, yet the responsibility of collection is entrusted to people who have no connection with education, who would believe that there is no arbitrary corruption? If one argues that this would disrupt financial authority, then finances should be supervised by the people, yet those directly involved cannot be questioned, leaving financial authorities or collectors to disburse funds at their discretion or delay payments arbitrarily. Is this what is meant by "not disrupting authority"? I dare to assert that if educational funds only strive for independence without participating in collection, they will be in name only.

Second, the issue of educational fund management

(1) In each county, public funds have traditionally been dominated by educational funds. Since the late Qing Dynasty, when local self-government was promoted, followed by the wars of the Republic of China, educational funds have often been encroached upon under the pretext of security or other so-called public welfare, greatly affecting education.

(2) The income from educational assets in each county often lags far behind the proportion of their total value, especially the assets of former academies (such as stipends and examination grants). Those familiar with these assets and related archives were mostly former local gentry in cities and government clerks. After the reform, many destroyed files and embezzled properties; the remaining ones are often controlled through collusion between tenants and managers. A common malpractice in cash management is delaying receipts and disbursements by one or two months, rolling over the delays, and depositing the accumulated cash to earn interest.

(3) The size of educational funds attracts local attention, leading to disputes over the appointment of education bureau directors. Newcomers tend to arouse resentment, while older officials are not always familiar with

education. This causes numerous disputes in appointing directors, much to the distress of government agencies. In fact, malpractice is not limited to either group.

(4) Management of funds is sometimes handled by the Education Bureau (or still called the Education Promotion Office), county government, public funds bureau, or a specially established educational fund management office. The flaws in management by the county government and public funds bureau are obvious. A separate educational fund management office is redundant and risks disputes between agencies.

In summary, to rectify the aforementioned drawbacks and consolidate educational funds, the following measures should be taken.

(1) The provincial educational administrative authorities shall issue a circular to all counties, instructing them to establish a Temporary Committee for Sorting Out Educational Assets. The committee shall dispatch members to work with the county magistrate to supervise the process, requiring that within a specified time limit, details such as the amount, source, price, annual income, interest, management status, and rectification methods of each item be clearly stated. For real estate, the location and boundaries shall be specified; for cash, the details of deposits shall be clarified. All information shall be compiled into detailed registers and submitted to both provincial and county authorities for record-keeping. In subsequent years, any newly increased assets shall be handled by the Education Bureau in accordance with the above procedures.

(2) The Education Bureau shall select knowledgeable education experts to form a Fund Allocation Committee, which shall formulate allocation standards at the beginning of each year and submit them to both provincial and county authorities for review and record-keeping.

(3) The county government, Education Bureau, and Education Association shall jointly establish a Fund Protection Committee to audit the revenue and expenditure accounts at the end of each year.

(4) Adopt modern bookkeeping methods.

(5) Monthly income shall be publicly announced, and an annual report shall be published.

2. Way of expansion

This consists in, beyond the existing educational funds, increasing taxes or appropriating funds from various local revenues. For example, in Changsha, a certain proportion of temple property, annual income from clan ancestral halls, and income from guild halls is appropriated, requiring them to establish primary schools either independently or jointly. Moreover, an examination of the compulsory education funds raised in various provinces shows that, for instance, in Shanxi, business donations, shop donations, and household donations constitute the main sources in towns, while land donations are the major source in rural areas; in Jiangsu, a special surtax on goods has been proposed; in Zhejiang, an additional tax on land and poll taxes has been planned, etc. All these are in line with local tax sources and are common to various localities. Using these to fund primary schools is quite convenient. In addition, appropriating a certain proportion of the estates of those who die without heirs is also easy to implement. Here, a list of approved levies in various counties as listed in the Overview of Hunan Provincial Educational Administration is reprinted (omitted) for reference.

As for the newly increased customs duties and surcharges on salt surplus, it seems that a certain proportion can be appropriated specifically to subsidize the establishment of additional primary schools in various provinces. A certain proportion of the returned indemnities can also be used to improve the equipment of existing primary schools. Today, politicians, celebrities, and scholars talk extravagantly about culture and science. It is earnestly hoped that they will launch a joint campaign for primary school education funds, so that the foundation can be established.

3. The extremely economical and efficient solution

The "economy" I speak of must be considered in conjunction with efficiency. It is not like negative regulations that merely limit the number of staff and funds based on the number of grades and students. If the schools established provide ineffective education, even if they use very little funding, it is still uneconomical. For this reason, I have serious doubts about today's schools.

Since the existence of schools, it has been recognized that mere book-reading does not constitute education, so various subjects have been added. In setting up these subjects, attention is only paid to the capacity, sunlight, and air of the school buildings. However, if there are no appropriate facilities as tools for implementing education—even if various subjects are offered and the school buildings have suitable capacity, sunlight, and air—how can the goals of education be achieved? Moreover, what is the point of having schools for education? As for the so-called "appropriate facilities," the minimum requirements must include adequate workshops, recreation rooms, sports fields, and school gardens, along with the necessary equipment for these. This is not limited to the traditional practice of allocating funds solely for salaries and office expenses. Therefore, to determine whether something is economical, we must examine the aforementioned facilities to see if they can serve their purpose at a relatively low cost, as well as evaluate the methods and capabilities in their implementation.

When discussing the efficiency of school education, the most obvious indicators are: first, student performance; second, the ratio of the number of students to the amount of funding. However, in educational statistics, there is no reliable and accurate standard for student performance. Remarks about performance are also vague and general. Merely relying on the ratio of the number of students to funding is insufficient to judge efficiency.

The current situation of primary schools in various localities that we should pay attention to is as follows:

(1) Only expanding the number of schools while ignoring the capacity of each school;
(2) Urban and rural areas mechanically allocating funds according to routine without considering the actual situation of the schools;
(3) The cost of living is rising day by day, yet many primary school teachers still receive salaries at the level of ten years ago, making it impossible to talk about encouraging progress;

(4) The salaries of public schools are mostly fixed and uniform across localities, with no appropriate incentives.

To promote the development of primary education, county funds should be used to subsidize and reward schools run by local communities with self-raised funds. There should be no distinction between public and private schools in providing such subsidies and rewards. Subsidies should not be given unless the founders have a sufficient basic fund.

Subsidies are divided into two types: first, one-time subsidies, such as subsidies for school establishment and temporary equipment. Second, annual subsidies. In addition to the general regulations based on the number of students and grades, subsidies must be provided for impoverished areas, rural joint schools with complete facilities that exceed the quota and are divided into groups, special classes set up for gifted or underachieving students, and grade expansions, etc.

Rewards are divided into two types: one is for outstanding teachers, and the other is for outstanding schools.

The standards for subsidies and rewards are closely related to the inspection standards. It is urgent for each province to select experts with profound knowledge and rich experience in primary education to formulate these standards, so that educational inspectors can classify schools and teachers accordingly. Only in this way can we ensure that names match realities and achieve immediate results.

Published in "Research Issue on Chinese Primary Schools" of *The Chinese Educational World*, Vol. 14, No. 2, August 1924. Tables were omitted during inclusion.

A Study on Readers of Primary School Chinese Literature

The currently prevalent national language readers, also known as readers, roughly fall into two formats:

One follows the old-style textbook framework, with both form and content gradually leaning toward children's literature. This is the improved version, commonly used in most primary schools.

The other has completely changed the look of old-style readers, featuring repetitive wording and content that emphasizes interest. This is the literary version, mostly adopted by new-style primary schools.

It must be said that both represent progress. However, there are several fundamental issues that I am eager to elaborate on here—whether they were taken into account before these readers were published.

1. The Relationship Between National Language Readers and Children's Literature

1.1 One must first understand what literature is

All human groups develop language first, then writing. Even before the emergence of writing, literary works had already come into being. Why? Because when people express their thoughts through chants or employ rhetoric akin to art, such expressions carry literary significance, differing from ordinary language. For instance, Chinese characters are said to have been created by Fuxi, yet the "Eight Odes" of the Ge Tian clan—songs passed down in oral form—were already circulating, with their titles preserved in Master Lü's *Spring and Autumn Annals*. This aligns with Zhang Shizhai's view that literature originated from poetry. However, once writing gained prominence, literati indulged in elaborate wording and intricate rhetoric to please readers, causing literature to drift farther from its roots in spoken language. In its decline, literature became a mere formality: its original function of expressing emotions was reduced to a tool for scholars to show off, obscuring the true meaning of literature. To counter the prevailing trends of empty rhetoric and sophistry, Neo-Confucian scholars advocated the rigid doctrine that "literature serves to convey Dao (the Way)." This over-correction further muddled literature by conflating it with history and philosophy, leaving its true essence fragmented. Thus, literature's relevance to life lies not in the function of writing itself, but in the artful construction of texts. In terms of writing's basic functions, it serves to express emotions and convey ideas; literature, however, captivates readers in the process of such expression and communication. As the saying goes, "Words without literary grace will not travel far." To study literature, one must first understand its origins, then grasp its artistic functions, and finally recognize its value to human life. Humans cannot suppress their emotions; when emotions overflow, they find expression in writing. Birds sing and insects chirp, each with its own motivation, and what moves the listener is the cadence and melody in their sounds. Literary works broadly fall into three categories: emotional expression, narrative, and argumentation. Narrative and argumentative texts, though distinct in form, emerged later to serve the practical functions of writing—they are not the source of literature itself. Hence, the skilled orators of the Spring and Autumn period were required to study poetry extensively; Sima Qian, in compiling *Records of the Grand Historian*, drew inspiration from Qu Yuan's *Li Sao* in pursuing its underlying purpose. Literary works, above all, value the spontaneous flow of genuine emotion, forming naturally as expressions of the heart. Mastery of words alone does not suffice to reach literary excellence. Folk songs and children's rhymes, casually composed by common people, have spread widely among the masses for a reason. In contrast, works like *Three-Character Classic* and *Thousand-Character*

Essay, though rhymed, are mere hodgepodges of disconnected phrases with no meaningful content—even traditional literati disdained them. This reveals the essence of a literary work: if the writing lacks profound thought, sincere emotion, or rich imagination, and fails to artistically convey the significance of life, it lacks aesthetic essence and cannot be said to possess literary value.

1.2 One must understand what children's literature is

The term "children's literature" has only drawn attention from China's education circle in recent years. Genres such as ballads, stories, fairy tales, fables, riddles, witty talks, novels, and plays have gradually been collected for children's reading. Among these, fairy tales have seen the most publications and detailed discussions. However, after reviewing various books—whether translated or original—none truly adopt children's colloquial language. As for Readers or readers for lower grades, they often claim to be "fairy tales" simply because their ideas are close to children's thinking or they use words children can speak. Children's literature has three essential elements: 1) It must align with children's thinking; 2) It must conform to children's language; 3) It must possess literary qualities. Without any of these, it cannot be called children's literature. The first two are self-evident. The third requires, as discussed earlier regarding literary value, artistic organization that expresses the meaning of life, with profound thoughts, sincere emotions, and rich imagination. Moreover, the thoughts, emotions, and imagination cultivated must be guided toward a bright and upright realm, ensuring that the aesthetic appeal of literature aligns with educational goals. Those who fail to understand this, and merely prides themselves on catering to children's psychology, will end up with "curiosity-driven" materials that fall into absurdity and superstition, or "playful" materials that become vulgar. Hence, recent Readers and readers, while increasingly catering to children's psychology, are drifting farther from educational purposes. This is not merely a concern for ignorant newcomers who doubt myths or conservative elders who sigh at textbook content—it is a fundamental issue.

1.3 One must understand the flaws of past national language readers

National language readers worldwide have gone through phases of emphasizing form and substance before gradually leaning toward literature. Chinese primary school language Readers have followed the same path. Those emphasizing literary form include Character Lessons with Illustrations and Introduction to Composition. Those focusing on textual form favored simplicity and brevity, such as early primary school national language readers. These are relics of the past and need not be discussed further. During the era of primary school national language readers, most aimed to balance form and substance, leaning toward substance. Since the shift to Chinese (vernacular) readers, there has been a trend toward literature. However, long-standing old habits still linger in the minds of editors and teachers. We must first recognize that Chinese education aims to cultivate proficiency in language and writing. Subjects like history, geography, and science are included because language must attach to concrete content; without diverse materials, interest may become monotonous. This does not mean confining scientific knowledge to Chinese classes, nor does it mean rigidly specifying the proportion of certain materials. It is also crucial to understand that learning difficulty is not determined solely by the number of new characters or text length. Language practice should not be limited to textbook models or rigid conversational forms. The first flaw (overemphasizing non-linguistic content) makes texts dull and dry, wasting time on explanations unrelated to language. The second flaw (overly simplifying form) leads to poor content and meaningless expression, leaving no room for reflection. Recent literary-style readers, as reported in newspapers, pay attention to repetitive wording and learning interest but still have three key shortcomings: 1) Vernacular language does not necessarily equal children's colloquial speech. 2) Misunderstanding the true value of interest: literary interest lies in aesthetic appeal, not mere entertainment. Truth, goodness, and beauty—though distinct—are interconnected; the finest works embody all three. 3) A one-sided view of literary elements: literary beauty arises from the integration of substance and form. Poor substance cannot create literary value; clumsy form diminishes it. For example, works like *The Old Man with a Broken Arm at Xinfeng* and *Fighting the Tiger at Jingyanggang* excel in both engaging content and artistic expression. Children's literature emerged late even in Europe and America, and China has no ancient traditions to draw from. Creating it requires more than just proficiency in Chinese, making it extremely challenging. It is no wonder that current national language readers fail to satisfy.

Based on the research on these three aspects, two principles for readers to be children's literature are derived: 1) Select children's teaching materials that are suitable for their learning psychology; 2) Employ literary edification to achieve educational goals.

2. The nature of First National Language Readers

To understand this meaning, we must first examine the results of the trial implementation of the two aforementioned types of readers. Children still do not take much pleasure in reading the improved-style readers. The literary-style readers fail to reach the realm where one can read them repeatedly without growing tired. This is a general observation, not to say that every lesson in the current readers is like this. The reasons for this are roughly as follows: the former type of readers has plain and uninteresting texts, while the latter type has short texts that often fail to present concrete facts and long texts that lay out their meanings entirely. Moreover, the sentences are not to the children's taste, and the rhetoric and structure are far from refined—these are especially common flaws. Fairy tales, stories, witty talks, fables, etc., are essential elements of children's literature. It is universally acknowledged that national language readers must adopt them as teaching materials. However, the interest that fairy tales, stories, witty talks, and fables bring to children each serves their own inherent purpose. It is not impossible to rely on the teacher's enthusiasm to make it easier for children to learn language and characters. But if the interest children feel in learning is purely derived from the inherent purposes of these literary forms, rather than from the language and characters they must know, or if the acquisition of language and characters must rely on the interest from these inherent purposes rather than arising from reading the texts themselves, then not only is the goal of teaching language and characters reversed, but the literature itself also loses any value in moving people. Today, those who study traditional Chinese literature do not understand what children's literature is. As for the so-called new literati, the inferior ones can only write in vernacular, while the superior ones merely delve into grammar. They are ignorant of how the unique characteristics of certain literary forms are constituted. It is no wonder, then, that the nature a national language reader should possess remains unclear. From this, my propositions can be stated as follows:

2.1 A national language reader is not children's literature for listening

Fairy tales and stories—such children's literature—are applicable in early childhood, not to mention the wide range of stories. Even fairy tales, with more and more being created, now vary in difficulty level. Some current works, with structures similar to short stories, are readable by teenagers. Children's literature for listening is suitable when children cannot yet read books. Its main purpose is to develop imagination, not to practice language and characters. Such works are created primarily to be suitable for children to listen to and enjoy, with little regard for other aspects. Furthermore, since storytelling can rely on gestures and actions for expression, even verbose content is acceptable. If primary school national language readers adopt texts of children's literature for listening, children will not be able to read them. If they excerpt one or two sentences and first tell fairy tales or stories, as in some literary-style readers, this can be a method in project-based teaching: when children, after listening to fairy tales or stories, become strongly interested in the language and characters used, they can then be taught those elements. Moreover, there is no way for teachers to forcefully determine which specific language or characters to teach. However, if a book is labeled a "literary reader" but abandons the original goal of learning language and characters by relying on other purposes, it deviates greatly from the path and loses the inherent value of literature. Observing that many still choose improved-style readers over literary-style ones, one can ponder the reason. Nevertheless, language and characters are an important foundation for human activities, requiring dedicated learning. Just as infants babble and practice naturally out of need, and children take joy in singing and do not find repeated recitation burdensome, it is clear that there are texts that children can enjoy reading.

2.2 A national language reader is not children's literature for reading

Children aged six, seven, or eight have no ability to read books. At nine or ten, they can read but with limited ability. Above ten years old, their reading ability develops, and their thinking evolves with age. For children's literature intended for reading, there should be two forms for those under ten: (a) texts with distinct paragraphs, varying meanings, and frequent repetition of words and sentences; (b) if repetition of words and sentences is difficult in each paragraph, the language should be concise, with pictures accompanying each paragraph to supplement what the text cannot convey. However, this is somewhat different from recently published children's pictures, which are specifically for young children. After the age of ten, ordinary fairy tales are no longer suitable. Magazines like Little Friends and Children's World, for example, have language that most children cannot read and ideas that are often inappropriate for both children and teenagers—a conclusion I drew after inquiring with many children. The language and content of children's literature for reading only need to be recognizable to children, without requiring the sentences to be pleasing to the ear. A reader, however, is different: it expects children to become familiar with the text and ponder over it repeatedly. Only texts with endless meaning beyond the words, suitable for recitation, or so enjoyable to read that one cannot stop, can reach this realm.

2.3 A National Language Reader is no Children's Literature of Singing

Mountain songs and boat songs are imitated and sung by country folk to amuse themselves, just as children do with nursery rhymes. Generally speaking, music harmonizes sounds, and poetry expresses aspirations. The subtlety with which nature shapes humanity resonates in rhythms—fast and slow, rising and falling—making people dance and gesture unconsciously. Common folk and children, sensing this subtlety, find immense joy in it. Thus, rhymed texts hold unparalleled value in harmonizing moods and inspiring aspirations. Such literature roughly falls into two categories: one with harmonious tones, easy to recite aloud, such as poems, songs, and drum lyrics; the other with rhythms matching musical scores, requiring mastery of temperament to compose, such as operas, arias (unique to traditional dramas), and musical lyrics. All these have distinct styles, differing from ordinary language and prose. Selecting a few pieces at random can indeed be enjoyable, but overemphasizing rhymed texts will hardly align with natural language. This not only defeats the purpose of learning language and characters but also risks presenting facts in a fragmented manner like *Three-Character Classic* or *Thousand-Character Essay*, which only breed weariness. Take drum ballads, for instance: singers and listeners merely appreciate the melodies, with no genuine emotional engagement. Even excellent musical lyrics can stir emotions, yet composing them demands expertise in rhythm and tone—an arduous task. Daily reading materials have no need for such complexity. Moreover, fine prose naturally carries harmonious rhythms, transcending the division between prose and verse. Therefore, children's literature for singing does not align with the nature of a reader.

2.4 A National Language Reader should be in the Form of Textbooks

The form of a textbook focuses on content structure and textual expression, leaving room for teachers to provide guidance. However, in childhood, the emphasis lies in arousing creative imagination; the function of literature is to inspire emotions. If a book merely serves as a tool for teaching characters, it is no more than a character lesson book and cannot be regarded as a reader. The current improved-style readers inevitably suffer from this flaw.

If the arousal of imagination and inspiration of emotions are based solely on narrative content rather than textual expression; or if the text merely conveys a sense of humor without stimulating creative imagination or evoking emotions that reflect the meaning of life, such a book is not a good reader either. The current literary-style readers are prone to this shortcoming.

Therefore, a national language reader requires guidance from teachers: it must enable children to deduce insights through their responses to the textual expression. The reason it is called a "reader" rather than a "textbook" lies in two aspects: first, it leans toward children's spontaneous activities, distinguishing itself from old-style books centered on teachers. Second, it emphasizes understanding content through recitation and study, differing from other textbooks that focus excessively on extracting content. Once these principles are clarified, the form can be defined.

From the above analysis, it can be affirmed that a national language reader must integrate various types of children's literature, reorganize them in natural language and common characters to facilitate recitation, and thus become a tool for teaching.

Furthermore, the reason why people in ancient China could achieve a thorough understanding of literature was largely due to the effects of chanting and pondering. However, if the composed texts fail to make children willing to read, enjoy reading, and read repeatedly without boredom, even chanting will arouse no interest, and pondering will yield nothing. In recent years, primary school students' performance in Chinese has been poor; no matter what methods are adopted, the results remain limited.

Upon reflection, we should, on the one hand, respond to the new trend of children's literature and, on the other hand, revisit the role of ancient chanting and pondering. Only in this way can we grasp the key to learning our national language and literature. Therefore, reforming readers is an urgent task. Neglecting this and merely engaging in in-depth discussions or debating writing techniques will be of no avail.

3. Research on Children's Language

Traditionally, compilers of primary school national language textbooks have taken short sentences as the sole principle for -grade texts, which may seem reasonable. However, if this is rigidly adhered to, it ignores the fact that adults' everyday speech contains relatively few long sentences. It is acceptable to say that short sentences are convenient for children to read aloud, but it is incorrect to equate short sentences with children's language itself. In terms of children's literature, content should align with children's thinking, and form should conform to children's language. Works that match children's thinking but not their language can serve as literature for listening or reading, but not as literature for reciting. A clear example is that rhymed texts like folk songs and boat songs delight children, while poetry and lyrics do not. A survey of various textbooks also shows that short sentences are limited to -semester texts. From my observations, the difficulties second and third graders face in reading aloud are: (1) Long sentences, especially those with multiple consecutive clauses. (2) Sentences that do not suit their taste, even if short. (3) Narrative texts with excessive consecutive sentences, which lack interest. Books on child psychology, when studying language development, focus only on very young children. Children under five or six already use extremely complex language, mostly centered on vocabulary accumulation. However, the words children use vary with their environment—they can be quantified but not categorized by fixed traits. Primary school teachers' surveys mostly focus on dialect correction and grammatical errors, which also vary by region. Few discussions exist on what constitutes "children's language." A few years ago, I began recording my daughter's speech daily from the age of one, planning to continue until she turns five or six. Since the project is unfinished, I cannot offer concrete conclusions. My research on children's language remains superficial, but my approach differs fundamentally from those who treat short sentences as the sole principle. I have two primary school students at home. By listening to their conversations, engaging them in various discussions, and observing other children, I have concluded: (1) Children's language emerges entirely from their own activities and perceptions of things. (2) Children's narratives list points separately without seeking coherence, unlike written narratives that rely on grammatical conjunctions for continuity. (3) Long sentences used by children consist of several short phrases, with unbroken tone but pauses. (4) Except for counting, these phrases (each usually under five characters) rarely exceed three in number, and even longer phrases contain at most three nouns. Children rarely use rhetorical adjectives (except in taunts) or turn-taking conjunctions. These principles form the basis of text structure. After drafting, I have my children read the texts, ask which words or phrases feel uncomfortable, revise accordingly, and then test them in schools—some texts even include revisions suggested by children. Children and adults do not speak entirely different languages; rather, adults can understand children's speech, but children may struggle with adult language. This subtle difference, if not carefully observed, can make even well-written vernacular texts difficult for children to recite. This is why Hans Christian Andersen's fairy tales, written entirely in children's vernacular, stand out in children's literature.

4. Research on Character Selection

In various countries, when formulating primary school curricula, extensive research has been conducted on the issue of character recognition. In China, however, most national language readers or textbooks are compiled by editors based on their own ideas. There is no standard to determine whether the characters used in these books are all commonly essential. Someone once tested university-educated individuals with ten uncommon characters from the seventh volume of a primary school textbook, and many of these characters were unrecognized by most of them. Even the draft of the National Language Curriculum Outline, which stipulates that primary school students should recognize approximately 2,200 characters, has been criticized for being overly vague. If this problem is not solved first, it will be difficult to ensure that children can learn the characters they should master through readers. Before explaining the standards, let's briefly discuss the issues related to character selection, which mainly include three aspects: 1) Commonly essential characters should be learned in national language readers, and there should be standards for selecting these essential characters. 2) Characters listed in each volume should prioritize those that are most urgently needed, and there should also be standards for their sequence. 3) Appropriate attention should be paid to characters that are commonly easily misused. Except that the third aspect belongs to the scope of practice, the first and second aspects are major issues in readers. Regarding the first issue, there are few published works on Chinese characters used in national language education in our country, and it is also difficult to collect private correspondence for research. Even if we adopt the method of character selection used in other countries, the lack of appropriate vernacular texts as a basis fundamentally undermines the effort, making it impossible to achieve a satisfactory solution. As for the second issue, there are three traditional viewpoints: first, teach characters with simpler strokes before those with more complex ones. Second, teach single-component characters before compound-component ones. Third, teach characters in their original meanings before their extended meanings. The first viewpoint was adopted in old-style textbooks, but now that reading and writing are not taught simultaneously in the early grades, the complexity of character strokes has little relevance to learning from readers. The second viewpoint is just as ineffective as the . As for the third, primary schools do not delve into the origins of characters, and the forms of characters have changed significantly in regular script; moreover, some original meanings are no longer in common use, so this viewpoint is also not feasible. If we consider the sequence of arrangement, focusing on words rather than individual characters, the urgency of a word's application is related to the substance of teaching materials rather than the characters themselves. If the standards for the nature of teaching materials evolve with the students' grade level, characters will no longer be a major issue. It should be noted that there are very few function words, and they can be clearly defined. Content words used as nouns vary with regions and occupations, and their usage contexts are easy to identify. For example, the characters (Zhe, short for Zhejiang) and first (Hang, short for Hangzhou) do not appear in some readers, but in Zhejiang Province, they should be taught as needed. In other provinces where there is no such need, even if students do not recognize them, it will not hinder their writing. The same principle applies to proper nouns related to history, geography, occupations, and surnames, which teachers can teach using natural teaching methods when appropriate opportunities arise. In addition, it is not difficult to verify commonly used nouns. Verbs and adverbs are key to forming sentences. All those expressing necessary meanings are indispensable, serving the same function as function words. They are universally used regardless of region or occupation, and synonyms that are not commonly used in daily life can be excluded. For characters needed in reading other books, students can look them up in dictionaries once they reach a higher grade, which is not inconvenient. Based on the above, I adopted a simplified method to set standards for character selection when compiling readers. Although this method is subjective, it may be more practically applicable than objective standards that lack appropriate materials. My steps for character selection are as follows: First, from *Kangxi Dictionary*, I selected over 6,000 characters that I recognized. Second, I divided these 6,000-odd characters into four major categories for the convenience of classification: 1) content words used as nouns; 2) content words used as verbs; 3) content words used as adverbs; 4) function words. When categorizing, I first examined the usage of each character in forming words or phrases, ensuring that characters that are not common themselves but can form common words or phrases are not excluded. Third, according to the things they refer to and their properties or states, I subdivided each of the four major categories into several subcategories. Characters with the same function were grouped into the same subcategory. Then, I removed characters with different forms but the same meaning, as well as characters with the same meaning but different forms. I also excluded characters that are not commonly used to describe daily things or actions. Finally, I classified the characters into three types: The first type: vernacular characters, which are essential for primary school students. The second type: literary characters, among which very few are vernacular, and they can be used as appropriate. The third type: characters that are unnecessary for primary school students. In total, the essential characters include over 600 function words, more than 500 verbs, nearly 700 adverbs, and over 1,000 nouns, amounting to more than 2,200 characters. This roughly aligns with the number of characters used in *Civilian Character Lessons* and the number specified in the draft curriculum. As for the sequence of arrangement, function words are ordered according to the stages identified in children's language research, and content words are ordered according to the standards of teaching materials. Although the selected characters may not exactly fit the needs of the entire country, they are generally free from major errors.

5. What A National Language Reader Needs from A teaching Guide

The format of teaching guides shall be discussed separately. What is addressed here is that the two major issues difficult to resolve in readers should be tackled in teaching guides.

5.1 The issue of character recognition

Current research on character recognition in primary schools focuses on two aspects: the number of characters to be learned and the frequency of each character's recurrence. Readers do pay due attention to these, but if texts are constrained everywhere by the pursuit of a perfect solution to these issues, the literary flavor will be diminished. Regarding the number of characters to be learned: Urban and rural areas, as well as regions with different customs, have varying needs. A character deemed essential in location A may be unnecessary in location B. Similarly, for synonyms (e.g., kan and qiao, diu and shuai) or words with different names for the same thing (e.g., fuqin and baba, daozi and guzi), a text can choose any one, while in speech, people may use whichever they prefer or is local. If a reader includes all such examples, it becomes a miscellaneous character book; if it selects some, it may be criticized for omissions in certain regions. However, if a teaching guide provides examples of characters related to farm tools, commodities, or local objects that can be taught alongside the text, allowing teachers to decide what to teach, the reader avoids both flaws, and students learn the characters they truly need. For synonyms or alternative names, if a reader includes all, vocabulary becomes confused; if it selects some, it may omit locally common terms. But if a teaching guide explains such synonyms or alternatives used in the reader and instructs teachers to present them according to local conventions, students will never lack sufficient vocabulary. Regarding the recurrence frequency of each character: According to learning psychology, a new word should reappear after 3–4 lessons, then 6–7 lessons, then after a month, and later after 2–3 months. Such recurrence is essential. However, rigidly enforcing this in text composition would make the text mechanical and drain it of meaning, even more so than outdated, uninspired texts. Instead, during teaching, lessons should be connected through exercises. By listing each character in the text, noting its recurrence frequency, and supplementing in the teaching guide any characters with insufficient or uneven recurrence, these supplements can be integrated into review without adding separate lessons. This not only aligns with learning psychology but also demonstrates variations in character usage through practice—achieving the best of both worlds.

5.2 The issue of practical writing

Today's educators recognize that learning practical writing should align with children's immediate needs. Yet, when discussing readers, they insist on including more practical writing. If practical writing becomes the main content of a reader, taught merely for the sake of reading, it clearly fails to arouse students' motivation. Without motivation, forcing them to learn rigid formats will yield little understanding. However, if a reader provides no examples at all, leaving everything to teachers' discretion, less capable teachers may miss opportunities to teach or not know how to teach when opportunities arise—sound in theory but problematic in practice. The solution is for teaching guides to identify, based on the text's context, what practical writing needs might arise, assess students' abilities, and provide graded examples of practical writing formats as supplementary materials. This way, all the aforementioned difficulties are resolved.

Published in *The Chinese Educational World*, Vol. 15, No. 3, September 1925.

On the Fundamental Reform of Primary Education

Chapter One On the Purpose of Education

I have long doubted that the organizational structure of today's schools, curriculum design, teaching methods, and disciplinary approaches in primary education are inadequate for achieving educational goals. Given the decline and corruption of education in our country today, advocating nationalism can indeed be a wake-up call. However, what is the content of nationalism, and what are the plans to achieve it? If the fundamental flaws in what we call "school education" today remain unrecognized, any such plans will be unimpressive. Any ideology will be nothing but empty talk, and perhaps its harms will emerge before its benefits are seen. How difficult it is to speak of education!

Here is a question that must first be resolved: What exactly constitutes a "school"? And why is a school necessary for education? These two questions are interrelated and can be addressed together. Is a school a place for cultivating academic achievements? Yet, is the academic knowledge cultivated in today's schools unattainable outside of schools? Is a school merely a convenient place to accommodate a large number of people seeking education? Or is it because schools have classrooms, playgrounds, libraries, and equipment rooms, providing designated spaces for study and recreation? If so, what is the true purpose of education that makes it necessary for people? If these doubts cannot be fundamentally answered, then both people's pursuit of learning and the establishment of schools will be far removed from the essence of educational goals. Why? Because the knowledge acquired in schools is not necessarily confined to schools; moreover, the utility of such knowledge and whether its impact is good or evil cannot be definitively judged by the world. Consider the masses and great figures in society today—most were not nurtured in schools. Those who only attended school for a few years have no more general knowledge than ordinary people. In fact, the higher one's knowledge, the greater the degree of evil they may commit. From this, why does the state provide such education through schools, and why is society willing to have people educated in this way? Today's politicians, warlords, and academic leaders in our country are exploiting the flaws of schools to manipulate public opinion. If we do not rectify this now, the breeding ground for all political evils will lie in education. Even if this is not entirely true, such formalistic, aimless education—forcing the state's outstanding talents to waste their energy on superficial decorations—is utterly meaningless.

Does this mean learning should be abolished, or schools should not be run? No. Whether a school is harmless and effective depends entirely on how education is implemented. From this, we can discuss the purpose of education. Those who have written about educational goals throughout history have divided them based on the foundations of life: some emphasize the individual, some the nation, some society, or the world. From the perspective of educational approaches, some focus on morality, some on practicality, or some on art. Although these viewpoints differ, their ultimate goal is to guide people toward progress. The debates lie in: what kind of person should be cultivated? Should education lean toward developing only a part of a person? And do the methods employed suffice to achieve the goal? Speakers offer different arguments, practitioners follow different paths, and to this day, no consensus has been reached.

There are many methods in education, but its core should be centered on cultivating "whole persons." A "whole person," in terms of life, should fulfill their fundamental functions; in terms of their own being, should have no physical or mental defects; and in terms of education, should undergo an integrated process. Yet today's educators, clinging to trivial gains like a chicken or a pig, hope for rewards as abundant as a cartful of grain—this is truly lamentable.

Chapter Two On National Education

National education emerged over a hundred years ago and spread across the world, with intensified efforts to advance it taking place in the last few decades. At its inception, it was rooted in the movement for democratic politics, aiming to eliminate the malpractice of education being monopolized by privileged classes. The main goal of the reform was, by and large, to transfer the authority over education to the state, making education accessible to all people. As for its content, it still followed the old-style learning procedures, regarding literacy as the sole key to education. Later, as scholarship and world trends advanced together and material civilization made progress, in a bid to enhance the common sense of citizens, various subjects related to knowledge and skills were gradually added. Moreover, as the world grew increasingly complex, it was realized that citizens with weak capabilities would be unable to survive in competition. Thus, the duration of compulsory education was extended, and continuing education was promoted. On the surface, every effort seemed to have been made for national education. But looking at the reality, the addition of subjects was limited to the scope of knowledge; even the extension of the schooling period only involved the level of knowledge. The growth of knowledge without a corresponding progress in morality has actually become a source of social unrest. What's more, the fragmentation of teaching materials and the cramming method of teaching are especially common drawbacks in today's primary schools! That is why global education statistics still measure the level of a nation's citizens by the literacy rate. It is true that a large number of illiterate citizens indicates that education is not universal, but if universal education is merely about literacy, one can well imagine the level of the citizens.

The evolution of national school education has moved from literacy education to knowledge education. With the gradual rise of theories emphasizing conduct, the educational trend has changed from the past. However, since these theories are derived solely from psychological changes, the improvements are only in the methods of acquiring knowledge. Their influence is no more than cultivating useful people, and has nothing to do with the fundamentals of being a person. *I Ching* says, "Enlighten the ignorant to nurture correctness." It also says, "Striking at ignorance is not beneficial for being a robber, but beneficial for defending against robbers." This means that being overly harsh in educating the ignorant will surely cause harm. Only by warding off external temptations to preserve one's purity and innocence is the way to nurture correctness. In recent times, Western psychologists mostly focus on phenomena and discuss the mind in isolation from human nature, and when this is applied to education, it inevitably leads to harmful consequences. Therefore, although their research findings can correct the mistake of being overly harsh, they fail to understand the meaning of "defending against robbers." They are merely preoccupied with analyzing appearances and seeking ways to make learning more effective, which is far from solving the fundamental problems of education.

China's national education is still far from being universal. The existing education is a mixture of literacy education and knowledge education, carried out in a piecemeal manner. On the one hand, it fails to apply the principles of learning psychology; on the other hand, it only disdains the past ways of learning without understanding the essence of the ancient sages' exhortations to the people to attend school and learn to be a person. It indulges in discussing school buildings and importing textbooks, thinking that learning should be sought in these things. Those who complete their school years obtain the right to vote, can write their names on the ballot, but cannot fulfill their fundamental duties as human beings or promote social welfare. What does this have to do with the responsibilities and obligations of citizens? Then, for those who are in charge of national education, when they advocate reforming private schools, what improvements do they make, and what effects do these improvements have? When they advocate banning private schools, one must ask how much better school education is compared to private school education? Not addressing the root cause but only the symptoms is nothing but unnecessary meddling.

Education in the Republic of China and democratic politics are interdependent. We cannot blame the government alone. Those in our country who claim to be scholars and politicians all advocate democratic politics. However, in their eagerness, they either advocate establishing universities, or at least middle schools, and none regard the popularization of primary education as an urgent task; others only seek to obtain the qualification of representing public opinion without making efforts to enhance citizens' knowledge. As a result, in chambers of commerce, labor unions, and student unions, all those who protest under the banner of the people, with their clamor and shouts, though their names sound good, generally have the mindset that "I am the state", only caring about the rights and interests of their own group and themselves, and do not hesitate to harm the people and the country, regardless of the widespread chaos. The wisdom and morality of the people are declining day by day. It is painful! If national education is not made universal, or what is pursued is not the national education we envision, but only the form of democratic politics is copied, then in the past, evil-doing was only on the part of the government; now, evil-doing extends to society, all under the pretext of public opinion to harm the people. Such a country will surely perish quickly.

Critics will say, "Now we should focus on popularization, and we can put aside the issue of quality for the time being." This is a specious view, which might have been feasible at the beginning of the establishment of schools in our country. But now, the abuses have reached an extreme, and if we do not realize the need to reform, it is foreseeable that each additional school will become an additional source of evil, which we must be wary of. Why? Thirty years ago, the drawbacks of material civilization were not yet fully detested by the world. World chaos was hidden and subtle. People's minds were not extremely frivolous. (In the early years of the Republic, I published an article in which I somewhat approved of pragmatism and attached a warning, which was published in *The Education Magazine*[9].) Therefore, literacy education was convenient for propagating knowledge, and knowledge education was beneficial for practical use. Achieving even one of these had some effect on popularizing culture and benefiting people's lives. But now, when is it? Culture, politics, economy, and the improvement of international relations have become common global issues. When an incident occurs, all parties only focus on their own interests, not hesitating to harm others to benefit themselves. The so-called citizens of civilized countries, the uneducated, and even the knowledgeable class all exhibit the same kind of abnormal psychology. As long as it is convenient for their private interests, they will do anything. Furthermore, the weaknesses of our country's traditional ethics have been fully exposed, and those who pursue new things only take pride in destroying everything. As a result, scholars are accustomed to not studying, people compete for profit, the whole country is in a state of panic, losing both the old and the new, with no place to belong. Education has lost its guiding role; even if it is popularized, can it be better than no education?

---

9 See page 34 of this book. — Translator's Note

Critics will also say, "Isn't the development of democratic political forces today the result of education?" But they fail to realize that political revolutions arise from the dissatisfaction of the masses. Although there are many visionary people who advocate them, the success of a revolution is not entirely attributed to the intellectual class. Various recent movements in our country have been pioneered by the academic community. However, later, the advocates were abandoned by the people because of corruption or monopoly. The reason is that the driving force behind these events lies in the use of political strategies, not the self-awareness of everyone's original intention. Therefore, knowledge can benefit the country, and also harm it. Education can enlighten the people, and also fool them. What we expect from national education is that national morality is more important than national knowledge. The so-called morality does not require rigid modeling. The so-called knowledge especially avoids being mechanical. The current education cannot be confidently said to be beneficial to the country and enlightening to the people.

Then, what should be done in education? The answer is: For education above middle school, revise the regulations and curricula, and allow private individuals to set up schools freely. The government only needs to consider the needs of employment, set up various examinations, so that all those engaged in public and social affairs, regardless of their status, are selected through examinations. For subjects that require special research, set up various academic laboratories. For those who have achieved expertise in specialized fields, formulate regulations to reward the creation of books. In this way, the cost will be lower than before, the application will be wider, and it will be more convenient for people to engage in research. As for national education, the government should assist localities and make every effort to implement it. At the beginning of its reform, all existing educational funds should be recovered and used to formulate local autonomy regulations, conduct household surveys, count school-age children, divide school districts, and manage school grounds. Furthermore, carefully select primary school educators with profound research, set up experimental schools, reorganize curricula, train normal school students, and then gradually promote them based on the trained personnel. It should be clarified that free establishment does not mean laissez-faire. Making every effort to implement it does not mean assigning full responsibility to the government. It is just that the government should adopt appropriate policies to promote education and make continuous progress, which is not merely a matter of dividing funds between public and private sectors. The detailed methods will be discussed in separate chapters later.

Chapter Three Educational Administration

The educational administration discussed here is specifically based on national education policies.

All changes in a country's education, though often driven by trends, are generally implemented nationwide through the power of the state, regardless of the form of educational administration. This is particularly evident in Chinese history.

Historical records state that before the Three Dynasties (Xia, Shang, Zhou), China's politics and education were most well-developed. During the Yu Dynasty, learning was associated with storing grain, and educational institutions were called xiang (schools) or milin (granaries), rooted in the virtue of filial piety. The Xia Dynasty trained scholars through archery, as described in Xingwei and Juexiang, and named its institutions xu (order), emphasizing the cultivation of conduct. The Shang Dynasty educated scholars through music, as mentioned in accounts of Kui and the Grand Music Master, and called its institutions xue (schools) or guzong (ancestral temples for blind musicians), focusing on moral perfection. In the Zhou

Dynasty, the imperial school was called biyong (Circular Moat Academy) or chengjun (Equalization Academy): biyong referred to harmonizing through Dao and clarifying through laws; chengjun denoted rectifying deficiencies and balancing excesses and inadequacies. Feudal lords' schools were called pangong (Half-Moat Academy), with pan meaning "to distribute," signifying the dissemination of politics and education here. From these records, we can deduce the following principles:

1) Education has a clear purpose, with all measures aligned to achieve it. Compare this to today's so-called educational tenets, school mottos, or class slogans—abstract, fictional phrases set as goals. Even when examining textbooks designed to achieve these goals, there is no unified plan for concrete expression. How great is the gap?

2)Governance was integrated into education: School education embodied the ethos of respecting virtue and valuing Dao, aiming to inspire the entire state to aspire and strive through shared ideals. Compare this to today's school education, which is confined to its own students, with educational outcomes isolated from society. Even empty talk of "socialization" remains far removed from real society; absurdly, some regard interfering in external affairs as students' "social service." How vast is this disparity?

3)Education provided standards for being a person. Compare this to today's school education, which merely arranges subjects, empty talk s practicality, and abandons the fundamental duties of being human. Subjects like ethics, citizenship, and classical studies, along with rules for self-governance, have little impact on students' physical and mental development whether retained or abolished. How striking is this contrast?

Details of the educational systems of the Yu, Xia, and Shang dynasties are lost to history, but the Zhou system is clearly verifiable. Its key principles are summarized as follows:

1)At age eight, all children—from the sons of kings and dukes down to commoners—attended school. (Zhu Xi's *Preface to the Commentary on the Great Learning*)

2)In the domains of the Son of Heaven and feudal lords, every community of 25 households or more had a school. (Xiang's *Record of Xinxue in Zhijiang*)

3)Primary education (xiaoxue) taught rituals of sweeping, greeting, and proper conduct, as well as skills in rites, music, archery, charioteering, writing, and arithmetic. Higher education (daxue) taught the principles of investigating things, rectifying the mind, cultivating oneself, and governing others. (Zhu Xi's *Preface to the Commentary on the Great Learning*)

4)Scholars were educated with rites and music in spring and autumn, and with poetry and history in winter and summer. Crown princes were taught military arts in spring and summer, and rituals of dance and music in autumn and winter. (*Book of Music*)

5)Officials aged 70 retired to their hometowns, where senior officials served as fushi (elders-teachers) and lower-ranking officials as shaoshi (junior teachers). Senior elders sat in the right wing of village schools at dawn, and common elders in the left wing. After all children had left for their duties, they returned; the same routine followed in the evening. (*Book of Documents: Great Tradition*)

6)When farming tools were stored, sacrificial music concluded, and annual tasks ended, all children attended school. They left 45 days before the Winter Solstice to assist with farm work. (*Book of Documents: Great Tradition*)

7)Students entered school annually, with evaluations every other year: in the first year, to test their ability to parse texts and clarify aspirations; in the second, to assess dedication to learning and harmony with peers; in the fifth, to examine mastery of teachings and respect for teachers; in the seventh, to evaluate discourse skills and choice of friends—this was called "minor achievement." In the ninth year, students who grasped categories, achieved mastery, stood firm in virtue, and never wavered attained "great achievement." (*Record of Learning*)

8)Outstanding scholars selected by local communities were promoted to the Minister of Education, called "selected scholars." The most exceptional among them were advanced to imperial academies, titled "excellent scholars," exempt from local duties and renamed "cultivated scholars." The Grand Music Master recommended the finest cultivated scholars to the king, who promoted them to the Minister of War, known as "advanced scholars." The Minister of War evaluated their fitness for office, reported the best to the king for final approval, and only then appointed them to positions.

9)Local authorities identified those who refused to obey teachings; after four warnings, they were exiled. The Junior Music Master oversaw royal students，exiling them after two unheeded warnings. (*Book of Rites*)

10) The imperial school, biyong, also served as the mingtang (Hall of Light) for court audiences, decrees, and sacrifices to emperors and ancestors; and as the lingtai (Spirit Tower) for calibrating musical pitches, climates, and calendars. Feudal lords' schools, pangong, hosted military assemblies, trials for officials and commoners, and sacrifices to founding ancestors. (Xiang's *Record of Xinxue in Zhijiang*)

11) Local governors led their people in studying laws on the first day of the first lunar month, rewarding virtue and talent, and correcting

transgressions. The same occurred during seasonal sacrifices to local shrines. In spring and autumn, they gathered people for rituals and archery contests at local schools. Community leaders assembled people to study laws on the first fortune day of each season, with additional gatherings during sacrifices. During national rituals to ethoss, they hosted feasts at schools to affirm age-based hierarchies.

12) The Zhou Dynasty had 360 official positions but no dedicated education officials. The Three Dukes deliberated on Dao, and the Three Elders taught—neither reporting to the Six Ministries—highlighting the paramount importance of education, distinct from routine administrative tasks.

13) The Minister of Education oversaw national teaching, and the Minister of War managed state affairs—their duties were distinct yet interconnected: during mobilizations, the Minister of Education trained scholars in warfare; when promoting cultivated scholars, the Minister of War evaluated their fitness for office.

From an examination of the first two points above, we can see that universal education was already practiced in the Zhou Dynasty. The reason for its successful implementation lay in the well-field system (a form of land nationalization) and a complete local administrative system, which made it easy to enforce.

From the third point, we learn that the ancient primary education focused on cultivating character and practical skills, closely tied to daily life—learning was for the sake of application. Not only did the later emphasis on studying classics fail to align with the purpose of cultivating virtue, but even pragmatism was superficial and missing the core.

The fourth point reveals that the differentiation and sequencing of subjects in ancient education reflected a deep understanding of "teaching according to aptitude" and "progressing in order."

The fifth point shows that the ancient reverence for teachers and respect for Dao first required teachers to possess true wisdom; respect was not a mere formality.

From the sixth point, we see that rural education in ancient times was aligned with local agricultural activities.

The seventh point indicates that ancient evaluations of students had clear standards that advanced with their years of study.

The eighth point demonstrates that in ancient times, selecting scholars and appointing officials were integrated, with morality as the primary criterion. This avoided both the superficiality of later imperial examinations and the modern grievances of graduates—some achieving success through luck, others being overlooked.

The ninth point makes clear that ancient schools aimed not just to enroll everyone, but to ensure all people obeyed teachings.

From the tenth point, we learn that ancient states held major events in schools, allowing the entire state to understand the source of politics and education, far beyond mere symbolic significance.

The eleventh point shows that ancient states never enforced decrees without prior education. Schools taught students daily, and periodic national gatherings reinforced law-abiding and ritual observance—this was the foundation of national education, far more profound than today's focus on primary schools alone.

The twelfth point reveals that while ancient politics and education were interconnected, each had its own essence and function. Education aimed to deeply influence people's hearts, not to coerce through laws—hence education officials were not subordinate to the six ministries.

The thirteenth point illustrates that ancient official positions, though divided in duties, were interconnected, ensuring all affairs functioned through mutual support. Times have changed, so systems must adapt, but the ethos behind legislation remains unchanged.

With the decline of the Zhou Dynasty, governance and education deteriorated. However, the tradition of respecting teachers and Dao persisted through generations, embedding itself in the national consciousness as a custom. Thus, though school-based educational administration declined, scholars continued private teaching: when a great Confucian emerged, disciples flocked to study with them, discussing Dao and virtue. Their teachings, often related to current politics, could still influence rulers and win the respect of the four classes (scholars, farmers, artisans, merchants).

By the Warring States period, powerful lords dominated politics, and independent scholars' outspoken critiques aroused rulers' suspicion. As a result, learned men could not demonstrate their abilities to promote governance and education. Instead, they devoted themselves to studying classics, analyzing current changes, articulating their views, and writing books to be preserved for future generations. Inferior scholars, however, used their knowledge to curry favor with authorities and seek official positions—this is why scholarship flourished uniquely during the Warring States.

The Qin Dynasty abolished the well-field system, so local communities could not maintain old institutions. Coupled with rampant fraud and unworthy officials, the so-called "unified customs" merely served the emperor's selfish desire to fool the people, abandoning education's true purpose. This led to the disaster of burning books and burying scholars.

The Han Dynasty inherited Qin's flaws. Though it honored Confucianism, established imperial academies, and sacrificed to Confucius, these were merely tools to control scholars. Thus, Confucians and officials followed separate paths, and governance and education diverged: provincial and county magistrates governed the people, while academicians and literary officials taught disciples—with no coordination between the two. What was taught was not what was used, and vice versa. Hence, Han's cultivation of scholars, like Qin's book-burning, stemmed from a policy of fooling the people. The ancient system of educating the people thus degenerated into a method of controlling scholars and deceiving the masses, completely extinguishing the essence of national education.

The Sui and Tang Dynasties, learning from the flaws of previous selection systems, introduced the imperial examination, luring scholars with official positions. This persisted through the Song, Yuan, Ming, and Qing Dynasties, drawing all talent into its net. Though exam subjects varied, the system overemphasized literary flair, failing to test practical wisdom. Scholars merely pandered to trends to compete for success, some exhausting themselves and dying without being selected. Yet the state spent nothing: the entire nation, observing how the government selected scholars, taught and studied accordingly, with education spreading even to remote villages. A poor but gifted child could still advance through a fixed path—not through power, money, intrigue, or coercion. Though the selection method missed education's purpose, its approach to encouraging learning and appointing officials had merits.

In the Western Han, imperial academicians were subordinate to the Ministry of Rites, echoing the Zhou system where chengjun (academies) fell under the Minister of Ceremonies. Provinces had academicians, and counties had literary officials—Confucian teachers appointed by local rulers, reflecting the ethos of village schools. However, rural students rarely entered imperial academies; discipleship positions were reserved for others, while nobles' sons were placed under the Ministry of Personnel, not educated in imperial academies. Moreover, the four examination categories followed different standards, leading to fragmented aspirations and superficial evaluations. Schools became merely a path to office, losing their ancient educational purpose.

From the Wei to Zhou Dynasties, with the state divided, schools existed in name only. The Sui and Tang solidified the imperial examination as the primary path: academy students, upon completing studies, were sent to provincial exams—differing from Han's academy system. Thereafter, imperial academies and private academies mostly housed exam candidates, with teachers skilled in writing exam essays. Exceptions like Hu Yuan, who divided studies into Confucian classics and practical affairs, attracted students not solely seeking fame—though such cases were rare. Notable critiques of the era's flaws include the following:

1) Using schools to embellish governance. For example, Emperor Wu of the Han Dynasty emphasized the Six Classics; Emperor Guangwu of the Eastern Han laid down arms to lecture on arts; Emperor Taizong of the Tang expanded school buildings to 1,200 rooms, attracting 8,000 students. Lü Donglai criticized such grand displays as mere spectacle—all driven by the selfish desire to adorn governance, completely betray the educational ideals of ancient kings. This is no harsh judgment.

2) Wang Anshi appointed education officials only if they pleased those in power. His disciples like Lu Dian received oral instructions in his study at night and repeated them in schools the next morning. The "Three Halls" system he established served to promote his partisans. Scholars who adhered to his New Interpretations of the Three Classics gained official

positions; those who rejected them were ostracized. When Cai Jing held power, he used educational laws to restrain scholars, treating them like soldiers coerced by military law, with layers of mutual control. Any dissent led to immediate dismissal of the offender. Feng Xie, currying favor with authorities, claimed "scholars hold no differing views" as a sign of the Imperial Academy's prosperity—a statement Cui Yi denounced as treacherous, misleading the throne.

3)Using schools to form cliques, sway public opinion, and manipulate state affairs. During the Chunxi and Jingding periods of the Song Dynasty, Imperial Academy students commented on politics at will, openly attacking even prime ministers and censors who displeased them. When restrained, they invoked Qin Shi Huang's "burying of scholars" to intimidate authorities, who dared not risk the stigma of "suppressing education." Though some political issues deserved criticism, students often exploited them to stir trouble. After the powerful minister Ding Daquan was ousted through their attacks, the Three Academies grew arrogantly powerful, rivaling the emperor—accepting bribes, protecting criminals, and undermining laws. Common people feared them like tigers; even merchants suffered in silence. When Jia Sidao became prime minister, he avoided confrontation by bribing them with generous stipends and land grants. Tempted by profits and cowed by his authority, students remained silent about his crimes, even praising him as a "wise mentor." Only after the military defeat at Lugang did they finally denounce him. Many who rose to prominence through such schools later proved to be national traitors—a moral decay that contributed to the Song's downfall. Similarly, during the Han Dynasty, over 30,000 Imperial Academy students, led by Guo Linzong and Jia Weijie, allied with Li Ying to openly criticize the powerful. At their peak, even nobles feared their censure and hurried to curry favor. But when enemies multiplied, over 200 were framed and imprisoned. Insightful observers saw this as the inevitable result of partisan strife—for which Li Ying and his allies bore partial responsibility.

In the final years of the Qing Dynasty, the imperial examination system was abolished, and schools were widely established. Graduates were granted official ranks equivalent to those from the imperial examinations. The Republic of China later introduced academic degrees and separate civil service examinations; in terms of institutional design, these were not entirely without merit. However, those in power and those running educational institutions were mostly unqualified. Laws and decrees became mere formalities. Schools existed only as places for teachers and staff to earn a living, and as preparation grounds for students to compete for fame and fortune—they had nothing to do with educating people. Graduation was solely a matter of completing the required years, unrelated to academic achievement. The government's promotion and maintenance of education were no more than window-dressing, bearing no connection to respecting teachers or valuing Dao. The root of moral salvation had fundamentally ceased to exist. Even when it came to selecting scholars and appointing officials, personnel decisions depended entirely on the whims of those in power. Illiterates and bandits filled important positions, while selecting the virtuous and capable was not a consideration. With schools established in this way, their existence or abolition had no bearing on the foundation of governance. Moreover, for education beyond middle school, even middle-class families struggled to afford the costs. Government-funded overseas study opportunities were mostly seized by those with influence. Regardless of whether such education was useful, it merely nurtured a privileged class—what was the point of such education?

In recent years, those running educational institutions have either entrenched themselves in academies or relied on foreign support, using the name and influence of certain parties or "new learning" to cultivate followers and enforce partisan education. They lure young people with money and power; some provinces even appoint special commissioners and set up secret agencies to recruit thugs, using party membership as a rallying cry. Seizing opportunities and exploiting issues, they manipulate the majority, incite student protests, and stage large-scale movements under various noble pretenses. Their hidden agenda is to destroy everything to facilitate the seizure of political power. Existing systems can be reformed, but not to serve private ambitions. Ideologies can be propagated, but not to suppress opposing views. What is practiced today combines all three malpractices of previous eras, exacerbating them further with the poisonous schemes of Qin Shi Huang, who burned books and buried scholars. They aim to make all four classes of society submit to and be absorbed into the ranks they have bought. Those outside their clique—if strong, are crushed without mercy; if weak, dare to anger but not to speak. This is indeed a great misfortune for education. As a result, corrupt officials, worthless politicians, outdated military personnel, opportunistic mediocrities, and incompetent scholars all exploit students as weapons and rush to run schools. The noble path of education has degenerated to its lowest point. In the past, Zheng Zichan destroyed rural schools, and Zhang Juzheng abolished academies—actions born of necessity. Yet the harmful influence of schools in those times was not as severe as it is today. Given the current malpractice，I dare predict that schools will not stop until they are completely bankrupt.

Is the current situation purely the result of trends? No, it is rather due to the lack of proper educational methods and the government's loss of control. Those above have no moral principles to uphold, and those below have no laws to abide by. Treacherous scoundrels, educational parasites, and frivolous youths occupy teaching positions, peddling superficial Westernization and the dregs of national essence. *I Ching* states, "When frost forms underfoot, hard ice will follow." This situation has developed gradually. Unless we abolish official schools, establish appropriate regulations, vigorously promote scholarship, strictly enforce examinations to cleanse the root causes and rectify academic conduct, and open wide the path for private education, there will be no way to save this declining trend.

Take primary education, for example. The Ministry of Education has clearly stipulated regulations regarding implementation procedures and compulsory requirements. Yet, it pays no attention to how these are actually carried out or what results they achieve. Compulsory education is to be implemented in phases over successive years, and the ministry's regulations lay this out in meticulous detail. However, the Ministry of Education merely sends a piece of empty paperwork to the education departments of each province, which in turn forward it to each county. Neither the ministry nor the provincial education departments concern themselves with how to assign responsibilities or ensure these responsibilities are effectively fulfilled. Even when it comes to such formal regulations, they disregard facts and ignore interrelationships, merely going through the motions with empty documents.

No wonder primary schools in each county remain as slack as ever year after year; some even struggle to maintain their current state. Compare this to the period before the abolition of the imperial examination system: in large counties, tens of thousands of people took the exams, and in small counties, thousands. Learners were ubiquitous even in remote villages and backward areas—the contrast is stark. To indulge in empty talk about education without changing the current system is like heading south when one intends to go north.

While the issues discussed here do not all pertain exclusively to primary education, they are interconnected, so they are addressed together.

1) In terms of the political system, regarding educational administration, the responsibilities of the central government and local governments should be clearly defined. They should not merely list the functions of jurisdiction but also specify the undertakings to be carried out.

2) In terms of official positions, those in charge of internal affairs should have assessments related to education. Those in charge of finance should have funding plans for the development of education; if they only allocate funds according to the budget, they deserve no credit. Those in charge of industry should plan to develop industry through education and promote appropriate undertakings.

3) The finances of the central government, provinces, and counties should be appropriately divided. There should be a standard for the balanced allocation of funds between education and other undertakings.

4) Competent educational institutions should establish appropriate organizational structures based on academic divisions and personnel appointment.

5) The implementation of national education should not be confined to primary schools, nor limited to enrolled students.

6) School education should focus on education that teaches people how to be good individuals.

7) For the organizations of legal groups and professional associations, their qualifications should be determined by the level of education, and their rights should be based on the progress of educational undertakings they have carried out.

8) Large-scale assembly venues should be set up in each school district where schools are located, for regular lectures attended by government officials, military personnel, farmers, workers, businessmen, and other people.

9) All government officials must have received appropriate education in schools and passed relevant examinations; otherwise, they shall not be eligible for selection.

10) Regulations on teachers' treatment should be formulated: ① Recommendation and appointment; ② Annual leave allowances; ③ Pension. The government must confirm plans to prepare for and promote private schools, so there is no stipulation on salary increases. However, the government must formulate detailed assessment standards and carefully select inspectors. Those eligible for the above-mentioned treatments must have served for a certain number of years and have achieved excellent results in previous inspection reports.

11) Normal schools should be public in principle, and detailed regulations for normal schools should be formulated: ① The curriculum must correspond to the purpose of training; ② Teachers in normal schools must have excellent works in the field of education, or have been teachers for many years with excellent teaching methods in various subjects; ③ The number of students admitted must correspond to local needs and be adjusted annually; ④ Students admitted must be restricted from joining political parties and from further studies within a certain number of years; ⑤ Graduation should be based on whether students have mastered the content specified in the curriculum, regardless of the length of study.

Published in *The Chinese Educational World*, Vol. 15, No. 6 & No. 8, December 1925, February 1926.

Implementation Plan for University Research Laboratories

1. Principles for the Establishment of Research Laboratories

1.1 Enabling the free development of intellectual abilities

Under the current educational system, there are two most obvious situations that deserve our utmost attention: 1) According to experimental results, those with excellent academic scores do not necessarily have proportionally high intellectual scores; 2) Observing the career performance of graduates, those who achieved the best results in school are not necessarily the most useful members of society.

To explore the reasons for this, we must trace it back to the commonly used teaching methods. These methods only make students accept the knowledge and facts imparted by education, turning them into intellectually dependent individuals. Learning and inquiry are separated from life, and there is no need to use intellectual abilities for exploration. The higher the level of the school, the more obvious this situation becomes. As a result, some students develop an attitude of indifference or resistance. The so-called “good grades” and “good students” are merely the results of being willing to obey and striving to absorb and memorize. In this case, there is no wonder that the two phenomena mentioned above occur.

It is universally acknowledged that university education aims to develop students’ mental life and cultivate an ethos of independent research. However, how to achieve this? Approaches like the Dalton Plan, which allows free work without the constraints of rigid methods and enables both intelligent and slow students to reach their full potential, are what we expect. Yet in universities, any learning group is formed to achieve cooperation through division of labor, and individuals cannot proceed independently.

Therefore, what we seek now is to cultivate a true research attitude. That is, educators must adopt an attitude of "refusing to lead" while earnestly assuming the responsibility of guidance, encouraging students to lead themselves and move toward a common goal. This so-called "mental power" comes from mental exercise. In other words, it is about how to guide, stimulate, impel, or unlock students' intellectual abilities, so as to achieve the goals of activity and independence, and make creations and inventions. This is the first principle for establishing research laboratories.

1.2 To enable knowledge obtained through techniques to become the result of one's own experience

In university teaching, there is certainly no need to use methods employed for teaching children. It is necessary to explore one by one: what constitutes the source of old experiences, what forms the psychological background, and what offers opportunities to expand experiences. However, when students choose certain courses to develop the ability to acquire new knowledge, involving processes such as cognition, generalization, and application, although teachers do not necessarily need to understand every step, they must examine the final outcome. Traditionally, lectures have been regarded as the sole method for universities to impart knowledge. Yet neither teachers nor students have any sense of whether the listeners have truly grasped the content. Even the new discussion-based method, though it roughly understands students' activities, only allows individuals to perceive fragmented and disjointed knowledge. Therefore, in the end, examinations are used as the standard to determine academic performance, which only causes both school authorities and students to waste a lot of time, generate various resentments. The result is that students are forced to memorize facts by rote, which hinders the development of intellectual abilities. Countless geniuses in the past have been stifled by schools, and many so-called scholars fail miserably when taking on tasks—isn't this the crime of past education? The value of knowledge lies in its role as a tool for solving problems. When one seeks knowledge from teachers, it must be for solving problems and avoiding errors in trial and error. If teachers teach independently, students learn independently, and courses exist in isolation, it is no different from placing dishes on a feast and saying "this is for you" but not allowing others to sit down and eat; or buying goods in the market and saying "this is for you" but not allowing others to hold and use them. Therefore, the issues we explore today are: first, how to obtain knowledge; second, that knowledge obtained from any problem must form an integrated structure; third, the ability to apply knowledge to solve problems. It should be understood here that all knowledge of things comes from the relationships between those things and external objects. To grasp the meaning of a thing, one must derive it from its uses and relationships with other things. Old psychology regarded sensation as the source of knowledge, but in fact, primitive functions cannot directly collect experiences. If knowledge is imparted in the form of isolated facts or vague theories, without allowing students to explore on their own, even if they gain something, it is of no use. Just compare the achievements of scientific laboratories with the truths sought through pure imagination and the practical application of knowledge imparted orally—one can see the difference in effectiveness. It is thus clear that learning methods must be similar to those used in laboratories. Only then can the knowledge gained possess vitality and exert value in life, becoming the result of one's own experience. This is the second principle for establishing research laboratories.

1.3 Seeking knowledge through doing things

The second principle emphasizes that the pursuit of knowledge should neither rely solely on passive acceptance nor mere meditation, which naturally fosters one's ability to get things done. However, this principle is specifically highlighted here because the work in a research laboratory involves continuous activities with a defined procedure. Within these continuous activities, there are additional tasks related to "doing things," which also extend to broader aspects of teaching and learning. Implementing the second principle is based on the theory of "the unity of knowledge and action" and serves the function of integrating "scholarship" and "practical work." It should be clarified that this integration refers to their interrelationship, methods, and procedures—not that work is equivalent to scholarship or vice versa. A common flaw in today's approach to learning is overemphasizing facts while neglecting their connections or interrelationships, forcing scholars to focus on erudition and rote memorization. Erudition itself is not harmful to learning, but if a person is merely praised for being erudite, it becomes problematic. Memory is also an indispensable part of the learning process, but if learning stops at memorization, intellectual activity becomes useless. Only by transforming the way of learning—guiding it toward the direction and process of "doing things," following a predetermined plan, and achieving the goal of acquiring knowledge—can what is learned become useful experience. As for the additional tasks related to "doing things": first, organizing such a learning group requires certain individuals to take specific responsibilities for administrative matters. Second, during the work process, various practical needs will inevitably arise. These are often overlooked by scholars, who consider them irrelevant to academic pursuits. In reality, for any work to proceed smoothly, be well-organized, and be carried out efficiently, proper administrative arrangements must be made from the start; otherwise, obstacles will clearly emerge. This is particularly significant for cultivating habits and attitudes. The essential abilities that every citizen should possess and the ethos of democracy that a civil society requires must be fully nurtured within such learning groups. The current methods, which rely on formal drills or intentional indoctrination, are inherently unable to achieve this goal. This constitutes the third principle for establishing research laboratories.

1.4 Cultivating the ethos of mutual assistance through division of labor

With the increasing development of democracy and material civilization, all social organizations take mutual assistance as their criterion. The satisfaction of human needs must rely on division of labor and cooperation to make up for their deficiencies. If we do not fully store this meaning in our hearts or familiarize ourselves with its allocation function, we will find ourselves incompatible with society. For example, the Dalton Plan only aims to realize the process of cooperation but fails to demonstrate its role through division of labor, which means it does not fully embody the purpose of mutual assistance, and its entire working mode is not applicable to universities. Moreover, if the work process does not involve a sense of design, it will never enable mutual activities to gain social experience from the results produced by social life. Therefore, what we should strive for further in the future is to formulate a new plan and form a learning group. All members of this group move toward a common goal and each has appropriate work. The division, integration, allocation, and mutual relations among them should be determined according to specific circumstances. Due to the organization of this group and the expectation of its purpose, people cannot stand aside but must strive to fulfill their responsibilities as members and encourage their own determination and courage to take initiative. Thus, the university is not only a place providing good opportunities and methods but also a place where responsibilities are enforced. This is the fourth principle for the establishment of research laboratories.

2. Laboratory Work

The work of a research laboratory is roughly divided into two parts: 1) Meetings; 2) Assignments.

First, let us explain the relationship between the two. Meetings are conducted collectively, while assignments are carried out individually or in groups; the two are causally interconnected. As for why meeting work is necessary, aside from its relevance to the broader sense of teaching (to be explained in the context of organization), its purposes are as follows:

1) To form the core of a learning group through assembly, serving as the sole hub for initiating and evaluating assignments. This thoroughly transforms the traditional authoritarian nature of lectures and the mechanical formality of learning, placing all members under a shared set of rules where each fulfills their responsibilities through active engagement.

2) To strengthen preparations for division of labor through collaborative foundations and to realize the ethos of mutual assistance. Specifically, the first step (discussion of objectives), second step (planning), and fourth step (appreciation or criticism) of the four-stage design process are adopted as guidelines for conducting meetings.

The key items in meeting work are as follows: 1). Reports; 2). Proposals; 3). Discussions. The relationship between these three items and teaching will first be illustrated with two diagrams.

Chart A illustrates the function of item 1, and Chart B illustrates the functions of items 2 and 3. Next, an analysis of the three items is as follows:

1) Reports The tasks of the research laboratory are: (1) self-study; (2) work divided among members. Regarding (1), although individual guidance is available during tasks, one must systematically verify the overall quality of their work. Through such systematic verification, the results are fully demonstrated in the presentation. This is the first essential purpose of a report. Regarding (2), since the entire content of each course is divided into several parts for separate completion, if each person is to gain relevant experience in the parts they have not worked on, it is necessary for everyone to contribute their insights from specialized research to the group. This transforms the teacher's lecture into student reports: on the one hand, it retains the efficiency of absorbing experience through listening, as in lectures; on the other hand, it offers the benefit of mutual exchange of experiences. This is the second essential purpose of a report.

In terms of form, reports can be divided into two types: (1) written reports; (2) oral reports. What is emphasized in meetings is the oral report. For any report, item (1) must be prepared first as the basis for conducting item (2).

In terms of substance, reports can also be divided into two types: (1) task reports, which form the main part; (2) administrative reports.

2) Proposals The value of any meeting is determined by its proposals. The research laboratory's meetings, organized as a learning group, are not limited to the norms of ordinary meetings and differ from what are commonly called "discussion groups" or "research societies." Their work plans, which vary with progress, serve as the source of initiating and organizing tasks. All participants should carefully plan the progress and methods of the work to achieve the expected goals. In particular, instructors should comprehensively coordinate and express their opinions to facilitate progress. This is why proposals are important.

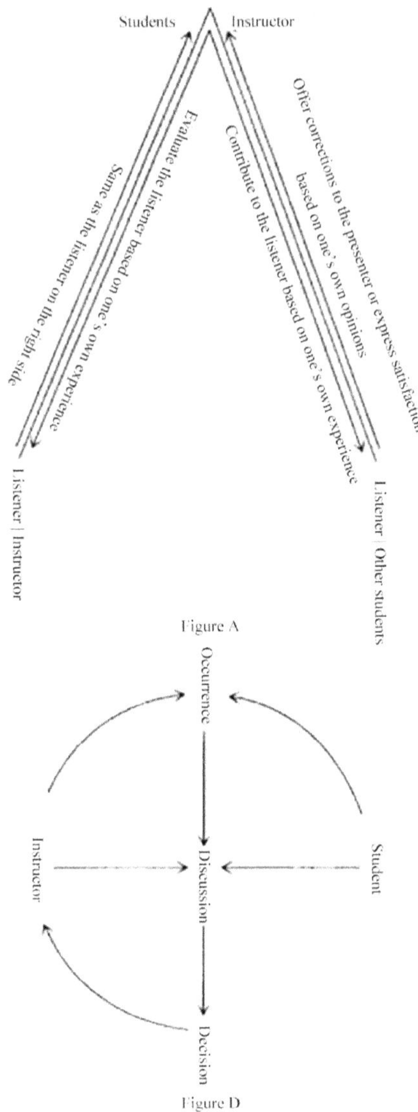

Figure A

Figure D

In terms of form, it can be divided into two categories: (1) Formal proposals. In addition to proposals put forward by instructors themselves, all issues raised in the work schedule must be separately proposed for discussion. Those that are insignificant can be answered individually on an ad hoc basis. (2) Unscheduled motions. These are raised after the conclusion of various discussions.

In terms of substance, it can be divided into three categories: (1)Goals of the ongoing work; (2) Plans for the progress of the work; (3) Facilities required for the work.

3) Discussions This adopts the method of discussion as a function included in the research laboratory system and also constitutes an important part of the meeting proceedings. Its purposes need not be elaborated on at length, and it is generally conducted on the following two occasions: (1) after reports; (2) after proposals.

Although the form of assignments seems similar to the Dalton Plan, its function is different. It is rather more like the laboratory system than the Dalton Plan. Its purposes are described as follows:

(a) It must be combined with meetings to complete the function of the work and to demonstrate the ethos of mutual assistance. That is, the start of assignments must obtain their progress and methods in meetings. The results of the assignments are then verified for their experience in meetings, and they can be exchanged with each other. Therefore, the assignments actually serve as the work of the third step in the design process.

(b) Through the division of labor within cooperation, people engage in work with responsibilities, each fully developing their own thinking and talents freely. In fact, with the ethos of the organization of such a learning group, they can dedicate themselves to the natural duty of serving society with their respective abilities, driving their sense of responsibility, rather than devoting themselves to work out of the vanity of competing for academic credits.

Assignments vary according to the nature of the work, and roughly fall into the following four categories. However, a certain type of work may belong to only one category or include several categories, which will not be discussed in detail.

(A) Reading

1.Classified by nature: a. Textbooks, b. Reference books

2.Classified by function: a. For understanding the outline, b. For selecting theories or facts related to the research

3.Classified by curriculum scope: a. The entire curriculum, b. A part of the curriculum, c. A part of the curriculum: which can be further divided into a part of the overall progress and a part of a specific stage of progress

4.Classified by method:

a. Intensive reading

b. Extensive reading

(B) Compilation

1. Classified by nature: a. Text, b. Charts and graphs, c. Physical objects.

2. Classified by source: a. Books, b. Newspapers, c. Surveys, d. Observations, e. Excavations.

3. Classified by course field: Same as 1-3.

4. Classified by function: a. Descriptions with a self-contained purpose system, b. Expecting to discover new issues through statistical results, c. For comparative research.

(C) Examination and Correction

1.Classified by nature: a. Research on the theories of experts, b. Research on specialized books, c. Research on special topics containing explanations and proofs

2.Classified by form: a. Style and form, b. Text (language), c. Content

3.Classified by course field: Same as (I)-3.

4.Classified by function: a. Explanation, b. Elaboration (or Extension), c. Revision (or Correction)

5.Classified by method: a. Selecting points that are divergent in sequence or mutually corroborative, b. Citing the diverse theories of various schools, c. Experimental verification or falsification

(D) Production

1.Classified by nature: a. Translation and narration, b. Plans/schemes, c. Charts and graphs, d. Theses/dissertations, e. Reports

2.Classified by method: a. Purely for the purpose of creation/production, b. Proceeding to applicable creation/production based on certain work of the first, second, or third type

3.Classified by course field: Same as (A)-3.

4.Classified by course function: a. Publishing one's insights/understandings, b. Organizing materials

When doing assignments, for the sake of facilitating the process and aiding learning, there are two things that should be noted:

(1) Using cards. No matter what kind of assignment you are working on, you will certainly use some reference materials, which are kept for later organization and may also be used for future reference. It is difficult

to memorize all of them, and placing each piece on the desk is also quite inconvenient. The best way is to imitate the card - using method of libraries: register the materials used in a proper format and store them by category. This is extremely economical for assisting memory and checking the original books.

(2) Making an outline. A report is required for each stage of every type of assignment. To ensure that the presenter speaks in an orderly manner and the listeners do not get bored during the presentation, adequate preparation is essential. To avoid the preparation being too fragmented, the most important thing is to make an outline. This is not only to ensure the correctness of the overall learning, but also serves other purposes.

3. Organization of the Research Laboratory

The research laboratory is organized into two parts: meetings and assignments, with meetings actually being the main body of such an organization. First, a diagram will be used to illustrate its functions.

(1) In terms of the overall supervision function, the meeting exercises various functions such as initiating, organizing, and verifying assignments, similar to how political power controls administrative power. The diagram (see Diagram C) is as follows:

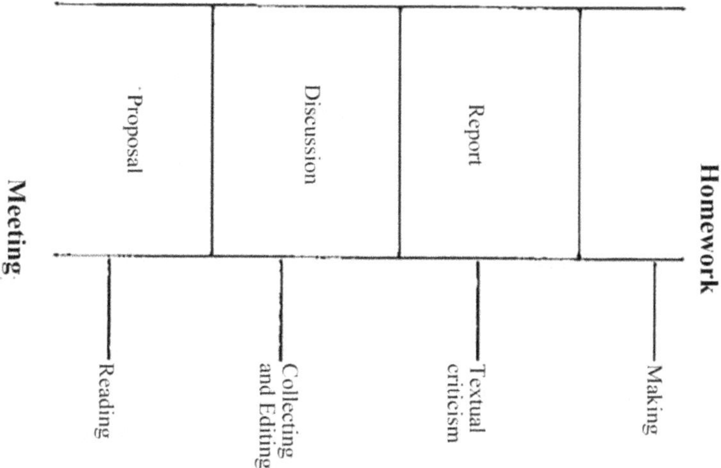

Diagram C

(2) In terms of activity function, the meeting body is like a nerve center. The three activities in a meeting—proposal, report, and discussion—are like sensory nerves in terms of their occurrence. In terms of resolutions, they are like motor nerves. The four activities in assignments—reading, collecting, textual research and emendation, and creation/production—are the various phenomena manifested by actions. The diagram (see Diagram D) is as follows:

The organization of assignments varies with different matters and times, and a general overview is as follows:

In terms of the scope of assignments: 1) All personnel take on the same work; 2) Work is undertaken in groups; 3) Work is undertaken individually.

In terms of the content of assignments: 1) The same work is carried out from start to finish; 2) Work is changed in accordance with the progress.

Regardless of the scope and content, the following points should be noted:

1)Each person shall give at least one systematic report at meetings within a month. Every week, each person shall fill in their own work status according to the work progress schedule and report to the instructor.

2)If a group has a relatively large number of people and a group leader needs to be appointed, the group leader and group members shall take turns to give attendance reports.

3)If an assignment involves undertaking a part of the entire course, a written report must be made and submitted to those who are not responsible for this part of the assignment for circulation and review. Each reviewer shall provide written comments, which shall be collected and submitted to the instructor. When the instructor organizes the reports, they will present these comments separately for discussion.

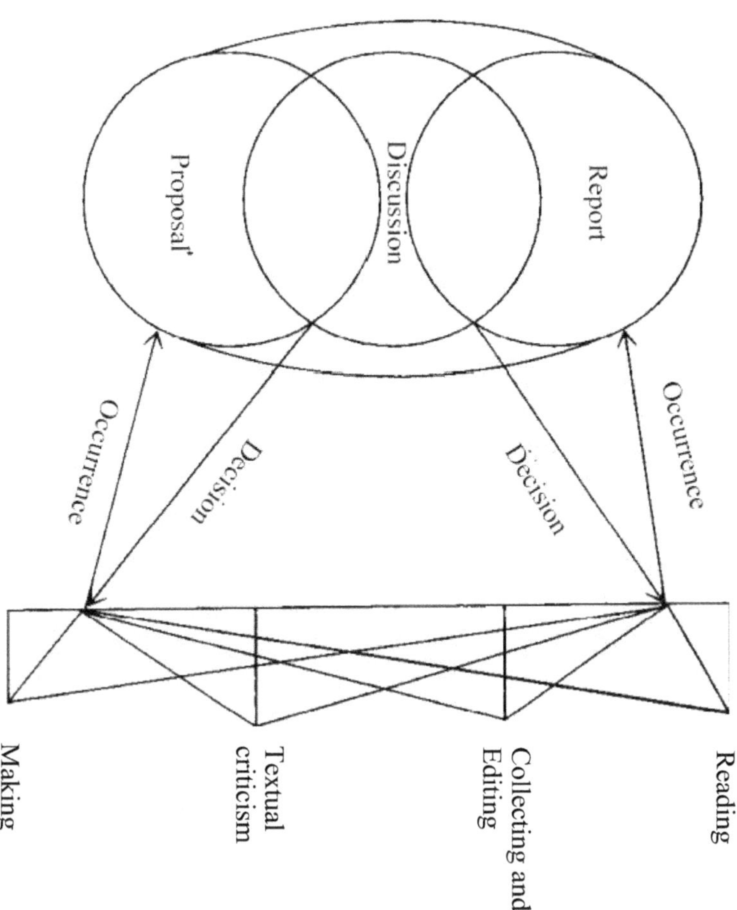

Diagram D

Meetings are the nerve center of the research laboratory, and their purpose has already been explained in the work of the research laboratory. However, such an organizational structure carries extensive significance. In essence, university education aims to cultivate sound character among students who can serve society and the country. As for how to cultivate such character, first, it must conform to the ethos of democracy, so that all teachers and students' activities are governed by the same set of rules, which serve as tools for training citizens under party rule. Second, everyone must have opportunities for practice at all times, without the need for special formal training outside of ordinary life, which would only leave traces of artificiality and affectation. This is the reason for the current organizational structure. The following is a record of the organizational structure of the Research Laboratory of the Department of Education for this semester, for reference:

1) The entire class elects one secretary, who, in consultation with the instructor, is responsible for convening meetings, preserving documents, and assigning work.

2) A regular meeting is held once a week to review the results of the current week's work and schedule the work agenda for the next week.

3) For each meeting, the class elects a temporary chairperson and a secretary (currently, these positions are held on a rotating basis).

4) When it is necessary to hold a plenary meeting for joint discussion for the convenience of research, a temporary meeting can be convened at any time upon the proposal of the instructor or two or more students.

5) For work that is relatively simple in nature and requires a longer time, the secretary arranges the order, and the entire class takes turns to perform the work. For temporary or more complex work, all members divide the tasks and collaborate.

6) Each person must fill out a work report form and submit it to the instructor at the weekly regular meeting.

Based on the experience gained, there are several points that should be noted:

1)The meeting procedures shall be conducted in accordance with The Preliminary Steps of Democracy. Everyone shall make their words and actions conform to the rules according to their respective positions at the meeting.

2)The meeting agenda shall be drawn up by the secretary and submitted to the instructor for approval before the meeting.

3)The temporary chairperson must review the meeting minutes and take responsibility for signing them.

4)Depending on the work situation, it may be necessary to appoint an additional general affairs officer besides the secretary, who will be responsible for keeping books and materials, handling arrangements for facilities, etc.

Next, under this organizational structure, the instructor, while in a position of consultation and advisory, actually bears the responsibility of command and supervision. Therefore, during the progress of work, the instructor should engage in research alongside the students. Moreover, the instructor must make overall plans and various projections regarding the progress and methods, so that when students express their opinions, raise questions for correction, or encounter difficulties, appropriate solutions can be provided. Alternatively, the instructor may use questions to inspire students to explore various different approaches, thereby identifying a more convenient and accurate path.

Naturally, the instructor must attend meetings and also be present in the research laboratory during the scheduled work hours to participate in research. All individual guidance and handling of students' completed work shall be conducted within these hours. Additionally, during a certain stage of progress, if there is a need for the instructor to give special lectures on specific issues or matters, provide special materials, or if the research involves connections and requires guidance from other professors, the instructor must proceed as appropriate based on the circumstances.

This aims to seek an overall solution to the problems in the current curriculum while also adopting the essence of collaborative teaching.

4. Time Calculation and Allocation

The so-called relatively new teaching method in current use is nothing more than indicating reference materials by chapters and putting forward research questions. However, there is no constraint on whether one must read the reference materials or answer the research questions. Even if assessments are conducted, the time required outside class does not correspond to that of other courses. Moreover, regarding the prioritization and selection of content, students can only make arbitrary choices, and it is impossible to restrict them to achieve a certain level of performance, let alone enable all those who take this course to demonstrate their abilities through their grades. If the work is required to be completed within the class hours, the amount of content taught in class is bound to be reduced. Such problems can be solved by adopting the laboratory work calculation method. Why? According to the general practice of university credits, one credit is given for one hour of class per week, while two hours of laboratory work count as one credit, which is also the case for calculating course credits under the Dalton Plan. Following this example, students in our university can obtain passing credits by taking 20 class hours per week. If all courses were conducted in the form of research laboratory work, it would take no more than 40 hours. The work time in the research laboratory, which accounts for more than two-thirds of the meeting time, allows for considerable freedom of activity and is not as tiring as listening to lectures. Additionally, by replacing lectures with practical work, there is no separation between receiving knowledge and practicing it, and there is no need for extra-curricular research. Thus, an average of 7 hours per day for 4 days and 6 hours per day for 2 days per week, compared with 20 class hours plus additional extra-curricular exercises and research, there is really no need to worry about overwork. Furthermore, such research-oriented learning inherently contains sufficient interesting value.

Allocation of Hours The current system is particularly prone to following conventions without realizing their drawbacks. Here is an outline of the situation:

1. Regardless of whether the number of hours allocated for each course is determined by the government, the school, or the teacher, if one asks about the criteria based on which such hours are set to achieve a certain level of performance, it can be safely said that no one can give a definite answer.

2. Under the course selection system, for the convenience of allocating time between professors and classrooms, the number of hours for each course is generally set at 3 or 6 hours. Consequently, the amount of content to be taught often has to be adjusted to fit the principle of time allocation, rather than being accurately aligned with actual needs.

With the research laboratory system, for any course, the number of hours required for each course must be estimated every semester by examining the subject of the course, the existing needs, the amount of content to be learned, and the expected performance. At the end of each semester, a faculty meeting must be held to review the existing results and discuss how to proceed with the courses in the next semester, ensuring that they are in line with the actual situation. It is not like the current system where graduation is granted as long as one attends classes in accordance with the regulations, earns enough credits, and completes the study period, regardless of the performance standards. As for the inconvenience in arranging the timetable due to the varying number of hours for different courses, this is only a problem under the current system. In the research laboratory, since the work time accounts for more than two-thirds of the meeting time, two classes can work in the same room without interfering with each other when it is not meeting time. Moreover, advanced courses, which usually have a small number of students, can also be accommodated. Since there is no worry about time conflicts, the number of research hours should be determined by actual needs rather than being restricted by the principle of hour allocation under the course selection system.

5. Scheduled Work Plan

In the research laboratory, instructors, adhering strictly to the ancient maxim of "teaching and learning mutually enhancing each other," fulfill their due responsibilities without controlling others' activities with their own opinions. However, students' assignments are ultimately of a learning nature; if they were merely governed by the collective opinions of meetings, the objectives pursued in the course and the corresponding performance standards would inevitably fail to be achieved. Therefore, at the outset of research, instructors must formulate a predetermined work plan to serve as the benchmark for the research laboratory's operations. Although the content of the plan may be adjusted as the work progresses, the overall framework should not be drastically deviated from. This plan is akin to a "fundamental law" in legal terms and, in pedagogical principles, serves to impart general concepts—thus embodying both meanings. Below, its basis, nature, and essential components are discussed separately:

5.1 Basis

(1) It should derive from faculty meetings, where the progress of all courses already studied is assessed to determine the direction for prioritizing or discarding content in the course work.

(2) It should be formulated from the students' perspective, estimating the knowledge they need to acquire, the time required, and the difficulties they will inevitably encounter, with the aim of achieving feasible results.

5.2 Nature

(1) Distinct from a teaching syllabus: A so-called "teaching syllabus" typically outlines the key points of a course's content. This plan, however, does not focus on content but rather stipulates the general framework for how work should proceed and the necessary preparations.

(2) Distinct from the Dalton Plan's work outlines: Work outlines under the Dalton Plan specify, in segments, a course's content and learning methods, allowing students to work independently based on them. This plan, by contrast, serves as the basis for initiating tasks through meetings. The phased progress and methods are determined by meetings according to the work's development. It adopts the ethos of the Dalton Plan's "work contracts" without replicating its form, enabling the design process to contribute to research work.

5.3 Essential Components

(1) The achievable objectives or expected outcomes of the work should be clearly stated, based on an assessment of the learning progress.

(2) The general content of the work should be summarized.

(3) Most of the reference materials required for the work should be pre-listed.

(4) The necessary phases of the work process and the hours required for each phase should be pre-determined based on estimates.

(5) The general methods to be adopted for the work should be pre-specified.

(6) The books, materials, and essential equipment to be procured for the work should be pre-planned.

(7) The number of credits the work will confer should be specified.

(8) The finalized work plan should be announced before course registration.

6. Work Process

The work of each course is indeed carried out through its assignments, but it can only be completed with the participation of meetings. The process varies depending on the nature and progress of the course. Here are some general examples for reference:

6.1 Reading Process (mainly intensive reading)

6.1.1 Indicating reading materials 1) Selecting reading books: The instructor selects one or more reading books. If more than two are selected, students can each choose one to read. However, students can also propose reading books and ask the instructor to decide. 2) Specifying reading methods: The instructor, either in writing or orally at a meeting, explains the purpose of reading, segmented reference materials, the number of hours required to finish each segment, and the reports to be made after reading each segment. Both items are determined in the meeting.

6.1.2 Book-reading procedures 1) Making an outline. 2) Raising questions: These can be corrected by asking the instructor during assignments or put forward during the meeting report. c) Judging the value of the reading books.

6.1.3 Reporting: Focusing on items 1) and 2) of 6.1.2.

6.1.4 Discussing: Both methods of 6.1.3 and 6.1.4 are conducted in meetings.

6.2 Collecting Process

6.2.1 Planning, all determined by meetings: 1) Discussing collection methods, which are determined according to the sources and nature (of the materials); 2) Discussing classification, styles, and items; 3) Discussing methods such as registration, arrangement, and preservation; 4) Discussing work allocation.

6.2.2 Carrying out the work.

6.2.3 Preparing reports: Determined according to items a, b, and c of the second type of functions of the research laboratory work.

6.2.4 Reporting.

6.2.5 Discussing: Both 6.2.4 and 6.2.5 are conducted in meetings.

6.3 Textual Research and Emendation Process:

(1) Discussing work guidelines, which can be proposed by the instructor or students, but must be decided by the instructor.

(2) Indicating reference materials, which are presented in writing or explained orally by the instructor.

(3) Discussing research methods: All the above are determined in meetings.

(4) Carrying out the work.

(5) Reporting.

(6) Discussing.

6.4 Creation/Production Process

6.4.1 Planning: 1) Creation/production guidelines; 2) Creation/production styles and forms; 3)Work allocation. All the above are determined in meetings.

6.4.2 Preparation: 1) Collecting materials: Appropriately adopting the process in 6.2. 2) Reading books: Appropriately adopting the process in 6.1. This item and item 1 must be used together or separately, depending on the work situation.

6.4.3 Carrying out the work.

6.4.4 Reporting.

6.4.5 Joint review and revision.

7. Equipment and Forms of the Research Laboratory

The most important thing for a research laboratory is its book collection and equipment. For each research course, the necessary books should be designated in accordance with the predetermined work plan. First, check for books not available in the library and prepare them in advance. When conducting research on a specific topic, all required books should be taken to the laboratory and returned in full after the assignment is completed.

The meeting area is set in the middle of the room, arranged in a long shape by joining several equal-sized rectangular tables with drawers on both sides, with stools placed around them. The number of tables and stools is determined by the maximum number of students enrolled in the courses offered in the laboratory.

For each course offered, a desk with drawers on both sides and two chairs must be provided for the instructor and secretary to work at, placed in a corner of the room. Additionally, a three-tier bookshelf should be provided, with the bottom tier designed like a bookcase for storing items. This bookshelf should be placed near the desk for the course.

Essential registers include meeting minute books, book registration books, performance record books, miscellaneous notes registers, and document pasting books. In addition, there are report and assignment papers (with specified formats to ensure uniformity) and registration cards (these can be considered as performance products; personal ones should be prepared by individuals themselves).

The essential forms are roughly as follows: 1) Weekly work progress report form, 2) Assignment performance calculation form, 3) Meeting performance calculation form, 4) Monthly work performance report form, 5) Resolution report form. (Forms are omitted)

8. The Three Attached Questions

Under the research laboratory system, three issues require special explanation: 1) The instructor's working hours, 2) The number of research laboratories, 3) The number of students enrolling in courses.

8.1 The instructor's working hours

Calculating two hours of research as equivalent to one hour of lecture inevitably means instructors must work more hours, which may invite objections. Consider this: under the lecture system, professors must prepare lecture notes, or even if using textbooks, one hour of lecture requires far more than one hour of preparation. Additionally, they must prepare questions and review answers after class. If research laboratories replace classrooms, all time spent before and after lectures can be saved. For research related to the course—such as checking other books or copying materials—instructors can direct students to share the workload during assignments, while they themselves synthesize the results. Thus, increasing working hours does not actually add to individual labor. Academically, it fosters mutual improvement between teaching and learning, and makes it easy to make achievements. Those who do not treat teaching as a commercial transaction should have no dispute with this.

8.2 The number of research laboratories

Research hours are double the regular lecture hours. If original classrooms are fully occupied with lectures, adopting the research laboratory system for all courses might seem to create a shortage of space. This concern is unfounded, however. For each course, meeting hours in the laboratory account for less than one-third of total work hours, fewer than original lecture hours. All types of assignments require two consecutive hours of independent research. During this time, even students taking two different courses can work in the same laboratory without interference. Scheduling can also be adjusted based on class sizes to accommodate everyone. Moreover, laboratories can open for two hours in the evening for independent work without inconvenience. With four morning hours and four afternoon hours daily, one day can accommodate research for four courses. Over a week, this allows for eight 3-credit courses. If each course holds two-hour weekly meetings, eight courses would require 16 hours, leaving 32 hours—with three-eighths of this time, two additional courses can run concurrently. Thus, one laboratory can host ten 3-credit courses. It is safe to say that traditional lectures rarely require more classroom hours than this.

8.3 The number of students enrolling in courses

Laboratory guidance combines individual instruction and group discussion, applied during meetings and assignments. Excessively large classes would reduce opportunities for individual presentations and hinder thorough guidance. Ideally, classes should have around 20 students to ensure effectiveness. Currently, over-enrollment in some courses stems from two reasons: first, a lack of structured requirements for core compulsory courses; second, under the lecture system, grades do not depend on student work—attendance and cramming lecture notes for exams suffice to pass. This allows students to enroll arbitrarily, often choosing popular or easy courses. The first issue demands resolution regardless of the laboratory system. The second can be addressed by adopting laboratories: 1) Research hours, being double lecture hours, make over-enrollment impractical. 2) Predetermined work plans are published before enrollment, letting students understand course expectations and avoid blind course selection. Combined with enrollment restrictions, this curbs excessive course selection.

Small class sizes are already recognized as essential for teaching. Yet current practice often places 100 students in lab or language courses, severely undermining effectiveness—a problem institutions must remedy. That said, specialized courses taught via lectures can accommodate any number of students, even as open classes for free attendance.

Published in *Journal of the College of Liberal Arts, Henan National University*, Issue 1, January 1930.

Plan for the Experimental School Affiliated to Henan University and Its Preparatory Work

1. General Description

Experimental schools have been a product of the past twenty years. After the revolutions in Germany and Russia, in particular, the entire states strove to achieve a thorough reform of education. Although their definitions and forms vary, they generally have three tendencies: first, practical tasks; second, communal living; third, integrated teaching. These aim to correct the errors of traditional education, which regards schools as mere places for instruction and isolates them from society. Even in capitalist countries like Britain and the United States, there is almost unanimous agreement on basic education. Such implementation must be supported by appropriate facilities to enable teaching and learning to proceed. As for how to embody the educational ethos of the new era, its principles and methods will be explained in the internal planning of the school. Here, we present the equipment plan to finalize the budget. However, it must be earnestly stated that if the Department of Education does not establish an experimental school, it will be as ineffective as if the science department had no laboratory, the agricultural department had no farm, or the medical department had no hospital. Moreover, senior students in the Department of Education must have sufficient internship time. Having a self-run school for internships can reduce the time spent on direct lectures. The funds required for an experimental school are not much different from the monthly salary of a full-time professor. Furthermore, this will enable the university's undertakings to also achieve the effect of social movements. Teachers and students from other colleges and departments who are interested in school education can also practice solving the practical problems they wish to address. Even if it costs more, the expenditure is indeed justified. If it is recognized that the Department of Education needs to be established, then an experimental school must be set up accordingly. If the experimental school is not run as proposed, setting it up will be of no value at all. The fourth-year students will graduate in a blink of an eye, so the establishment of the school can no longer be delayed. We hereby present our opinions and respectfully request a decision.

2. Organization

The number of students in the national primary school ranges from 120 to 160. They are divided into four classes based on their actual age, with reference to their intellectual and academic abilities. An attached supplementary school is set up, which focuses on literacy. For the participation situation, industrial supplementary subjects are offered and divided into six groups: (1) morning class, (2) afternoon class, (3) Group 1, 3, 5, (4) Group 2, 4, 6, (5) weekend group, (6) evening school group. Each study session lasts for two hours.

In terms of the number of faculty and staff, there are four general teachers, each in charge of a class in the primary school. There are three specialized teachers: one responsible for manual work, one for music, games and sports, and one for school gardening and teaching natural science. In the future, even if the senior primary school adds two or three classes, no additional teachers will be hired. There is one clerk. The directors of each group in the attached supplementary school are concurrently held by the above-mentioned staff respectively. There is one school worker and two gardeners.

Matters concerning curriculum design and facilities are proposed through discussions among professors of the Department of Education, College of Liberal Arts (but guidance from professors of the College of

Agriculture or other colleges and departments is required) and then decided by the primary school teachers' meeting. The implementation of resolutions and the progress of school affairs are discussed and implemented by the teachers' meeting, which is composed of primary school teachers and interns, with one person elected as the chairman. The progress of the curriculum is discussed by the responsible teachers and students. Matters related to student management are discussed by each class teacher, students and representatives of the school self-government association. The self-government association is organized by all students, and its representatives are limited to higher grades (but it shall be implemented after a certain period of training). For administrative discussions, school workers may also attend but need to undergo a certain period of training. In addition, there is a joint meeting of the parents' association (which must be promoted by the school through various methods and must not be a mere formality), jointly organized by the teaching staff, the self-government association, the parents' association and professors of the Department of Education, held at the beginning and end of each semester.

Third-year students of the Department of Education serve as teaching assistants and must account for at least one-fourth of their study time each semester. Fourth-year students serve as assistant teachers, accounting for at least half of their study time each semester, with no pay. Second-year students who have completed teaching methods and educational psychology can also work as teaching assistants.

The curriculum of the supplementary school is taught by primary school teachers and interns, and fourth-year students outside the university's Department of Education who are willing to teach are also allowed.

Cleaning, storage, copying, binding, livestock rearing, cultivation and other tasks are undertaken jointly by teachers, interns and students. Fixed curriculum timetables and textbooks are abolished.

3. Equipment

3.1 Buildings and Premises

(1) Playground and School Garden According to the American scholar Wootton, a primary school should cover an area of at least 720 square zhang (a traditional Chinese unit of area). Half of this area should serve as the school grounds, and the other half as a public park (i.e., the school garden) open to citizens. It is proposed to use 300 square zhang of land: the buildings in the northwest courtyard of the university may be converted into school premises, or part of the current preparatory school buildings may be utilized. Additionally, an open area in the northeast of the northwest courtyard will be designated as the primary school playground and garden. The College of Agriculture will be invited to assist in its management. The school garden will function as an agricultural or flower garden and be open to public visits.

(2) Teaching Rooms A general classroom, also used for the supplementary school. An assembly hall, also used for games, indoor exercises during inclement weather, and large gatherings. A specimen room, where natural objects (plants, animals, minerals), various commodities, and man-made artifacts will be displayed in a corner. A library, with a corner dedicated to primary school children's books, picture books, and newspapers. An achievements room, where children's various works will be displayed in a corner to serve as reference materials for evaluating academic performance across subjects. A manual arts classroom, specifically equipped for skill-based work. (The above four rooms are all specialized classrooms.)

(3) One combined office and meeting room.

(4) Residential quarters sufficient for faculty and staff.

(5) Livestock sheds and a greenhouse for flowers and plants, adequately equipped for teaching purposes.

3.2 Equipment and Supplies

(1) Furniture and utensils for each classroom.

(2) Playground equipment, more comprehensive than those found in facilities in Kaifeng.

(3) Equipment for the manual arts classroom.

(4) Tools and produce for the school garden, livestock sheds, and greenhouse.

(5) Natural and man-made objects for the specimen room, as well as display fixtures.

(6) Children's books for the library, along with display furniture.

(7) Reference books for teachers and teaching aids.

(8) One harmonium, two thermometers, two barometers, and two clocks.

(9) Other necessary items such as beds, tables, chairs, stools, and various miscellaneous articles.

4. Expenses (Omitted)

5. Preliminary Plan for Preparatory Work

5.1 Covenant

(1) This work shall be limited to one month (from November 1st to 30th, 1930).

(2) All third- and fourth-year students of the Department of Education must participate (however, those who are overly uninterested in this work need not be forced to join). Second-year students or students from other departments who are interested in this work may join freely.

(3) After joining this work, participants must divide tasks and collaborate diligently to achieve the collectively desired goals, and must not shirk responsibilities or retreat in the face of difficulties.

(4) This work shall be realized through social activities. Each individual's initiative must not be constrained by the former concept and habit of sitting quietly to study.

(5) Whether this work shall be carried out in groups or through collaboration shall be discussed separately in a plan.

(6) If the work requires guidance or assistance from faculty and staff, upon request from the participating group, the Dean of the College of Liberal Arts shall make every effort to arrange for it.

(7) This work group may formulate additional organizational rules.

(8) The credits to be awarded for this work shall be determined by the departmental meeting based on the actual hours of group and subgroup work, the results achieved, and the reports from group representatives, following a comprehensive evaluation by the instructor.

5.2 Tasks

5.2.1.Regarding Equipment

(1) Books—Investigate the equipment, organization, management, reading, and guidance conditions of primary schools in Kaifeng; record the names, prices, and publishers of various books (reference may be made to the university's winter vacation papers); prepare an investigation report and a proposed design plan.

(2) Handicrafts—Investigate the teaching materials, methods, and equipment (including tools: names, styles, uses, manufacturers; desk styles, dimensions, and overall arrangements) in primary schools (including upper primary schools) that offer handicraft courses; prepare an investigation report and put forward design suggestions.

(3) Gardens and Fields—Investigate the equipment, layout, working hours, work conditions, and related teaching (relevant to the curriculum, so it is advisable to investigate simultaneously) of primary schools in rural areas and middle schools; at the same time, investigate the cultivation, breeding, and internship conditions of the university's farm; prepare an investigation report and put forward suggestions.

(4) Sports—Investigate the area, layout of sports fields in primary schools and public places, as well as the names, styles, dimensions, placement, and arrangement methods of sports equipment; prepare an investigation report and a proposed design plan.

(5) Desks and Chairs—Investigate the styles, dimensions, and arrangement of desks and chairs in various primary schools; prepare an investigation report and a proposed design plan with reference to examples in relevant books.

5.2.2 Regarding the Curriculum

(1) Practical Materials

Investigate the living conditions in nearby rural areas, such as production, farming, livestock breeding, handicrafts, industrial distribution, people's housing, food, clothing, labor conditions of the elderly and children, and agricultural work in different seasons. This should be coordinated with the Extension Department of the College of Agriculture to collect relevant materials and reports. Meanwhile, conduct separate surveys and organize data on nearby historical sites, scenic spots, and travel routes.

Investigate historical sites in Kaifeng's urban and suburban areas—their locations, contents, and histories; markets—locations, business operations, local products, Chinese and foreign goods and their sales, employees' work and treatment; workshops—locations, products, raw materials, manufacturing and sales, laborers' gender, age, work, and treatment; public business institutions—locations, contents, operational status, staff work and treatment; public tourist attractions—locations, contents, and management; famous wells—locations, surrounding conditions, and water drawing situations. Prepare survey reports and organize the materials.

Investigate the water flow, embankments, river management work of the nearby Yellow River, as well as nearby waterways, and organize the data.

(2) Reference Materials

Collect primary school textbooks, teaching books, and children's readings published by various bookstores, and prepare a survey report.

Collect curriculum organization plans and unit design plans published in books and journals (starting from 1922), compile them into a volume, prepare a survey report, and put forward opinions.

To support the above work, start by taking out all books on primary school education and various previous educational journals from the library (including recalling all lent items). Additionally, investigate publications on primary school education from the past decade (using bookstore catalogs, advertisements in books, and personally known books) that are not available in the library. The library shall be required to purchase these separately within a time limit. All newly purchased books, together with existing ones, shall be stored in a separate room for easy access.

Published in *Henan Education Monthly*, Vol. 1, Issues 2 and 3, November and December 1930.

Revised with merges and abridgments when included in this book.

A Matter That Requires Special Attention from Primary School Teachers and Staff Across the Province

To all:

Every day at school, you are either busy giving lessons or handling administrative work—truly, you never stop being busy! However, despite all this busyness, there is one extremely important thing that you have not yet attended to!

When you implement teaching, handle school administration, or read educational books, do you often encounter difficulties? When difficulties arise, shouldn't you be eager to resolve them? At this point, you must surely say: "We face quite a few difficulties, and we really want to solve them, but who can we ask? And who would be willing to answer us?" It is indeed a fact that when you feel stuck, no one is there to help you find solutions.

For this reason, while we few have not conducted extensive research on primary school education, we are eager to discuss primary school education issues with you! As long as you are willing to reach out with questions, we will respond with utmost sincerity!

The plan we have formulated is as follows:

First, we intend to organize a "Primary School Education Issues Discussion Group." We ask you to voluntarily send us your name, native place, age, gender, qualifications, work experience, current position, and any suggestions you may have for our future discussion and research plans, listed in detail.

Second, by the end of March, we will carefully review each

submission we receive, compile statistics, and determine the next steps based on the majority opinion.

Third, we will act in accordance with the statistical results. Each month, all inquiries and discussed issues will be published in this journal.

What do you think of the above plan? Finally, we would like to add that regarding any issue related to primary school education that can be discussed, we will provide earnest responses— and sometimes, we might even turn to you for advice on practical problems! If we can get this initiative off the ground, we will see it through to the end. We hope you will pay special attention to this!

Li Buqing, Gao Weiyue, Gao Zhisheng, Ding Peizhi, Huo Luting, Wu Jiazhen, Yu Xiangwen, Wang Haihan, Du Yaoxin, Zhao Zijie, Qi Xihou, Feng Xuanzi, Cai Hengxi, Sun Huaiyang, Li Daoxiang, jointly announced.

Contributions should be sent to Comrade Li Daoxiang, Editorial Office of Henan Provincial Department of Education.

Published in the combined Issue 18 and 19 of *Henan Educational Administration Weekly*, Vol. 1, January 1932; also published in *Henan Education Monthly*, Vol. 1, Issue 5, February 1931. This article was published in several consecutive issues in these two journals.

The Common Tendencies of Modern Primary School Education

Brothers and friends, today I am here to talk to you about the issue of "the common tendencies of modern primary school education." There are a few points I need to clarify in advance:1) The scope of this topic is very broad, and what I will talk about today will be somewhat biased towards teaching; 2) The common tendencies of primary school education I will discuss can also be said to be the tendencies that general education should have. However, since primary school is the foundation of education, these tendencies are relatively more distinct; 3) I am speaking from the standpoint of methodology. But the methods mentioned here are the means to achieve goals, and they are specific methods derived from factual issues. In recent years, various experimental schools have been springing up like mushrooms all over the world. These experimental schools are not the Chinese-style ones; they are established to experiment with a certain theory or a certain proposition. Although each has its own characteristics, they generally share the following three common tendencies:

1. Work and Activity

Previous education was all about "intellectualism," that is, it emphasized knowledge. But what is knowledge? Are the phenomena of all things in the world knowledge? Or is what is recorded in books considered knowledge? No, these are the sources of knowledge. True knowledge must involve the ability to recognize or understand the phenomena of things and the records in books. Therefore, acquiring knowledge is a concept or action formed by stimuli and responses. In terms of stimuli, can the teacher's words and the text in books be stimuli? Obviously, they are not limited to these. In terms of responses, if students show no activity in relation to the taught materials, or only answer when ordered by the teacher without forming new experiences, can this be considered a response? A proper response? Can "intellectual-oriented" education go beyond the scope mentioned above? Therefore, teaching must be based on children's experiences; if it is not based on children's experiences, children will not gain true knowledge at all.

In the past century, Europe has particularly emphasized practical subjects, shaking off the previous trend of valuing literature and history, which has contributed to material civilization. However, the overall life of human beings is still deteriorating day by day, which is precisely the drawback of emphasizing intellectualism. Moreover, at a time when egalitarianism is being loudly advocated, we should absolutely break the traditional idea that mental labor is noble and physical work is inferior. The principle of work and activity is that human activities require not only mental power but also manual, physical, and limb strength. Therefore, in the implementation of education, some people advocate taking handicrafts as the center of teaching, with other subjects starting from handicrafts, and some even advocate conducting teaching in factories. These all build education on manual activities. Recently, there has been an emphasis on the activity of the four limbs, with travel and observation as important teaching methods. As for educators with a broad perspective, they regard work and activity as a teaching process.

2. Integrated Teaching

Knowledge in the universe is a unified, whole, and real entity that cannot be divided into individual subjects. However, in schools, it is divided one by one, which is far from real life. Therefore, many people are skeptical of this division, and thus two reform methods have emerged:

1) Connection of subjects – This is to connect separate subjects, such as the connection between handicrafts and painting, and between history and geography. But this method is not thorough and cannot fundamentally break the shackles of separate subjects.

2) Project-based teaching – Project-based teaching can break the separation of subjects and form an integrated activity. However, without adequate preparation or with incompetent teachers, it is unlikely that children will have universal participation in activities; only a few top students will be active. Moreover, breaking down subjects suddenly is also difficult in practice. The experimental teaching in Germany – integrated teaching – which centers on natural observation or handicrafts, is relatively easier to implement.

3. Communal Living

The so-called purpose of education in the past was undoubtedly "to learn to be a person." After all, what kind of person to be and how to evaluate the moral standards for being a person are indeed difficult things. Because moral standards evolve over time. For example, the religious moral standard is to respect God or gods; the ethical and social moral standard is to value virtue and trust sages. Whether such morality is good or not goes without saying, as it is a matter of the times. The cultivation methods of ancient moral standards can neither maintain faith nor conform to the psychology of modern people. Then, moral standards or ways of being a person should certainly be sought in the society of communal living. This new society must be formed based on the free will of each individual in the group to arouse a sense of social interests, responsibilities, and to be publicly believed in, respected, and obeyed by society.

Schools are a hub for transitioning from family to society. If school education has no labor and communal living, and no sense of common interests, perspectives, or responsibilities, is such education effective? Is it valuable? Friends, just think: currently, school teaching is separated from moral education, with academic performance and conduct trained separately, and there is a distinction between in-class and out-of-class activities. In addition, methods such as grading, punishment, and rewards all promote individualism. We criticize old education every day and talk about new education, yet we are all living within the framework of traditional education. This is something we should be aware of and pursue to change.

This is a transcript of a lecture delivered by Li Lianfang in the spring of 1931 at the Henan Provincial First Normal School, recorded by Li Yaozhang. —— Editors' note

Published in the "27th Anniversary Special Issue" of *Weekly of Henan Provincial First Normal School*, May 1931.

Report at the First Meeting of the Primary School Experiment Guidance Department

The primary school experiment has been discussed many times over the past few months. After much anticipation, today we are finally presenting a general plan to our colleagues from the three pilot primary schools. This is a matter of administration; however, for those of us in the field of education, especially those specializing in educational research, it is something we should all regret.

There is no need to report in detail on the proceedings of the meetings regarding the primary school experiment. Now, I will briefly explain the purpose of how we will proceed, which can be divided into two points: first, the purpose of undertaking this work; second, the purpose of the work that should be done at present. When it comes to the purpose of undertaking the work, it can also be divided into two points:

The first point is the reason for changing the original proposal to pilot the experiment in three schools and the key considerations for future work. Initially, when we proposed conducting the experiment, we intended to gather a group of researchers passionate about experimentation through the authorities to assist a single primary school. We also planned to transfer several technically proficient individuals with practical experience in primary schools to work together in one place, aiming to carry out more thorough work and provide reference materials and plans for other schools. This was not meant to show preference for any particular school. However, after discussions with representatives from the participating schools, it was decided by vote to pilot the experiment in three schools (School 1, School 4, and School 10). As a result, the originally planned concentration of efforts and thorough implementation has become difficult for the instructors, who can only contribute their spare time to assist with the experiment. Therefore, for future work, the colleagues directly responsible for and collaborating with the three schools must take greater responsibility. The planning and implementation of weekly or semester-based work plans will be the responsibility of the colleagues at each school. Instructors will only review the work plans proposed by each school in advance and discuss the reports on the outcomes of weekly or unit-based work. If there are special matters in the proposed plans or unexpected situations during implementation that require assistance from the Guidance Department, we will provide suggestions to the best of our ability. This is not an attempt by the Guidance Department to shirk responsibility; it is simply a practical reality.

The second point is the reason for starting the overall experiment with only the first and second grades of primary school and the key considerations for this phase. This is not because we lack the personnel or funds to extend the experiment to all grades, but rather because, in terms of experimental procedures, it is not feasible to carry out a comprehensive experiment in higher grades until the experiment in lower grades has been completed and relevant issues have been addressed. During the experiment in lower grades, all colleagues from the three primary schools must clearly understand that even if they are not directly responsible for teaching lower grades, they should dedicate some of their spare time—like the instructors, or even more so—to assist the colleagues directly in charge. This includes helping to formulate plans, find teaching materials, arrange facilities, and handle all related preparations. It is important for everyone to understand that helping them is helping yourselves. This is not to say that if you help them now, they will help you in return, creating a mutual exchange. Rather, the experimental work in lower grades is a preparation for the experiment in higher grades. If their experimental work achieves considerable success, it will reduce many difficulties for your future experimental work in higher grades. Moreover, their pioneering work truly needs assistance. Since you have not yet taken direct responsibility for the overall experiment, you are in a position to help them. Success in the lower-grade experiment is not just the success of the individual teaching in those grades; it is the beginning of success for the entire school's teaching and a vertical success for education as a whole. I hope everyone will share this responsibility and not think that lessons not assigned to you have nothing to do with you. There is another important point to note: while the responsibility is shared, the equipment funds provided by the authorities are exclusively for lower grades and cannot be used, even in the slightest, for other grades. This is not a disregard for higher grades; when the time comes to experiment with higher grades, separate funds will be allocated for equipment. Given the current limitations on funds, we must not distribute them as if they were "benefits to be shared equally," as this would reduce efficiency. If the school authorities become distracted and fail to focus, this experiment will completely fail.

Regarding the purpose of the work that should be done at present, it can be divided into two parts:

(1) Partial experiments are divided into two categories: small-issue experiments and curriculum reform experiments. Teachers of all grades can choose to conduct one or two of them.

For small-issue experiments, four principles were proposed during the preparatory meeting, which all of you are already aware of. Let me now elaborate on them with specific examples. For instance, in Chinese reading instruction, it has been proven that characters should be presented in complete sentences from the beginning for students to recite and learn, and that reading and writing should not be taught simultaneously. This has been correctly verified, so there is no need for us to experiment on it.

However, questions such as when reading and writing can be connected, and what steps should be taken to connect them, remain. Specific issues can be broken down into aspects like dictation, 默写， and excerpt writing. Another example: when starting to learn characters, how to pronounce them, how to distinguish their forms, and how to explain their meanings? Why are the ancient methods of reading and the character-learning methods used in the early days of school education no longer applicable? In principle, Western-style language teaching methods are not problematic, but they have been misapplied by educators who do not understand Chinese characters, leading to increasingly poor results in language learning. This has become a serious issue in the foundation of education.

First, Chinese characters are formed by combining individual radicals, which is more than a hundred times more complex than phonetic scripts formed purely by combining phonetic letters. Moreover, the number of characters formed by radical elements (so-called radicals) is large, and their forms have changed significantly. It is no longer possible to first distinguish radicals as in the Shuowen Jiezi (an ancient Chinese dictionary). However, to distinguish the forms of characters, one must understand their constituent elements. Second, the form of Chinese characters is related to their meanings, and the same character can have different meanings depending on usage, which can cause problems in explaining meanings and distinguishing forms. How should we reform the teaching methods of Chinese language and characters based on educational principles? This urgently requires experimentation. By analogy, if every teacher conducts one or two small-issue experiments each semester, either individually or jointly with several colleagues, these experiments, accumulated and integrated over time, will be sufficient to innovate education.

Curriculum reform can be carried out by subject. If you feel that you lack the ability to reform the entire system of a subject you teach, I can propose a relatively simple method: for each teaching unit, record details such as how to organize teaching materials, how to conduct the teaching process, what responses are received where, what effects are achieved in which aspects, how to prepare for the class, how to arrange practice sessions, and your final reflections. Then, sort out the experiences you have gained and propose them for discussion. Although this is not a direct reform, it has a considerable impact on reform.

(2) Comprehensive experiments, specifically the lower-grade experiments. various schools are planning to conduct such experiments. Details of these have been outlined in the experimental plan. However, this plan, formulated based on the input of many people, varies in detail, with numerous omissions and oversights. Let me now highlight several key points that have gained relatively consistent consensus:

First, the daily learning curriculum is child-centered. What children need to learn is determined by their core needs and issues. Moreover, attention should be paid to the interrelationships between various learning contents. Unless special practice is required, there should be no isolated study; even practice should serve practical needs. This differs from the old approach of selecting unit materials from various subjects and applying fixed teaching methods accordingly. Instead, it aims to enable children to grasp the inherent value of subjects through learning activities.

Second, the tools for reading, writing, and arithmetic should be introduced gradually, adapting to learning opportunities and assessing children's abilities. Learning should take place whenever opportunities arise, regardless of time constraints. These tools must never be divorced from current core issues or become impractical.

Third, learning is not aimed at acquiring knowledge for its own sake, but at meeting immediate needs. It enables children to find answers to problems in books and science, explore the meaning of various things in nature and human society, develop an understanding of human responsibilities through daily life, get accustomed to group life through the learning process, and gradually cultivate the qualities required of a citizen. Practical knowledge will naturally be gained through their experiences, making it vibrant and a source of enhanced wisdom and control.

Finally, I would like to share a personal view: What should our curriculum standards be? What should our standard of living be? I believe that part of our education is a leftover ornament from China's traditions, and another part is Western-style education imported from capitalist societies. Both are mere forms lacking in ethos and absolutely incompatible with the new era. Various experimental education models in Europe and America still bear strong traces of capitalist society, not to mention so-called "civic training." Even the primary school curriculum in the Soviet Union, if we set aside its emphasis on class struggle, seems to embody more genuine educational significance than our officially prescribed curriculum standards. We do not possess the ability of primary school teachers in Hamburg, Germany, to cultivate children's capacity for judging social values. If we refer to the Soviet primary school curriculum, replacing the concept of "class struggle" with "labor-capital harmony" to develop a new curriculum, it may prove more effective than mindlessly following old paths such as advocating Confucianism or Christian teachings in educational principles and implementation guidelines—paths that are fundamentally incompatible with educational principles.

Published in *Henan Education Monthly*, Vol. 2, No. 3, December 1931;

Also published in Li Lianfang et al., *Experimental Primary School Education*, "Special Issue on Experimental Education" by the Primary Education Experiment Guidance Department of Henan Provincial Department of Education, January 1932

Foreword to the *Education Weekly*

The realization of the Three People's Principles has become a cliché. In what way is today's educational system and school facilities different from those that are non-Three People's Principles?

Those who talk about party affairs all say they are cultivating democratic forces. These forces are tied to the people. If we do not start with basic education, can this be a proper way of cultivation?

All powerful empires have made great efforts in national education and production using scientific methods, yet their societies still inevitably develop first abnormally and unemployment increases day by day. What problems exist in their educational policies?

The national political system is incompatible with education and society. Is there a need to entirely inherit the educational system of such capitalist countries?

It is true that China's social revolution should not involve class struggle. However, is it reasonable to implement class-based education? Even if education is said to be classless, if it only facilitates the enrollment of children from powerful and wealthy families, does it not form a class-based education?

Everyone says that feudal thoughts should be broken. These thoughts form the inherited psychology of humans, and everyone falls into them without realizing it. In particular, the development of intelligence and talent tends to be used for authority. How should such illusions be thoroughly reformed through education?

Recently, those in charge of politics, in their antipathy towards educational phenomena, tend to focus on issues such as morality, discipline, and banning heresies, triggering a retro movement. I am not opposed to the past, but I have doubts about the content and methods of raising such issues. Even if education was extremely strict 25 years ago, why could it not maintain its original state? Now, instead of finding a proper path, returning to the old ways—can this solve the problem?

Schools and society, education and politics, students and faculty—all have become extremely contradictory phenomena. The higher the status of the school, the more we hear about educational principles and praise excellent schools. If we take them as norms, can they really avoid the aforementioned contradictory phenomena?

The new life that humans strive for, on the one hand, aims to advance material civilization, and on the other hand, to prevent the ethos from being dominated by material things. This has become an overall problem. How should education solve it?

The realization of a new society requires education to enable ordinary people to have the ability to adapt to the new life and maintain the society; for special people, they should be able to contribute to society with advanced knowledge. The cultivation of such special people must ensure that those receiving higher education truly have the ability for advanced studies and are not restricted by their circumstances. The ability of ordinary people to adapt to a new life must be acquired through appropriate vocational education after completing general education. If such universal education is not implemented, can a true people's politics be established? Even if we try to force an explanation, this cannot be achieved overnight. However, does the current implementation of educational administration have the slightest hint of universal education?

Education cannot yield results overnight. It is said that social reform must be rooted in education one by one, especially primary education. Those who are impatient should not think it is too distant. However, if we reform society without going through education and only adopt revolutionary means, the majority of people will not know what revolution is. Either the result will be bad, or they will be hostile to it. In particular, initiating revolution and suppressing revolution have purely become issues of power struggle. The people suffer from both but turn a blind eye. Even if a new society is realized and promoted by revolution, the impact will only be superficial. If we understand that the realization of a new society lies in the full development of the intelligence of all people, and the tool for this lies in overall education, then we have thought halfway through the issue of educational reform. However, the one-sided views of the world such as "saving the country through science", "education is omnipotent", "education is independent", and "education is noble" have nothing to do with the issue of educational reform proposed today.

On the occasion of the launch of this publication, I do not know where to start. I write these random thoughts to arouse the attention of those interested in educational research.

Published in Li Lianfang and Tai Shuangqiu (eds.): *Education Weekly* (No. 3 of the special supplements to Henan's *Republican Daily*), Issue 1, March 31, 1932.

Reflections on Children's Day

Since people broke away from the ape-like existence and entered human society, the ability to control nature and dominate the world stems from two roles: one is the role of humanity, and the other is the role of the state.

There is a National Day to commemorate the state, but what other appropriate day is there to commemorate humanity besides Children's Day?

Whenever a somewhat authoritative gentleman arrives in Kaifeng, the policemen from the Public Security Bureau go door to door to pass the word that flags should be hung and welcome notes written; the party headquarters also put up many slogans along the street, offering excessive flattery. However, today is April 4th, which was designated as Children's Day by the central government long ago. I took a rickshaw, going from home to school and then back home, but I didn't feel the slightest bit of a special atmosphere. Could it be that my old eyes have grown dim, making me unable to see the preparations made for these children?

I heard that during the commemoration of Children's Day the year before last, the streets of London, England were covered with slogans about happiness everywhere. The King and Queen visited in person, and the mayor and his wife were especially enthusiastic. President Hoover of the United States even opened the White House to welcome children from across the country to visit.

China can really be regarded as an outdated country, where only authoritative gentlemen are worthy of people's flattery. Especially in recent years, the government has spared no effort in promoting this trend.

What is even more noteworthy is that wherever we go in the streets and alleys, we see parents beating and scolding their own children. Why are the children beaten and scolded? Are they born bad, or have they been infected by this adult society? Is this adult society created by the authoritative gentlemen throughout history? Therefore, I have endless thoughts about this Children's Day, and I don't want to say any more.

Published in *Education Weekly*, Issue 2, April 6, 1932

Three Principles of the People and Educational Reform

All institutions under party rule are aimed at the Three Principles of the People. When talking about education from the party's standpoint, people often deviate from the inherent issues of education and take publicizing policies and expanding party power as their goals. When discussing the Principles from the educational standpoint, people tend to focus on theoretical research or simply adopt theories as teaching materials, without exploring how work and institutions should implement the ethos of the Principles. Therefore, the more discussions there are about education and the Principles, the more emphasis is placed on formality, and the farther they drift from reality. This is a common fallacy resulting from the separation of teaching and moral education. However, the world fails to perceive this and often acts in a way that runs counter to the correct path. Nowadays, education under party rule is particularly plagued by this drawback. If we do not awaken to this, it will be like "going south by driving the chariot north" (acting in a way that defeats one's purpose). In studying the issue of educational reform, we should derive basic concepts from the overall theory of the Three Principles of the People, and all reform issues should be constructed based on these basic concepts, rather than seeking solutions in a fragmented manner.

The entire theory of the Three Principles of the People contains four basic concepts that we must understand. Here is a summary of their main points.

1. The targets of the Three Principles of the People are military force, bureaucracy, and capital—imperialism.

The politics formed by military force, bureaucracy, and capital inevitably intertwine and collude. To break it down:

Military force serves as the tool for building a state, and its politics revolve around invading other states or ethnic groups as a strategy for self-defense and expansion. During times of national chaos, it becomes purely an instrument for individual self-interest.

Bureaucratic politics rely on wielding administrative power to uphold their privileged influence. Hypocritical democratic politics and class dictatorship serve the same function.

Capitalist politics focus on extracting profits and monopolizing unearned material comforts.

The root cause of these three political systems lies in humanity's struggle for survival, where the one-sided development of individual traits has, over time, become ingrained as social heredity, forming a domineering impulse within human nature. In the past, this could still be restrained by societal sanctions such as traditions and maxims. However, modern education, shaped solely by ornamental and mechanical methods, has even eroded these restraining influences.

As the world evolves, the domain of the domineering impulse expands, and its methods grow ever more sophisticated. This so-called domineering impulse refers to the suppression of others' desires, rights, and survival to fulfill one's own. Since political and economic systems are inseparable from human life, they become the most fertile ground for the development of this impulse—and the primary reason why political parties seize power as their ultimate goal.

Consequently, political and economic structures have undergone repeated changes, yet even today, no form of state has freed itself from the shackles of humanity's domineering impulse. Every individual action and public institution bears traces of selfishness, vanity, deceit, envy, and animosity.

In states with partisan politics, parties rise and fall in succession. Though each serves its own interests, they must still rely on one or two populist policies to win elections. In states with class dictatorship, despite the tyranny of the ruling faction, their policies inevitably benefit one segment of the population.

However, in a one-party dictatorship that does not align with any particular class, the slightest misstep means that all state decrees become driven by the domineering impulses of a few rulers. This is not unlike the ethical framework of the autocratic era, where "the ruler guides the subject, the father guides the son, and the husband guides the wife"—all manifestations of the domineering impulse. Even leadership and command, if derived purely from authority, are nothing but disguised expressions of this same impulse.

2. The Three Principles of the People are rooted in nationalism, with democracy and people's livelihood as their instruments.

Since the foundation lies in nationalism, it must be grounded in the current state of the nation, its inherent culture, and its shortcomings to cultivate its ethos. Consequently, the goal of democracy is to establish a politics of the whole people, preventing the bourgeoisie, the intellectual class, the powerful, and the cunning from monopolizing political and administrative power, thereby avoiding the pitfalls of sham democracy or class-based bureaucratic dictatorship. The aim of people's livelihood is communism, where industrial development seeks to improve the living conditions of the entire state—not to satisfy the special demands of any class, lest it foster capitalist ambitions or incite class struggle.

Since the instruments are democracy and people's livelihood, the nationalist pursuit of international equality does not, like statism, rely on military force and diplomacy or exploit temporary popular xenophobia. Nor does it appeal to cosmopolitanism in hopes of national independence. Instead, it seeks to dismantle both internal and external oppression through political and economic means, thereby achieving national liberation and advancing the realization of cosmopolitanism.

Thus, from a substantive perspective, the Three Principles of the People form an indivisible whole—a coherent doctrine. From a functional perspective, they operate in an interlocking manner, mutually reinforcing one another. As the Premier stated in his Guilin speech: "To solve the national question, we must simultaneously solve the democratic question; to solve the democratic question, we must simultaneously solve the livelihood question."

3. The Ethos of the Three Principles of the People Lies in Equality

(Equality in international status, political status, and economic status—see First Lecture on Nationalism)

3.1 The Foundation of Equality

First, it must encompass the entire populace—that is, "the state must be shared by all, governance must be jointly administered by all, and benefits must be enjoyed by all." (Second Lecture on People's Livelihood)

Second, it must not be constrained by objective conditions—that is, "every individual should receive equal starting opportunities, after which each may achieve according to their innate intelligence and ability." (Third Lecture on Democracy) If objective circumstances, due to restrictions of status or wealth, lead to clear instances of mutual harm and enmity, merely instilling a subjective sense of mutual affection in humanity to eliminate hostility is impossible. Therefore, "when the power of religion is exhausted and charity proves ineffective, revolution becomes the only means to achieve a fundamental solution." (Fourth Lecture on Democracy)

3.2 The Social Nature of Equality

First, the fundamental capacity of society—that is, "if every individual becomes a productive member, the problem of people's livelihood can be resolved." (Fourth Lecture on People's Livelihood)

Second, the ethos of social service—that is, "everyone should regard service as their purpose, not seizure. Though natural endowments of intelligence and ability may vary, when the moral sense of service flourishes, those with greater talents will serve more and benefit society more, while those with lesser abilities must still contribute to the best of their capacity—this is how true equality can be achieved." (Fourth Lecture on Democracy)

4. The Historical Perspective of the Three Principles of the People is Social Evolution

"People's livelihood is the central force of social evolution, and social evolution is the core of history... The struggle for human existence is the true cause of social progress, not class struggle." (Lecture on People's Livelihood)

Thus, the conditions for evolution, as outlined by the Three Principles of the People, are as follows:

(1) Unceasing Human Effort “Throughout history, the reason all humanity strives is to secure survival. Only through uninterrupted effort can society achieve unending progress.” (Lecture on People’s Livelihood)

(2) Expansion of Collective Unity “The 400 million people of China must first unite, then extend this solidarity to weaker states, joining forces to subjugate first tyranny with justice. This is our responsibility in advancing global evolution.” (Fourth Lecture on Nationalism)

(3) Harmonization of Economic Interests “Social progress occurs when the economic interests of the majority are harmonized rather than in conflict.” (Lecture on People’s Livelihood)”Purely revolutionary means cannot fully resolve economic issues.” (Second Lecture on People’s Livelihood)

(4) Emergence of New Systems “Society evolves precisely because new systems continually arise.” (Lecture on People’s Livelihood) Examples include social and industrial reforms, public ownership of transportation and communication, direct taxation, and socialized distribution—all concrete manifestations of modern social evolution.

Based on the four fundamental concepts outlined above, education must be reformed. The first two principles define the direction, while the latter two provide the foundational guidelines—thus giving rise to the following two key questions:

First, what kind of education should be implemented? Second: How can education for all the people be achieved?

Before addressing these questions, there are three prevailing trends that must be recognized:

(1) The influence of democratic development, which emphasizes the rights that all people should enjoy.

(2) The influence of social revolution, which prioritizes the scientization and socialization of production and consumption.

(3) The influence of psychological experimentation, which focuses on manual operation, physical movement, and environmental stimuli.

The first two trends pertain to the background of education—society—while the latter concerns the subject of education—the child. The convergence and interconnection of these three elements shape the necessary direction for education in the new era, ultimately achieving the goals of Three Principles of the People-based education.

5. Addressing the first issue

5.1 Transforming Thought First, it is necessary to eradicate the deeply ingrained misconceptions inherited from society—those fallacies that have become accepted as truths and are firmly embedded in the national psyche. These inherited misconceptions have been perpetuated over time by feudal systems, bureaucratic politics, and privileged classes, directly or indirectly reinforcing their desire for dominance. Let us analyze them as follows:

(1) Obedience as a Virtue This was the attitude imposed on the people under autocratic rule, demanding unconditional submission without allowing them to exercise their own judgment. Particularly, governments, teachers, and parents, who presume themselves wise and capable, often fall into this error. Consequently, individuals in society—distinguished by gender, age, status, circumstance, or ability—are conditioned to believe that the weaker or less privileged should adopt this mindset. Over time, even those who are neither wise nor capable, once in positions of authority, come to regard dominance as their inherent right. Education thus becomes

passive and mechanical, unwittingly steeped in these entrenched social habits.

(2) Exceptionalism as the Goal of Advancement In states where universal education has not been implemented, parents send their children to school, striving for higher education in hopes that they will become extraordinary talents—a desire shared by the children themselves. Their aim is simply to elevate their social status and secure a superior standard of living, mirroring the mentality of the imperial examination era. If education serves only individual gain, schools become factories for class stratification, further equipping individuals with the means to suppress others.

(3) Manual Labor as a Lowly Occupation This mentality originated during aristocratic rule and was amplified by bureaucratic governance, driving the populace to distinguish themselves from the common people. On one hand, the intellectual class disdains productive labor; on the other, the laboring class is denied access to knowledge. Even after feudal hierarchies collapsed, rulers and the ruled remained in opposition, leading to increasing social division. From agriculture to industry and commerce, laborers were exploited as prey. As more people avoided labor, a single individual's rise to prominence would sustain an entourage of idle dependents—relatives and servants living off rents and privileges. In public affairs, this breeds corruption. While past systems at least had checks and balances, today such restraints are entirely dismantled. The saying, "When the master attains enlightenment, even his chickens and dogs ascend to heaven," has become a rampant reality.

Beyond these surface phenomena, the deeper issue is the anti-evolutionary psychology ingrained in the state—a collective preference for wealth and luxury without productive labor, neglecting manual skills and physical work. Some even consider abstract theorizing the essence of spiritual cultivation, resulting in individuals who lack holistic physical and mental development. How can such people hope to compete in the new era to come?

5.2 Cultivating Capabilities To develop individuals into useful members of society, enabling them to adopt new lifestyles through shared living models, thereby promoting social evolution and fostering national ethos. This consists of two essential elements:

(1) Social Tools

a. Political Competence In practical terms, this means training in the exercise of the Four Powers (referring to Sun Yat-sen's political framework). The methods for cultivation are twofold. Fostering political interest: Current social issues should be incorporated into lessons to stimulate students' motivation for inquiry, but overt propaganda and flattery must be strictly avoided. Imparting political knowledge: The forms and functions of the Four Powers should be taught through practical activities, allowing students to gain concrete experience at appropriate opportunities. However, participation in politically motivated social activities should be avoided to prevent deviation.

b. Enhancing Productive Capacity
Individuals must be trained as productive members of society. During schooling, general education should instill disciplined work habits, while vocational education should provide practical skills. This ensures that in production, scientific methods are employed to increase efficiency, and that in labor, individuals maintain enthusiasm for their work.

(2) Social Ethos

a. Empathy Empathy must align with universal human standards or arise from shared social interests. Exploiting one group to benefit another is not true empathy. Therefore, empathy originates from love and manifests in cooperation. In an increasingly complex society, development and harmony depend on the expansion of empathy. Schools must cultivate this foundation by:

Encouraging intellectual and emotional engagement.

Selecting historical facts for instruction—not to conceal wrongdoing but to enlighten through comprehensive knowledge.

Activities such as caring for animals, cultivating plants, and sharing toys can all nurture empathy.

Collaborative projects should replace competition, fostering mutual stimulation, knowledge exchange, and teamwork.

Daily academic efforts should stem from intrinsic motivation, not coercion or rivalry, thereby eliminating the roots of social ills.

b. Responsibility Along with empathy, responsibility replaces external authority as a cornerstone of democratic society. Though distinct in meaning, responsibility and service are functionally the same:

Responsibility is internal conviction; service is external action.

Without understanding responsibility, one cannot truly serve.

Ancient Chinese philosophy rooted family and state governance in self-cultivation (xiūshēn), but later distortions reduced it to rote memorization, contributing to societal decline.

Blind obedience (past) or misconstrued power shifts (present) both fail to instill genuine responsibility.

c. Creativity Creativity arises from latent potential, not exclusive to a gifted few. For example, school projects that involve planning and executing tasks independently demonstrate creativity. Schools must provide structured freedom, adequate resources, and opportunities to acquire knowledge through experience. Scientific methods should guide learning, with hands-on work fostering traits like precision, courage, deliberation, initiative, discipline, and daring—all mutually reinforcing qualities.

Achieving These Aims Education must be built upon the foundation of society as a whole, and all human education must derive from an integrated system. Yet current educational systems worldwide have evolved from distorted social structures, leaving lasting flaws. To fulfill the mission of reform, these deficiencies must first be identified and addressed, as elaborated below.

(1) Reforming the Formalistic Education of Bureaucratic Politics The bureaucratic society rules over the people entirely through external authority. The most important form of this authority is law. While law is indispensable for maintaining social order, relying solely on legal power to enforce compliance means that obedience stems purely from fear—or worse, the law itself may be shaped by the interests of a privileged few, serving the convenience of those in power. Under bureaucratic rule, all institutions align with its policies. Even so-called scholars construct theories based on this social backdrop, which are then revered as doctrine. School education is no exception, devising rigid regulations where rewards and punishments become the sole means of control. Yet, managing students through rules contradicts the very essence of education. Over time, however, this malpractice has become entrenched, leading to a separation between teaching and discipline. The so-called "good teacher" is reduced to a mere knowledge dispenser, while character cultivation becomes an empty formality—a peculiar phenomenon resulting from the Western-style education imported into China. Today's emphasis on "moral education" is merely a superficial evolution of this trend. Since authority prioritizes formality, all human activities are constrained by

fixed structures. Uniform curricula and mechanical teaching methods are natural outcomes. Moreover, the system incentivizes bureaucratic careers—official appointments are tied to academic credentials, significantly impacting secondary and higher education. Students in agriculture, industry, or commerce no longer study for practical careers, nor are they limited to such paths. Many endure schooling despite dissatisfaction, clinging to diplomas solely for social advancement.

(2) Reforming the Distorted Education of Capitalist Society Modern European and American educational systems, shaped by capitalist societies, exhibit the following issues:

First, compulsory primary education is enforced, while secondary and higher education remain optional. Compared to states without universal education, this may seem progressive. Yet, compulsory schooling—often glorified as "national education"—originated from nationalism, aiming to cultivate citizens for national supremacy rather than human equality. Even recent extensions like supplementary or adult education merely address the inadequacy of primary schooling in fostering livelihood skills, rather than ensuring all individuals fully develop their potential. Consequently: The diligent poor, though qualified, are barred by circumstance. The idle rich, though unfit, gain access—with inequality worsening at higher levels. Most people are excluded from the full educational system, unable to contribute their talents to society. Meanwhile, those pursuing doctoral, master's, or bachelor's degrees are often not the truly gifted but profit-seekers—hindering both social progress and academic advancement. The repercussions are profound.

Second, directly productive education inherently bears class character Such education typically offers vocational training at the primary level and industrial specialization at the secondary level. While designed to meet the efficiency demands of different social classes—serving a functional purpose in addressing immediate needs—it ultimately fails to resolve social issues and may even exacerbate societal tensions. Why? Because individual needs arise from private economic conditions, leading education to foster a harmful universality: people rely on acquired skills for personal material gain rather than societal prosperity. Consequently, individual desires remain perpetually unsatisfied, creating a standoff between those who hold power and those who refuse marginalization, rendering labor-capital harmony unattainable. Though specialized production education remains necessary in our complex society, it should be viewed only as a stopgap measure—not the ideal vocational model.

(3) Reforming the Leisure Education Inherited from Ancient Aristocracy The persistence of viewing scholarship as a leisurely pursuit stems from academia's aristocratic origins. Early schools catered to the elite, where erudition meant memorization for ceremonial roles. This legacy glorified abstract discourse and cultivated a disdain for labor, entrenching a mind-body duality. Even today, schools rely on servants for manual tasks, and students in practical fields depend on hired labor. Traditional study, beyond leisure, focused on governance—esoteric "wisdom" divorced from ordinary life. Pure theory and rote memorization dominate, even in specialized disciplines.

(4) Reforming the Rote-Based Education of Classical Tradition Before science's rise, ancient texts were the sole cultural repository. But their misuse made books the only knowledge source and oral transmission the sole tool. Universities epitomize this: liberal arts cling to texts; even applied fields prioritize theory over practice. They lack the free inquiry of old academies, the skill focus of trade schools, and societal impact—becoming relics of aristocratic leisure, state propaganda tools, and capitalist strongholds. Dubbed "temples of learning," they squander public funds to breed political factions. Reform demands radical action—like

France's 1792 dissolution of universities. Modern universities should: Transfer applied skills to vocational schools. Reserve academic research for institutes. Merging these functions compromises both.

(5) Reforming Subject-Based Logical Systems in Education Modern curricula, bloated by historical accretion, prioritize disciplinary precision over human needs. Isolated subjects:

Fail to reflect real-world complexity. Stifle interest by obscuring interconnections. Misguide beginners with oversimplified content. True education should: Cultivate broad knowledge organically. Anchor learning in human activities and natural-social relationships—not rigid subject systems. Current "depth" often means irrelevance, making curriculum reform urgent.

The foregoing discussion emphasizes rectifying past errors, rather than advocating a form of pragmatism devoid of core principles or merely asserting that purely theoretical and liberal curricula are inadequate for modern life. Below, we outline three key principles to guide implementation:

(1) Schools should be regarded as the center of society. Only when a new society emerges can people enjoy a new life. Revolution can be expected to bring about a new society, but it cannot guarantee that what is realized will definitely be a democratic society. Especially in countries where there is no class struggle, revolutionary elements are mostly people who were frustrated at that time, or they rely on and utilize certain forces. After seizing political power, in order to consolidate their own positions, they have to exclude dissidents. As a result, they completely forget their original intentions, making the current government a hotbed of deterioration and corruption, even willing to sacrifice everything without hesitation. To reduce such drawbacks, the only way is to base all the

facilities of the new era on education; and to ensure that the education of the new era truly conforms to the goal of civilian politics. This meaning is by no means like the emperors' monopoly on educational power, the Communist Party's seizure of leadership, or the religious-style propaganda of doctrines, which completely take means as ends. Therefore, the aspirations should be as follows.

First, education should not be dominated by political forces. Since the separation of officials and teachers, the higher the official position, the knowledge does not necessarily advance with it. Since the abolition of the imperial examination, teaching has become a profession. From the former perspective, education should not be independent of politics, but educational undertakings must not follow the temporary wishes of officials. From the latter perspective, officials are not fixed, while the teaching profession is permanent. A permanent profession should not be manipulated by unstable officials. Although in the past, education inherited the mentality of the imperial examination and was deeply influenced by Western-style capitalist methods and mechanical technologies, with profound harmful effects, there is an urgent need for a thorough reform. However, this is an academic issue. If we do not respect people with academic knowledge, do not recognize that political status and Western-style academic degrees cannot represent academic knowledge, and only adopt political means, such as requiring that certain positions must be held by party members; all facilities are subject to the government's orders; and even party organizations or student unions with political purposes, which are not organized by academic personnel, are actually considered to have the inherent duty to guide schools. I do not believe that education, a century-old cause, will not be exploited by ordinary political careerists and corrupted by those who are uneducated and incompetent.

Second, educational plans should advance in tandem with all political systems. For example, surveys on the livelihood of school-age families and public welfare and health campaigns should progress in conjunction with civil affairs. The establishment of vocational education and student enrollment in courses should be coordinated with the construction of agriculture, mining, industry, commerce, transportation, and the development of factories and companies. If political organs act independently and education becomes isolated, it is enough to prove that politics has lost its unity, and no education can have complete facilities and good results. As for the government's employment, it is dominated by forces. Peddlers and errand boys can all hold high positions. Those who lack common sense are in charge of government affairs. Even so-called believers can obtain qualifications overnight by relying on military power or currying favor with dignitaries. Even if there are good laws, they cannot be implemented.

Third, schools should be established for society. In today's education, in terms of administration, the government regards educational undertakings as the responsibility of government agencies, which are not to be interfered with by teaching staff. Teaching staff consider school facilities as their inherent power, which are not to be interfered with by local people or students' parents. In terms of content, it follows the opinions of supervisors and specialists and copies existing texts. There is no in-depth consideration of the suitable needs of the local society and whether students can develop fully according to their abilities. As a result, schools are becoming increasingly distant from society, educational culture and civil undertakings are not coordinated, and once students enter school, they almost become born favorites, while their studies are not sufficient to contribute to society. It is no wonder that education has become a tool of the leisure class and the capitalist society, with deep-rooted problems. If we do not reverse the above-mentioned drawbacks, start anew, and make school buildings and facilities sufficient for the use of public organizations, and make emerging social undertakings rely on local schools, then it is better not to run education at all.

(2) Education should be built on the foundation of students' lives. Students' lives vary due to differences in age, aspirations, and environments. However, through their fundamental functions, they can enable the goals of communal life to keep moving forward. It is necessary to acquire intimate knowledge in response to the environment, and further gain the ability to transform the environment through learning. This allows individual natural development to emerge from social development, rather than taking money and bread as substitutes for the pursuit of knowledge. From this, there are two basic principles:

First, spontaneous activity. Nowadays, from primary schools to universities, all teaching is passive and mechanical. The result is that some students become indulgent, which is a case of "extremes meet." It is essential to eliminate the various drawbacks of the old-style education, such as rigid book recitation, fixed curricula, separation of teaching and discipline, and overemphasis on rationality. All learning should correspond to students' needs, abilities, and interests, be controlled by their own consciousness, and proceed purposefully to develop their experience. Or, through problems arising from practical tasks, students can seek knowledge and acquire systematic experience. Only in this way can the inspiration in teaching lay the foundation for the development of civilian politics. Merely pursuing universal access or improvement in form has nothing to do with democracy.

Second, all-round development. Today's education, on the one hand, suffers from fragmented subjects that cannot be integrated into useful and broad knowledge. On the other hand, it tends to be narrow, leading only to distorted development. The former is a drawback formed by general education, while the latter is caused by vocational education and the course selection systems in specialized universities. Therefore, universities in various countries strive to establish comprehensive cultural courses for the first and second years, and allow sufficient specialized research in the third and fourth years, while providing self-study opportunities tailored to students' abilities. For primary and secondary education, they help students discover their strengths through various basic exercises over a certain period, and then encourage them to develop to the fullest extent according to their individual aspirations, becoming tools for serving society. Any distorted education or education that promotes a mechanical life, which has nothing to do with communal life, should be rejected. However, education based on the political ideology of the Three People's Principles still relies on the outdated systems and methods of capitalist society—how can we not reflect on this?

(3) Character should be built on the foundation of knowledge and ability. When discussing character, it is associated with moral issues. Past education did emphasize character, yet its effects were not evident. This was not merely because the forms of morality were incompatible with the times, but actually because the methods of cultivation were not based on knowledge. It only focused on ancient maxims and aphorisms, or resorted to ascetic practices and strict self-discipline. As a result, morality was separated from knowledge and ability. The morality cultivated became artificial behavior, and the knowledge and ability acquired became tools that could be used for either good or evil. Therefore, in future education, if we want to cultivate a certain character and improve individual behavior, the highest goal of education will never be achieved unless we develop a proper attitude through a deep understanding of the relationships between things and acquire normal habits through the process of doing practical

work. The cultivation of habits focuses on laying the foundation in early childhood. Although the theory that this starts at the age of three or six may not be a conclusive view, if a child is exposed to bad customs in the family and society from an early age, and we expect an ideal character to be cultivated in school, the effect will be minimal. As for education at and above the middle school level, the situation gets worse and worse, and there are reasons for this. This is why the country's efforts to establish public nursery schools and public kindergartens for early childhood education have become the most urgent issue today. However, among ordinary people, those of a higher status only hope that their own children will have good character, while those of a lower status seek to obtain qualifications for higher education to improve their social status, without considering the state of education for the general public or the foundation of education. This is failing to address the root of the problem.

6. Addressing the second problem

6.1 Equality of Opportunity

(1) The number of publicly funded schools, gradually expanding to reach universal access, should align with the intellectual capacity of the entire population. Compulsory education, as currently implemented, requires phased establishment; the poorest children will only gain access once universalization is finally achieved. Even if this distant goal were realized (which remains uncertain), social stratification would already be entrenched through education, making true equality impossible. Moreover, limiting universalization to primary education alone effectively reserves higher education for the bourgeoisie, rendering political revolutions irrelevant to the masses. Claims of insufficient national funds ring hollow—limited resources must serve the entire people, ensuring access depends on opportunity, not circumstance. Arguments that higher education should wait until primary education is universalized ignore

education as a national imperative requiring consistent policy. Piecemeal, fragmented approaches hinder societal progress and breed conflict. Critics dismissing higher education universalization as "utopian" due to unfulfilled primary education targets overlook political will. If "people's governance" remains a facade under party rule, expansion is futile. The failure of compulsory education over two decades of Republican rule—merely nominal despite official rhetoric—reveals that financial constraints are not the root cause. Genuine commitment would prioritize education as a solution to social ills, using public funds for public good and calibrating expansion to children's needs (as outlined in Henan's proposed aid program for impoverished gifted students).

(2) Educational access must transcend economic barriers, ensuring neither family circumstances block enrollment nor schooling destabilizes family livelihoods. Blanket tuition waivers are inadequate; scholarships, grants, and loans often become tools for institutional control over students. Two remedies are critical:

- For impoverished primary students: Provide supplies, modeled on charitable schools.

- For indigent secondary/higher students: Fund living expenses, adapting Soviet vocational school models.

Such support must avoid fostering dependency or entitlement, operating in conjunction with holistic aid frameworks that preserve dignity.

(3) Higher education should prioritize merit: diligent, impoverished students must gain entry, while wealthy but incompetent ones should be excluded. Current systems, which tie access to financial means, reserve advanced education for the privileged. Higher education, tasked with advancing scientific and professional excellence, demands selection based on exceptional ability, not status.

Today's admissions rely on narrow, one-time exams that fail to reflect the state's diverse talent. This reduces universities to diploma mills, corrupting academia and exacerbating social problems—an urgent need for reform.

6.2 Everyone as a Productive Member

(1) The Meaning of Productivity Productivity has direct and indirect forms. For example, engaging in education constitutes indirect productivity. Thus, the essential elements of a productive member are: first, that what one learns can contribute efficiently to society; second, that emphasis is placed on division of labor rather than sharing unearned benefits. However, the core remains the ability to engage in direct productivity.

(2) Methods for Cultivating Productive Members These methods fall into basic and specialized categories.

Basic productive capacity is fostered through general education. In educational theory, concepts such as vocational cultivation—emphasizing manual work, practical tasks, and curricula rooted in natural and social foundations—all share this orientation. Educational duration that is too short fails to solidify foundational skills, while excessive length strains national finances. Remedial education is often provided through supplementary programs outside the regular system.

A major contradiction lies in secondary education. Theoretically, it aims at general education, but in practice, it juggles vocational preparation, university entrance training, preservation of traditional secondary school models, and forced alignment with educational theories—resulting in the current junior and senior high school system. Senior high schools focus on university or vocational preparation, with curricula containing general knowledge that differs in nature from the "general education" of junior high. Though junior and senior high are hierarchically linked and share overlapping goals, their curriculum design and teaching methods often prioritize status over purpose.

To fulfill the aims of general education, junior high should be integrated into primary education by abolishing the upper primary level, dividing primary education into two four-year phases, or restructuring it into three three-year stages (lower, middle, upper). This would clarify the goals of primary and secondary education and simplify implementation: integrating junior high into primary education would improve curricula and teaching methods; for primary education, it would raise teacher qualifications and eliminate divides between primary and secondary education sectors. To adapt to social needs, supplementary education could be offered in the later phase of primary education, using flexible methods similar to those of the past.

Specialized productive capacity is cultivated through vocational education. Vocational categories vary with social needs, and individuals' vocational aptitudes emerge in youth—making senior secondary education the key period for vocational preparation. Education must ensure equal access to vocational training for all and address diverse individual needs through equitable systems.

Current senior high school programs, with academic tracks for university entrance, cater to an elite-oriented model; vocational tracks (agriculture, industry, commerce) focus narrowly on technical skills, serving the middle class in a capitalist society. Vocational schools today predominantly enroll students from families unable to afford higher education, regardless of their academic aspirations or abilities. Moreover, these schools rarely align with society's full range of vocational needs, while non-vocational education institutions function as profit-driven factories rather than nurturing talent for advancing scholarship. This leaves secondary students adrift, with educators unable to provide adequate guidance.

Separating secondary education into parallel general and vocational tracks—similar to the dual-track primary education system—fails to cultivate appropriately productive members for all and contradicts the principles of populism.

6.3 Remedial Education for School Dropouts

(1) Supplementary Education This should develop in parallel with the regular education system. For example, attached to institutions of higher education (universities and specialized colleges), there should be Type A supplementary schools, established for those unable to receive regular higher education. Attached to secondary schools (senior high schools), there should be Type B supplementary schools, for those unable to receive regular vocational education. Attached to the advanced stage of primary education, there should be Type C supplementary schools, for those unable to complete the regular advanced primary education. For details, reference can be made to my work Notes on Investigating Japan's Vocational Supplementary Education.

(2) Literacy Education for Illiterates This is designed for illiterate adults, such as the mass experimental schools. However, their establishment must be the responsibility of public institutions and public schools, which would make the endeavor cost-effective and easy to implement. If regarded as an independent project, it would either remain a mere formality or, if developed, easily become a substitute for primary education. As for literacy campaigns that rely solely on empty propaganda, they are of no practical benefit.

In summary, the transformation of education through the realization of education based on the Three Principles of the People requires further analysis and discussion. Nevertheless, the path to reform can be roughly glimpsed from the above.

Published in *Education Weekly*, Issues 2–9, from April 6 to June 1, 1932.

What I Hope for the Inaugural Work of the Kaifeng Education District

The regulations for the Kaifeng Education District have been formulated by the Henan Provincial Department of Education, which, in collaboration with Henan University, has submitted them to the provincial government for record and implementation. This is a matter deserving of great attention. However, no matter how much attention is paid, if the method of implementation is not understood, it will be no different from establishing so-called special municipalities or ordinary municipalities in various places, which merely adds a few people's rice bowls; or it will be like setting up various committees in general institutions, which are simply nominal, a case of covering one's ears while stealing a bell.

When it comes to starting the work, to cut the long story short, the focus should be on qualitative transformation rather than quantitative increase. I am not opposed to quantitative growth, nor am I unaware that without increasing the quantity, the goal of universal education for all cannot be achieved. However, if we solely focus on quantitative expansion, even after expending herculean efforts, education still cannot be popularized. Even if it could be popularized, whether it would count as genuine education is an even bigger question. It should be noted that universal education for all is not what ordinary people call universal education, which merely concerns quantity. If the essence of education still inherits the form of the ancient feudal society or imitates the model of Western capitalist societies, such education would only get worse as it is promoted, let alone talk about universal education for all.

Everyone recognizes the importance of education and feels that past education has failed. Nevertheless, what they consider important about education is the cause rather than learning; what they regard as learning is associated with universities and specialized studies, while primary education is seen as something trivial with no profound theories. Ordinary people think this way, and so do specialists, even those with doctoral, master's, or bachelor's degrees who claim to be education experts. They have no concrete research or experience in primary education but still boldly talk about so-called education.

To remedy the failure of past education, in terms of people's mindset, there is the so-called issue of spiritual education. In terms of making a living, there is the so-called issue of vocational education, which is also a material issue. What I want to say is not about how important these two issues are, but whether spiritual education can be effective through strict training or verbal lectures, and whether vocational education can be considered successful just by mastering professional skills. Moreover, how to integrate these two issues into one and manifest them in the teaching process, so that students' character is formed through acquiring knowledge and skills, and knowledge and skills do not become tools for people to compete for status. In terms of neo-Confucianism, this is the unity of knowledge and action; in terms of psychology, it is the unity of body and mind; in terms of teaching, it is the unity of teaching and discipline.

What has been said above is indeed a problem for education as a whole, but it must start from the basics. Therefore, if primary education is not thoroughly reformed, all schools will be in trouble. Adult supplementary education (i.e., mass experimental schools) in the current way can hardly be called education. However, what the dignitaries and scholars consider as the failure of education is only the problem of being unable to control young people and the problem of choosing subjects; they do not feel at all that all the facilities and various courses in schools have completely lost the true meaning of education. If readers do not believe this, just ask: are not those who talk about spiritual education now treading the path of restoring the old? Are not those who talk about vocational education treading the path of capitalist countries?

Now, focusing solely on primary schools, integrating the above two issues into one is what European and American countries are striving to experiment with. For example, the plan proposed by the Primary School Experimental Guidance Department also has the same tendency. However, due to various difficulties, it has not embarked on the right path. I hope that in this inaugural work, talents will be concentrated, all staff of the committee and all primary school teachers will cheer up, and under the leadership of capable leaders, they will earnestly do some relatively thorough experimental work. They should also conduct various investigations and collections to provide various teaching materials, and conduct detailed inspections of each school, make an overall plan, so that all schools can catch up. I particularly hope that the education administrative authorities will not stint on reasonable expenses, provide all the needs for creation, and not handle it as a routine matter. They should also carefully appoint committee members, preferring vacancies to inferior appointments, and not allow those who are unworthy of their positions. Now, I write down these two hopes at the beginning of the article, which is my small contribution.

Published in *Education Weekly*, Issue 3, April 13, 1932.

Contributions to the Primary School Teachers in Kaifeng

Gentlemen: The dilapidation of our country and the peril of our state are now thoroughly exposed for all to see. Although the important figures of the Party and the country declare that they will not lose the slightest bit of national sovereignty; yet, the current situation has reached such a point that events are beyond their control. No matter how loyal and dedicated they may be, they cannot safeguard the country's complete territory and rights. Our only hope lies solely in the survival of the state.

Under the current severe circumstances, specifically speaking, there are two approaches: the youth's advocacy of taking up arms to defend the country, and the advice from the esteemed gentlemen of promoting material science to save the state. If either of these can be achieved, or if both can proceed in parallel without conflict, they could indeed be policies for national survival. However, upon careful reflection, they are still like treating the head when the head aches and the foot when the foot hurts. In abstract terms, the call for sincere unity is the most grand-sounding slogan, but unfortunately, it remains too abstract.

Gentlemen: You are the only hope for nurturing the state, and it is also your sole responsibility, as well as the only way out for the Republic of China. At this point, no one in the country dares to openly say that education should not be pursued, yet few know how to conduct education and understand that primary education is the most important. Even those who repeatedly emphasize the importance of primary education only mean that everyone should receive education, without knowing what constitutes effective education. Especially those who specialize in educational research do not engage in practical research on primary education; while those actually engaged in primary education set aside educational theories when running schools. This is not me making lofty remarks; the facts are indeed so.

Speaking further about national issues, on one hand, people say that the moral standards of the world are not what they used to be, and on the other hand, that old ethics are oppressive. On one hand, there is advocacy for inherent morality, and on the other hand, it is despised as barbaric by nature. In particular, important figures in the government and party headquarters, who have mostly not even read through the academic records of the Song, Yuan, Ming, and Qing dynasties, merely pick up fragmented meanings from the Premier's teachings and advocate for China's old morality. Such contradictory statements each have their own positions and functions, and I will not criticize them for now. What I want to say is, how should we behave as individuals and as citizens? Is it like the lecture-style or reading-style methods used in ordinary schools, or the strict training methods like the Public Security Bureau's security laws used by most educators, which can achieve the goal? If we think they can, we should not oppose old-style education, let alone talk about educational theories and teaching methods. If we think they cannot, why do those engaged in education stick to the old ways? Is it really that just changing the organizational form counts as school reform? What is the difference between this and thinking that a government agency has adopted a committee system and thus achieved democratic politics, or that becoming an official of the Party and the country means it is a revolutionary government?

There is an old Chinese saying: "Enlighten the young to cultivate correctness." Modern psychology also tells us that "children's habits are mostly formed by the age of three or four." We need to know that the difficulty in running schools above the middle school level today is largely not due to the country itself but to a poor foundation. Not only is it harder to correct habits than to cultivate them, but even learning tools are getting worse day by day. Especially regarding physical and mental development, the higher the school level, the lower the average level. If we examine the general situation of students, most of the first and second graders in primary schools are more lively and make more progress than when they were at home. This is because, although ordinary schools are not entirely satisfactory, their environment is better than that of ordinary families. From then on, most students are infected with bad habits as they grow older. As a result, the knowledge they acquire is used solely for personal gain, or even becomes a tool for doing bad things. Looking at society from another perspective, social progress is becoming more and more complex day by day. Even ordinary people must have appropriate life skills to meet the needs of the times. Such life skills cannot be cultivated by just reading a few rigid books. If children are made to live under idolization from an early age, not only will dropouts only know a few rigid characters without any practical use, but even those who continue their studies will have most of their talents stifled, and day by day, they will seek a way out in wrong paths or fantasies. Let's just look at the top graduates from both Chinese and foreign schools today; how many of them have made inventions or creations? Moreover, those who do bad things and betray the country are mostly from the intellectual class. Today, more than 80% of the authoritative figures in the party and government are under 40 years old. Except for a few who came from a background of outlaws and have not received school education, even most of the military police and representatives of mass organizations have received education. If education were effective, the revolution would never have succeeded in this way.

Even imperialist countries rely on the development of national education and efforts to expand. I don't know if there is another fundamental way to implement democratic administration and subjugate first imperialism without urgently developing and reforming primary education. Although the vocational education and talent education advocated by the esteemed gentlemen are also beneficial, if basic education is ruined, even if we don't agree with the radicals' view that vocational education creates slaves for capitalists and talent education is a factory for the aristocratic class, the lack of basic knowledge and skills would make such distorted education do more harm than good.

Gentlemen: In our society where both the great and the small are poor, there is essentially no such thing as proletarian interests. However, for civil servants and intellectuals, the higher their salaries and positions, the more disconnected they are from the sufferings of the people. Their background is the bourgeois society, and their stance is dominated by power. After the revolution, all legislation and administration are still reformed by these people with high positions and large sums of money. They certainly do not deny primary education, but in their minds, there are only the magnificent undertakings admired by the world, and they do not take primary education seriously.

Gentlemen: Your lives are close to the common people. Your responsibility is to prepare the citizens, and the hope for the future of the state lies entirely on you. Even if the country is dilapidated, as long as the cultivated national capabilities can gradually balance with those of the world's states, even if there is temporary humiliation, the state will eventually revive.

Gentlemen: Do not think that your status is low; there is no group of people in society with more authority than you. The old and evil forces are subjugate n, and new and good forces are cultivated. Politics is only a form; in fact, it is mostly formed by the citizens nurtured by your consciousness. Only through the formation of your correct consciousness can there be a thorough transformation and bring society to light. However, I hope that you will rely on your insights and strength to transform society, follow the correct path of education, cultivate children, participate in society, and lay the foundation for social transformation. Do not harbor political ambitions and use educational opportunities as a tool for propaganda.

Gentlemen: Do not be discouraged either, thinking that because you are not doctors or bachelors, or university or specialized professors, it is difficult to conduct in-depth research. If you open the history of education, you will find that most educators gained their experience from primary schools. As long as you make appropriate preparations before each teaching session every week and every term, conduct appropriate inspections during the session, and reflect appropriately after the session, and verify everything with the educational principles and cases you usually study, over time, this will be the best material to contribute to the academic community of education.

Now I want to talk about how education can be effective. Aren't ordinary new youth constantly criticizing old-style education? I want to ask what the current popular teaching methods have that are different from the old lecture-style ones. Some claim to use the heuristic method, but what is the effectiveness of the answers obtained through questioning compared to the results of the old-style memorization? What's more, those who show off the so-called autonomous teaching—are children really not still in a passive position? In terms of content, teaching knowledge such as history and geography from books with the method of blindly copying and practicing characters is fundamentally useless for practical life. In particular, basic civic training is carried out through rigid and mysterious indoctrination. These methods are all tricks once played by Confucianists and Christians. They take them as the only way to new education, which has ruined education and even destroyed the Premier's teachings completely.

What I have said above does not cover the entire scope of education. There are two more points worthy of our study. One is that the ultimate goal of education is to shape children's character. I don't know how the standards of moral education can be established without connecting it with teaching. The other is that people's life experience is concrete and fluid. For the subject-based curriculum, which breaks down the entire experience one by one, with fixed teaching materials and fixed time, according to what standards can children's basic knowledge and skills be formed?

The slogans of your schools are all about child-centered education and nurturing democratic forces. Examine your implementation; apart from a few verbal lessons, are you not standing on a reactionary position? If you do not want to cultivate reactionary elements, you must change the orientation of education. In January of the 21st year (of the Republic of China), the Primary School Experimental Guidance Department published an experimental issue. Although it did not make a great contribution, it opened a broad road on that issue to achieve the goal of your slogans, which is perhaps wider and flatter than the new road from the South Gate to Longting. It is hoped that the primary school teachers in Kaifeng will work together to study it.

Published in *Henan Education Monthly*, Vol. 2, No. 7, April 1932.

Appeal to Compatriots: Propose June 6th as Teachers' Day

▲ Also known as the Double Sixth Festival!

▲ All people across the country should participate in the celebration together!

In social movements, it is common to designate a permanent commemorative day. For instance, Labor Day, Children's Day, and Women's Day all serve to unite the masses in striving for the improvement of the living status of a particular group. These not only directly benefit that group but also indirectly benefit the entire society. This is because people in society are often blinded by prejudices and content with the status quo, frequently failing to perceive the hardships in the lives of specific groups. Without widespread movements, it is impossible to change social trends and attitudes to achieve the effect of improvement. Hence, the establishment of commemorative days is indispensable.

We deeply feel that education personnel in China today bear an extremely heavy responsibility and face severe social criticism. However, their lives are highly unstable, their positions are precarious, and they lack opportunities for self-cultivation. All these factors affect their work, preventing them from fulfilling their responsibilities. This is not only the personal suffering of education personnel but also a great loss to the entire society.

It is common knowledge that the salaries of primary school teachers are insufficient to support their families. Even university and middle school teachers often face life crises due to delayed salary payments. When they fall ill, they cannot afford medical treatment, yet schools still withhold their salaries. When they are elderly and unable to handle heavy workloads, schools dismiss them from their positions. The cost of living and family burdens increase year by year, but schools have no system of seniority-based salary increments. Unfortunately, if they die in office, their families are left in poverty, with their wives and children suffering from cold and hunger, as schools have no pension provisions. As a result, the children of university professors cannot even enter universities, and the children of middle and primary school teachers cannot afford to attend middle or primary schools. What could be more unjust than this! This is why teachers' lives are extremely unstable and urgently need improvement.

Regarding the status of teachers, facts show that their retention or dismissal often depends on students' likes and dislikes and other special factors, regardless of their educational achievements or loyalty in work. They have no protection whatsoever. Furthermore, due to political changes, frequent replacements of school principals, partisan strife, and social exclusion, they often live in constant fear of losing their jobs overnight. This makes it impossible for them to make long-term plans or accumulate profound achievements, let alone engage in academic research or improve teaching. Even social employment is maintained by contracts, but teachers' appointments lack any guarantees. This is why teachers' positions are so precarious and urgently need improvement.

Moreover, the cultivation of excellent teachers entirely relies on social support. However, the common practice is to assess and eliminate teachers who are deemed insufficient in self-cultivation, with little effort made to remedy their shortcomings. For those with better self-cultivation, they are burdened with extremely heavy teaching tasks, leaving them no time for research. Such practices are tantamount to cutting off teachers' paths of self-improvement and wasting their valuable talents. As a result, even those with outstanding academic abilities will be permanently buried and unable to develop, while those with lesser abilities will never have the hope of advancement. This is not due to teachers' self-abandonment but rather the improper treatment by the state and society. Hence, teachers' lack of opportunities for professional development is an issue that urgently needs to be addressed.

Feeling deeply about this, we aim to unite people across the country to work together for a solution, hoping to draw the government's attention and arouse social awareness. We propose June 6th as Teachers' Day, so that we can pool wisdom and efforts to seek fundamental solutions. We urge all education personnel, whether primary, middle, or university teachers, as well as education administrators, to participate unanimously, so that we can achieve the effect of "unity is strength."

The reason for choosing June 6th is that it is also known as the "Double Sixth Festival," which is more appealing for advocacy. Moreover, it coincides with the end of the academic year, when plans for the next academic year are yet to be finalized. This allows us to put forward suggestions to educational authorities and voice our difficulties to society, hoping for gradual improvements year by year.

The goals of this festival movement are as follows: 1) Improving teachers' treatment; 2) Safeguarding teachers' status; 3) Enhancing teachers' opportunities for self-cultivation. These are just the outlines of the movement, highlighting its purposes. The detailed measures will depend on public opinion.

Although our voices may be weak, this issue is of profound significance to the rise and fall of national education and the stability of society. Thus, we dare not shirk the responsibility of advocating for it. Every compatriot in the country has children or younger generations, who, after entering school, entrust their education to teachers. Therefore, we believe that people will rise up to support and participate in this movement that is closely related to our common interests, becoming the backbone of education personnel.

We hereby solemnly declare this to all our compatriots across the country, hoping for your attention and understanding.

Signed by 352 people including Wang Shulin, Li Buqing, Li Qingsong, Wang Maozu, Tai Shuangqiu, Hu Shuyi, Xu Keshi, Ma Ketan, Xia Chengfeng, Zhang Yaoxiang, Zhang Fang, Zhang Gengxi, Cheng Qibao, Peng Baichuan, Meng Wentong, Zhao Zhenfu, Lu Jiye, Xie Xunchu, etc.

Published in *Education Weekly*, Issue 6, May 4, 1932.

A Document Submitted to the Ministry of Education by Li Buqing and Other Initiators of Teachers' Day

It is observed that in modern social reform movements, a permanent commemorative day is always established. For example, Labor Day, Children's Day, and Women's Day all serve to unite the masses in striving for the improvement of the living status of a certain group of people. They directly benefit this group and indirectly benefit the entire society, which is indeed a noble intention and an excellent approach.

We, Buqing and others, deeply feel that education personnel in China today bear an extremely heavy responsibility and face severe social criticism. However, their lives are highly unstable, their positions are precarious, and they lack opportunities for self-cultivation. All these factors are sufficient to affect their work and prevent them from fulfilling their responsibilities. It is only by establishing a permanent festival that we can change social trends and attitudes to achieve the effect of improvement. We respectfully present this to Your Excellency, the Minister.

Since the separation of officials and teachers, what has been advocated by custom is the position with peace, wealth, honor and glory. As for the prevalent trend, those who can amass huge fortunes through industry and commerce also hold superior power in society. The so-called great scholars and pure Confucian scholars, when they live in an unfavorable era, often suffer from displacement and are almost disdained by the world. Even if they have works, some still await recognition from prominent figures, and countless numbers of their hidden virtues and obscure brilliance are eventually lost without being known.

If teaching ends up like this, unless one is an extraordinary person, who would be willing to teach students with peace of mind, only to end up in poverty, sorrow and death of old age? Even though university professors have relatively generous monthly salaries, compared with those who seek favorable positions or engage in speculative businesses and earn tens of thousands of gold a year, the difference is as vast as between the sky and the earth. It goes without saying that the salaries of primary and middle school teachers are insufficient to support their families.

The reason for this situation, it can be said, is that most occupations take ordinary life as the standard. However, if education is merely a means to make a living, then those engaged in education, unable to become bureaucrats due to insufficient influence, will inevitably become like petty officials; and unable to make education a business, they will inevitably turn it into a form of peddling. Under such circumstances, expecting them to concentrate on self-cultivation, set an example for others, is extremely difficult.

Moreover, with incomplete regulations on treatment and delayed payment of salaries becoming a common practice, it is no wonder that most teachers are restless, always ready to change jobs at the sight of better opportunities. This has gradually become a common trend. This is from the perspective of education itself.

As for the political trend, it is increasingly moving towards the development of people's rule. If we do not base it on education, people's rule will be nothing but a mere pretext. All constructions of the country and society will not be planned in accordance with education, nor will they rely on education for supply. In the worst case, construction will become a means for officials to seek profits, or go against the goal of social and economic interests.

Therefore, the way to remedy this is that both the government and the people must regard education as the center for promoting political reform and social transformation. Only then will they know how to respect and select teachers. And teachers themselves must cultivate their virtues, establish themselves and help others, regard education as a lifelong career, and enable education to have permanent value. There is no more important task at present than this.

Having realized this, we, Buqing and others, have invited education colleagues from Beijing, Shanghai, Kaifeng and other places to discuss repeatedly. We all believe that establishing a Teachers' Day is an urgent matter. The date of this festival is proposed to be June 6th, because the "Double Sixth" is easy to advocate. Moreover, it coincides with the end of the academic year when all plans are being finalized, so that we can put forward suggestions to the party and government authorities and explain our work to society in general, hoping for gradual improvement year by year. As for the detailed measures, they await the formulation by the Ministry.

For these reasons, we submit this petition, requesting Your Excellency, the Minister, to approve the designation of June 6th as Teachers' Day, following the example of Labor Day, Children's Day, Women's Day, etc., and issue an order to the whole country to hold celebrations uniformly. We present this with urgency and await your decision with great anxiety.

Published in *Education Weekly*, "Special Issue on Teachers' Day," June 6, 1932.

Why do we need to designate a Teachers' Day?

The reason we want to establish a Teachers' Day is not to speak up for teachers, but indeed to plan for the country. This festival embodies the significance of the state's new life. Let me present three reasons for it:

First, from the perspective of teachers themselves. The current political evils, directly speaking, are caused by warlords and politicians. Fundamentally, they are all people who have received education; some have aided tyrants in doing evil, while others have turned a blind eye, leading to such phenomena. Teachers throughout history must bear responsibility for this. To make every teacher clearly recognize their responsibilities, strive to cultivate their virtues, and set an example for others while improving themselves, merely improving their treatment and safeguarding their rights is not enough. It is necessary for the entire society to explicitly demonstrate a collective will in this regard. Only when teachers feel that they have an inescapable responsibility will they not shirk it; and only when they receive a kind of spiritual solace will they redouble their efforts. Therefore, the establishment of Teachers' Day is more profound and meaningful than even the Christian Sunday.

Second, from the perspective of society. China has always valued scholars, originally because scholars were regarded as people with knowledge and moral integrity. However, since scholars began to be seen solely as a ladder to wealth and status, they have ceased to be true scholars. Nowadays, this tendency has worsened: knowledge is no longer valued, and only those with money and power are recognized. Apart from bureaucrats and active-duty soldiers, wealthy merchants and big entrepreneurs occupy the most important positions in society. Recently, workers and students have also gained superior influence through organizing groups. Only teachers are in a precarious position: they are neither among the elite nor the common people. If they join workers' organizations, they are dismissed as "parasites" because they are not manual laborers; if they associate with students, they are scorned as "old fogeys" because their student days are long gone. Though they are called "outstanding individuals," without party membership, they lose their qualification to lead and almost have no independent rights among the people. The people talk about social reform every day, yet they deprive the core figures of society of their stance. Just imagine what kind of country this would become. To correct this mistake, we must uphold the original essence of valuing scholars to restore the national ethos. Therefore, by establishing a Teachers' Day following the example of Labor Day, social attitudes will change, and social trends will naturally shift.

Third, from the political perspective. The concepts of "rule by virtuous men" and "strong government" have become things of the past; they have been thoroughly exploited by ambitious politicians and no longer have any value of existence. What we hope for in the future is a "scientific government," where all its organizations and facilities are based on real facts and form correct ideals. All officials, high and low, should be rooted in professional knowledge and scholarship. This echoes the ancient idea of the unity of officials and teachers, the so-called "those who excel in learning should enter officialdom, and those who excel in officialdom should continue learning" — the two cannot be separated. The failure of the previous period of political tutelage was entirely due to the lack of learning and skills, falling into the trap of "governing the country in the same way as conquering it by force." The intellectual class has simply become a tool for the authorities. Instead of empty disputes over constitutional government and following the old path of false people's rule, it is better to vigorously promote education, integrating politics and scholarship. If we establish a Teachers' Day to show respect for teachers and emphasis on learning as the foundation of building a state, then politics shaped by scholarship can gradually achieve our goal, leading us together toward a world of great harmony.

What I have said above does not fully cover the significance of Teachers' Day. However, these three reasons alone make it necessary to establish this commemorative day as soon as possible for the sake of the country. Teachers, rise up!

Published in *Education Weekly*, "Special Issue on Teachers' Day," June 6, 1932.

Explanation of the Name "Kaifeng"[10]

Kaifeng, historically a territory of the ancient Zheng State, was built by Duke Zhuang, and its name literally means "opening up and consolidating borders." At a time when foreign aggression is pressing in, and our territories beyond the Pass are shrinking by hundreds of miles each day, we think of how our ancestors opened up and secured these borders, bequeathing them to later generations—yet now we can barely hold onto what we have. Let us read The Last Lesson by the French author Alphonse Daudet, or recall how King Goujian of Yue nurtured his people and prepared for revenge through education and governance. Who could fail to be roused by such examples, and seek to inspire our fellow countrymen?

The Shuowen Jiezi (Explaining Characters and Analyzing Forms) states: "Feng (to consolidate) refers to enfeoffing nobles with land." Its extended meaning includes "to strengthen" or "to solidify." "Kai (to open)" means "to stretch out"—as in stretching a bowstring. Now that our military and political reforms are complete, all efforts at national reconstruction must first eradicate feudalistic thinking to cleanse our state's ills, and break the mindset of complacent isolation to forge ahead. With national crisis looming, our state must not wait passively for destruction. We must "open up" to strengthen the weak, and "enlighten" to awaken the ignorant. If we neglect educational experimentation and rely solely on propaganda, it is like "painting a cake to satisfy hunger." If education remains stuck in old routines, focused only on superficial order,

10 This article was written by Li Lianfang for the inaugural issue of *Kaifeng Ten-Day Journal* (which was renamed *Kaifeng Education Ten-Day Journal* after publishing 12 issues). The original title is *Explanation of the Name*. ——Translator's note

or if we tout experimentation but pursue it piecemeal and fragmented, it is like "climbing a tree to catch fish."

This publication is named Kaifeng, and like an arrow on a drawn bow, it is not shot without purpose. We hope readers, upon hearing its name, will grasp its meaning: national reconstruction depends fundamentally on educational experimentation in primary schools and among the people. This is more crucial than slogans like "saving the state through air power", "saving the state through science", or "saving the state through industry." Its significance extends far beyond the local city of Kaifeng.

If the educational experiments advocated in Kaifeng can arouse sympathy from educators nationwide for national rejuvenation, and if we work together to transform our four hundred million compatriots from closed-mindedness to enlightenment—recovering our territories and advancing toward a world of great harmony—then this publication will have fired the first arrow of this mission.

Published in *Kaifeng Ten-Day Journal*, Volume 1, Issue 1, November 1, 1932.

Textbook Research[11]

Opening Remarks

Today, I am here to talk with you all about textbook research. Textbooks are a means to achieve educational goals, and education is an aspect of national administration. Whether textbooks are appropriate or not directly relates to the quality of education and indirectly affects the rise and fall of the country. Although the current educational goals in China are very new, the methods still follow the old path, so there has been no significant progress. Now, we will conduct research on textbooks in the hope of finding appropriate educational methods to serve as the basis for improving education.

1. Trends in Education

1.1 Errors

In the past, textbook research was subsumed under teaching methods, focusing on the psychologization of textbooks—exploring what is possible, desirable, or actionable. This cannot be deemed entirely wrong. Education began to emerge as a science with Herbart, and it has evolved and advanced ever since. However, over time, only formalistic frameworks remain, leading to the following two errors:

(1) Matching specific teaching methods to specific textbooks. Schools generally categorize textbooks into those focused on knowledge, skills, or morality, emphasizing organization for knowledge-based materials, practice for skill-based ones, and reasoning for morality-based ones. While we cannot deny the unique nature of different textbooks,

11 From July 1 to August 7, 1932, Li Lianfang was invited by Henan Provincial Rural Normal School (Baiquan, Huixian County) to give lectures on "Overview of Rural Education" and "Administration of Rural Schools." This article is a part of his lectures, transcribed by Wang Yuzai.

forcing inappropriate textbooks to fit rigid teaching methods—such as mechanical instruction or "candy-coated" teaching—will never yield good results.

(2) Using specific textbooks to cultivate specific abilities. A single textbook is interconnected in multiple ways and cannot be arbitrarily divided. The formation of a character trait is a multi-faceted process that cannot rely on a single aspect. Past teaching, based on the biases of faculty psychology, used vague standards like imagination, judgment, and aesthetics to arbitrarily split textbooks, hoping that different materials would cultivate different abilities. For example, using "cleanliness textbooks" to teach children cleanliness, or "patriotism textbooks" to foster patriotism—focusing only on tools while ignoring inherent meaning—is truly inappropriate.

Although formal teaching methods (the five-stage teaching method) and faculty psychology are things of the past, their traditional influence persists, posing a major obstacle to implementing new teaching methods.

New project-based learning, influenced by the traditional five-stage method, has also become rigid in form (e.g., fixed processes like construction, appreciation, research, and practice) and fails to be applied flexibly. Some even rigidly assign specific processes to specific units, which is extremely erroneous. Notions like "subject-based projects" or "department-based projects" also follow the old path of faculty psychology.

The Dalton Plan has not escaped the confines of faculty psychology either.

Educators in China lack systematic research on teaching methods, so even when adopting new approaches, they still follow old paths. Below is a diagram centered on textbooks:

(1) 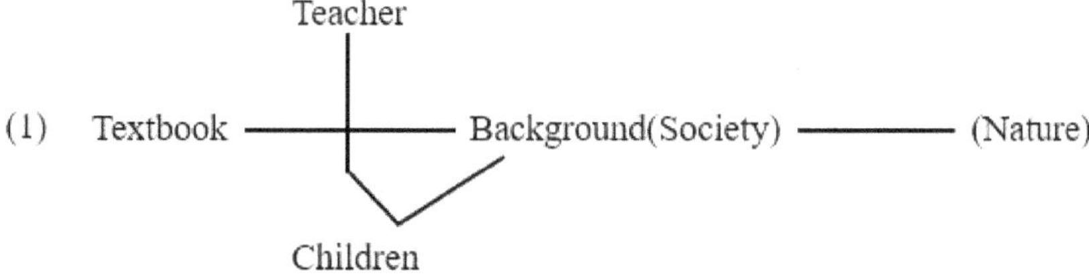

(2) 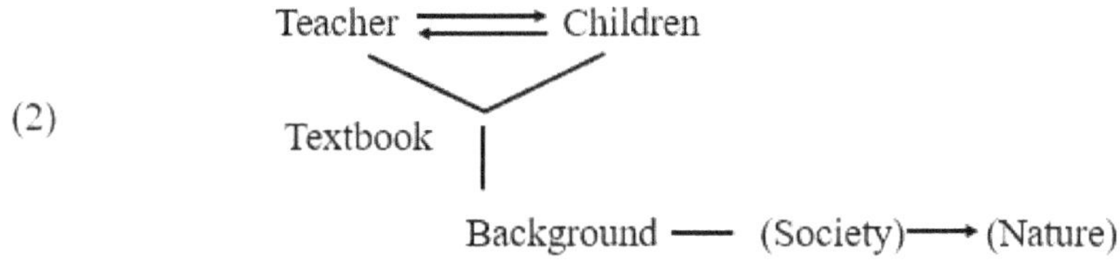

1.2 Shift in Direction

(1) The traditional mistake of only changing the signboard without altering the content has been mentioned earlier.

(2) The mistake in the formation of fragmented teaching materials. Current education, in an attempt to meet individual needs, compiles various teaching materials based on differences between urban education, rural education, and education for merchants, workers, and farmers. However, such an approach that merely goes around in circles with the teaching materials themselves will not yield good results.

Current teaching is static rather than dynamic, book-based rather than practical, fixed rather than flexible. These issues cannot be solved by merely addressing teaching materials. To break away from static, book-based, and fixed teaching, we must distinguish between tools and raw materials.

(3) The future shift in direction: "Environmental adaptation." As mentioned above, there are common mistakes in current teaching. Going forward, the direction must be changed, with the primary principle being

"environmental adaptation." Teachers must provide an environment for students, enabling them to develop in multiple aspects. Children with different aptitudes and abilities should all receive appropriate and individualized development, so that "after receiving education, students can make correct judgments on anything in society." By cultivating students' ability to transfer skills, they will never be unable to survive no matter how rapidly society changes in the future.

2. Subject-based and Integrated Approaches

Current curricula are entirely dominated by subjects. Below is an analysis of the origins and evolutionary trends of subjects:

2.1 Origins of Subjects

2.1.1 Evolution from higher education

(1) The emergence of formal education. Formal education evolved from informal education in the past. The apprenticeship system in Chinese shops, for example, was a form of informal education, where learning was fully aligned with real-life needs. In primitive societies, people learned production skills and group rules within families or communities, characterized by three features: shared living, shared recreation, and collective defense against threats. Its educational goal was collective survival, with an ethos of group orientation. As times changed, this goal of collective survival gradually faded, and education became a pastime for individuals.

As society aged, cultural accumulation grew, and communication expanded, preserving and advancing such experiences could no longer be achieved through direct participation. Thus, formal, organized education emerged.

Over time, accumulated experiences became too vast for any single person to transmit entirely. Instead, specialists were tasked with teaching categorized knowledge, gradually evolving into a subject-based system.

(2) The invention of writing. Writing is a powerful tool for exchanging and transmitting knowledge. After its invention, written records of social experiences multiplied. For ease of reference, these records were categorized into books, giving rise to subjects.

(3) Specialization in scholarship. Developing social undertakings required specialists, who passed down categorized knowledge to subsequent generations. This advanced scholarship further—examples include Western rhetoric, geometry, and grammar, as well as China's ritual officials, music officials, and historians, all of whom were specialists.

Today's categorized subjects, evolved from higher education by narrowing the scope of advanced disciplines, reflect both experts' insights and analytical syntheses. They represent logical frameworks of knowledge, not real phenomena; outcomes, not processes. While suitable as tools for adults, they are irrational for teaching children.

2.1.2 Evolution from social changes

Greater social needs led to more subjects:

(1) Increased categories: e.g., national language, arithmetic, history-geography, nature studies, drawing, and handicrafts.

(2) Changes in scope:

A. Fragmentation: e.g., dividing "national language" into four subjects—national language, history, geography, and natural history.

B. Merging: e.g., combining history, geography, civics, and hygiene into a "social studies" subject; merging natural history, physics-chemistry, and physiology into "natural sciences."

(3) Qualitative changes: e.g., from "classic reading" to "moral cultivation," "civics," and "party doctrine"; from "classical Chinese" to "national language"; from "drawing" to "visual arts" and "fine arts"; from "handicrafts" to "practical arts" and "work activities."

In summary, the evolutionary trends of subjects are: 1) categories expanding from simplicity to complexity; 2) content broadening from narrow to wide; 3) activities shifting from static to dynamic, from sensory reception to physical and manual engagement. How to integrate these into unified learning that adapts to children's needs? This demands our careful study.

2.2 Mergers and Splits in Primary School Subjects

Analyzing learning content by educational goals reveals three dimensions: I. tools; II. knowledge and skills; III. character. Every subject encompasses knowledge, skills, and tools, with integrated knowledge and skills forming character. The relationship between these three in primary school subjects throughout their evolution is as follows:

(1) Knowledge and skills embedded in tools. This was tied to the social context. In underdeveloped industrial and commercial societies, people led simple lives; basic literacy and knowledge sufficed for daily needs. Moral standards were rooted in ancient maxims (ethics were critical in patriarchal societies), and memorizing classical texts fulfilled this purpose. Thus, primary curricula unified tools, knowledge, skills, and character. However, this embeddedness of knowledge in tools trapped Chinese education in a book-centric model.

- Subjects in ordinary primary schools (1903, Guangxu 29th year): Moral cultivation, composition, calligraphy, geography, arithmetic, classic reading, history, and physical education.

- Subjects in elementary primary schools: Compulsory—moral cultivation, classic reading, national language, arithmetic, physical education; Elective—drawing, handicrafts, music.

(2) Separation of knowledge/skills from tools. In underdeveloped societies, curricula focused on liberal arts, with no distinct separation between knowledge-based and skill-based subjects. Though "practical schools for the poor" existed in some cities, they were rare. After the 15th-century Industrial Revolution, traditional education grew obsolete, prompting more practical subjects in primary schools. In China, during the late Qing (Guangxu and Xuantong reigns), elementary schools lacked natural science courses. After the Republic's founding (1912), the Ministry of Education mandated subjects: national language, moral cultivation, arithmetic, physical education, music, handicrafts, and drawing—marking the start of separating knowledge/skills from tools.

In 1923, the National Education Federation meeting in Yunnan resolved primary subjects: national language, arithmetic, society, history, geography, civics, hygiene, nature studies, practical arts, visual arts, music, and physical education. Knowledge-based and skill-based subjects now stood as equal, separate entities.

This separation expanded students' knowledge but shattered educational unity, complicated school organization, divided teaching from moral education, and reduced opportunities to practice foundational tools.

3.Tools embedded in knowledge and skills. Tools are foundational to understanding all sciences but are boring to learn. To spark children's interest in symbolic tools, learning must stem from their needs. The 1929 provisional curriculum standards mandated primary subjects: party doctrine, national language, society, nature studies, arithmetic, work, fine arts, music, and physical education. These standards detailed teaching methods for each subject, emphasizing curriculum integration and project-based learning—thus embedding tool instruction within knowledge and skill acquisition.

From late Qing to 1929, primary curricula progressed steadily. However, two persistent patterns emerged:

One is Book-centric focus: Chinese curriculum designers often copied foreign models, never breaking free from rigid textual frameworks despite changes.

The other is Subject-based division: The entire curriculum remained rooted in subject divisions; despite adjustments, its core structure and traditional influence persisted.

Under a fragmented curriculum, critical questions arise: Can educational unity be preserved? Can character development be addressed? Is school life holistic? Should teaching and moral education be separated? These demand urgent attention.

3. Drawbacks of Subject-Based Division

Subject division is a method used by highly educated individuals to organize research materials for the convenience of study. However, it is ill-suited for primary education, which should be centered on life. Its drawbacks are as follows:

3.1 Tendency toward formalism

The content of each subject consists of existing materials, which are the crystallization of scholars' insights. Not only do children find it difficult to understand such content, but even if they can understand it, they may not be able to apply it in practice. Under the subject-based system, an integrated thing is split into many fragments based on its different properties. How can such teaching help solve specific problems? Moreover, when compiling curricula, the editors of each subject often determine the content and difficulty level by academic year based on their own subjective opinions, completely ignoring the integrity of life. As for issues like how much time should be allocated to local teaching materials, they are not even worth asking about in reality.

Focusing solely on the teaching materials themselves can never meet children's current needs. Their only effect is to make children acquire fragmented knowledge or abilities. Using such unchanging content to cope with the rapidly changing social life is absolutely impossible. Then, what is the significance of such education?!

3.2 Failure to form concrete experiences

Everything has its own characteristics, and these characteristics are manifested through the whole. Although any part of a thing may seem small, it is interrelated with other parts. When children first enter society, they have little experience of what they hear and see. Their perception of the universe often takes the parts they have personally witnessed as the whole. To make children's responses to things meaningful, valuable, and effective, we must stimulate them with concrete things.

Wisdom is formed through emotions and actions. Learning fragmented things has nothing to do with emotions or actions. No matter what things are divided into different subjects, they are only parts or aspects. If things are disassembled, children cannot form concrete experiences during learning, and there will never be good results.

3.3 Diminishing interest in learning

Regarding the understanding of interest, people generally have three misunderstandings:

(1) Misunderstanding about teaching materials themselves: They think that teaching materials that are vivid, changing, and with a humorous touch are interesting, otherwise, they are not.

(2) Misunderstanding about children themselves: They think that things that conform to children's psychology should be learned by children. In fact, what children like is not necessarily suitable for them, and most children do not necessarily like the same thing.

(3) Misunderstanding about motivation: Nowadays, most teachers or those who compile teaching methods try to arouse motivation with a few witty words. In fact, this is a big mistake, because motivation cannot be aroused by empty words.

True interest lies in persistent efforts, which is intrinsic rather than imposed from the outside. To make children have persistent efforts in learning, two conditions must be met: (1) relevance to themselves, that is, being able to satisfy their own desires; (2) a connection between the expected results and their attached desires.

The subject-based structure does not meet these two conditions, nor can it show the integrity of things. Therefore, children will never have a strong interest in it. Furthermore, the problem of diminishing learning interest caused by time allocation is even more unavoidable.

4. Value of Integrated Curriculum

4.1 Holistic life Under subject-based curricula, the learning process is often lost. An integrated curriculum teaches through holistic life experiences, encompassing both material and spiritual dimensions. Within a single unit, it coordinates relationships across various aspects, avoiding the drawback of fragmentation.

4.2 Attitudes, ideals, and knowledge as co-attributes of teaching materials Attitudes and ideals hold crucial positions in teaching. Subject-based instruction focuses solely on knowledge, neglecting attitudes and ideals. In integrated teaching, appropriate attitudes are required to carry out practical tasks during activities; planning and allocation begin with an overarching theme, generating specific issues through autonomous thinking. This approach ensures balanced attention to attitudes, ideals, and knowledge.

4.3 Coordination of action and reason Subject-based teaching separates body from mind, knowledge from ability, and in-class learning from out-of-class experiences. Integrated teaching seeks to unify body and mind, align knowledge with action, and merge in-class and out-of-class learning into a seamless whole.

4.4 Centered teaching materials Integrated teaching materials have a central focus, eliminating the problem of fragmentation and disorganization.

4.5 Taking local materials as a starting point In the past, many educators emphasized intuitionism and sensationalism but leaned excessively toward analyzing objects, rendering their value limited. Integrated teaching is rooted in the environment: it enables children to understand the significance of actions toward things within their surroundings, then expands to help them utilize and control the environment. Such cultivated wisdom remains applicable throughout life.

4.6 Clarification of large-unit project-based learning What distinguishes project-based curricula from others lies in their use of large units. The characteristics of such units are:

(1) They are not isolated facts;

(2) They are not a hodgepodge of facts;

(3) They are not confined to 20-minute or 40-minute lessons;

(4) They are not simplistic outlines;

(5) They are not fixed schedules or rigid principles.

5. Basic Classification of Teaching Materials

Purpose: All things that can control the environment and become life issues are either matters or objects. Individual things belong to either the natural or social realm. However, learning issues are not this simple. From an educational perspective, most are socially significant, and society is closely connected to nature. In the past, children were forced to learn abstract concepts such as morality and civics, which were disconnected from concrete matters and objects—this is highly inappropriate.

For learning to form a unit, we must focus on two aspects: (1) the teaching materials themselves; (2) the learning context—whether attention is focused generally or individually.

Tools beyond society and nature must be integrated with society and nature to form practical tasks.

(1) Raw Materials spatial: Nature (school gardens, fields, mountains, waters, forests, scenic spots, natural phenomena) and society (bodies, peer interactions, neighborhoods, families, schools, historical sites, temples, villages, roads, factories, shops, public institutions, public constructions, charitable organizations, notices, newspapers). Temporal: Past and present. Categories: Household affairs, school affairs, occupations, etc.

Ancient classical education and modern vocational education both carry class biases, which is a major reason students lack interest in gardening. This harmful phenomenon must be corrected immediately. We should help children develop ethical thinking through activities and enable them to learn agriculture and understand their environment through project-based learning.

(2) Tools Substance: National language: Characters, calligraphy models; Arithmetic: Numbers, terms, counting tools; Music: Lyrics, scores. Usage: National language: Grammar, syntax, writing; Arithmetic: Four operations, integers, fractions, decimals, units of measurement; Work: Tool usage, manufacturing methods; Physical education: Basic skills.

Substance and usage are inseparable. No form of usage (whether involving fingers or the body) can exist independently of substance. In integrated teaching, raw materials are dynamic, while tools are unified and fixed. Tool learning must be embedded in overall activities, allowing children to develop basic abilities through practice.

(3) Special Exercises. In traditional teaching, subjects are isolated, and knowledge is separated from practice. Educators often use isolated training—having children practice difficult parts of the curriculum independently, which causes great frustration. In integrated teaching, to cultivate children's basic habits, long-term and short-term tasks are designed, with training integrated into regular units. For harder knowledge or skills, separate practice units are created.

(4) Commonalities and Specialties. Primary education involves debates about commonalities and specialties, as follows:

(a) Foundation of learning: We reject the view that primary school is merely preparation for secondary education or going to a higher school. In reality, not all primary graduates continue to secondary school; we can only say primary education is closely linked to the basics of learning.

(b) Preparation for life: This is an outdated notion, inconsistent with modern educational principles. Teaching children adult knowledge is wrong, but we cannot deny that primary education relates to adult life.

(c) National education: Primary education aims to foster shared perspectives and abilities among all citizens, but this does not require unified textbooks. Shared goals can be achieved even with diverse materials.

(d) Educational administration: Unified textbooks make it easier for authorities to assess education—this is undeniable. However, local conditions must be accommodated without violating core principles.

(e) Vocational issues: In industrially advanced countries with fine-grained division of labor, many advocate adding vocational subjects (agriculture, industry, commerce) for efficiency. However, primary education should help children recognize shared life goals; it can only adapt generally, not use specialized materials to meet individual needs.

In summary, integrated teaching uses diverse raw materials with unified goals. Under the same objectives, different materials adapt to children of different grades and environments—this approach avoids major errors.

6. Basic Designs

Design-based teaching is essentially about dealing with certain things or objects, but the natural process cannot be ignored. Here, we will elaborate on the two aspects of things and objects:

Making something:

(1) Its significance lies beyond the goal (e.g., the purpose of a task is for exhibition);

(2) The work produced at that time serves as a tool for activities (practical tools for games);

(3) Needs arise from certain tasks or contact with the environment—for example, raising livestock requires a birdcage, and writing requires a notebook.

Doing something:

(1) The entire activity process is tasked with achieving the goal;

(2) Specific activities emerge under a general goal;

(3) Playful actions achieve the desired purpose, such as story performances, real-life simulations, postman role-plays, or small store designs.

Regarding something:

(1) Observation is the main task, such as visiting a meeting or a place;

(2) Experimentation is the main task, such as testing seed germination.

Regarding some matter:

(1) Investigation is the main task, such as surveying the surroundings of the school;

(2) Collection is the main task, such as collecting books, pictures, physical objects, or flower seeds.

"Making something" and "doing something" are objective, where activities generate problems; "regarding something" and "regarding some matter" are subjective, where problems generate activities. These two aspects promote each other, ensuring the continuity of activities.

Concluding Remarks

Design-based teaching is a more progressive teaching method at present. In studying design-based teaching, we should, on the one hand, clearly understand its theories, on the other hand, start with small issues for experimentation, and simultaneously adopt and utilize other new methods. Only in this way can design-based teaching become increasingly refined, and the future of education gradually shine with brightness.

Appendix: Reference Books on Project-Based Teaching Methods

1. *Outline of Educational Philosophy*, by John Dewey, translated by Meng Xiancheng, Commercial Press;

2. *On Soviet Primary School Curriculum*, translated by Cui Zaiyang, Commercial Press;

3. *The New School in Europe*, by Carleton Washburne, translated by Tang Xianzhi, Zhonghua Book Company;

4. *Schools of Tomorrow*, by John Dewey, translated by Zhu Luonong and Pan Zinian, Commercial Press;

5. *Project-Based Teaching Methods in Primary Education*, by Shen Youqian, Zhonghua Book Company;

6. *Project-Based Teaching Methods*, by Yang Lian, Zhonghua Book Company;

7. *Essentials of Project-Based Teaching Methods*, by Cao Chu, Zhonghua Book Company;

8. *On Organizing Primary School Curriculum with Project-Based Approach*, translated by Zheng Zonghai and Shen Zishan, Commercial Press.

Published in *Rural Reconstruction*, Volume 1, Issue 6, September 1932.

Slogans for "Children's Day" in Kaifeng Education Experimental Zone

1. Children of the whole state, unite!
2. Children are the future masters of society.
3. To belittle children's education is to destroy the lifeblood of the state.
4. Children are not appendages of their parents.
5. Long live Children's Day!

Published in *Kaifeng Experimental Education Monthly*, Volume 1, 1993.

Declaration on the Establishment of the Kaifeng Education Experimental Zone

In general, a state that has enjoyed the longest and most glorious history in the world of survival competition must possess its own distinctive characteristics that enable it to stand on its own. When it is in decline, external forces can conquer its country but cannot annihilate the state itself. For although the government that leads to the state's downfall is formed by the state, if the national characteristics do not perish along with it, the state's revival can still be expected.

Since the founding of the Huaxia (Chinese) state, our people have promoted etiquette and education, developing into a great country. Though we went through disturbances by the Five Barbarians, and usurpations by the Yuan and Qing dynasties, we regained our territories before long and achieved invisible assimilation of the conquerors. In the past, the cultural level of our state was far higher than that of other states. Even if we were temporarily suppressed by military force, we ultimately overcame them with our superior culture. The change of dynasties only shook the ruling class and had nothing to do with the people's livelihood. Hence, the ancient teaching "He who cherishes us is our sovereign; he who oppresses us is our enemy" remained valid even when the ruler changed. Nowadays, the times have changed drastically. Due to the underdevelopment of politics, the inherent culture of our country has shown increasingly obvious cracks. Western science, in conjunction with capitalism and imperialism, is advancing with each passing day. Its overflowing influence is enough to shake up countries that are complacent and conservative. People with shallow knowledge, dazzled and enchanted, copy the appearance while discarding the essence, wanting to destroy all our inherent traditions. Up to now, this has become a fashion among the intellectual class, to the extent that some even regard the four cardinal virtues of propriety, justice, integrity, and shame as poisonous remnants of feudal ethics. This trend is even more intense than the phenomenon in the Northern Qi Dynasty where children learned the Xianbei language, or that of the Roman nobles imitating the Greek style.

The Book of Documents says: "They annex the weak, attack the ignorant, seize the chaotic, and insult the dying." If the decline of our country is indeed caused by the inherent nature of the entire state, then we would be like sheep and pigs at the mercy of others, and there would be no such thing as national crisis. If not, then we are humans just like others. For example, the exiled Jewish state can still survive by attaching themselves to other countries, unlike the Red Indians who have been completely wiped out. Why? Because their state has its own distinctive characteristics for independence.

The characteristics of our state, such as perseverance and hard work, magnanimity, and loyalty, have been nurtured by the ethos of our ancestors and influenced by the vast land, becoming social heredity over time. It is obvious that through their unity, they tamed the ancient barbarian states, and through their individuality, they competed with today's civilized states. In particular, social discipline and national decrees are all formed based on ethical concepts. Now that the world is interconnected, the tools for humans to adapt to the times cannot remain unchanged and rigid. However, regarding reform and improvement, political revolution can only change the form, while the subtle transformation must be achieved through education. This cannot be managed overnight, nor can it rely on politicians who are skilled in manipulation to achieve national liberation and cope with the current hardships.

Furthermore, regarding education, ancient education focused on written characters, which was determined by the times. However, the required tools and the way of being a person were acquired through memorization. Moreover, teachers were supposed to pass on the way, teach knowledge, and resolve doubts; mere memorization was not enough to be a teacher. Therefore, teaching and moral education were combined, and knowledge and practice were not separated. With the rise of the imperial examination system, the tradition of teaching was abandoned, but the lecture system in academies still retained some of the old traditions. When European culture spread eastward, the imperial examination was abolished and schools were established, which coincided with the spread of Western intellectualism. In terms of principles, utilitarianism was advocated, and all subjects were included. In terms of methods, formality was emphasized, with clear stages. The so-called learning psychology was entirely used for understanding knowledge. Those called good teachers were nothing more than force-feeding like stuffing ducks or cajoling like giving candies. In human life, emotions are the source of all actions. The internal or external responses of the body system are closely related to neural impulses. In ancient times, education was based on established teachings, emphasizing restraining anger and desires, which indeed made learners feel that life was cold, and naive and lively children might even feel incompatible. In particular, emotions must be controlled by reason, and reason is actually a product of knowledge. However, if we ignore the correlation of the overall physiology of the human body, knowledge may become a tool for individuals to do evil, and emotions will remain in a state of impulsive life. This is why today's strongest countries, despite their extremely civilized appearance, still have the whole state satisfying themselves with beastly instincts, all due to this unhealthy education.

As for knowledge, if we analyze it into categories, they are separate parts of an integrated thing. The logical system is the arrangement after analyzing things. Regarding the former, all our interactions with the world involve dealing with integrated things. If learning is all about separate parts, common sense and experience are enough to prove whether such fragmented experience can form a comprehensive effect, or if it can, whether it can form an immediate effect. Although we cannot experience every action of dealing with the environment during learning, we must cultivate the ability to deal with integrated things so that we can control the environment and be at ease wherever we are. Regarding the latter, when we understand various things, we all expect to have logical thinking. But this is the final process and must arise from practical experience, so that what we gain is not just the learning of language and characters. Today's education, even in the teaching and learning of knowledge, is still in a state of confusion and groping. Even if the selected teaching materials are practical, the process is wrong, and it is rare that learners can truly absorb them.

Education in our country is particularly guilty of copying the appearance while discarding the essence. In terms of system, we take that built on bourgeois and nationalist foundations as a model, without any implication of implementing people's politics. In terms of teaching, learning and moral education are separated, school curricula are not connected with social activities, knowledge and ability improvement have no relation to personality perfection, teachers treat teaching as selling goods, and students take entering higher education as a way to raise their social status. On the one hand, various regulations are restrictive, all of which are enough to suppress individuality; on the other hand, various competitions are created, all of which induce selfish motives. In a society without a foundation of the rule of law, filled with an atmosphere of individualism, wrong practices become accepted as right. It is impossible to expect that a shot of stimulant can cure the chronic disease of apathy and make the blood flow smoothly and the limbs move in strong coordination.

Alas! The country is on the verge of destruction, and every common person has a responsibility. The prosperity of all countries begins with national education. The government is responsible for popularizing education, and the methods of teaching are also accountable. From the 7th to the 13th year of the Republic of China (1918-1924), primary schools in our country had quite a new look. However, the experimental methods originally lacked a central ideology, and imitators often failed to consider the environment and only pursued forms, so they were not valued by the people. Mass education has only recently been regulated, and its implementation has not achieved any significant results compared with the previous simple literacy schools and civilian literacy education. We deeply feel that current education needs fundamental reform, and the national crisis has strengthened our determination to reform. We start with primary schools to lay the foundation of education, and also involve mass education in the hope of achieving mutual benefits.

Reform is not imitation. At the very least, there are two points to note: first, there should be the emergence of new life. If we do not understand the shortcomings of the old, the existing mistakes, and what the state lacks or most needs, then the so-called new may not be able to correct the past mistakes. The past mistakes are as discussed above, and we should change direction and strive to realize them concretely one by one. Second, we should pursue practical results and relative economy. For example, regarding the tool of writing, if Chinese characters are not abolished, their structure is completely different from that of phonetic characters, so learning them is naturally different. Today's discussion on national language teaching, in terms of reading, writing, and composition, completely abandons the experience of experts over the ages and adopts foreign language teaching methods that are of a different nature, claiming them as new methods. Even in character selection and Chinese testing, the compilers, who basically do not understand Chinese philology, rashly apply the form of scientific methods. This itself raises the question of correctness, not to mention practical results. People often sigh that students' writing skills are getting worse recently, without realizing that the mistake is entirely based on primary schools, and primary school teachers have formed a bad habit, not realizing that their teaching methods are wrong day by day. As for relative economy, in the teaching process, we do not need to analyze parts and observe their mechanical movements, but should ask whether individual learning arises from the needs within the entire unit. Because learning out of need will lead to focused attention, and thus no time will be wasted. Therefore, tool subjects, except for practice, should be learned according to the needs of the unit, and should not be set as independent subjects to be learned at fixed times. The above-mentioned mechanical movements of analysis cannot control the entire teaching process. Recent experiments, such as reading aloud and silent reading, have different uses depending on materials and situations. For example, horizontal and vertical writing, whether the length and width are equal, whether the content is equal, whether the subjects' habits are equal, and their value in ordinary learning is very small. Using this to compare learning economy is far from practical results.

What we should solemnly state here is that we do not adopt the judgments of metaphysical psychology, but we should know that in the teaching process, no matter what kind of actions children take, they all show their overall and unified activities. The mystery in activities cannot be fully predicted by imagination. Although experimental psychology can help strengthen learning tendencies, it cannot solve the entire teaching process. We also do not adopt the views of pedantic Confucians, who focus on pure moral theory. However, we should know that for the perfection of personality, the ethos of cultivating virtue and pursuing learning advocated by Neo-Confucians in previous dynasties is indeed worthy of emulation. We should carry forward this ethos, place it in the path of children's tendencies discovered by modern psychologists and the process of physiological development, and develop the expected behavioral standards based on their possibilities. This is the national character cultivated by ideals, and also the commonality that humans in the world should have. Furthermore, to promote the neurological research in psychology, we should pay attention to the connection and regulation between the original functions of the system and the comprehensive functions of the cerebrospinal system, so as to control our learning and life.

As for inspiring our state to rejuvenate itself in the face of severe national crisis, the only way is to strengthen our determination and courage to fundamentally reform education, and there is no need for other attempts beyond the above discussion. Why? If the people's ability to adapt to and control the environment is cultivated in various ways, enabling them to have correct concepts and quick abilities in dealing with things, they can cope with any changes at any time. If we only use special teaching materials and methods to arouse emotions, it can only impulse for a while and cannot maintain long-term persistence. If we are not careful, it may be like a fire spreading across the prairie, arousing actions that go beyond the normal track, which is completely contrary to the purpose of education. With this in mind, we take this as our experimental policy, hoping to throw a brick to attract jade and gain enlightenment.

Published in *Education Weekly* on November 3, 1932; also published in *Kaifeng Education Ten-Day Journal*, Volume 1, Issue 1, on November 1, 1932.

Basic Understanding That Teaching Units Should Have

The term "teaching unit" holds a significant position in teaching. However, when it comes to the question of what the essential elements of a teaching unit are, not only do teachers engaged in practical teaching pay little attention to it, but even those who discuss teaching methods also skip over it. I believe this is a question well worth studying.

In the past, when the five-stage teaching method was prevalent, trainee teachers, when preparing lesson plans, invariably took the unit as the basis of teaching. Although they attached great importance to the unit, the so-called unit at that time referred to dividing the learning process based on a compiled lesson of teaching materials, without considering the essential elements that constitute a teaching unit. Therefore, despite emphasizing the teaching unit, people did not truly understand it. As a result, teaching methods became formalized and fragmented, which was inevitable.

Some might argue that in the past, when teaching methods discussed teaching materials, didn't they address the organization of teaching materials? That's correct, but this pertains to the compilation of the entire curriculum. Due to the different natures of materials in various subjects, each has its own specific research, which is not the issue of a single unit of teaching materials. Although unit teaching materials are sometimes mentioned in discussions about organization, they are not the main focus of research. How, then, can people be expected to pay attention to the essential elements of a teaching unit!

To understand the teaching unit, one must first distinguish the content of various similar terms. For example, teaching details, activity outlines, key assignment items, action units, etc., are inherently different from the teaching unit. However, these terms are easily confused, and their contents sometimes overlap or diverge, leading to misunderstandings among those engaged in practical work. The four terms listed above encompass the necessary quality and quantity of curriculum content. Teaching details, activity outlines, key assignment items, etc., differ in name but are similar in essence. Whether enumerated for subject-based or integrated courses, they are generally outlines of teaching materials, occasionally touching upon teaching forms. As for how to form a unit, there is no plan. Action units, on the other hand, are a method of compiling to break down subject-based curricula. Under specified objectives, they are analyzed into various activities or problems, such as the notes listed under each subject's objectives in Cheng Xiangfan's An Introduction to Primary School Curriculum (Commercial Press, 1923). These two types only involve analysis, not organization, and do not address the various interrelated aspects. The contents listed can, in practice, have one item divided into several units, several items combined into one unit, parts of several items formed into one unit, or one item serving as a note condition for many units. Although a certain item listed separately may have the framework of a teaching unit, it cannot be regarded as a teaching unit solely for that reason. In summary, a teaching unit in an integrated curriculum is a project, while in a subject-based curriculum, it is a topic in a subject's teaching materials, i.e., a lesson in a textbook.

Since a project is a unit, the essential elements of a teaching unit can be explained using the definition of a project, and it is not a teaching unit formed from teaching forms. There are various definitions of a project. Among them, more specific ones include: focusing on activities with concrete achievements; not limited to concrete achievements but solving problems through purposeful activities that generate valuable objects or knowledge; and taking practical operations as the basis. Adopting any of these as the essential elements of a teaching unit is highly valuable. To elaborate further, they are: (1) having a basic concept as the center for gathering facts; (2) forming a process of developing ideas during the progress of main actions; (3) problems being concrete, with ideas manifested in the activity process; (4) organizing and applying knowledge based on a certain purpose; (5) practical results being contained in the concrete situations or things of real life; (6) having transferability, i.e., the success of one project serving as the key and explanation for many similar undertakings; (7) being able to gradually expand from a small, partial, concrete foundation to a large, overall explanation. If a teaching unit is formed according to these conditions, then the relationship and sequence between each learning task and the entire curriculum will be connected, and there will be concrete results. Even under a fixed curriculum, teaching will not be like the current practice of teaching strictly according to the textbook.

However, there are two points about the current popular project-based approach that affect the teaching unit and must be clarified. The first point arises from following the old teaching methods, such as the four methods of construction, appreciation, research, and practice. The originator of this idea undoubtedly had unique insights, and it is quite useful for studying teaching methods. However, in primary education, the application of these four methods has become a variant of the stage-based approach. It should be noted that a unit as a project focuses on a central purpose, and the teaching materials are absolutely not like the isolated nature of subjects. Moreover, the problems arising in the process must be solved together. If it is said that a certain unit must adopt a certain method, it will not work. Furthermore, the entire plan should include sub-plans. During implementation, discussions, criticisms, appreciations, etc., must adapt to the sequence of the plan, be divided into several steps, and be used alternately. They are by no means limited to a certain time or a certain period, especially language activities and physical movements. If they are not coordinated and formed in different stages, then no matter how hard the movements are, they will lack thinking, which is no different from the mechanical practice of handicrafts in the secular world. Each language activity takes too long, leaving most children with nothing to do, making it difficult to maintain order. This is a common drawback of the heuristic method.

The second point is the misunderstanding of large units. In fact, the function of a project does not lie in the size of the unit. What makes it different from the subject-based curriculum is that a project as a unit is not a classification of teaching materials but is built on the entirety of things. Although it has the possibility of integrating various subjects, it does not have to integrate them to form a project. Even in the scope of integrating subjects, it is not necessary that the larger the unit, the more subjects it includes. Forced connection will lose the true face of the entire thing. For example, when MacMurry discusses project-based teaching methods, he advocates five functions of large units, which are actually the standard meanings of a project. However, in project-based teaching, there are always several main projects in each semester that take more time, which is an inevitable fact.

As mentioned above, a teaching unit should generate children's activities from purposes or problems, not just stipulate the learning process from pre-planned teaching materials, which has been clearly stated. Therefore, its minimum requirements can be determined as follows:

(1) For each learning activity, there must be a common activity purpose. This purpose is not to give abstract meanings but to form specific activity goals.

(2) Based on this purpose, adapting to the activity situation of children at this level, there must be an appropriate process. This process is not a formal procedure but requires specific work for each part of the activity to be formed by the new activities generated step by step.

(3) In each process, regardless of the main or auxiliary aspects, what children should learn and what should be accomplished in the end? These results do not come out of nowhere, and the activity performance is not necessarily based solely on mechanical work as achievements. In particular, it is necessary to assess whether labor and time are wasted.

If a learning activity does not meet the above three conditions, or only formally meets them without showing children's spontaneous activities, no matter how good the teaching materials are, it is a waste of time. Another point to note is that the function of teaching is not only to impart knowledge and skills but also to show children's true personalities through all actions within the scope of activities in the lessons. This issue may be discussed in a special article in the future; here, only the purpose is pointed out. As for the school holding large-scale meetings, which are not based on children's activities and cannot enable them to learn anything, that is an even more serious mistake. Now I specifically put forward three points:

First, all activities in the school should be divided into items to form teaching units. Do not think that teaching units are only a form of what is commonly called formal lessons. Daily affairs or moral education issues should not be handled in a fragmented and simple way. A moral education goal should be paid attention to at all times and cultivated in various aspects, but we cannot forget specific planning because of this. For example, the issue of cleanliness, if turned into a project of organizing the classroom or public places, with various activities each time and things that echo each other throughout the semester in this project, I think it will be more effective and interesting than the so-called cleanliness inspection. In particular, the good opportunity of integrated teaching should not be lost. Such as the items specified in the school calendar of each school can be used as common projects. Even if there is no school calendar, there are several memorial days and large-scale regular meetings every semester, aren't there? What good project opportunities these are! It's a pity that when schools encounter such opportunities, either the school handles them on their behalf or they pass as a day of entertainment.

Second, for any teaching unit, it is necessary to examine the entire process to see what new activities can be generated. If more specific old experiences can be applied in a certain process, teachers should record them separately to avoid unnecessary discussions in new situations that waste time. As for the new activities that should be generated, it must be believed that they can serve as the key to similar explanations. I very much hope that every teacher, when experienced people visit or ask, can report such situations, and this teaching will surely succeed.

Third, if a teaching unit takes more time, although it is continuous work, it does not have to be a whole-day lesson. For example, the project of raising silkworms and planting flowers takes a long time, and a lot of knowledge and skills are obtained from the work, and many moral education issues can be integrated into it to develop habits. Such projects are spread over several months, with work needed every day, without a fixed time, until completion. If it is not started from the beginning or is interrupted midway, the significance of teaching is lost. I call it long-term, short-time daily lessons, and strongly advocate doing one or two such projects every semester, which will surely achieve the goal of integrating teaching and moral education.

Many visiting teachers randomly observe a few minutes in a teaching unit, do not study the related courses before and after each part, conduct a comprehensive assessment, and casually make comments, which is too reckless. However, for teachers with no training, it is hard to talk about this. Finally, I boldly say that whether you are visiting or teaching, please ask yourself: do you clearly understand the essential elements of the teaching unit?

Published in *Kaifeng Education Ten-Day Journal*, Vol. 1, Issues 2 & 3 (combined), November 15, 1932.

Speech at the Talk Meeting of Provincial Primary Schools and Mass Schools in the Urban and Suburban Areas of Kaifeng

Today I am here to speak on behalf of two persons: first, on behalf of President Xu Xinwu of Henan University; second, on behalf of Mr. Xu Shifeng, standing committee member of this association. Let me first speak on behalf of President Xu.

President Xu believes that the Department of Education at Henan University has always confined itself to closed-door research, with no connection to schools or educational administrative agencies. As a result, the theories learned cannot be constantly verified against facts. Therefore, he specifically collaborated with the Department of Education to establish an experimental zone, allowing students of Henan University to have more research opportunities. Furthermore, Henan University originally planned to hire two professors to take full responsibility for experimental guidance. Unfortunately, most of the hires did not materialize, leaving only a few professors to assist here—they are not fully dedicated, nor do they have much time. For this, Henan University apologizes.

Second, let me say a few words on behalf of Mr. Xu. All primary school teachers here are busy with heavy workloads and meager salaries. Now, due to the work of this association, we have added more troubles to you all. Even if you do not mind the trouble, this association has such feelings. However, the reason why this association is stepping up this work is precisely because among the intellectual class, primary school teachers have the busiest work and the lowest pay—especially in urban primary schools, and Kaifeng is no exception, with even heavier workloads and poorer treatment. It is precisely under such circumstances that we can talk about educational reform on the road to national rejuvenation, and what is experimented out will be the most economical and practical. Because past education is full of bourgeois colors, teachers with good salaries and easy work will never have a real sense of this. Moreover, the problem of heavy workloads and meager salaries cannot be solved in isolation. If we can find a bright path through educational reform, this problem will naturally be resolved. Therefore, we resolutely established the Education Experimental Zone and invite everyone to work together. This is the first point to clarify.

Although this association is jointly organized by Henan University and the Department of Education, its work can never be fully undertaken by just a few committee members and secretaries. It requires teachers from all schools to put forward more practical educational issues, conduct joint research, and find joint solutions. We cannot say for sure that we will succeed, but only through collective research by the majority can there be hope for success. To do this, it is essential for all school principals to take the lead. This is the second point to clarify.

At the start of any work, there must be appropriate investigations to serve as a basis for improvement. If this association needs to conduct various surveys in your schools, please inform us of the true situation. Do not mistake these surveys as evaluations. To improve education, we must identify real problems to have objects of research. Whether they are right or wrong is another matter, but being truthful, reliable, and unembellished is the research attitude we must uphold from the beginning. This is the third point to clarify.

As for the process of establishing the experimental zone, it is necessary to give a brief report. When Zhang Youshan and Huang Renchu were directors of the Henan Department of Education, there was a proposal to establish an experimental zone, but it was never realized.

During the tenure of former Director Li Jingzhai, it was brought up again at an educational conference, and an experimental plan was formulated. Last year, an Experimental Guidance Department was established, but due to a lack of dedicated personnel, no significant results were achieved. During this summer vacation, Mr. Tai Shuangqiu revisited the proposal. It was only after President Xu of Henan University invited Mr. Li Jingzhai to discuss it with Director Qi Zhenru that the zone was finally established. Director Qi is very pleased with this initiative but has taken an extremely prudent attitude. From the beginning, he appointed Mr. Xu Shifeng as a standing committee member. Mr. Xu, due to unfinished matters in Beiping, is temporarily staying there. Once his affairs are completed, he will return to Kaifeng to take full responsibility and formulate an overall plan for Kaifeng's education.

Regarding the work of this association, the immediate tasks include investigating children's bad behavior, implementing health education, and investigating the implementation of large-unit teaching. As for the investigation on the implementation of large units, such as the "Chrysanthemum Competition," the investigation has been completed and is currently being sorted out. Other matters will be launched soon.

Finally, there are three more things to clarify to everyone:

First, the purpose of the investigations is to understand the implementation situation in each school, serving as a basis for solving practical teaching problems. Please provide us with as much real information as possible.

Second, regarding subjects such as nature and society, we plan to invite teachers from all schools to form research groups. Committee members and secretaries of this association will assist in joint research.

Third, the Kaifeng Ten-Day Journal of this association has launched a call for books and a column for correspondence research. We hope everyone will write down practical materials and problems frankly. This association will publish them on your behalf to facilitate joint solutions.

The number of people in this association is small, and our capabilities are limited. We earnestly request your guidance and advice.

Published in *Kaifeng Education Ten-Day Journal*, Volume 1, Combined Issues 2 & 3, November 15, 1932.

Reply to Wang Zihe

Elder Brother Zihe,

Your letter, which extracts three key points from your entire year of experience and elaborates on them incisively and profoundly, is truly remarkable. In our country, those engaged in primary school experiments often focus on trivial issues or merely put on a show. Such insightful reports, published in a raw and unvarnished manner, are quite rare.

The three reflections in your letter are: first, we should not be confined to the form of syllabi and engage in unnatural knowledge cramming; second, we should arrange a project-based environment where children can observe, discover, explore, and research freely; third, children's diligence arises from their interest in what they learn. The examples you provided to illustrate these three points are thorough and comprehensive. However, regarding the third point, you mentioned that "in the previous period, due to the school's equipment, the children always felt uninterested in 'duty patrols' and had nothing to do." This is what teachers from various schools said last year, and it is indeed a fact. Nevertheless, in my personal view, I always feel that the difficulties everyone talks about are not derived from understanding the project itself but are rather assumptions made by applying old habits to new life. Let me put forward my two reflections:

The first reflection is that the function of teaching lies in controlling children's lives. Any conscious action of a child manifests as an integrated and unified activity, and daily teaching should aim at this. In the past, due to the division of subjects, teaching only imparted fragmented knowledge. Even if we transform various subjects into different activities or merge several subjects into a few departments, if we take separate parts as learning units, it is still easy to lose the integrity and unity. Take "duty" and “patrol” as examples. In our usual research, we can focus specifically on their nature. However, if they are implemented as an isolated course, no matter how well-equipped the school is, children will not be interested, nor will they find much significance in them. This is why moral education should be integrated into teaching. Therefore, “duty” and “patrol” can certainly be carried out within the scheduled time, but if the work does not arise from the purpose of a teaching unit, it is simply unnecessary. A clear example is that children are not interested in the cleanliness inspections conducted by various schools. Teachers fail to realize that the specified items need to be flexibly used and appropriately combined, permeating the purpose of a teaching unit, so it is natural for them to have illusions.

The second reflection is that although it is desirable for primary schools to have complete facilities, teaching does not necessarily require such facilities to be carried out, especially project-based teaching. Otherwise, project-based teaching would simply be a method of bourgeois society, and there would be no need to study it. We should know that in such a vast nature and society, teachers can make full use of the environment, which provides enough things for children to learn. Therefore, what teachers need to do in arranging the environment is to delimit a scope from the vast environment at any time to arouse children’s questions. Thus, teachers should utilize the environment to design various projects. As for the facilities that must be provided to meet teaching needs, it is certain that when everyone is highly interested in a problem, they will naturally find ways to obtain them together. However, teachers need to spend some time preparing how to distribute such work. The example you mentioned in your letter, that this semester you used the seeds collected last year and those found by the children for cultivation, irrigation, recording, and observation, is a good case in point. Unfortunately, most teachers of lower grades, after casually reading two or three irrelevant examples, without thinking, take a variant of heuristic lesson plans and stubbornly claim to be implementing project-based teaching, which is a great disservice to project-based teaching. There were many such cases in the chrysanthemum exhibitions held by various schools this time. There is a Chinese proverb: “Admit what you don’t know, and what you know is true knowledge.” This is the ethos that teaching must possess.

Finally, I am very much looking forward to your plan to compile a “children’s life calendar.” However, I have two suggestions:

(1) The “children’s life calendar” of the Tenth Primary School this semester does not pay much attention to activities, and there are many aspects in its content that can be discussed.

(2) The term “children’s life calendar” always seems inappropriate. Because children’s lives cannot be regulated by us, and teaching is a two-way matter. We should not ignore children, but we should also not forget our own responsibilities. I hope you can think of another term.

Lianfang
November 1st

Published in *Kaifeng Education Ten-Day Journal*, Volume 1, Combined Issues 2 & 3, 1932

To Xiangmin

Mr. Xiangmin,

Your second letter mentions me and expresses expectations, which I dare not accept. However, my inclination to engage with the primary education community, and by extension with mass education, stems from a long-held view: in national undertakings, there is nothing more crucial than the basic education of citizens. Moreover, the foundation of educational scholarship must begin with understanding primary education, and it must center its research on actual teaching practices.

I have often been puzzled by so-called educational scholars in our country who do not observe teaching practices as an integrated, systematic whole to advance education. Overestimating my own limited abilities, I have conducted research based on this conviction. Every time a new theory emerges, I must repeatedly examine its crux; though I may not fully grasp it, I cannot say I have not delved into its essence. From the late Qing dynasty to the present, I have occasionally published works, mostly on topics either unaddressed by my compatriots or differing from the views of domestic scholars. Beyond this, I have no desire to speak—I have never parroted hearsay or boasted of insights. The outlines I propose are unlikely to resemble the hollow, vague goals in the Ministry of Education's curriculum standards, such as "healthy physique" or "good character," which lack specific meaning.

If anyone raises concrete questions based on my arguments, I am eager to exhaust my knowledge in ongoing, iterative discussions. Without such questions to debate, I would not know how to make my words sufficiently detailed. My lectures at this summer's workshop would have followed this approach, had language barriers not interfered. I welcome any advice you may offer.

Li Lianfang
November 28th

Published in *Kaifeng Education Ten-Day Journal*, Volume 1, Issue 4, December 1, 1932.

Preface to *Special Topics in Educational Research*

How deplorable today's university education is! It pursues the reputation of breadth and erudition without substance. In terms of learning, it substitutes hearing for seeing and seeing for doing. Professors rush around all day preparing lecture notes and scripts, yet in the end, students clearly gain nothing—they may even fail to achieve the function of memorization. How deplorable today's university education is!

When I took charge of the affairs of the College of Liberal Arts at Henan University, I once wrote an essay on the university research room system, hoping to implement it in specialized courses. However, things went against my wishes, and it was not successfully carried out.

This spring, Mr. Zheng Zhuxu[12] taught education and offered a course on special-topic research, which did not rely on lectures as the teaching method—a approach that aligns with my advocated research room system. At that time, six students enrolled in the course, conducting research for two hours each week. After one semester, despite their heavy coursework, each student completed an essay based on their research. Their attainments vary in depth, and naturally, the content has both strengths and flaws. However, their purpose was to seek advice, and they never intended to publish these works. Nevertheless, compared to those under the rigid examination system, where monthly grades are based on a few brief answers, there is a world of difference.

---

12 Namely Zheng Ruogu, a native of Luoshan, Henan. He obtained a Master's degree in Education from Washington University. He was then a professor in the Department of Education at Henan University, and later served successively as the department chair and dean of the College of Liberal Arts. ——Translator's note

Student Cai Hengxi, who is in charge of editorial work at the Education Department, selected these essays to publish as a special issue, which was not the original intention of the authors. There are six essays in total: An Introduction to Educational Philosophy by Huang Zengxiang; Zhu Xi's Philosophy and Educational Thought by Wei Hongxu; The Past and Future of the Independence of Henan's Educational Funds by Yang Jiabin; Chinese Society and the Path Forward for Its Rural Education by Pan Weixin; A Study on the Teacher-Student Relationship in Schools at All Levels by Song Chuanbin; and A Study on Primary School Curricula by Dong Deshu.

Li Buqing (Lianfang), Dean of the College of Liberal Arts at Henan University, inscribed this in the period when Leonid meteors were streaking across the sky, in the 21st year of the Republic of China (1932).

Published in the "Special Topic on Educational Research" special issue of *Henan Education Monthly*, Vol. 3, No. 2, December 1932.

Inscription at the Beginning of the New Year Volume

The way of heaven circulates ceaselessly; after a full year, the four seasons begin anew. Thus, in the unfolding of human affairs, annual planning is of paramount importance.

The year is said to bring "change"—all things present their new life. Whether this new life evolves or not depends entirely on the efforts exerted by humans, and how they influence innate transformation and acquired development. If left to grow and perish naturally, without possessing special qualities, there is nothing that does not decline day by day.

The methods of transformation and development vary appropriately with the environment, just as "oranges, when transplanted beyond the Huai River, turn into trifoliate oranges." Observing this natural phenomenon and reflecting on the state of education, those who cling to a single approach without understanding change should desist.

Primary education and mass education are the cornerstones on which the state's fate rests. Education in our country has been misled once by traditional habits and again by the pernicious influence of the capitalist system. Wrong practices have become accepted as right, like a drunken dream. Without reform, we cannot save the state from peril. Those in charge of the lifeblood of education bear a responsibility far greater than that of ordinary individuals.

The past is gone. As we usher in this new year, we reflect on the past and plan for the future. Proposals for initial reforms, such as those in this volume, are indeed crucial undertakings. In fulfilling this duty without hesitation, I shall watch with eager anticipation. Therefore, I compose this ode as a new year's tribute:

At the start of this year, all things vie in beauty.

To reform education, unifying moral guidance and teaching is the first priority.

Treat knowledge as a tool; needs must focus on the present.

Select the essential and utilize the vast, discarding all empty forms.

The new life begins its journey; dawn shines atop the Iron Pagoda.

Published in *Kaifeng Education Ten-Day Journal*, Volume 1, Combined Issues 6 & 7, January 1, 1933.

Suggestions for the Initial Reform of Primary Schools in the Urban and Suburban Areas of Kaifeng

▲ Work – In accordance with the original regulations, each school can set aside one-fourth to one-fifth of its teachers every day for independent research.

▲ Equipment– The primary schools in urban and suburban areas can spare 50 classrooms for special facilities of mass education, with surplus funds from various routine expansion expenses available.

▲ Curriculum – Children can take appropriate courses by subject or topic without conflict, and these courses are suitable for cultivating productive skills, labor habits, and a sense of cooperation.

When it comes to educational reform, two issues arise: first, the workload is too heavy; second, there is a lack of funds and space to expand special facilities. These have almost become common complaints among primary schools in general, and are particularly prevalent in Kaifeng. I believe we must first examine whether such a situation has been caused by a wrong path taken all along or by genuine difficulties. Hereby, I have compiled the facts related to this issue from various primary schools in Kaifeng. As I have not conducted a detailed study on all the realities of the current mass schools, I will not include them for the time being, but perhaps they can be inferred from this.

Comparison Table of the Number of Classrooms, Grades, and Teachers in Provincial Primary Schools in Kaifeng

Item / Quantity School	Classroom			Grade			Teacher		
	Special	Total	Ordinary	Advanced	Total	Elementary	Homeroom teacher	Total	Subject teacher
No.1 Primary School	2		12-	4		8	-12		5
		14			12			17	
No.2 Primary School	2		9-	3		6	-9		3
		11			9			12	
No.3 Primary School	1		10-	4		6	10		4
		11			10			14	
No.4 Primary School	2		12-	4		8	12		3
		14			12-			15	
No.5 Primary School	2		8	3		5	8		3
		10			8			11	
No.6 Primary School	3		17-	6		11	17		7
		20			17-			24	
No.7 Primary School	1		8-	2		6	8		3
		9			8			11	
No.8 Primary School	1		10、	3		7	10		4
		11			10-			14	
No.9 Primary School	1		7-	2		5	7		2
		8			7			9	
No.10 Primary School	2		9-	2		7	9		3
		11			9			12	
No.11 Primary School	unclear		8	2		6	8		3
		3			8			11	
Boys' Affiliated Primary School	3		13-	4		9	13		4
		16			13			17	
Girls'	1		9-	3		6	9		5

Item / Quantity / School	Classroom			Grade			Teacher		
	Special	Total	Ordinary	Advanced	Total	Elementary	Homeroom teacher	Total	Subject teacher
Affiliated Primary School		10			9			14	

Note: The dotted line indicates that the number of ordinary classrooms, the number of class teachers, and the number of grades are equal.

Based on the above table, the points that should be noted are as follows:

1. Each grade must have a regular classroom, which is a common fact in all schools. As for special classrooms, two schools have three, and five schools each have one or two. The number of special classrooms does not correspond to the number of classes in the school. In addition, facilities that function similarly to classrooms, such as auditoriums, libraries, or achievement exhibition rooms, are generally available in all schools.

2. The ratio of the number of teachers to the number of classes in each school is based on the regulations of the Henan Provincial Department of Education in July of the 19th year of the Republic of China (1930). Specifically, for senior grades: 3 teachers for 2 classes, 4 teachers for 3 classes; for 4 classes, 5 teachers for junior grades and 6 teachers for senior grades; for 5 classes, 6 teachers for junior grades and 7 teachers for senior grades; for 6 classes, 8 teachers for junior grades and 9 teachers for senior grades; for 7 classes, 9 teachers for junior grades and 10 teachers for senior grades; for 8 classes, 10 teachers for junior grades and 12 teachers for senior grades; for 9 classes, 11 teachers for junior grades and 13 teachers for senior grades; for 10 classes, 13 teachers for junior grades and 15 teachers for senior grades; for 11 classes, 14 teachers for junior

grades and 16 teachers for senior grades; for 12 classes, 15 teachers for junior grades and 18 teachers for senior grades. These regulations stipulate that for senior grades, 1 additional teacher is assigned for every 2 classes; for junior grades, 1 additional teacher is assigned for 4 classes, 2 additional teachers for 6 classes, and 3 additional teachers for 10 classes.

In terms of courses and class hours, there are minor differences among schools. However, since the schools have not provided special explanations for the reasons behind these differences from the ministry's regulations, nor have they made accurate estimates of efficiency, others cannot identify any distinctive features. Therefore, the discussion of this issue has to be based on the subjects stipulated by the ministry and the weekly teaching schedule, which are listed below.

Grades / Weekly Hours / Subjects	Lower Grades Grade 1, Grade 2	Middle Grades Grade 3, Grade 5	Upper Grades
Civics	60	60	60
Hygiene	60	60	60
Physical Education	150	150	180
Mandarin	390	390	390
Social Studies	90	120	180
Science	90	120	150
Arithmetic	60150	180340	210
Manual Labor	90	120	150
Art	90	90	90
Music	90	90	90
Total	11701260	14401380	1560

Furthermore, the Henan Provincial Department of Education stipulates that primary school teachers must teach 20 hours per week (more than 1,200 minutes).

According to the aforesaid regulations, when comparing the number of class hours stipulated by the Ministry for each grade with the minimum number of hours each teacher must undertake as prescribed by the Education Department, the first grade is still 30 minutes short, the second grade is 60 minutes over, the third grade is 180 minutes over, the fourth grade is 240 minutes over, and the senior grades are 360 minutes over. In total, the number of hours stipulated by the Ministry for the four years of primary school is 5,250 minutes. If calculated according to the Education Department's stipulation that 5 teachers are assigned to 4 primary classes, the total number of hours they should undertake amounts to 6,000 minutes. After deducting the hours that should be studied by each grade as stipulated by the Ministry, there is still a surplus of 750 minutes. Now, taking 1,200 minutes as a benchmark, the number of hours each teacher undertakes per day is no more than three and a half hours. Even if the classes are taught consecutively, it takes less than half a day's work. So, the so-called "too busy with work" certainly does not refer to the number of teaching hours. It is said that teachers are busy with preparations, but nowadays, for knowledge-based courses, they just teach straight from existing textbooks and teaching guides, requiring little preparation, not to mention skill-based courses. This is certainly not the reason for being too busy. However, many teachers nowadays are indeed very busy. Except for those who are busy under special circumstances due to their poor basic qualities or their extraordinary efforts, the general causes of the widespread phenomenon of being overly busy mainly lie in the following aspects:

(1) Too many class periods: Although the official daily teaching hours are only three to four hours, or even less than three hours, there are always five to six or six to seven class periods every day, distributed in the morning and afternoon. As a result, the non-teaching time in between is all wasted in the midst of busyness.

(2) Too busy with after-class handling: I am not saying that there should be no after-class handling work. However, for such handling work as it is now, I wonder if there has been any proper assessment to know how much efficiency children have gained from it. I always suspect that teachers do such work just because they are afraid of inspections by the authorities or reproaches from parents, thus forming a kind of routine work.

(3) The difficulty of being a class teacher: Subject teachers, apart from giving regular classes, can even skip meetings, and have nothing to do with children otherwise. Only class teachers have to fill in forms, handle assignments and all matters related to their class. If they take their responsibilities seriously, they can hardly finish the work all day long.

Before putting forward an overall reform plan, I would first like to elaborate on my views on the above three points:

(1) Regarding the first point – Excessively fragmented class periods: Approximately 15 years ago, primary school classes in China were conducted in one-hour units. Children either arrived late or left early, spending half a day at school each day. Since the number of class hours stipulated by the Ministry was only around four hours, teachers could ignore students once their classes were over. As a result, society generally felt that schools were less responsible than private tutors.

Now, classes have been divided into periods. Although the total learning hours remain the same as before, the number of periods has increased, with more breaks in between. Consequently, the time spent at school in the morning and afternoon is longer, and the problems of the past no longer arise. However, there are several points that deserve attention. Firstly, the duration of each period is entirely determined by the nature of the subject. Due to the excessive number of periods, it is inconvenient to adjust them temporarily. Secondly, each learning session is relatively short, which naturally prevents excessive fatigue, but it can sometimes dampen students' interest in learning. Thirdly, for teachers' workload allocation, it is advisable to distribute classes evenly between morning and afternoon. However, since each grade has subject teachers, if one or two days per week are not set aside for each teacher to work only half a day, teachers will inevitably lack time for research.

(2) Regarding the second point – Overly busy with after-class handling: Teachers only have 3.5 hours of classes per day, which is just half a day. Even though their classes are spread throughout the day, setting aside half of the non-teaching half-day for after-class affairs would certainly be sufficient.

(3) Regarding the third point – The difficulty of being a class teacher: I believe this is entirely caused by the subject-based system. While dividing teaching responsibilities by subject is inevitable, the educational flaws arising from such division must be corrected urgently. Firstly, class teachers and subject teachers should share equal responsibilities, and the burden on class teachers should be reduced to avoid uneven distribution of work. Secondly, teaching can start from the subjects one is responsible for, or assign teaching tasks to individuals based on the overall unit. However, no unit should derive its teaching process from an isolated subject; instead, it should enable students to acquire interrelated knowledge and skills. Therefore, for each teaching unit, all teachers of the grade must reach an agreement before class and assist each other during instruction. In

particular, for symbolic exercises, even subject teachers should take responsibility under the coordination of the class teacher, and this responsibility should not be limited to management issues alone.

What has been said above focuses solely on teachers. However, for educational reform, school administration is also highly relevant, especially regarding issues of classrooms and equipment. It is widely acknowledged that current school facilities are too basic to carry out experimental work, yet few realize that much of this ordinary equipment is largely wasted. If this traditional mindset is not broken, there is no point in talking about educational reform. I now randomly list the work schedule of a certain grade in a certain school, where the parts marked with grid lines indicate the time when the grade's classroom is empty and unused.

Monday	**Tuesday**	**Wednesday**	**Thursday**	**Friday**	**Saturday**
Morning Exercises	Morning Exercises	Morning Exercises	Morning Exercises	Morning Exercises	Morning Exercises
Morning Assembly	Morning Assembly	Morning Assembly	Morning Assembly	Morning Assembly	Morning Assembly
Mandarin	Arithmetic	Mandarin	Arithmetic	Mandarin	Weekly Meeting
Arithmetic	Mandarin	Arithmetic	Mandarin	Arithmetic	Mandarin
Geography	Music & PE[2]	Art	History	Geography	Nature
	Nature	Art	Scout Activity	Nature	History
	History	Mandarin	Nature	Music & PE	Party Doctrine
	Party Doctrine	Geography	Music & PE	Mandarin	Mandarin
	Mandarin	Music & PE	Mandarin	Civics	Scout Activity
	Abacus Calculation	Work Class	Mandarin	Work Class	Hygiene
				Work Class	

In the weekly schedule of this grade, there are 64 periods in total, among which 33 periods do not require the use of the grade's classroom (morning assemblies are not limited to being held in classrooms). This means that the grade's classroom is left empty for most of the day, which may not be necessary. Or is it really unavoidable that the classroom has to be left empty? This situation is roughly the same for other grades, as well as for all grades in primary schools in Kaifeng. By extension, it can be inferred that the same applies to primary schools and schools above the secondary level across the country. Moreover, there are many school buildings not used for teaching that remain empty all day long.

Despite such idle facilities in schools, a check of the budgets of educational authorities reveals that large sums of temporary construction funds are allocated each year because schools report a shortage of premises. In fact, the number of actually unused premises is even greater than the so-called "shortage." However, people are accustomed to following old practices, and even if insightful individuals point out this issue, they remain obstinately blind to it.

The reform measures I am proposing now are not merely aimed at saving funds. Rather, it is because only when human and financial resources are fully utilized can ideal education be realized. It should be noted that the pernicious influence of traditional education is still prevalent nationwide. In terms of teaching, part of it stems from the leftover ills of imperial examination-based education. Yet, the emerging intellectual class, while constantly criticizing the corruption of old systems, follows old paths in their own practices, just in a different form. A larger part of the problem comes from the pernicious influence of the Western capitalist society, which continues to persist. In particular, so-called educational scholars and scientists, accustomed to the forms of capitalist society, believe that academic undertakings, in whatever form they take, must involve substantial expenditures. Even if there are some academic achievements, it is questionable whether the money spent is commensurate with the results achieved.

Admittedly, acquiring knowledge today, even at the primary school level, is not like the old days of studying, where one could get by with just a few elementary textbooks. However, I would ask: when setting up a school, if the premises and utensils needed by children are left unused, waiting for opportunities to be used, or only used for part of the day, such waste is comparable to teachers wasting their labor and time. This alone fully demonstrates that education has become an ornament. Therefore, the measures I propose, which I consider as initial reforms, are based on this understanding.

We all know that the purpose of education is to cultivate well-rounded personalities. However, the best results of current education are only manifested in the acquisition of knowledge and skills. Even knowledge and skills, if learned solely from textbooks in classrooms, will inevitably pose problems when applied in practice, which is widely acknowledged. Therefore, integrating the above ideas, I put forward my proposal as follows:

All schools in urban and suburban Kaifeng adopt a multi-grade system, and this system is applicable to them. Therefore, I advocate that each school should adopt a dual system, dividing all students in the school into two parts and classifying the tasks of each grade into three categories. Let me take a hypothetical 12-grade primary school as an example to illustrate this.

1. How are students divided into two divisions? That is, students in the first half of the six academic years are classified as Division A, and those in the second half as Division B; alternatively, students in the first,

second, and third grades are in Division A, and those in the fourth, fifth, and sixth grades are in Division B. The significance of this division is as follows: first, the two divisions take turns attending classes, with the same number of study hours maintained. By using half the equipment, twice the number of students can be accommodated, thus saving funds. Second, whether it is school buildings or utensils, they are fully utilized throughout the day without idleness. Third, the courses are naturally alternated, which can more easily reduce children's fatigue. Fourth, no school building or utensil is monopolized by a single grade, thus avoiding conflicts between grades.

2. How are assignments divided into three categories? That is, according to the subjects prescribed by the ministry, they are grouped into three different places for teaching. The first category is coursework in ordinary classrooms — Chinese, arithmetic, and social studies. The second category is coursework in practice venues — nature studies, manual labor, and art. The third category is coursework in collective venues — civic training, hygiene, physical education, and music. The subjects included in each category are grouped because their main purposes are relatively similar, not because they are absolutely independent of each other. In fact, in actual teaching, coursework of the first category can sometimes be learned in the second or third category of assignments, and coursework of the second or third category can sometimes be taught in the first category of assignments. This depends on the processes involved in the unit. Therefore, the facilities for the twelve grades are arranged according to the three categories mentioned above. The first category requires three ordinary classrooms. The second category requires three practice venues: one workshop or workroom, one nature laboratory, and one school garden or farm. The third category requires one sports ground, which can preferably accommodate one-third of the

school's students, and at least one-fourth. One library is needed, which must be at least twice the size of an ordinary classroom, where academic achievements can be displayed. One recreation room, which can be shared with the auditorium. Music classes are also taught here, and it can accommodate students from the sports ground in case of rain or snow. During class time, Division A works in the third category of venues, while half of Division B works in the first category of classrooms and the other half in the second category of venues. The same applies when Division B and Division A swap assignments. The significance of this is: first, the entire school's facilities can be used as learning venues, meaning that all facilities have educational significance. Second, when the two divisions swap assignments, no group is idle or engaging in aimless activities for the entire time. Third, each of the three categories has special meanings related to different assignments, and only the first category can use the old-style teaching method, which naturally breaks the prejudice of text-based or book-based teaching.

The methods and their significance have been discussed above. However, there are additional explanations needed regarding the application of this method. Because this method is based on the meaning that education is life, aiming to generate the functions of ideal education through organization. It is not without an educational philosophy as its background, merely focusing on the form of methods. Although it is simpler and easier to implement than any other method and is not prone to becoming formalistic, if those running the school do not truly understand the underlying principles, it will still be difficult to apply it freely. Further explanations are provided below.

1. Schools should make full use of their existing facilities. If, due to environmental constraints, certain facilities required for the classification of assignments cannot be provided—for example, most schools lack

spacious areas for a school garden—alternative measures should be adopted. In such cases, one more ordinary classroom than specified above can be temporarily reserved instead of setting up a school garden; or the school garden can be merged with the nature study room. One approach is to use the school's open space for cultivation, limiting its use to one grade per semester; another is to forgo school garden work and only conduct nature study experiments. This logic can be applied by analogy to other facilities. However, the recreation room and library must be reorganized; otherwise, the classification will be meaningless.

2. Schools with a minimum of 7 grades and a maximum of 17 grades must adjust the organizational model based on the 12-grade example mentioned above, with slight modifications. Except for schools with only 7 grades, which do not need to adopt the dual-system division into two divisions, in the classified assignment system, only 2 ordinary classrooms are needed, and other facilities can be reduced as appropriate according to the previous regulations, or parts of the second and third categories can be merged. For other schools with fewer than 12 grades (specifically, fewer than 10 grades), 2 ordinary classrooms are required. For schools with more than 12 grades, a maximum of 5 ordinary classrooms are needed.

3. The swap of assignments between Divisions A and B should be based on 90-minute units. During each unit, one division engages in the first and second categories of assignments, while the other division participates in all three categories. Within these 90 minutes, the first and second category assignments for a division must be swapped, and it is more convenient to swap the entire group of students in each category. For the division engaged in the third category of assignments, only physical education and music should be conducted in graded or combined-grade groups at fixed times, with the number of participants not exceeding half of the total number of students in that division across all sessions.

Activities in the recreation room and library can allow for more flexibility; however, proper arrangements should be made before class, and students must engage in purposeful activities under the supervision of on-duty staff during class. Alternatively, the Dalton Plan can be partially adopted in these two rooms, but it should be noted that only methods such as assignment designation, guidance, and evaluation should be used, not other formalities of the system.

4. Students of all grades arrive at school for the morning assembly, after which they split into two divisions to swap assignments. The two divisions swap assignments twice in the morning and twice in the afternoon, with each session lasting 90 minutes, totaling 6 hours. Although the learning hours for students are increased, since the assignments are divided into three categories—where the second category does not cause fatigue and the third category allows for flexibility—students will not feel overburdened. The teaching hours in classrooms are reduced. According to the regulations, there are 6 teachers for 4 senior classes and 10 teachers for 8 junior classes, totaling 16 teachers. With three categories of teaching, one teacher is directly responsible for each venue, working 4 hours a day, totaling 64 hours. Three teachers are left with only 2 hours of classes in half a day, amounting to 6 hours, and one teacher who works 4 hours can be reassigned to assist in collective venues. By further reducing the required teaching hours for each category, more teachers can be freed up.

5. The subjects included in each of the three categories, based on the weekly hours specified by the ministry for each grade, are listed below.

		Grade 1	Grade 2	Grade 3	Grade 4	Upper Grades
Category 1	Mandarin	390	390	390	390	390
	Social Studies	90	90	120	120	180
	Arithmetic	60	150	180	240	210
	Total	540	630	690	750	780
	Daily Average	90	105	115	125	130
Category 2	Nature	90		120		150
	Manual Labor	90		90		150
	Art	90		90		90
	Total	270		300		390
	Daily Average	45		50		65
Category 3	Civics	60				60
	Hygiene	60				60
	Physical Education (PE)	150				180
	Music	90				90
	Total	360				390
	Daily Average	60				65

According to the above standards, the first category has a maximum of 130 minutes and a minimum of 90 minutes; the second category has a maximum of 65 minutes and a minimum of 45 minutes; the third category has 65 minutes for senior grades and 60 minutes for junior grades. Then, within the specified time for classified assignments, two problems will arise. First, the standard study hours should not reach such a limit, as students are prone to fatigue in the first category of assignments in ordinary classrooms. The remedy is to include self-study within the specified time, allowing children to engage in purposeful free practice, and junior grades should use more competitive exercises.

For the second category of assignments, there are not so many tasks, or not many subject teachers for direct instruction. Our reform measure is precisely to take this category of assignments as the core, so the hours will naturally be increased. Moreover, there are several remedies: first, for this category of assignments, children can perform tasks individually or in groups, and direct instruction is not required everywhere. Second, regarding symbolic exercises, comprehensive teaching methods should be used, and sometimes teachers of general subjects can assist. Third, when there is extra time after completing tasks, students can go to the recreation room or library with the teacher's permission, especially for junior grades.

As for schools with fewer than 12 grades, the second and third categories can be combined for use, so there is even less of a problem. It should be stated additionally here that this dual system, first, depends on proper classification and arrangement, and second, on appropriate daily schedule allocation. It is also necessary to adjust the situation and replace it two or three times per semester. Otherwise, the first point will become a textbook-copying Dalton Plan, and the second point will become each grade occupying a classroom with self-study interspersed.

6. In the classified assignments, the second and third categories are the most active places for children, and they are also the main places where moral education is integrated into teaching. Therefore, there are significant changes to the issues that traditionally constituted teachers' responsibilities. First, for skill-based subjects such as physical education, handcraft, gardening, music, and fine arts, not only should the time be increased and methods improved, but also character cultivation should be achieved in the process of skill proficiency. Except that the guidance in the library is undertaken by teachers of the first category or by form teachers on a rotating basis, all heads of places for the second and third categories must be subject teachers. Therefore, the selection of subject teachers is more important than that of any other teachers. In my opinion, attention should be paid here when adding staff according to the specified standards. Second, although form teachers can still be held by teachers of general subjects, their responsibilities are only limited to the curriculum

planning and total score statistics of the grade. As for the management of the grade, it should be shared by all teachers of the grade, who handle temporary matters respectively, instead of being entirely borne by form teachers.

7. Although each assignment in each category is based on grades as units, the timetable can be changed within an appropriate period. According to children's individual abilities and progress, they can be promoted or demoted between classes. Those who are demoted in the first category may be promoted in the second or third category; even within the same category, they can take appropriate courses by subject. Sometimes, relatively senior and junior grades can be mixed to conduct certain assignments, so that they can help each other.

8. Such improvements are naturally applicable to the simultaneous implementation in multiple schools. The principal of each school takes handling administration as their sole responsibility. Regarding curriculum planning, homework arrangement, and teaching methods, multiple schools can be integrated and guided by experts respectively. Moreover, administrative tasks must take teaching as the starting point, avoiding the drawbacks of traditional teaching being controlled by administration. On the one hand, teachers with any ability can easily fully demonstrate their capabilities; on the other hand, capable principals, even if they are slightly inferior in academic knowledge, will not affect the progress of teaching. With this method, there may be a possibility of a rift between principals and instructors. However, the legitimate power of principals still exists, and their responsibilities are greatly reduced. If they are reasonable, there will never be a rift. In short, in urban areas, there are many similar schools. Without handling it in this way, everything is uneconomical, and it is an inevitable fact that good schools can hardly influence bad ones, while bad ones can easily restrict good ones.

What has been stated above is derived from the American Gary-style organization. However, it must be solemnly emphasized that this two-division alternating work system is not a variant of the half-day school, but a crystallization of the two-division system (old-style), group division system, self-study guidance system, Dalton system, and project-based system. For the essence of this system lies entirely in exerting the functions of classified assignments. Therefore, in multi-grade schools with fewer classes, there is no need to divide into divisions; as long as classified assignments are implemented, the number of ordinary classrooms can be reduced.

Some people will surely say that such a reform would require a lot of temporary funds for the facilities of the second and third categories, right? That's true, but I would ask: what kind of education would it be if children's schoolwork only uses ordinary classrooms! Moreover, the renovation costs required by my method do not need to be arranged separately; it is sufficient to take the money originally intended for expanding ordinary classrooms and use it in a different direction.

First, among the 13 provincial primary schools, 9 still have fewer than 12 grades, and classes will certainly be added in phases. According to the usual practice, adding classes means adding classrooms and desks and chairs. These 9 schools with fewer than 12 grades, even the one with the smallest number of 7 grades, have more ordinary classrooms and desks and chairs than those used by 12 grades. Using the money wasted on adding classes for proper facilities while still adding classes in the same way—shouldn't this be done!

Second, isn't there an urgent need to expand mass education? The first major obstacle is the lack of premises. Even if premises are found, renovation and equipping them require a lot of temporary funds, not to mention building new ones. If my reform method is adopted, these 13 primary schools have a total of 145 ordinary classrooms and utensils. After converting some of them for the second and third categories, based on the current number of classes, the maximum number of surplus classrooms would be 7, and the minimum would be 2. Approximately one-third, about 50 classrooms, can be used for mass education. With a more economical approach, and by using the classrooms of various schools at night, 100 classes can be run during the day and 100 at night, which can accommodate almost 10,000 people. Allocating these 50 classrooms to mass education schools and using the temporary funds for renovation to subsidize the facilities of the second and third categories in each school—I think it wouldn't even require that much money. Furthermore, by integrating mass education with primary schools, all elderly illiterate men and women in children's families can receive education in the same place, making the school a social center. What a great opportunity to transform society that would be!

I shall say no more here. It is my hope that all gentlemen responsible for educational administration, those running schools, and those leading the people will read this proposal with an open mind and calm heart, and reflect on what thoughts and reactions it evokes.

Published in *Kaifeng Education Fortnightly*, Vol. 1, Issues 6 & 7 (combined), January 1, 1933.

Speech at the Inaugural Meeting of the Teaching Research Association

Dear principals and teachers,

Just now, Director Qi, Principal Xu, Principal Zhao, and Principal Xing have spoken many words of praise for us, which we truly do not deserve. On behalf of all colleagues in the experimental zone, I would like to express our gratitude to everyone.

You are all the ones actually engaging in activities on the stage, while we in the experimental zone are merely cheering you on from the sidelines. To achieve overall results, it still depends on each of you showcasing your skills.

The significance of holding today's inaugural meeting of the Teaching Research Association lies in three points:

First, it serves as a platform for advocacy. At the initial stage of the establishment of the experimental zone, we should encourage all parties to express their views on education as much as possible. This was originally the proposition of Mr. Xu Shifeng[13], and the establishment of the Teaching Research Association is based on this proposition.

---

13 Xu Shifeng, a native of Nanyang, Henan Province, graduated from Beijing Normal University. In the early 1920s, he followed Li Lianfang to work in the Henan Provincial Department of Education as Secretary-General, engaging in the experimentation and design of teaching methods. Later, he successively served as Principal of Henan No.1 Normal School, Director of the Affiliated Middle School of Zhongzhou University, Professor of Henan Sun Yat-sen University, and Director of the Department of Education at Henan University. He advocated for and once took charge of the Kaifeng Urban Primary School and Mass Education Experimental Zone. Subsequently, he became a Professor at Beijing Normal University, concurrently serving as Director of its Affiliated Middle School and Chief Administrator. He also held the positions of Dean of Academic Affairs and Acting President at Fu Jen Catholic University. His works include *Behaviorist Child Psychology* and *Collected Essays on Secondary Education*, among others. —— Editors' note

Second, there are only a few colleagues in the experimental zone, with limited time and weak capabilities. To conduct comprehensive research on education and achieve overall improvement, it is essential for everyone to work together. The initiation of this Teaching Research Association aims to unite everyone in joint research and demonstrate overall achievements in education.

Third, each school has its own individual research efforts. However, when schools work independently, their efforts are scattered, and there is no way to exchange ideas. Even if schools form voluntary alliances, teachers are all occupied with their own lessons. Without dedicated personnel to organize everything, difficulties may arise in the process. Therefore, our office has taken on the responsibility of initiating this association.

The recognition that primary education deserves attention and the perception that current education is failing have almost become a common feeling among everyone. Yet, while people generally feel that primary education is important, they have not realized that primary education involves profound knowledge. I believe that primary education is not only the most important but also more difficult to research.

The main reasons for the current underdevelopment of primary education are:

First, most educators are unwilling to think deeply, simply following routines and repeating mistakes.

Second, there is a fear of failure. Although some people are willing to make improvements, following old paths will not draw criticism, while adopting new methods may lead to severe attacks once failures occur. Thus, they dare not attempt new approaches. This conservative mindset is indeed the greatest obstacle to educational innovation. We must work together to break this state of apathy, fear of difficulties, and desire for comfort.

Regarding the research approaches of the Teaching Research Association, I believe there are three points:

First, overall reform: completely overhaul the school curriculum, schedules, teaching methods, and teaching materials for thorough transformation. However, such experiments cannot be expected of ordinary people; instead, we need everyone to support those conducting the experiments to help them accomplish their work.

Second, partial reform: retain the original curriculum but select several common tasks or issues for research, or specifically conduct a few large-unit experiments.

Third, subject-specific reform: evaluate the value of existing teaching materials and textbooks, eliminate those that are inappropriate, and conduct systematic research anew.

The above three points are the opinions of colleagues in the experimental zone, put forward for your reference in the future. Finally, we hope that each school will elect representatives within a week in accordance with the organizational regulations of the Teaching Research Association and inform our office, so that we can convene various teaching research meetings before the winter vacation. This is our most earnest hope.

Published in *Kaifeng Education Fortnightly*, Vol. 1, Issues 6 and 7, January 1, 1933.

Reply to Gao Tianxi on the Issue of Single-Grade Teaching

Mr. Tianxi,

In response to your question regarding the single-grade curriculum for four school years, I hereby provide the following reply:

I am not aware of how your curriculum is arranged, but based on the situation described in your inquiry, it is presumably arranged with different subjects taught simultaneously. The so-called "different subjects" are defined by their distinct teaching formats. For example, arithmetic, handcraft, art, etc., are arranged alongside Chinese language lessons, with their respective class hours precisely matching. However, the remaining class hours allocated to general knowledge (changshi) lack corresponding subjects that can be taught concurrently, thus giving rise to problems. Otherwise, according to the ministry-prescribed hours, Chinese language should have more class time than general knowledge, so why is it that only general knowledge cannot be completed? If it were merely an issue of the individual workload of each subject, unrelated to curriculum scheduling, there would only be the problem of not finishing the curriculum. The difficulties encountered in the form of teaching here are the same as in regular teaching. By focusing solely on the principles of single-grade teaching, I may be able to resolve all these issues.

The point of attention in single-grade teaching is the problem of grade-level organization, which depends on the number of classes in the school and the number of teachers. If there is only one teacher, the grade-level organization need not be taken too seriously. If there are two or more teachers and, say, four classes of students, most of the courses should be divided into two groups, while a small portion of the courses can be taught individually or collectively as appropriate. Such division and combination can be based on grade levels or abilities.

In terms of curriculum arrangement, teaching the same subject at the same time or different subjects at the same time—i.e., teaching different lessons to different classes in the same classroom at the same time—involves two immutable principles that must be observed:1) Avoid certain practices, such as having multiple groups speaking aloud simultaneously.2) Make adjustments, such as when demonstrating to one group, ensuring that the other groups are engaged in self-study that truly requires independent work.

In accordance with these principles, when allocating courses for the same time period based solely on the nature of the subjects, even teaching different subjects may sometimes violate these principles. Even if the first principle is met, it is extremely difficult to satisfy the second. If applied properly, even teaching the same subject to different groups at the same time can conform to these principles. This goes without saying for subjects like handcraft, art, and arithmetic; even Chinese language, which encompasses reading, writing, and composition, can be taught in this way. Only general knowledge tends to pose problems, and this is due to the use of traditional textbook-based teaching methods. In fact, general knowledge is subsumed under various subjects, so its independent content is limited. Even if, due to the teacher's own constraints, textbook-based teaching must be used, it should be appropriately integrated with Chinese language lessons. Many lessons in commercial textbooks merely involve literacy training and should be deleted entirely. For those focused on imparting knowledge, a small amount of time can be allocated to organizing written exercises. I am not advocating for exclusively teaching the same subject at the same time, but rather emphasizing the need to allocate courses in accordance with the two principles mentioned above.

The steps for curriculum allocation are as follows:

(1) Carefully examine the interconnections between the units of each subject across all grades, extract them, and integrate them into comprehensive teaching materials. Estimate the time required for each integrated unit and separately calculate the time needed for independent units of each subject.

(2) For the units identified above, carefully determine which can be taught collectively to specific grades.

(3) Identify units that require special demonstration, special practice, or grade-specific instruction.

(4) Allocate units to the same time period based on either the unit content or the nature of the subject.

(5) Adopt ability grouping in addition to grade-level divisions, with adjustments every two months during the semester.

(6) Due to variations in class hours across grades and the need for flexibility in scheduled study time, set aside specific periods each day or every other day for grade-specific demonstrations or practice. When teaching one grade individually, clear guidelines must be established in advance for self-study tasks for the other grades.

This approach integrates group teaching, self-study guidance, and other recent innovative methods. The traditional single-grade teaching method, which focused solely on whether subjects were the same or different when arranging the curriculum, had many shortcomings. Prior to 1916, single-grade teaching was widely promoted in China, and several books on the subject were published. From the schools I observed at the time, although some had reasonable curriculum arrangements, in reality, when teaching four grades in the same classroom, each grade only received genuine instruction for a quarter of the time, with most of the remaining time wasted. Today, those engaged in single-grade teaching who follow traditional methods without thorough research are likely encountering similar issues. I hope that teachers of single-grade classes will adopt my suggestions, which may help avoid such problems. If, due to limitations in energy or expertise, teachers cannot fully implement my proposals, simply reflecting deeply on the two principles mentioned above and applying them to curriculum allocation and daily teaching—while setting aside a small amount of time for grade-specific instruction—will fundamentally resolve issues such as incomplete coverage of certain subjects.

Published in *Kaifeng Education Fortnightly*, Vol. 1, Issues 6 & 7 (combined), January 1, 1933. The title is added by the editor.

Reply to Mr. Sen's Inquiry

——Regarding School Education Policies[14*]

I am a person who has achieved nothing in education, so how can I be worthy of your high expectations? Honored by your thinking highly of me and humble inquiry, I dare not but pour out my foolish thoughts. However, I shall speak frankly on matters, and my words may be unpleasant to the ear. I hope you will not misunderstand—this is my sincere wish.

Before answering your questions separately, there are a few points to note:

First, society consists of "me" or "us." Do not exclude "me" or "us" when criticizing society.

Second, do not hold subjective views. Whether discussing knowledge or affairs, if one takes one's own position as the sole perspective, what is considered right or wrong will easily be tainted by emotions.

Third, one should reflect. No matter how influenced or criticized by the outside world, if one first excuses oneself, it will inevitably lead to a tendency to cover up mistakes.

I shall answer your questions based on these three points.

——As stated in the opening remarks, I respectfully reply as follows:

First, you stated that the term "society" is not "red propaganda," but I do not understand why such a statement was necessary. As in the first paragraph of your opening, even if people are obtuse, how could they be suspicious or fearful merely upon hearing the word "society"? If that were

---

14 *The subtitle is added by the editor.

the case, would the ministry-prescribed "society" subject in primary schools not be a serious violation of regulations?

Second, you stated that you observe [matters] with a scholar's attitude, fearing that others might suspect you of standing on a class position, and even more afraid that others might also stand on their own positions. This seems extremely cautious on the surface. However, in reality: (1) Is a scholar's attitude formed by detaching oneself from a position? (2) Does truth vary with one's position? If one ignores whether words contain truth and only cares about the speaker's position, one is setting up a stance to block opposing views ahead of time.

Third, you argue that education is a product of society, implying that the failure of education stems from the influence of social forces. Here, one must ask: Is education a product of society, and should it be a product of society? If the conclusion is absolute, then the formation of society would have nothing to do with education, and there would be no need for education to reform society. Furthermore, are social forces born of nature or of human action? If they are human-made, and if education is effective, is the society we have today related to past education? Moreover, have those engaged in education today truly exerted their efforts to advance society? If not, yet they attribute [failure] to society, I am deeply skeptical.

——As stated in the section on school education policies, I respectfully reply as follows:

First, the education policies list the Three Principles of the People... and other items side by side. Are they independent of each other, or do they form a continuum? The questioner may have had a specific intention, but to the respondent, these intricate goals are more vague than a general purpose, making specific discussion impossible.

Second, if the listed policies do not contain elements contrary to the stated purpose, one should first check whether their implementation is consistent with their claims. If what schools display—apart from slogans or occasional remarks—lacks comprehensive implementation to match their policies, and even unconsciously violates the listed goals by adhering to traditional methods, merely using these goals to silence criticism, then the goals become nothing but tools to cover up shortcomings. Therefore, I advocate that when examining policies, one should focus on one's own implementation rather than directing criticism at society; one should examine overall and consistent implementation rather than becoming excited over isolated incidents.

——As stated in the section that it is unreasonable for parents' family education policies to dominate schools, I respectfully reply as follows:

I am not sure what this question refers to. If, as in the final conclusion, parents do not express opinions to the school but issue orders through the Education Department, and this is called "using power to dominate schools," this requires separate discussion. The reasons why parents do not express opinions to the school may be: (1) Is the school not trusted by society? (2) Has the school always regarded parents' opinions as insignificant? (3) Even without the first two reasons, must parents' opinions about the school be limited to expressions directed at the school? Orders issued through the Education Department can be examined in terms of form and content. In terms of form: (1) Are parents utilizing the Education Department's orders? If so, this is a matter for the authorities to handle. (2) Is there an issue of improper procedure in the issuance of orders by the Education Department at the instigation of parents? If so, this concerns the validity of such orders. In terms of content: if the opinions are correct, they should be acknowledged even without an official order; if incorrect, they should be protested even if officially ordered. To condemn official orders merely because parents did not express their opinions to the school is unreasonable. While parents' attitudes may be criticized, the attitudes of principals and teachers in such cases are hardly better. As for the establishment of parent-teacher associations supposedly providing opportunities for parents to express opinions, if schools are satisfied with this, the opportunities provided are meager indeed. Moreover, parent-teacher associations have become a formality—who would voice dissatisfaction amid all the ostentation? Regarding the relationship between family and school education: children with poor family education may indeed affect their reception of school education. However, the claim that current school education policies are constrained by family education policies, and that teachers' implementation is interfered with by parents, thus violating so-called education policies, is something I have not witnessed. The parents referred to in the letter are certainly those with the influence to speak to the Education Department. Such parents may not all understand education, but most have received an education. To claim that their views on education are all inferior to those of current principals and teachers is hardly accurate. People's encouragement of their own children is no less sincere than teachers' guidance of students. While some may spoil their children, they do not necessarily demand the same from schools, nor can they realistically do so. Furthermore, teachers are also parents, and parents may also be teachers—does a change in position drastically alter one's educational perspective? To dismiss their criticism of schools as a failure to understand educational significance or national and ethnic public interests is excessive. While schools cannot cater to every parent's opinion—and in reality, they do not—this does not mean parents should be barred from asking about school affairs, limited to expressing opinions only at parent-teacher associations. The words in the letter may have been written in anger, but measured against the so-called scholar's attitude of calm thinking, such remarks are inappropriate.

——As stated in the section that it is unreasonable for social customs to dominate education, I respectfully reply as follows:

First, regarding the title: to recognize this as unreasonable contradicts the opening statement that education is a product of society. If the earlier statement describes a phenomenon and this one presents a theory, no old educational theory has ever advocated that education should be dominated by social customs. The reason such a phenomenon exists is not that social forces overwhelm schools, leaving them helpless, but that those engaged in education are perfunctory and incompetent, unable to inspire [society] with an ethos adapted to the new era. One must ask: in today's school education—whether in administration, teaching, or discipline—has there been implementation of an ethos adapted to the new era, consistent with its goals? Even if the form is fashionable, has anyone assessed its effectiveness to confirm real progress? Instead of seeking this, resenting the evils of social customs is of no practical help.

Second, regarding the content, it can be divided into three points:

I fully sympathize with the criticism of static education. However, shifting blame by citing irrelevant traditional maxims instead of examining school practices is evasion. In fact, society has never taken this as the sole standard, nor have schools adopted it as an educational policy. Yet education everywhere reveals the drawbacks of being static—who is responsible for this? Observe the teaching of games, sports, and handicrafts, all of which exhibit mechanical methods—this is food for thought.

The criticism of formal meetings: this is not a social custom but the false democracy flaunted in recent years. In fact, holding meetings several times a week, apart from the chairman's ritualistic opening remarks like "Dear gentlemen" or "Dear students," provides no practice in the basics of civil rights.

The criticism of the "wastepaper basket." Superficially, I agree with your view, but in substance, I differ. Regarding language teaching: I oppose textbook-based teaching, teaching dead characters, and teaching language through fixed subjects. However, language is a tool to unlock all knowledge. The traditional demand for children's literacy skills—also a general social demand—has not diminished, though methods are highly debatable. As for the Dalton Plan: while it has weaknesses, it has considerable value in education. Domestic books and discussions on this system are limited and not particularly erroneous. Yet schools in Kaifeng merely copy teaching manuals, a practice unheard of in other implementing schools. Instead of blaming themselves for failing to deeply understand, study, and prepare adequately, implementers attribute their failure to social traditions, the fashion for new methods, and the temptation of trivial teaching method manuals. Though there may be reasons hard to explain， this is hardly consistent with a scholar's attitude. I believe that to avoid falling behind, one should study diligently and act earnestly. Any attempt to defend shortcomings will ultimately lead to backwardness. Academic pursuits, unlike the power struggles of politicians and soldiers, allow no room for opportunism.

——As stated in the section that it is unreasonable for authorities to focus only on appearances, I respectfully reply as follows:

I have no objection to the arguments in the original letter. However, I would add that to break free from superficial education, one need not solely blame the party authorities or pin hopes on the authorities, but should start with ourselves—especially myself. This does not mean struggling against the authorities, but engaging in thorough research, rejecting superficial methods, and truly demonstrating results. While authorities are the main cause of schools' tendency toward superficiality, principals who merely follow routines, seeking not to make mistakes and even exploiting this to gain merit, have also contributed. Those engaged in education, though they may sense the pointlessness [of superficiality], cannot stop this trend if their own work shows no distinctive achievements.

——As stated in the section on poverty and facilities, I respectfully reply as follows:

Simple facilities are indeed common, but I disagree that this is the main reason teaching becomes divorced from reality and focuses on textual recitation.

First, are the existing facilities in various schools—whether idle or useless—largely wasteful?

Second, in terms of utilizing the environment without special facilities, have natural and social resources been fully employed in teaching?

Third, in non-verbal subjects like handicrafts and art, do current school practices lead away from reality?

Fourth, regarding language teaching itself—Is it inherently divorced from practical tasks?

——As stated in the section on the hardships of teachers and students, I respectfully reply as follows:

Teachers' lack of job security, which affects their work, indeed deserves full sympathy. However, using this to shirk our responsibility toward our duties or society is something I absolutely cannot endorse. If we follow this logic, vulnerable states without security should simply resign themselves to decline. Moreover, teachers' lack of security is not purely an educational issue. To expect political and social problems to be solved before reforming education is not a fundamental solution. And who but those engaged in education should undertake educational reform? This is why I consider educational reform more urgent than teacher security.

The claim that teachers have too many "masters" is perplexing. Principals control schools, and teachers control students, almost like governments over people, wielding supreme power. From my observations, I have yet to see any principal create a new policy or any teacher develop a new teaching method that was blocked from implementation—unless they refrained from creating out of fear of non-implementation. But without concrete demonstration, who would believe in their ability to create? To say they are suppressed by superiors: perhaps principals' and teachers' personal activities are manipulated, but internal practices indeed allow for free reform. To say they are suppressed by parents: as previously noted, this is rare, and judgment depends on the motives and circumstances. All teachers have siblings or children in school; putting themselves in parents' shoes, would such sweeping condemnation not make them cry injustice? To say they are suppressed by educational visionaries: if teachers were engaged in extensive research, visionaries' words would be mere nonsense. Moreover, implementers merely follow tradition and have never tested any theory to prove its uselessness, so how can they know it is 空想 (fantasy)? If they could truly refute it, how could the theory seduce them? To say they are suppressed by aristocratic defenders of old customs: schools in Europe and America may have capitalist backers, but public primary schools in China do not exclusively admit children of special classes, nor are they controlled by any special class. Even if some students, influenced by old society, have aristocratic habits and dislike manual labor, it is entirely up to teachers to exert subtle influence and lay the foundation for national rejuvenation. In fact, most children enjoy manual work; their reluctance stems from poor teaching.

Regarding students: who dares to violate policies based on educational purposes? Those in charge only have administrative power over education and do not interfere in internal affairs; no one else asks about it. If this is seen as contradictory, it is merely a psychological contradiction of implementers. As for issues like punctuality... simplicity, I do not understand the intention. Literally, there is no doubt about the difference between forging ahead and shrinking back, honesty and hypocrisy, extravagance and simplicity. Perhaps the disparity in children's family circumstances makes it difficult to achieve uniformity in extravagance vs. simplicity, but even if simplicity is emphasized, there is no need for rigid standards. Activity vs. stillness varies with circumstances and has no inherent positive or negative value. "Thrown in the wastepaper basket" and "jumping high" are incomparable. Only early rising vs. lateness seem contrasting, but their significance differs. Lateness must be judged against punctuality to cultivate the habit of timeliness; while lateness is bad, what good is early rising? It is also inefficient. If the intention is to promote early rising, a specific time should be set, not based on arbitrary semester start times, and measures must be reasonable. The promotion of early rising in Kaifeng primary schools has been criticized on all fronts. From what I've heard, the main reasons are: (1) Schools reward early arrivals, leading students to carry lanterns and wait outside for doors to open; those living nearby sign in then go home to rest; those living far away, arriving an hour before class, are still reprimanded for lateness. (2) Lateness is punished arbitrarily, sometimes by other students, causing humiliation. (3) So-called "self-study" lacks teacher guidance; sometimes teachers are still asleep while students noisy among themselves, with the most tedious task being aimless review. Due to competition to arrive first and excessive punishment, children often lack sleep, harming their health. Arriving too early, when households are still closed and streets empty, risks accidents. These criticisms do not come solely from special classes; I have heard them from no fewer than thirty people, including friends, workers, and merchants. Education researchers, child health doctors, and reviews of morning school hours in other countries all find this practice inappropriate. Therefore, the educational experimental zone has proposed to the Education Department that reasonable adjustments be made to retain the ethos of promoting early rising while eliminating the harms of competition and excessive punishment. If schools have such practices but refuse to admit fault, and your letter's reference to early rising and lateness alludes to this—while also condemning parents' comments as unreasonable and labeling parents as aristocrats—what kind of psychology is this? I earnestly hope you will reflect calmly.

——As stated in the section that educational reform should begin with education policies, I respectfully reply as follows:

The previous section attributes reform solely to authorities and scholars, who indeed bear responsibility. However, I believe principals and teachers share this responsibility. If they adopt the government's tone of blaming people for ignorance, what then? In fact, regardless of position, everyone has responsibilities. The progress of new undertakings depends not on a powerful few but on the efforts of the majority. Even if authorities are incompetent, they rarely deliberately obstruct new undertakings. Scholars are not limited to those outside teaching; many educational scholars in advanced countries emerged from primary school education. If teachers do not strive individually, even with ideal authorities and scholars, education cannot be reformed. I hope primary school teachers, upon whom the state relies, will not pin hopes on authorities and scholars but first look to ourselves—then there is hope for our state.

The latter section attributes poor education to social systems and education itself, exonerating teachers. While education is influenced by systems, those engaged in it have an even greater impact. Can one truly say that poor society and education have nothing to do with teachers' complacency and perfunctoriness? Even within the current system, have teachers done their utmost to reform within their capacity? If as claimed, current education needs no reform. Otherwise, are teachers comparing themselves to executioners? Executioners kill people but are not responsible for whether it is justified. Teachers directly harm children and indirectly endanger the state—this responsibility cannot be shifted to others.

Finally, I would add: I do not deny the difficulties teachers face as described in your letter. However, blaming others without self-criticism, and evading responsibility excessively, inevitably leads to evasive language. Hence, I urge you with these blunt words. Society degenerates because of people. Our degeneration is not because society corrupts people, but because people corrupt society! Because my expectations of teachers are high, my criticism is sharp. I have no other motives. I earnestly hope you will understand my sincerity and forgive my bluntness.

Published in *Kaifeng Education Fortnightly*, Vol. 1, Issue 9, January 21, 1933.

The Rural Education I Advocate

Without further ado, I will put forward general opinions in four aspects: organization, staffing, facilities, and curriculum.

1. Opinions on Organization: Advocating the Co-location of Primary Schools and Mass Education Schools

This is not only to save manpower and expenses but also to ensure that the two types of education do not hinder each other but rather complement each other. How do they not hinder each other? During the Qing Dynasty, when simple literacy schools were run, drawbacks emerged: learners sought school supplies provided by the government; those running the schools, tempted by easy achievements due to the simplicity of facilities, even disbanded primary school classes or embezzled funds earmarked for expanding primary schools. I hear that today's so-called "mass education experimental schools" are not immune to such problems. If co-located, classes and curricula must adapt to actual circumstances, preventing overlap or encroachment. How do they complement each other? In sparsely populated areas, separate schools may fail to form classes, but combined, they can offer divided sessions. With a centralized location, staggered class times allow families to take turns supervising household duties; simultaneous classes enable older students to care for younger ones. Moreover, family engagement in primary schools has long been a hollow promise. By incorporating mass education, school education becomes a matter for entire families, naturally making the school a social hub.

2. Opinions on Staffing: Implementing Single-Grade or Multi-Grade Teaching

This approach is not only suitable for separate operations but also allows flexible merging or splitting of the two school types based on coursework. For example, older students can lead specialized agricultural or craft courses, while upper primary students can guide specialized literacy or arithmetic classes. What I wish to clarify is: First, groups within a single grade are mobile, not fixed. Second, single-grade teaching is not merely about scheduling the same or different subjects simultaneously; it integrates individual tasks and group teaching into project-based curricula. How rural education benefits from single-grade staffing is widely understood and needs no further explanation.

3. Opinions on Facilities: Guided by Local Economic Conditions

These suggestions align with single-grade staffing. Since primary and mass education schools are co-located with staggered classes, a two-session system can be adopted. School Buildings: At minimum, one large room capable of accommodating a single grade, with appropriately sized windows on the left as a general classroom; an open space for recreation; and 3 – 4 additional rooms for specialized classes and teacher housing. Work spaces: At least 4 – 5 mu (≈0.27 – 0.33 hectares) of garden and 2 – 3 mu (≈0.13 – 0.2 hectares) of farmland. More garden space is preferable because rural primary and mass education should center on hands-on work, and cultivation or animal husbandry—less strenuous than farming—suits daily activities. Teaching Tools: All should be simple and aligned with local livelihoods.

4. Opinions on Curriculum: Centered on Agricultural Work

Three types of work—horticulture, farming, and crafts—can coexist, with emphasis varying by grade: lower grades focus on horticulture, middle grades on farming, and upper grades on crafts (closely linked to agriculture). A central teaching unit should integrate natural and social sciences; even tool subjects like language and arithmetic must serve work-related goals and needs. Through such holistic activities, students develop essential national virtues. In single-grade teaching, note that when lower grades join middle/upper grades in core tasks, middle/upper students should lead; when middle/upper grades involve lower grades, the latter participate as learners.

These modest proposals, though unremarkable, point to a path of thorough reform. Those who emptily shout "go to the countryside" or promote "vocational education" fail to grasp education's true meaning. Today's normal school curricula only drift further astray. My only hope is that rural normal schools will reform thoroughly soon—only then can the rural education I advocate become a reality.

Published in *Rural Reconstruction*, Vol. 2, Issue 2, April 1933.

Another View on the Treatment of Primary School Teachers

In the past, a state's strength depended on the extent of universal national education. Therefore, all governments of so-called civilized states regarded universal education as their paramount policy. For without it, a state's people could not compete with others in terms of military power and economy on the world stage; having education is ultimately better than having none. As social problems have become increasingly severe, traditional education, in all aspects, has only intensified the elements of human sin. Thus, the issue of education lies not only in its quantity but also in its quality. This "quality" cannot be achieved by merely following the Europeanization of pragmatism or production, as that would be addressing the symptoms rather than the root cause. Nor can it be advanced by returning to China's ethical concepts or the Buddhist theory of emphasizing tranquility.

Countries around the world are competing in primary education experiments. Although they have not fully grasped this essence, their common tendency has gradually shifted toward using learning to solve all aspects of human life. It can be asserted that the universal human demand for social salvation lies not just in having education, but in the quality of education. The reason why primary education must be emphasized is that human intelligence and habits are initially formed in primary school. If the foundation is flawed, it will be extremely difficult to improve later. Cultivating this foundation is the responsibility of primary school teachers. Hence, a state's lifeline is tied to national education, and primary school teachers are the "mothers of the state."

If a government wishes to strengthen its country but does not prioritize education, or values education but underestimates primary education, it is like dredging a river without first unclogging its source—dryness will come in no time. However, if primary education is valued but only follows the path of universalization from the previous century, focusing on quantity over quality, then having education will be of little effect compared to having none in today's world of peace and chaos. This quality-oriented education cannot evolve based on traditional concepts. While its initiation requires one or two deeply insightful scholars, its promotion depends on ordinary practitioners who are willing to take responsibility and engage in extensive research.

To expect ordinary practitioners to take responsibility and conduct more research—ensuring that each school fulfills its purpose and each student achieves results—depends entirely on the government's incentive measures. If there are no proper incentives, or no incentives at all, a few capable individuals, living in an environment of perfunctory routines, will see their hard work go unrecognized and their initiatives mocked as meddling. Initially, they may be eager to try, but over time, they will fall into the same pattern of complacency. The decline of national affairs stems from the degradation of public morality, and this is how it begins.

Today, our state faces severe crises. The government and intellectuals, in responding to current events, mostly focus on superficial solutions. No matter how comprehensive their strategies, they cannot ultimately save the state from hardship. In fact, addressing national crises lies not in the present but in the future. As long as the younger generation we cultivate is not as weak-willed and selfish as we are today, even if the country is destroyed and the state scattered, this vast state will eventually rejuvenate. If national politics and social undertakings are not integrated into education, nothing can be accomplished. The vitality of education depends on whether children can lay a solid foundation in due measure. If we truly focus on this and act now, all future children will become useful members contributing to the state and society, rather than products of family advancement or power struggles—and they will not be abandoned by humanity.

The standard for the treatment of teachers in Henan provincial primary schools originally stipulated a promotion every five years, which many consider inconvenient. First, the five-year limit is too long. In today's situation, nothing is secure; even if there are guarantees, they often remain on paper. As a result, teachers' appointments and transfers are chaotic. Less competent teachers, escaping attention, often retain their positions. Moreover, with the rising cost of living, capable teachers, burdened by family responsibilities, cannot wait passively for this "mirage of comfort." Second, seniority and merit rarely go hand in hand. Due to a poor environment and the authorities' lack of clear evaluation standards, practitioners easily get by with perfunctory work, forming a culture where "avoiding mistakes is considered merit." Over time, those with longer tenure often prioritize routine over academic growth and experience. A five-year promotion system will inevitably lead to valuing seniority over merit. Checking the promotion records of the Henan Education Department confirms this.

Colleagues in the experimental zone, aware of this situation, proposed revisions. Their goal is to establish appropriate incentives to promote education and lay a century-long foundation for the state, not to complain or seek rewards on behalf of desperate primary school teachers. I hear Director Qi [15] has taken this proposal seriously, but due to reservations in department meetings and reviews, further discussions are pending. Those involved surely have their difficulties, which outsiders

15 That is Qi Zhenru (Xingyi), a native of Luoyang, Henan Province, who was then serving as Director of the Henan Provincial Department of Education. —— Editors' note

cannot fully understand. However, despite its seeming triviality, this matter is of great significance. The arguments presented here are not delusions. I believe that if the Chinese people have the will to rejuvenate the state, and the authorities bear the responsibility of reforming education, revising primary school teachers' treatment should be a prerequisite for promoting reform.

Some may argue that primary schools currently show no results, but results (or lack thereof) are a separate issue. The key question is: Is it crucial to regulate primary school teachers' treatment? Should the original standards be revised? If no valid objections exist, retaining the old system is merely a disguised defense of personal biases. Furthermore, precisely because primary schools lack results, educationally, this affects the quality of secondary and higher education; nationally, it impacts the survival of the state. Without proper incentives, all reforms and experiments will be stymied. This is why I do not hesitate to speak out loudly to the Education Department.

As for the excuse of funding: the five-year promotion rule was issued in 1929 and is now due for revision. The proposal to emphasize merit over seniority would only require a limited increase in expenditure. If it is beneficial, efforts should be made to implement it. Moreover, allowing the tradition of valuing seniority over merit to persist—rewarding mediocrity and discouraging talent—will only worsen the situation, which the authorities must consider.

Others may claim that rural primary school teachers are poorly paid, and provincial teachers, already better off, would exacerbate inequality if promoted too quickly. However, addressing inequality requires adapting to circumstances. Using this as an objection is like arguing that because there are starving people in the wilderness, the government should not function on an empty stomach. In short, primary education urgently needs thorough reform. Revising teachers' treatment standards with proper incentives will inspire diligence, making reform possible. Without this, nothing can be achieved, and our state will only sink further into decline. Alas!

Published in *Kaifeng Education Fortnightly*, Vol. 1, Issues 13 & 14 (combined), May 1, 1933.

Work Plan for Kaifeng Urban Primary School and Mass Education Experimental Zone[16]

1. Plan for Dahuayuan Education Village

1.1 Experimental Objectives

To pilot community-centered education, develop rural economy, enrich farmers' lives, strive for the rejuvenation of the Chinese state, and realize a fair society.

1.2 Implementation Principles

(1) Treat the entire village as an integrated educational venue, abolish the form of a "school," and break down the fragmented system of family, school, and social education.

(2) Target all villagers as educational recipients. Implement mixed education to discard the traditional concept of separating primary education from adult education.

(3) Integrate education into daily life. Provide tangible or intangible education anytime and anywhere according to the actual needs of society. Abolish all practices such as fixed class schedules, winter/summer vacations, semesters, and school years.

(4) Based on the direct or indirect economic activities of rural society, design large-unit projects. Without violating psychological principles, focus particularly on cultivating character for social production, training skills for social production, and mastering various knowledge related to

---

16 All departments of the experimental zone have work plans designed. Here, three of them are excerpted, collaborated on by Li Lianfang, Tai Shuangqiu, etc. — Editors' note

social production. Literacy education shall only play an auxiliary role; abolish all subject-based systems and textbook-based systems.

(5) Promote a "mutual teaching system," guide villagers to teach each other, so as to expand educational undertakings and improve educational efficiency.

1.3 Outline of the Organization

The organization of this Education Village consists of three divisions: Research, Education, and Cooperation. A Director is appointed to oversee the implementation of experimental work. The responsibilities and staffing of each division are as follows:

1.3.1 Research Division

This division has 1 Chief Officer and 3 Assistant Officers, with the following responsibilities. (1) Investigating the occupations of residents in the area, types of local products, production conditions, and living needs. (2) Researching methods to improve local products in the area. (3) Researching household crafts suitable for residents in the area to engage in. (4) Developing large-unit teaching designs. (5) Other related tasks.

If the research results are valuable, their application will not be limited to a single village. Therefore, the funds required for research work should be determined based on the nature of the projects. Initially, it is planned to appoint 1 officer with agricultural and industrial training and 3 officers with educational training to share the responsibilities.

1.3.2 Education Division

This division has 1 Chief Instructor and 1 Assistant Instructor, with the following responsibilities. (1) Organizing villagers and promoting various educational activities. (2) Disseminating research results to improve villagers' lives. (3) Other related tasks.

The scope of work of this division corresponds to both regular school education and social education. To align with China's economic conditions and facilitate future promotion, the expenses of this division should be kept as economical as possible, adhering to the principle that they shall not exceed the proportional funding normally required by villagers for school education and social education. The instructors shall be experienced primary school teachers who have graduated from normal schools.

1.3.3 Cooperation Division

This division has 1 Chief Officer and 1 Assistant Officer, with the following responsibilities. (1) Managing credit cooperatives. (2) Managing production cooperatives. (3) Managing marketing cooperatives. (4) Managing consumer cooperatives.

The work of this division is not limited to a single village, so the required funds should be determined based on the nature of the projects. Before production cooperatives are established, venues for training production skills can be operated in collaboration with villagers—either entrusted to them under the guidance of this division, or existing venues can be used with appropriate subsidies.

In addition, a Rural Education Instructors Training Course will be established and attached to the organization of this Education Village. Detailed regulations will be formulated separately.

1.4 General Situation of Dahuayuan Village

Dahuayuan Village is located outside the Songmen Gate of Kaifeng. A brief account of its land, population, and economic conditions, based on survey findings, is as follows:

1.4.1 Land

The village covers an area of approximately 10 square li (about 2.6 square kilometers). The terrain is flat, with no mountains, forests, or rivers, but there are numerous burial grounds. Cultivated land totals around 30 qing (about 200 hectares), of which 10 qing (about 67 hectares) are sandy soils, located in the northwest corner of the village. Each household owns an average of about 40 to 50 mu (about 2.7 to 3.3 hectares) of farmland; households with more than 1 qing (about 6.7 hectares) are quite rare.

1.4.2 Population

There are 119 households in the village. Among them, 113 are engaged in farming, and 6 are unemployed. Each household has at least 4 members, with an average of about 7, and some have as many as 25. The total population is 880, including 468 males and 412 females. The age distribution is as follows:

Under 6 years old	106
6 - 10 years old	87
11 - 20 years old	152
20 - 50 years old	373
Over 50 years old	162

1.4.3Economic Conditions

The main agricultural products of the village are wheat, beans, peanuts, and sorghum, followed by radishes, watermelons, and Chinese cabbage. Sideline occupations are limited to peddling, vending, chicken-raising, pig-raising, and weaving, with meager income. As a result, the lives of the villagers, except for a very small number, are extremely poor.

1.4.4Potential for Future Development

There are numerous productive undertakings that could be developed in the village. Here are some of the key ones:

(1) Willow Planting

Approximately 10 qing of sandy land in the village is currently used for growing peanuts, yielding minimal profits. If converted to willow cultivation, the area could become a thriving forest within three years. Willow branches can be used to make buckets, carrying cases, and other items, generating substantial profits.

(2) Weaving

The village's busy farming season runs from April to October, leaving ample free time in other months. The village cooperative could provide cotton, looms, and other supplies on credit, allowing villagers to engage in weaving during agricultural slack periods. The products could then be sold through the cooperative on consignment, with net profits used as cooperative shares for each household. These shares could further fund the development of public productive enterprises, gradually making each household an owner of such enterprises and avoiding exploitation by usurers.

(3) Chicken Raising

The village produces sorghum, which is highly economical for feeding chickens. According to local farmers, raising one chicken yields a profit of at least 1 yuan per year. However, chicken plague often occurs in spring and autumn, with no effective prevention measures, and managing large flocks is inconvenient. Thus, no households in the village specialize in chicken raising. With proper guidance on plague prevention, introduction of high-quality breeds, and the establishment of collective chicken farms with joint management, chicken raising could become a significant supplementary source of income for the villagers.

1.5 Methods for Implementing Education

1.5.1 Several thatched cottages will be built in the center of Huayuan Village to serve as the administrative office of the Education Village and the villagers' meeting hall. The meeting hall, capable of accommodating approximately 100 people, will have a storage room adjacent to it for storing various supplies used in teaching activities. All facilities in the meeting hall and office should be kept simple, with priority given to items made by the villagers themselves.

1.5.2 Under the guidance of education instructors, organizations such as the Public Justice League, Service Society, Children's Association, or similar groups will be established as institutions to promote educational activities. Detailed regulations will be formulated separately.

1.5.3 Educational activities requiring collective participation will be held in the villagers' meeting hall or in the open fields.

1.5.4 Except for special cases, all members of these groups must practice production skills, which will be arranged by education instructors and conducted at various production sites.

1.5.5 All knowledge related to educational activities will be learned and practiced at any time—at production sites, the villagers' meeting hall, or other locations—as needed for the activities.

1.5.6 Under the arrangement of education instructors, members of each group will, based on their individual circumstances, go to designated households or fields to participate in the following activities:

(1) Publicize the importance of household production;

(2) Introduce methods of household production;

(3)Introduce methods for improving production;

(4) Guide production activities;

(5) Disseminate knowledge related to educational activities;

(6) Distribute raw materials for production cooperation to each household;

(7) Take the products of each household to the cooperative for sale;

(8) Publicize the importance of purchasing local goods;

(9) Guide how to purchase local goods;

(10) Publicize the importance of frugality;

(11) Guide how to practice frugality;

(12) Other matters related to economic activities.

1.5.7 Instructors must investigate the personality and family situation of each villager. When necessary, they should adjust the types of economic activities for villagers to provide them with opportunities for diverse practice.

1.8 Budget (omitted)

2. Education Plan for Xinghuayuan Town

2.1 Social Overview

Xinghuayuan Town is a small autonomous district under Kaifeng County, located in the northeastern part of Kaifeng city. The town comprises two streets: Xinghuayuan and Xuanjiang Hutong. The streets are narrow with poor road conditions, and both sides are densely lined with production workshops of ordinary craftsmen. Over 70% of the town's population are productive laborers, but due to outdated methods, their products have a limited market. Most people live in extreme hardship;

some even work day and night without getting enough to eat. Coupled with underdeveloped education and a closed mindset, despite possessing the national virtues of diligence, simplicity, and perseverance, they show obvious signs of decline under the mutual oppression of economic hardship and lack of knowledge. This town well represents the prototype of production groups of traditional urban craftsmen in China.

According to surveys, the details of its household registration and occupations are as follows:

2.1.1 Population Survey Statistics

(1) The town has a total of 235 households, among which 121 are engaged in industry or commerce.

(2) The total population of the town is 1,332, with 700 engaged in industry or commerce.

(3) There are 981 males and 351 females. Among them, 242 are under 15 years old, 705 are between 15 and 40 years old, and 335 are over 40 years old.

2.1. 2 Occupation Statistics

Occupation Statistics Table of Xinghuayuan Town

Occupation Types	Number of Households	Number of People	Remarks
Pen-making Industry	7	72	
Cloth Shop	1	2	
Carpenter	26	162	
Tinsmith	2	6	
Mason	1	2	
Brush and Bone Craftsman	2	11	
Paperhanger	2	9	
Painter	3	8	

Book Trade	1	2	
Cigarette-making Industry	1	4	
Tea House	2	12	
Ready-made Clothes Shop	2	12	
Fried Pancake Shop	2	12	
Grocery Store	6	25	
Barber Trade	1	4	
Government Sector	25	63	
Education Sector	14	72	
Military & Police	13	35	
Business Sector	18	117	
Industrial Sector	103	587	
Non-employed	62	462	Mostly children and women
Total	235	1332	

Statistics Table of Industry and Commerce in Xinghuayuan Town

Occupation Types	Number of Households	Number of People	Remarks
Coppersmith	50	282	
Blacksmith	2	7	
Silvcrsmith	1	8	
Dyer	3	28	
Painting Trade	8	46	
Engraving Trade	1	2	
Steamed Bun Shop	1	2	
Total	121	700	Women and children without occupations are not included in the headcount.

Production Capacity Table of Xinghuayuan Town

Monthly Income (in Silver Dollars)	Number of Households	Remarks
Over 200 Silver Dollars	None	
100–200 Silver Dollars	6	
50–100 Silver Dollars	32	
10–50 Silver Dollars	114	
Under 10 Silver Dollars	21	
Total	235	Non-employed individuals are not included.

The above three tables were surveyed by the mayor of Xinghuayuan Town. Although we cannot be certain about their reliability, the general situation is probably correct.

2.3 Educational Goals

Both theory and facts tell us that the wave of the industrial revolution is about to engulf all traditional handicrafts in China. Not only have rural household handicraft sideline industries long since disappeared, but even the extensive urban handicraftsmen are everywhere feeling the horror and sorrow of being on the verge of extinction. The facts are as follows:

(1)The new machine production methods have eliminated the clumsy manual techniques.

(2) The exquisite exports of the mechanical industry have replaced the shoddy local products.

(3) "Trusts" and other reasonable economic organizations have destroyed the feudal guild system.

(4) The results of education implementation over the past 30 years and the trend of the world's new education have clearly exposed the ineffectiveness of past education and its incompatibility with the current social needs of China.

Therefore, if we want to save China's handicraft industry from danger, develop the economy of urban people, and correct the mistakes of past education, we must:

(1)Implement education centered on society and life — The content and methods of education should be centered on the entire society, labor production, and practical life, so as to avoid the harms of fragmentation, opposition, superficiality, and emptiness.

(2) Improve the production techniques of handicraftsmen — Through the gradual improvement of existing production techniques, enable them to use appropriate machines, so as to catch up and avoid falling behind.

(3) Improve the products of handicraftsmen — Investigate the supply and demand situation of production products in the general society, and thereby improve the products as much as possible to meet such needs.

(4) Improve the economic organization of handicraftsmen Break the feudal guild system and the decentralized management mode, and adopt an open cooperative system to concentrate and enhance the power of social production.

(5) Change the attitude towards life of handicraftsmen — Address the fact that ignorance and poverty reinforce each other, improve citizens' common sense, cultivate social morality, and foster an open and progressive attitude towards life, so as to enrich people's lives.

Therefore, based on the social conditions of Xinghuayuan Town, we have formulated an overall educational goal: to pilot social production education, so as to enrich citizens' lives and realize an ideal society.

2.4 Principles of Implementation

(1) Take productive labor as the center of educational activities. Use educational forces to improve production, and implement education through production activities, so that education and production undertakings are integrated into one.

(2) Involve all townspeople in educational activities, so that children's education and adult education are integrated. Encourage self-education and mutual teaching to achieve the effect of mutual support and common progress.

(3) Take the entire town as the venue for educational activities. Integrate the forms of family education, school education, and social education, and apply them as appropriate to concentrate educational forces and improve educational efficiency.

(4) Take the entire life of citizens as the scope of educational activities. From all aspects of citizens' lives, apply various appropriate methods to implement various effective education, so that education and life are integrated into one.

(5) Attach equal importance to the improvement of production capacity and the cultivation of production habits, so that production and consumption can adapt to each other, and thus develop living habits of smooth economic operation.

(6) Use and cultivate the talents and financial resources of the whole town in an economical and effective way to manage the educational and production undertakings of the whole town.

(7) Take promoting production cooperation as the pioneer of activities, improving production goods as the backbone of activities, enhancing production skills as the focus of activities, and increasing social production as the goal of activities.

2.5 Implementation Measures

2.5.1 Administrative Organization:

2.5.1.1 The Education Administrative Committee of Xinghuayuan Town shall be the highest authority for educational administration in the town. It shall consist of 9 to 11 members, appointed by the Experimental Zone Committee from individuals with the following qualifications. 1) The mayor and deputy mayor; 2) Townspeople who are enthusiastic about public welfare and advocate for education; 3) Faculty and staff of the Provincial Experimental Mass Education School; 4) Experts with extensive research and experience in social production education; 5) Members and staff of the Experimental Zone Committee.

2.5.1.2 The functions and powers of the Education Administrative Committee are as follows. 1) Determine the guidelines and plans for educational implementation in the entire town; 2) Decide on methods for raising funds for educational undertakings in the town; 3) Review the budget and final accounts of educational funds for the town; 4) Supervise and guide the progress of educational undertakings in the town; 5) Encourage and guide all townspeople to engage in various educational activities; 6) Deliberate on proposals regarding education submitted by educational instructors and townspeople of the town; 7) Handle other important educational matters.

2.5.1.3 The Education Administrative Committee shall have 3 standing members, elected by all committee members, who shall convene meetings and handle daily affairs.

2.5.1.4 Under the Education Administrative Committee, there shall be two divisions: General Affairs and Undertakings. A Chief Executive shall be appointed by the Experimental Zone Committee to manage the affairs of both divisions under the direction of the Administrative Committee.

Duties of the General Affairs Division: 1) Matters related to surveys and statistics; 2) Matters related to documentation, accounting, and general services.

Duties of the Undertakings Division: 1) Matters related to general education; 2) Matters related to vocational education; 3) Matters related to supplementary education; 4) Matters related to special training education; 5) Matters related to cooperative planning and implementation.

Detailed plans for the two divisions shall be formulated by the Education Administrative Committee from time to time in accordance with the above provisions and implementation procedures. Initially, the General Affairs Division shall not have a dedicated staff member but shall employ one clerk to handle documentation, accounting, and general services. The Undertakings Division shall concurrently be responsible for surveys and statistics. The Undertakings Division shall initially have 3 full-time instructors, 2 part-time instructors, and 2 single-grade primary school teachers. Staffing shall be expanded as the undertakings progress. All personnel shall be appointed separately by the Experimental Zone Committee.

2.5.2 Activity Methods and Procedures

(1) Take school education as the main institution for activities aimed at transforming the town's undertakings and people's lives.

(2) Conduct a comprehensive social survey of the town, with special emphasis on economic surveys, such as types of occupations, production and consumption situations, and profit and loss of income and expenditure.

(3) Based on the results of the social survey, register various production activities into several categories and divide them into groups accordingly to facilitate the implementation of designs and training.

(4) Establish credit, production, marketing, and consumer cooperatives respectively according to the common needs of each group or household.

(5) According to the needs of each production group, utilize the strength of cooperatives to provide appropriate knowledge and skill training respectively under certain precise designs.

(6) Determine the training venues based on the nature of the training, such as using schools, tea houses, factories, town halls, family guest rooms, etc.

(7) After mastering the necessary knowledge and skills for a certain need, specify the direction of activities and start work, with responsible instructors explaining and guiding at any time.

(8) Conduct various training related to social production as appropriate, such as language training, recreational training, civic training, and housework training.

(9) During the process of various training, fully publicize the importance of social production, the significance of cooperatives, the necessity of improving production skills and products, as well as the main points of cooperation between us (those running the experimental zone) and the townspeople.

2.5.3 Regular Budget (omitted)

3. Plan for Compiling Flexible Teaching Materials for Primary School Subjects

3.1 Rationale

Teaching materials are the sole tool for achieving educational goals, and teaching methods and efficiency also hinge on teaching materials. Therefore, progressive primary schools everywhere strive to compile appropriate teaching materials themselves. The curriculum standards issued by the Ministry only outline general frameworks without specifying concrete teaching materials, nor do they account for local specificities. Various textbooks available in the market are mostly broad in content and disconnected from reality. Their adaptation relies entirely on on-the-ground implementation. Thus, existing fixed teaching materials are hardly suitable for primary schools in Henan.

Since the establishment of this committee, Director Qi Xingyi has encouraged the compilation of appropriate primary school teaching materials. This was repeatedly emphasized at the inaugural meetings of the principals' discussion forum and the teaching research association. Entrusted with this task, we are committed to contributing our efforts and have therefore formulated a specific plan for compiling flexible teaching materials for various primary school subjects in Henan. We intend to gather experts in primary education from across the province to compile subject-specific teaching materials suitable for Henan's primary schools, tailored to local conditions and adhering to the principles of the ministry-issued curriculum standards. The plan is as follows:

3.2 Plan

3.2.1 Compilation Guidelines: Compile flexible teaching materials based on the ministry-issued curriculum standards and adapted to local needs.

3.2.2 Types of Compilation:

3.2.2.1 Revised Textbooks: Not limited to full revisions; select specific lessons from certain textbooks and correct inappropriate content.

3.2.2.2 Supplementary Materials: Systematically describe specific topics in the form of booklets, divided into two categories: 1) Local needs; 2) Current affairs needs.

3.2.2.3 Children's Reading Materials: Include adaptations, translations, and original works, all suitable for modern children's reading:

(1) General Knowledge Readers: A. Natural science knowledge; B. Social knowledge.

(2) Literary Readers: A. Children's picture books; B. Children's stories; C. Short stories.

3.2.2.4 Large-Unit Project-Based Lesson Plans:

(1) Original project designs.

(2) Organized and refined valuable project designs scattered in books and newspapers.

3.3 Compilation Methods:

(1) Staff of this district must, in accordance with items a, b, c, and d above, determine in advance the number of topics they will undertake each semester and the number of materials to be completed monthly. These materials must be submitted monthly to the committee for review.

(2) Invite experts and experienced teachers to participate in compilation.

(3) Solicit manuscripts (remuneration and review rules for this item and item 2 will be separately stipulated).

(4) Review manuscripts from items (1), (2), and (3) will be the responsibility of committee members, who will present review opinions for voting at regular meetings. Experts may be invited for review when necessary.

(5) A designated staff member of this district will collect manuscripts, oversee printing, report on all affairs at each regular meeting, and handle matters in accordance with resolutions.

(6) Printing will be in the form of booklets or loose-leaf sheets.

3.4 Budget (omitted)

Published in *Kaifeng Education Fortnightly*, Vol. 1, Issues 13 & 14 (combined), May 1, 1933.

Opinions on Labor Courses and Teaching

Mr. Sun Juemin, a labor education teacher at the Tenth Primary School, has completed the compilation of The Syllabus for Labor Education Teaching Plans. This journal will publish it as a special issue, hoping to promote the improvement of craft and art teaching and inspire the subsequent implementation of teaching plans for other subjects. Mr. Sun has conducted concrete and in-depth research on primary school crafts and arts, as can be glimpsed from his syllabus. My own views on primary education tend somewhat toward centering teaching around manual training. However, as I am not proficient in such techniques, I hesitate to elaborate extensively. That said, in actual teaching practice, the isolation resulting from subject-based division—even with improvements—inevitably leads to narrowness of perspective. In principle, this reduces education to vague goals; in process, it becomes an empty formality. This has become a common trend in today's "new-style" teaching. Thus, based on my long-held educational views, I offer further thoughts on Mr. Sun's proposed syllabus, hoping to "cast a brick to attract jade" and contribute something of value.

The ministry-issued curriculum standards originally referred to "labor education" as "work education." Its categories included school affairs, household chores, farming, and crafts. In the general instructions, it stated that farming or crafts could be offered as a standalone subject (named accordingly), with other necessary tasks integrated into related subjects. Additionally, lower grades could merge art and labor education into a single "work subject." The key teaching methods emphasized that this subject should fully integrate with social studies and science; discussions and research must be combined with hands-on practice and investigation, rather than being treated as an isolated activity prone to empty talk. These points form the foundational understanding for developing a labor education curriculum.

To determine how labor education should be taught, we must first clarify its significance in holistic education. In modern educational thought, labor has become a common methodological trend—whether rooted in social or psychological factors—aimed at reforming the traditional knowledge-centered education and replacing it with action-centered education. However, this trend achieves its purpose only when embedded in holistic education; it cannot be realized through a single course or rigid format. In subject-based teaching, certain courses may indeed be more suitable for labor education. Yet, to fulfill this educational vision, labor must serve as the core subject, with all arrangements and teaching activities branching out from it.

The ministry-issued curriculum lists labor as one of ten subjects, accounting for less than one-tenth of total class hours. Building the function of holistic education on such a minor subject is formally incomplete. If offering one type of activity suffices, traditional manual training courses could easily replace it, making "labor education" merely a name change. As for the categories, school affairs and household chores are listed alongside farming and crafts, though many tasks are interconnected—for example, clothing and food relate to farming, and production relates to crafts. If units are designed around rigid categories, fragmentation becomes inevitable. While the ministry's goals and teaching methods might theoretically support labor education, practical implementation and effectiveness assessment would raise numerous issues.

If education authorities and curriculum drafters recognize that Chinese education is deeply entrenched in elitist, book-centered habits and believe labor education can remedy this, they should embed labor's essence into the entire primary school curriculum to establish a foundation for productive education and foster an ethos of democratic citizenship. Subjects most suited to labor—such as science, manual training, and art—should be reformed accordingly. Merely renaming a subject or expanding its scope (whether called "labor" or "work") would remain vague and impractical, even undermining labor education's true value.

Mr. Sun's labor education plan divides the subject into two parts: art and crafts. This allows me to articulate my views:

First, separating art and crafts in planning: While the two subjects have distinct natures and can be taught independently in practice, their learning units, though divisible, must be grounded in integrated teaching. Since art and crafts are merged into one subject, their materials should be organized holistically. Art activities—such as painting and collage—when combined with crafts, form a natural part of project-based learning. A nominal merger with separate materials and processes renders the integration meaningless.

Second, confining labor education solely to art and crafts: As discussed earlier, while these subjects are well-suited to labor education, isolating them from other subjects risks obscuring labor's true value. This issue stems from adhering to the ministry's nomenclature and need not be dwelled on. However, to embody labor education's significance in practice, curriculum design must address three aspects:

1. Formal learning: This refers to the core content of a unit. For art and crafts, it includes three key elements—materials, techniques, and tool use—long emphasized in teaching, which should be specified by grade level and progression.

2. Incidental learning: Art and crafts involve creative activities that, in the process of acquiring knowledge and skills, shape character more overtly than other subjects. For instance, if teachers allow students to seize or damage tools or waste materials during crafting or animal care, even

successful formal learning would be undermined by moral harm. This splits practicality from personal growth. True educational reform hinges on recognizing the value of incidental learning. Guidelines must anticipate, based on formal learning goals, how students should interact with others and objects, enabling them to discover these principles through action rather than ignoring opportunities for growth.

3. Key connections: Unlike incidental learning, this refers to links between labor education and other subjects. To achieve holistic learning, key points of integration should be identified and aligned across subjects, with roles (primary/secondary) shifting as needed.

Mr. Sun's plan only partially addresses the first aspect, neglecting the other two. Without the second, teaching and character training become disconnected, diminishing labor's impact. As for teaching processes, his division of art into appreciation, research, and creation, and crafts into research and construction, reflects popular project-based models. Adapting these flexibly to materials is beneficial, but rigidly applying them to entire units would replicate the outdated "five-stage teaching method." I have discussed this at length elsewhere and will not elaborate here.

Finally, labor education is indeed a prevailing trend in modern education, but not all labor activities inherently hold educational value. While art and crafts involve creativity, merely emphasizing these subjects does not guarantee fostering children's creativity. Project-based learning can reform curricula, but empty formalism may yield worse results than outdated teaching methods. These three points are offered to draw attention to labor education, concluding my thoughts.

Published in *Kaifeng Education Fortnightly*, Volume I, Issue 18, September 1, 1933.

Single-grade Teaching[17]

Meaning of Naming: All students in the school are organized into a single grade.

Definitions:

1) Multi-level single-type grade: Students in the same grade or with the same proficiency are grouped into one grade.

2) Combined grade: It refers to the integration of several grades among multiple levels, applying the meaning of single-grade organization.

3) Combined teaching: It is not limited to the use of single-grade organization but adopts its teaching methods.

From the perspective of establishment — economy.

From the perspective of teaching — self-study.

Reasons for the previous underdevelopment:

1)Merely recognizing the economic stance and not delving into the teaching value of itself.

2)Teachers conduct teaching while maintaining popular educational concepts.

17 This is the manuscript of Li Lianfang's lecture at Henan Provincial (Baiquan) Rural Normal School. ——Translator's note

1. Grade Organization

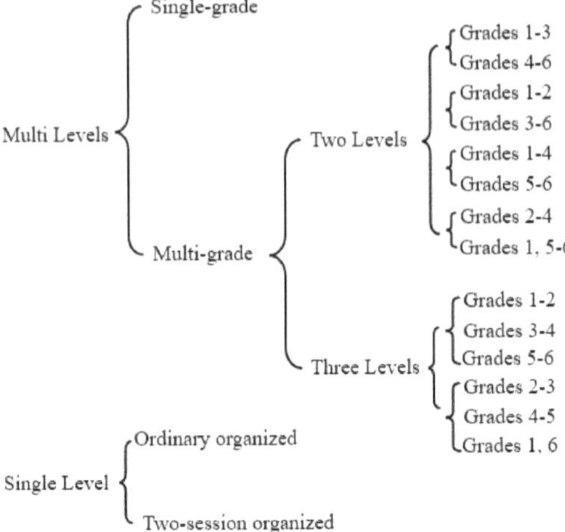

Single-level Class

1.1 Ordinary organized single grade

(1)

Grade 1					
Grade 2					
Grade 3					
Grade 4					

1o'clock 2o'clock 3o'clock

4o'clock 5o'clock

(2)

Grade 1					
Grade 2					
Grade 3					
Grade 4					
Grade 5					
Grade 6					

1.2 Single grade with two-session organization

(Grades 1 and 2 form the second session, and so on for grades 3, 4, or 5, 6.)

(3)

Grade 1						
Grade 2						
Grade 3						
Grade 4						
Grade 5						
Grade 6						

(4)

Grade 1					
Grade 2					
Grade 3					
Grade 4					
Grade 5					
Grade 6					

1.3 Single grade with two-session arrangement

(Grades 1 and 2 form one session, and grades 3 and 4 form another session.)

(5)

Grade 1						
Grade 2						
Grade 3						
Grade 4						
Grade 5						
Grade 6						

(Grades 3, 4 and 5,6 form two sessions)

(6)

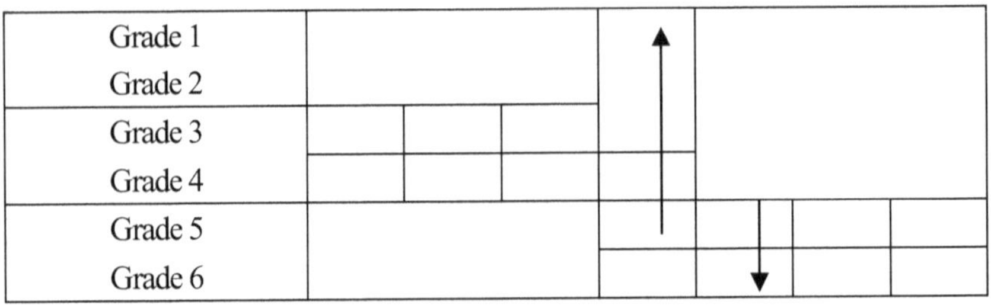

Grade 1						
Grade 2						
Grade 3						
Grade 4						
Grade 5						
Grade 6						

1.4 Single grade with two-session arrangement

(Grades 1,2,3 and 4,5,6 form two sessions)

(7)

Take Grades 1-6 as an example

Take 4 grades of a primary school as an example

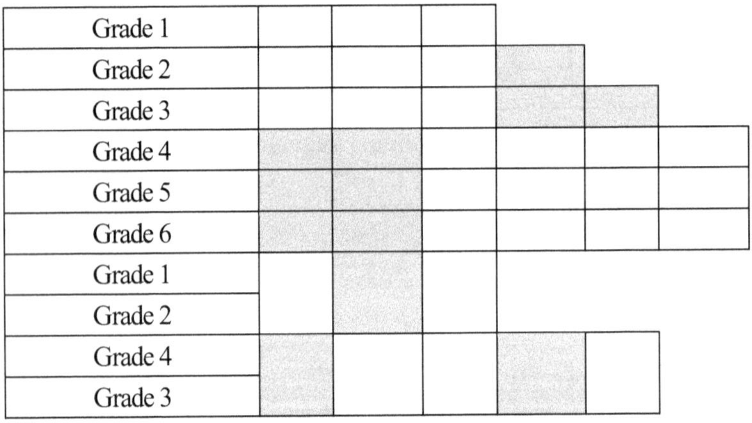

Grade 1						
Grade 2						
Grade 3						
Grade 4						
Grade 5						
Grade 6						
Grade 1						
Grade 2						
Grade 4						
Grade 3						

2. Subject arrangement for scattered classes

2.1 Teaching during common time

(1) For more suitable subjects or their parts, although it is more convenient to teach physical education, crafts, and fine arts with different teaching materials at the same time, it is not impossible to use the same teaching materials for a small part of each semester, led by senior students. Civics regarding collective training, unexpected events, and

commemorative festivals, and singing regarding common lyrics are all suitable for common teaching. Calligraphy in Chinese is also quite appropriate, but composition should not be done in the same time too often.

(2) Teaching time is not limited to a certain subject, nor does it take up all the class hours of any subject.

2. 2 Group teaching

If there are students from three or more grades, it is advisable to adopt the two-session single-grade mode, so that the number of students being taught at the same time is halved due to grouping, which will reduce difficulties. However, according to the teaching materials and methods commonly used in single-type classes, the efficiency of each group in simultaneous teaching will depend on whether there is direct instruction.

In China, primary education is underdeveloped, and most schools that implement single-grade teaching are usually lower primary schools, with only two grades in each group. The teaching time is divided into two parts (before and after), each focusing on one grade for teaching. If we discuss separately according to this principle:

For Chinese language, writing, reading, and composition each have their independent teaching components. When Group A is having reading class, Group B can be doing composition or writing; conversely, when Group B is doing composition, Group A can be engaged in reading or writing.

In arithmetic, under direct instruction, half of the time can be allocated to exercises, which also facilitates alternating arrangements.

For nature studies and social studies, when explanations are given using written texts, some time can be set aside for organizing and recording; if it involves on-site observation or collection, it is suitable for individual guidance, and sometimes can be connected with drawing or Chinese language.

Group activities such as crafts, fine arts, and physical education are more convenient, but the following points should be noted:

(1) Parts of teaching time that should be specially highlighted

a) Matters for starting learning;

b) Matters for special exercises;

c) Training for new students upon enrollment.

(2) Main teaching materials for combined use in groups

a) Teaching materials with continuity organized in a circular manner;

b) Teaching materials with expansibility organized in design units.

(3) Predetermined matters

a) Key points of assignments: Specify all unit key points or subject-specific details at the beginning of each semester.

b) Lesson plans: Prepare lesson plans in advance each week, including the teaching topic, preparation matters, new teaching materials, exercise materials, procedures, etc.

All the above are listed in Group A and Group B respectively for easy comparison.

2.3 Controlling Self-study

(1) Division of self-study: The self-study emphasized in ordinary organized single grades is attached to simultaneous teaching. If the two-

session system is adopted, there should be three types of self-study: Half self-study, Intermittent self-study, and Self-study before and after noon.

(2) The main tasks of self-study should be integrated with direct teaching to form a unit.

(3) Except for half self-study, specific items of self-study should be instructed in advance.

(4) During self-study, children should have freedom as long as they do not disturb others. Especially for the second and third types of self-study, they should be allowed to do arbitrary work.

(5) For students in the second grade and above, group leaders can be selected to take partial responsibility for guidance and supervision under the teacher's command.

(6) Regarding the purpose of self-study for various subjects:

For reading: On the day of direct teaching, there should be at least half an hour of self-study to review or preview lessons before and after class.

For composition: Students are not allowed to do other homework unless there is no need to copy and correct.

For writing: Students are not allowed to write characters that have not been taught; teachers must check their work during break time.

For arithmetic: The number of exercises should not be excessive, and cards should be used for easy checking.

For history and geography: There should be self-study before direct teaching.

For nature studies: The focus should be on review.

For arts and crafts, especially traditional Chinese painting: Children can be allowed to study freely, which is most suitable for lower grades.

For physical education: Senior grades or group leaders can be assigned to lead the most enjoyable games.

3. Seating arrangement:

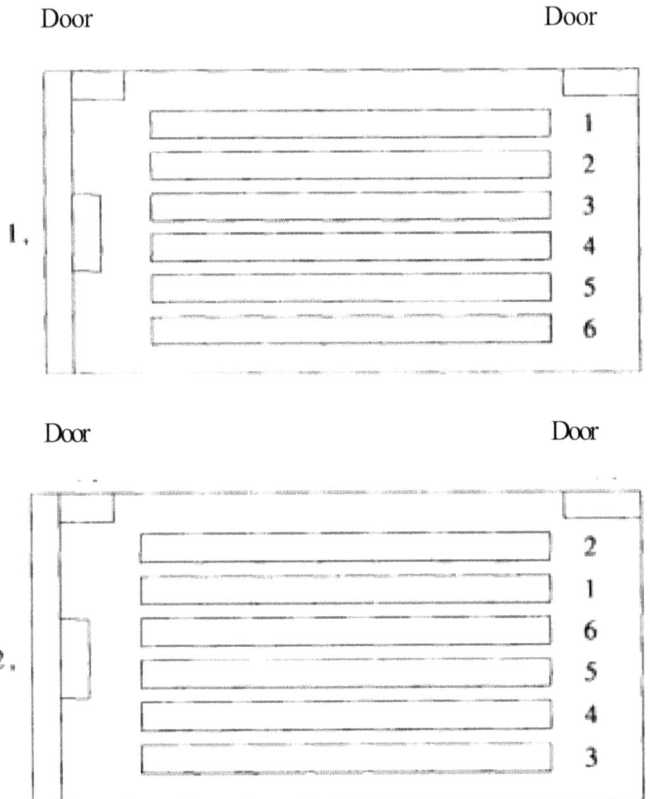

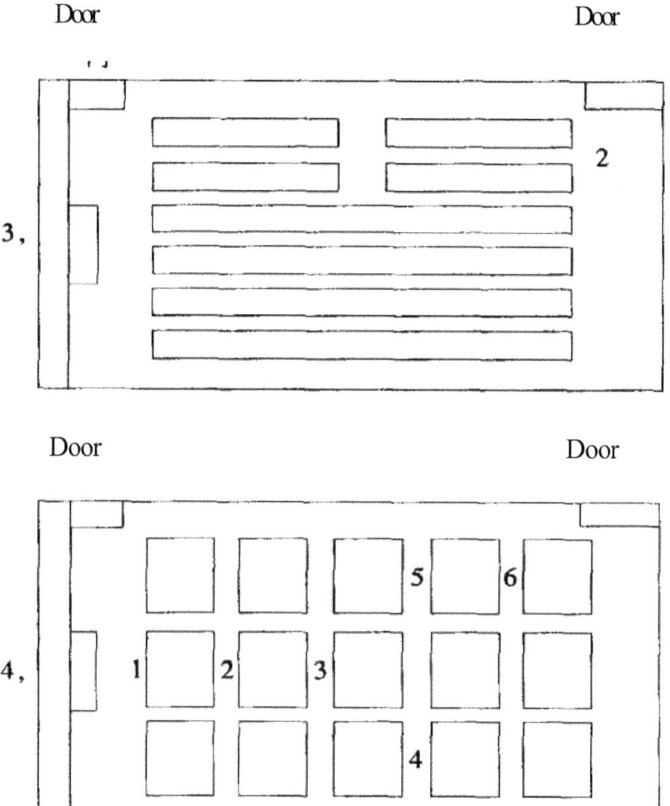
Door
Door
2
3,
Door
Door
5
6
1
2
3
4,
4

Appendix: The main points of my reply to Xihua teachers in Issues 6 and 7 of *Kaifeng Fortnightly*.

Arranging the curriculum:

1. What should be avoided — such as having multiple groups making noises at the same time.

2. What should be adjusted — such as one group receiving demonstration teaching while another group studies independently.

Allocating the curriculum:

1. Separately examine the units of each subject in each grade, carefully review their mutual connections, put them forward one by one, integrate them into comprehensive teaching materials, estimate the time each subject should take in total, and then calculate the independent time each subject should occupy.

2. For each of the separate units mentioned above, carefully check how many units can be taught jointly to certain grades.

3. Carefully examine the special demonstration teaching or special exercises required for each unit, as well as the special teaching needed for each grade.

4. Arrange subjects for the same time period according to the nature of unit teaching materials or subjects.

5. Group students by school year and also by ability; the grouping must be changed every two months during each semester.

6. Due to the different time allocations for each school year and the need for temporary flexibility in the scheduled study time for each grade, the special demonstration teaching or practice time for each grade must be specified daily or every other day. However, when a certain group is

receiving separate teaching, there should be clear and pre-determined regulations for the self-study tasks of other grades.

Two-session Teaching

Definition: It refers to dividing children who exceed the specified number of a class or children from two or more grades into two parts, which are taught by one class teacher.

Purpose: It is an alternative form of organization, but it is very important when popularizing education.

Forms: Taking grade organization as the only form, in terms of grades, there are differences between the whole and the part; in terms of teaching time, there are differences between full-day and half-day; in terms of organization, there are differences between single-type and combined-type; in terms of academic ability, there are differences between the same grade and different grades; in terms of teaching tasks, there are differences between one teacher and two teachers; in terms of overall education, there are differences between primary education and mass education, as well as between separate implementation and mutual implementation. In addition, there are those who classify courses, but it is inconvenient to discuss them without understanding my theory of the dual system, so they will not be discussed for the time being.

Whole two-session system

1. Divided by lower primary grades

<table>
<tr><td>1</td><td></td><td></td><td></td></tr>
<tr><td>2</td><td></td><td></td><td></td></tr>
<tr><td>3</td><td colspan="3"></td><td></td><td></td><td></td></tr>
<tr><td>4</td><td colspan="3"></td><td></td><td></td><td></td></tr>
</table>

2. Divided by the sixth grade

1						
2						
3						
4						
5						
6						

3.Divided by grades 1-5

1						
2						
3						
4						
5						
6						

4.Divided by grades 1-6

1						
2						
3						
4						
5						
6						

Partial two-session system

5. Same as items 3, 4, 5, 6 under sections B and C of the single grade

Half-day two-session system

6. Refer to diagrams (1) - (4)

Full-day two-session system

7. Same as items 7, 8 under section D of the single grade

Half-full two-session system

8. Same as item 4 under section B and items 5, 6 under section C of the single grade

Single-type two-session system

9.Example of semi-periodical division

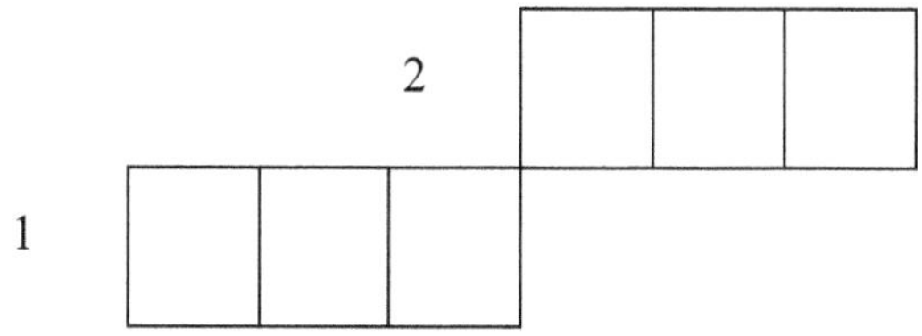

2

1

10.

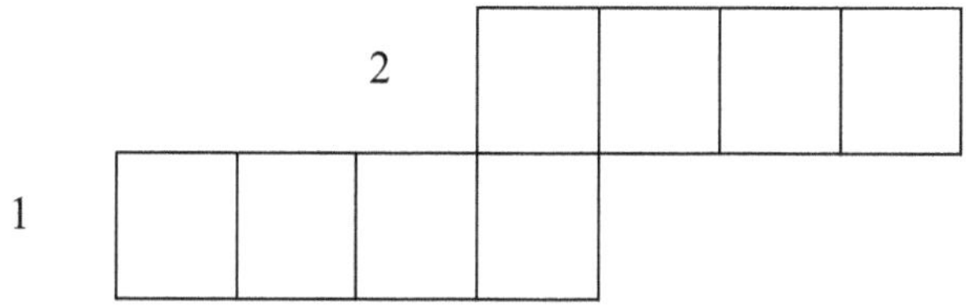

2

1

11.Example of full-day division

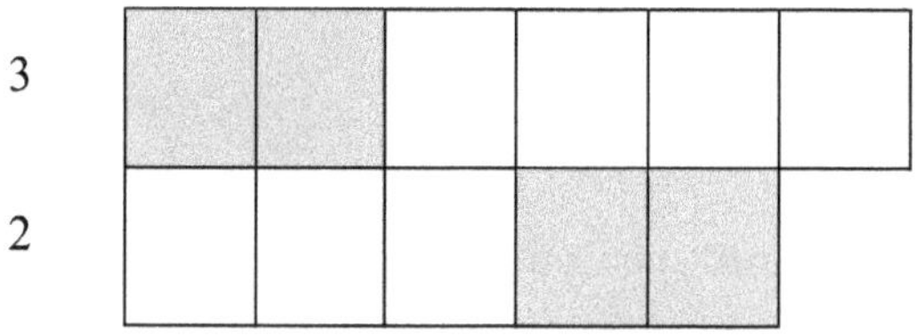

3

2

12.

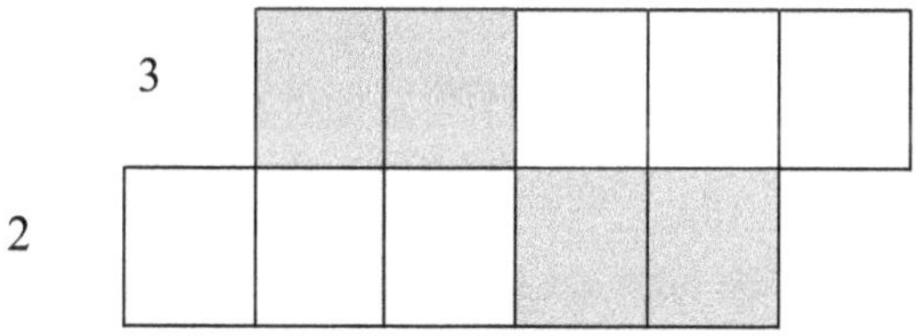

3

2

13.

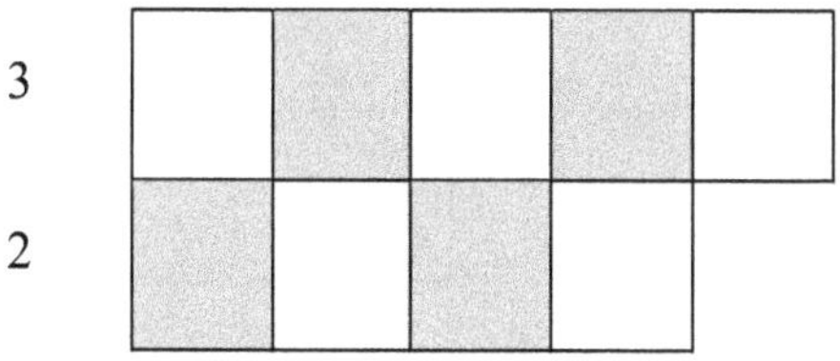

3

2

Combined two-session system

14. Same as items 9–13 of the single-type two-session system, except that grades 1 and 2 or grades 2 and 3 are divided into Group A and Group B. The grades included in each group follow the model of the whole two-session system.

Mixed two-session system

15. That is, a two-session system where the single-type and combined-type operate in parallel: Group A adopts the single-type, while Group B adopts the combined-type, as specified in items 3 and 4 of the single grade (Section B).

Two-session system for the same grade

16. (Taking Grade 1 as an example) The single-type two-session system is generally applied, except that the two grades are changed to the same grade, such as Grade 1A and Grade 1B.

Two-session system for different grades

17. Applicable to the combined-type and mixed-type two-session systems.

Two-session system for separate implementation of primary education and mass education

18. For the organization of primary education or mass education, any of the above-mentioned forms can be adopted for the two-session system of separate implementation of primary education and mass education.

19.

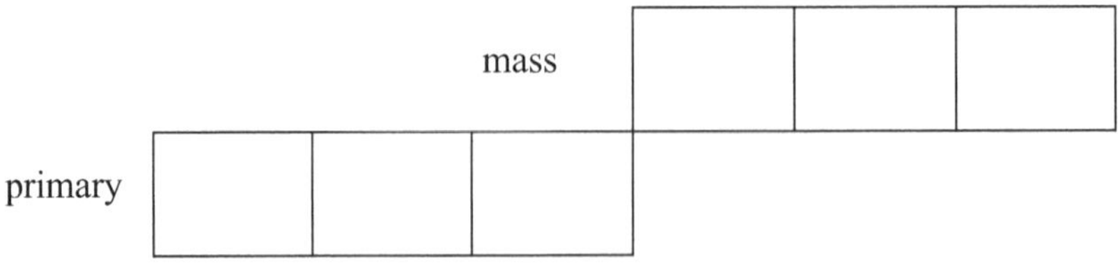

mass

primary

20.

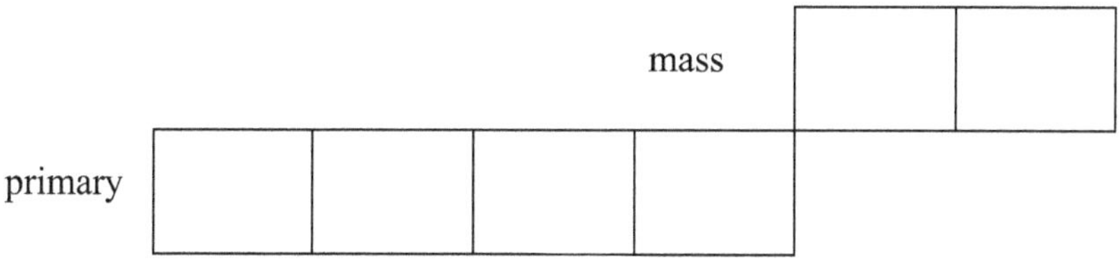

mass

primary

21.

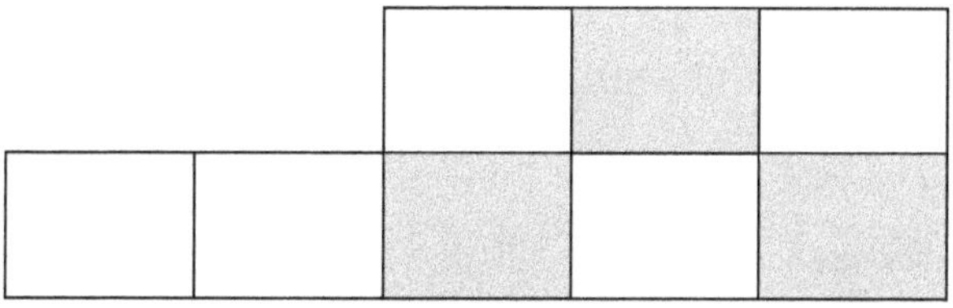

Two-session system with one teacher in charge

22. All the above forms can be taken charge of by one teacher.

Two-session system with two teachers in charge

23.

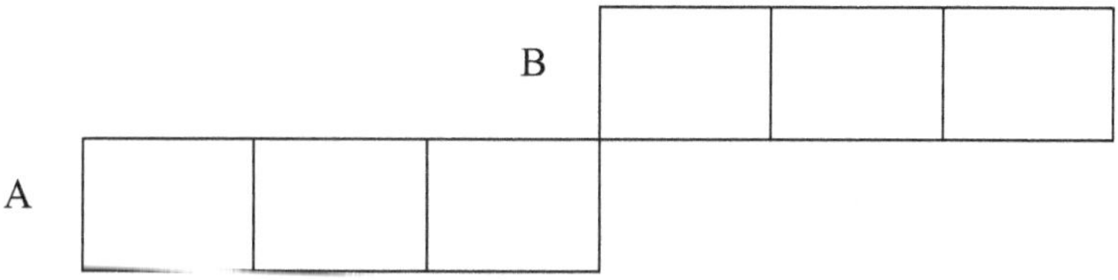

B

A

Three-session system with two teachers in charge

24.

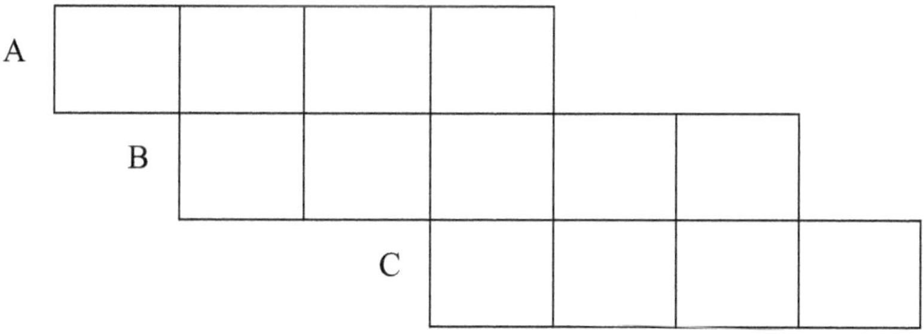

A

B

C

25.

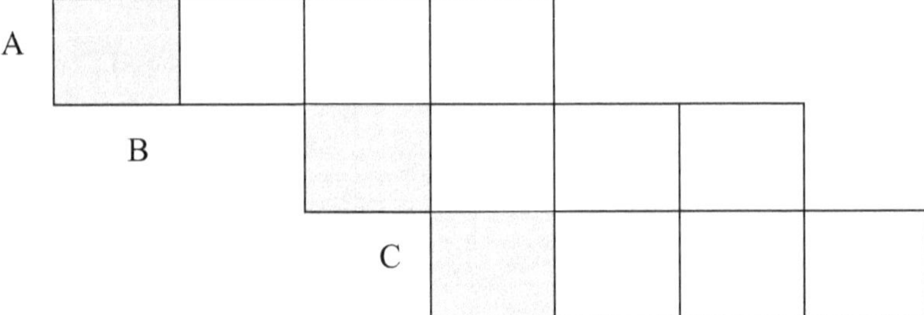

Practical Problem:

For a half - day session, it is most suitable for public education; for a full - day session, it is most suitable for senior grades in primary school.

The sub - departments should be promoted starting from single - type grade levels and gradually extended to combined - type ones.

Adequate practice should be provided for self - study preparation.

If the separate teaching time for both parts reaches four hours, only the number of classrooms can be reduced.

Appendix:

1.The main idea of the circular issued by the Ministry of Education stipulates that the two-session system shall be implemented starting from the 22nd academic year. It roughly states that, except for the existing primary schools in provinces and cities that still use the full-day system due to local needs, they should be converted to the half-day or alternate-time two-session system as much as possible. The alternate-time system was implemented in schools with relatively spacious classrooms and premises.

2.News about the two-session system in Shanghai.

(1) In urban areas, several designated schools were selected to pilot the alternate-time two-session system, starting from lower grades. In rural

areas, several schools with overcrowded students and narrow school buildings were designated to pilot the half-day two-session system.

(2) For teachers whose teaching hours are increased due to the implementation of the two-session system, their salaries shall be increased proportionally.

(3) The fees to be paid by students under the two-session system may be appropriately reduced.

(4) The following schools were designated to pilot the alternate-time two-session system: Wuben Affiliated Primary School (2 classrooms), Jingye Affiliated Primary School (2 classrooms), Nongtan (1 classroom), Bide (2 classrooms), Daizhu (2 classrooms), He'an (2 classrooms), Dexin (1 classroom), Shuji (1 classroom), Qimei (1 classroom), Shangwen (1 classroom).

(5) The following primary schools were designated to pilot the half-day two-session system: Yinxiang District (Yucai Peide), Yinhang District (Yinhang), Wusong District (Wusong), Jiangwan District (Hongjiang), Pengpu District (Pengpu), Zhenru District (Zhenru), Pusong District (Shicun), Fahua District (Honglu), Caojing District (Hua), Yangsi District (Yangsi), Tangqiao (Tannan), Yangjing District (Yangjing Zhenxiu), Luxing District (Sanxiu), Gaoxing District (Peiying), Gaoqiao District (Gaoqiao). All two-session system courses shall be handled jointly by Supervisor Xie and Commissioner Zhou.

3.Overview of the full implementation of the two-session system in Hyogo Prefecture, Japan.

In Japan, there are currently about 1,390 schools implementing the partial two-session teaching system and approximately 120 schools adopting the full two-session system. Although this system has been promoted for a long time, it has not become widely prevalent. Recently, due to budget cuts, three provinces jointly issued an order, drawing nationwide attention to the system. However, in Hyogo Prefecture, as early as after the Russo-Japanese War, the half-day two-session system was widely adopted. In the 40th year of the Meiji era (1907), the prefectural order was revised, replacing it with the full-day two-session system. Recently, advocated by officials of the prefectural government, it is believed that this system can achieve educational outcomes equivalent to those of single-grade classes and promote the sound development of education. For example, in Akashi County of the prefecture alone, there are already more than 80 school grades implementing this system. The following is an excerpt of the stated purposes for its implementation:

The two-session teaching system is not only adopted due to economic reasons and a shortage of teachers, but also for more important reasons. Although the Ministry of Education stipulates that each grade should be assigned one full-time teacher as a principle, the educational influence of an excellent teacher should not be limited to just one grade. On the surface, it seems that children are taught by the teacher, but in fact, they also learn from other children. That is to say, in the two-session teaching system, the educational influence of excellent teachers can be expanded in scope. Although the above statement may be somewhat exaggerated, it is indeed worth pondering over its educational value.

Published in *Rural Reconstruction*, Vol. 2, Issues 15 & 16 (combined issue), September 1933.

Written Before This Survey Report

To investigate how homework is handled across different subjects, the Henan Provincial Department of Education collected exercise books and notebooks (including those for calligraphy, diaries, compositions, arithmetic, etc.) from provincial primary schools. These materials were then submitted to the leaders of this district and all students of the Department of Education at Henan University for thorough inspection. The inspection results were recorded using a temporarily designed form. Mr. Zhao Zuo'an, a clerk in this district, compiled statistics, analyzed the data, created tables, provided explanations, and finalized the survey report. After I reviewed and corrected it, I added further remarks as a supplement.

The survey materials were collected on-site by officials from the Department of Education, who oversaw the process as teachers selected five books each (representing top, middle, and bottom performers) from their respective grades. This method ensured that the samples were neither randomly selected nor tampered with. Even when doubts arose about whether certain works belonged to the current semester, inspectors carefully flagged them for verification. Thus, the materials can be deemed relatively authentic and appropriate, worthy of general trust.

The investigation into homework handling was driven by two primary concerns. On one hand, primary school teachers often cite homework management as their most time-consuming task outside of teaching. We sought to quantify the extent of this burden. On the other hand, we aimed to understand the actual impact of such after-school workloads on students. Additionally, we hoped to explore the prevailing methods of homework management and assess their educational value—this was a secondary but meaningful objective.

The survey focused exclusively on quantifiable items to facilitate recording and statistical analysis, as numerical data is generally considered the most reliable measure of real value. While some aspects of homework cannot be fully captured by numbers, establishing a baseline through quantitative data would enable more accurate subsequent qualitative analysis.

Few issues in primary education demand more urgent attention than students' after-school homework and teachers' after-hours homework management—a trend that has become widespread. Teachers endure this burden despite their resentment; parents harbor doubts but dare not criticize; and education authorities and school principals even use homework performance as a key criterion for evaluating teacher and student success. As to habits of perfunctoriness and dishonesty that students hereby develop, teachers cut corners, neglecting lessons or reducing class time to manage homework. Even when teachers and students take homework seriously, questions remain unaddressed: Is the feedback effective? Does diligent homework completion harm students' health? No one has verified these issues. The practice persists merely because it has become customary—even the most negligent teachers feel compelled to spend at least some time maintaining this formality. However, pity the children, trapped in homework that serves only to meet quotas. The costs far outweigh the benefits—a tragedy that is truly heart-wrenching.

Scope and Intent of After-School Homework. After-school homework, as defined here, primarily refers to tasks recorded in exercise books or notebooks. Initially, homework was intended to supplement the curriculum for advanced students or to facilitate preview and review, with clear connections to in-class lessons. Its management was not limited to after-school correction; teachers were expected to provide direct, tailored guidance, distinguishing between collective and individual needs. Today, however, the line between homework and in-class work has blurred. After-school correction has become a mere formality for teachers. Even if exercise books and notebooks appear flawless, their value as evidence of genuine learning is highly questionable.

Teachers complain about homework but cannot avoid it; parents doubt its value but dare not object. Inspectors and principals rely on it to assess performance, while the harm it inflicts is ignored: students learn to cut corners and deceive; teachers sacrifice teaching time to manage it. Even earnest efforts raise questions—Is feedback effective? Does diligent work harm health? No one has verified these. Homework was originally meant to extend learning for advanced students, with clear links to lessons. Now, it is a mindless ritual. Children suffer most: their efforts to "get it done" yield little benefit, a tragedy beyond words.

The report's tables and analyses convey much between the lines. Two striking observations merit reflection:

(1) Lack of Standards in Assessment: Most corrections rely on vague grading without clear criteria. Methods requiring more time are rarely used, revealing a troubling disregard for effort and genuine learning value.

(2) Inappropriate Composition Topics: Many writing prompts mimic the abstract, opinion-driven style of magazine essays (e.g., "Preface to This Survey Report"). Worse, some topics leave harmful impressions on children, such as "A Son Who Killed His Mother" or "The Enemy in My Soul." Both the substance and form of these topics urgently need reform.

This report aims to use survey findings to address problems, with no intention of evaluating schools or teachers. However, comparison is necessary to identify solutions. Readers may glean insights from the data, but those directly involved in teaching will best understand its nuances. I wish to emphasize: this survey is not meant to judge 优劣 (superiority or inferiority). Please do not misunderstand its purpose.

Published in *Kaifeng Experimental Teachers' Monthly*, Vol. 1, No. 1, October 1933.

Work Report of This District Over the Past Year

1. Introduction

The establishment of the Kaifeng Urban Education Experimental Zone aims to integrate three entities: the Provincial Department of Education, the Department of Education at Henan University, and Kaifeng's provincial educational institutions. On one hand, it seeks to promote collaboration between administrative initiatives and academic research; on the other, it aims to verify theories through practice and vice versa.

The initiative was proposed by Director Zhang Youshan, finalized by Director Li Jingzhai, and formally established under Director Qi Xingyi. It was first advocated by Mr. Xu Shifeng, followed by Mr. Zheng Zhuxu, and later by Mr. Xu Xinwu and Mr. Tai Shuangqiu.[18] I have been involved in its development from start to finish, which I consider a great privilege.

The experimental zone embodies both institutional and academic attributes, encompassing administration, research, and implementation. Such an undertaking cannot be approached superficially; it requires collective effort. Since its founding last winter, Mr. Xu Shifeng was elected as standing committee member. With a small staff, initial work focused on formulating plans and publishing a fortnightly journal to disseminate ideas. However, Mr. Xu was unable to return due to his duties at Beijing Normal University, and I lacked the capacity to manage both roles. Over ten months, preliminary work proceeded hastily, resulting in little tangible progress despite colleagues' efforts. Remedial measures were often needed, for which I deeply regret.

---

18 Xu Xinwu was President of Henan University; Zheng Zhuxu (Ruogu) and Tai Shuangqiu were professors in the Department of Education; Xu Shifeng was Dean of the Department.—Translator's note

As the academic year concludes, I submit this report in accordance with regulations, reflecting on the past to inspire improvement in the coming year. The following is a categorized account.

2. Surveys and Statistics

2.1 Survey on Chrysanthemum Exhibition Practices. In late October last year, provincial primary schools in the city held chrysanthemum exhibitions. Given the significant time and funds invested, the Experimental Zone questioned their educational value. To determine whether schools leveraged these exhibitions as teaching opportunities, a survey was conducted in October 1932 using specially designed forms. After completion, data was analyzed, a report compiled, and recommendations published in the combined second and third issues of the Zone's Kaifeng Education Fortnightly. This aimed to inform future exhibitions.

2.2 Survey on Workshops' Achievements. To assess whether items produced in school workshops were practical and whether materials used were domestically made, the Zone designed forms for on-site investigations. The goal was to aggregate and analyze results to establish improvement standards.

2.3 Survey on Moral Education Implementation. Moral education is a critical issue in education, requiring focus on substance rather than form. To understand its implementation across schools, the Zone designed a survey form covering: 1) objectives of moral education; 2) administrative structure for moral education; 3) implementation status; 4) assessment methods; and(5) challenges and specific suggestions. This survey was conducted by students from Henan University's Department of Education.

2.4 Survey on Homework Correction Methods in Primary Schools. In recent years, primary school students' homework has increased significantly, making homework management a major burden for teachers. Ineffective correction wastes both teachers' effort and students' time, hindering rather than enhancing teaching efficiency. Thus, three weeks after the winter semester began, the Zone requested the Department of Education to collect 15 homework samples (per grade and subject) from provincial primary schools in the capital. These samples—including compositions, diaries, calligraphy, arithmetic, and Chinese notes—were analyzed by all students of Henan University's Department of Education. Statistics have been finalized, with findings to be published shortly.

2.5 Survey on Color Blindness Among Primary and Secondary School Students. 1) Schools and participants: 2 secondary schools and 16 primary schools, totaling over 4,570 students. 2) Tools and methods: 10 color charts designed by Japanese scholar Hirohara were used. Students were divided into groups (approximately 10 per group) and registered individually. 2) Survey period: June 17 to 28. 4) Statistical report: Data is being processed, with a report to follow upon completion.

2.6 Survey on Current Status of Primary Schools. To understand the internal conditions of Kaifeng's provincial primary schools and mass education schools, the Zone conducted a detailed survey covering school profiles, principals, teachers, number of grades, funding, and student enrollment. Statistical charts were published in the fortnightly journal.

3. Experimental Research

3.1 Experimental Research on the Dual System. After publishing Preliminary Reform Proposals for Kaifeng Urban Primary Schools—proposing the dual system—on New Year's Day, the Zone submitted a formal proposal to the Department of Education, which approved the experiment and designated Provincial No. 10 Primary School as the pilot. The Zone then formulated regulations for an Experimental Design Committee, composed of Zone staff and No. 10 Primary School faculty. Excluding lower grades (which were implementing project-based learning), the experiment began in February for all other grades. Due to delayed planning and unchanged class numbers, adaptations were made, including: 1) dividing upper and middle-grade students into Groups A and B; 2) developing a dual-system timetable; 3) allocating classrooms; and 4) grouping students by ability. After one semester, details are documented in No. 10 Primary School's experimental report.

3.2 Research on Common Character Errors Among Children. Chinese characters are prone to confusion in structure and pronunciation, posing difficulties for children and adults learning to write. Without statistical data, teachers cannot preempt such errors, leading to frequent mistakes in students' writing and ineffective letter-writing classes in mass education schools. To address this, the Zone is investigating common character errors in provincial primary schools and mass education schools. The goal is to compile statistics, create practice materials, and help teachers and students better distinguish and avoid errors. Survey methods and forms, developed by specialists from the Chinese Teaching Research Association in collaboration with the Zone's staff, have been distributed to schools.

3.3 Research on Commonly Confused Homophones and Near-Homophones. Chinese has numerous characters with similar forms, often causing misuse and misunderstanding—especially among children. To help children recognize these characters and reduce errors, the Zone developed a research framework covering: (1) objectives; (2) research methods; (3) statistical methods; (4) applications; and (5) deadlines.

Forms for summing up such characters were distributed to schools before the summer vacation, with Chinese teachers responsible for data collection. Results will be organized and published by the Zone.

3.4 Research on Composition Topics. The Chinese Teaching Research Association initiated this survey to assist teachers in designing composition topics. Guidelines and forms were distributed on July 10, with Chinese teachers tasked with recording topics from students' composition books during the summer vacation. Results will be analyzed by the Association after the new semester begins.

3.5 Review and Research on Children's Books. Children's books significantly influence intellectual development. However, many current publications are outdated, inconsistent with contemporary thought, or overly complex. Worse, some inculcate superstition, timidity, cruelty, or passivity. To address this, the Zone is reviewing children's books, grading them, promoting high-quality works, and banning harmful ones. Most reviews will be completed soon, with a special publication to follow.

4. Designs and Proposals

4.1 Design of the Dual-System Organization for Primary Schools. According to statistics from the 18th academic year, there are over 41,441,000 school-age children in China, but only 212,300 primary schools nationwide, with a mere 7,108,000 students enrolled in lower primary grades. This means over 80% of school-age children are out of school. Such a lack of educational accessibility severely hinders the improvement of national literacy. Furthermore, many primary schools focus on superficial decorations rather than substantive education, wasting teachers' efforts, time, funds, and facilities. Without addressing these issues, primary education can hardly achieve meaningful results.

To tackle this, the Zone formulated a preliminary reform plan for Kaifeng urban primary schools on New Year's Day of the 22nd academic year (1933), aiming to enroll more out-of-school children and enhance educational effectiveness. The plan was approved by the Department of Education, which designated Provincial No. 11 Primary School as the pilot for implementation.

4.2 Design for Compiling Adaptive Teaching Materials. Most primary school textbooks are purchased from commercial publishers, but they often fail to meet local needs due to differences in seasons and regions. Thus, the Zone drafted detailed methods, prepared a budget, and proposed to the Department of Education that starting from the next academic year, locally adaptive teaching materials be compiled. These materials will first be tested in Kaifeng's primary schools and promoted province-wide once proven effective.

4.3 Proposal for Developing Subject-Specific Tests for Primary Schools. To meet the needs of primary schools across the province, the Zone proposed to the Department of Education the development of subject-specific tests for universal use. A detailed plan has been submitted to the Department.

4.4 Proposal for Establishing a Children's Science Museum. Recognizing the critical need for science equipment in primary schools, the Zone drafted a proposal in spring of this year, including detailed equipment plans and a budget, and submitted it to the Department of Education. The goal is to formally establish the museum in the first semester of the 22nd academic year.

4.5 Design for Implementing Health Education. The physical strength of citizens is vital to a state's survival. While active exercise strengthens physical fitness, hygiene is a more fundamental and essential measure. The Zone believes that hygiene habits must be cultivated in schools. Therefore, it formulated a health education implementation plan, statutes for a Health Education Committee, and a budget, which have been submitted to the Department for review. Implementation will begin once approved.

4.6 Design for the "Big Garden Education Village". To experiment with "society-centered education," the Zone selected Dagarden Village (east of Kaifeng's outer city) as the pilot site. A detailed plan and budget were submitted to the Department of Education for approval, aiming to build a new educational village in Kaifeng's suburbs in the short term. This village will focus on improving rural economy and enriching farmers' lives.

4.7 Proposal to Revise Salary Standards for Provincial Primary School Teachers. The current salary standards for provincial primary school teachers lack incentives, leading to a state of decline in primary education. Thus, in December of the 21st academic year (1932), the Zone proposed revisions, focusing on two aspects: 1) establishing evaluation criteria; 2) formulating salary increment methods. The goal is to encourage professionalism, motivating teachers to strive for progress and commit to lifelong teaching.

4.8 Production Education Plan for Xinghuayuan Town. To experiment with urban production education and improve industrial skills, the Zone selected Xinghuayuan Town as the pilot site. A plan and budget were submitted to the Department of Education for review, with implementation to begin once approved.

4.9 Proposal to Revise Students' Morning Arrival Time. In children's education, knowledge impartation and health preservation are equally important. However, Kaifeng's primary schools encourage students to arrive earliest in the morning, which harms children's health and development, with far-reaching negative consequences. To address this, the Zone wrote to the Department of Education, urging all primary schools to revise morning arrival times to prioritize children's hygiene.

4.10 Editing of the Fortnightly Journal. Since its establishment, the Zone has published a fortnightly journal to document its work and research. It is scheduled to release two volumes annually, with 18 issues per volume (800 copies each, 20–60 pages per issue). To date, 18 issues have been published, completing the first volume.

5. Convened Meetings

5.1 Forum with Principals of Provincial Primary Schools and Mass Education Schools. To ensure schools fully understood the Zone's experimental work plan, a forum was held on November 10, 1932, with principals of provincial primary schools and mass education schools. Director Qi attended and delivered a speech; Committee members Mr. Li Lianfang and Mr. Tai Shuangqiu reported on the Zone's work and explained the significance of its establishment.

5.2 Inaugural Meeting of the Teaching Research Association. On December 10, 1932, the Zone held an inaugural meeting to organize a Teaching Research Association for teachers of Kaifeng's provincial primary schools. Approximately 300 attendees participated, including representatives from the Department of Education, Henan University, the Zone Committee, and all teachers from urban primary and mass education schools. Organizational regulations and bylaws were approved.

5.3 Plenary Meeting of the Chinese Language Teaching Research Association. On June 17, 1933, the Zone convened a plenary meeting of Chinese language teachers from Kaifeng's provincial primary schools. The meeting approved research guidelines, proposed research topics, and resolved to complete tasks such as submitting opinions on compiling

Chinese textbooks (as requested by the Ministry of Education) and developing self-compiled Chinese textbooks within a specified timeframe.

5.4 Executive Meeting of the Chinese Language Teaching Research Association. On June 29, 1933, the Zone held an executive meeting of the Chinese Language Teaching Research Association, attended by over 30 executive members from various schools. After electing a chief executive, members discussed research topics proposed at the plenary meeting. Three topics were selected for summer research: (1) statistical study of commonly confused similar-form characters; (2) statistical study of common character errors in children's compositions; (3) research on composition topics. Specialists were appointed to draft research outlines and design survey forms, which were distributed to schools to initiate the research.

6. Participation in the Work of the Education Department

(1) Compiling examination questions for the unified examinations of primary schools in the provincial capital.

(2) Participating in the unified examinations of primary schools in the provincial capital.

(3) Participating in the unified graduation examinations for primary and secondary schools organized by the Education Department.

(4) Participating in the inspection team for primary schools in the provincial capital.

(5) Conducting detailed review of examination papers for unified examinations.

Published in *Kaifeng Experimental Education Monthly*, Vol. 1, No. 1, October 1933.

Abbreviated when included.

Reply to the Education Department on the Latest Implementation Measures for Guiding the two-session Teaching in Primary Schools

Pursuant to:

We acknowledge receipt of your office's letter dated August 25, 1964, which states: "Pursuant to the ministry's order, the two-session system shall be implemented starting from the 22nd academic year to enroll more children and expand education. All provincial primary schools shall first reorganize and trial-implement the system for the first and second grades. We hereby request guidance on its implementation and ask that you inform us of your measures."

It should be noted that one semester before the ministry's order was issued, our district committee had proposed to your office the dual-track system drafted by Lian Fang, which already included the two-session system and aligned with the trends of new education, ensuring that the two-session system would not be promoted as a mere formality. The purposes and methods were detailed in our previous letter. Now, in response to your communication, we believe that the effective implementation of the two-session system can also facilitate the gradual realization of the dual-track system, and we are willing to assist in this endeavor. However, the supervision of schools in implementing the system is entirely under the authority of your office. If schools wish to consult us, we will provide full information to the best of our knowledge. That said, we must solemnly state that our district cannot be held responsible for whether the system is implemented or whether its implementation conforms to the guidance provided.

Regarding the implementation measures you inquired about, we can only outline the essentials of the two-session system itself. In terms of grades, there are distinctions between full and partial implementation. In terms of teaching hours, there are differences between full-day and half-day sessions. In terms of organization, there are single-class and combined-class models. In terms of teaching responsibilities, there are differences between having one teacher and two teachers. In terms of education itself, there are distinctions between primary education and mass education, as well as between separate and mutual implementation. The key lies in grade organization and curriculum arrangement, which often need to be combined to form a more appropriate model. These are illustrated separately in the diagrams below.

The full two-session model is as follows (numbers indicate grades; blank spaces without horizontal bars indicate no classes. The same applies below):

The lower primary grades are divided into two parts.

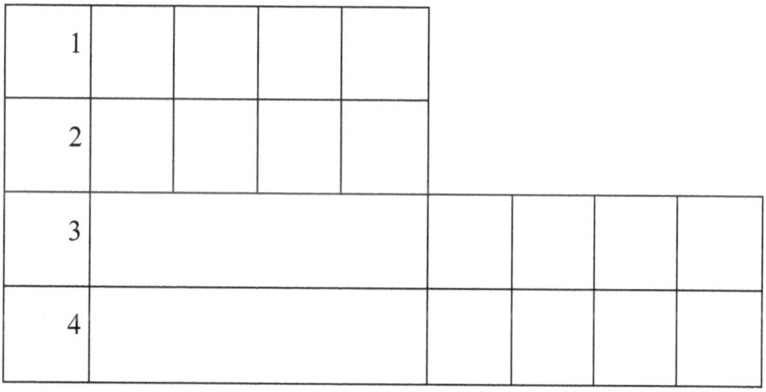

1								
2								
3								
4								

(1) This is a system where the first and second grades have classes in the morning, and the third and fourth grades have classes in the afternoon.

1								
2								
3								
4								

(2) This is a system where the first and third grades have classes in the morning, and the second and fourth grades have classes in the afternoon.

The combined six grades of lower primary and upper primary can also be organized as described above: either three grades can be arranged in the same time slot instead of two, or any two grades and four grades can be scheduled in the morning and afternoon respectively.

The partial two-session model is as follows:

Take the first and second grades as an example.

1								
2								
3								
4								
5								
6								

(3) The second grade can also swap schedules with the first grade, and the same logic applies to other grades.

Grade 1,2,3,4 form two sessions

1								
2								
3								
4								
5								
6								

(4)

The full-day two-session system is as follows (the half-day two-session system can be clearly understood by referring to the previous diagram): Take the first and second grades as an example.

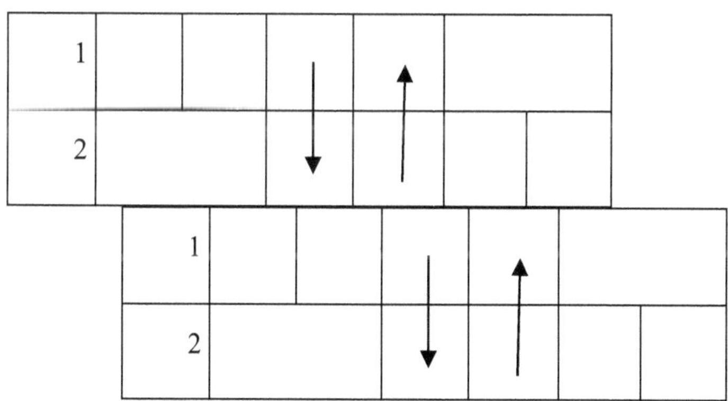

(5)→Table of Combined-Class Teaching

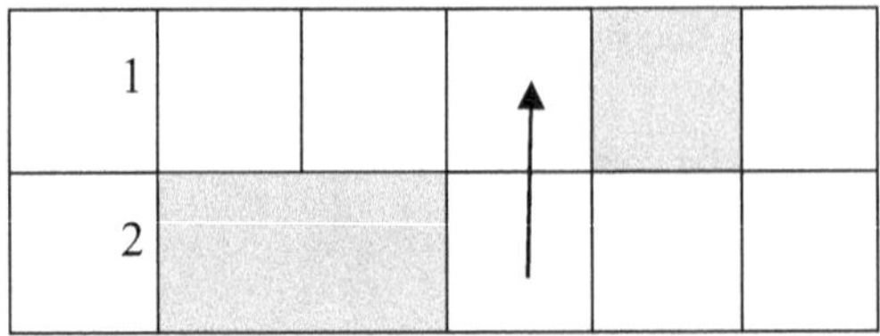

(6)Table of Free Work or Self-Study

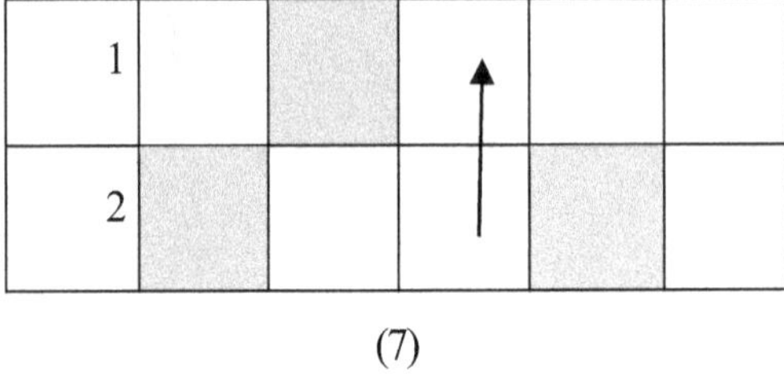

(7)

(5), (6), and (7) are diagrams of the two-session system that are suitable for recent use, among which diagram (7) is the most appropriate.

The multi - grade double - session system is as shown on the left (the single - grade system is self - explanatory in the preceding diagram):

Multi - grade double - session system for two grade levels.

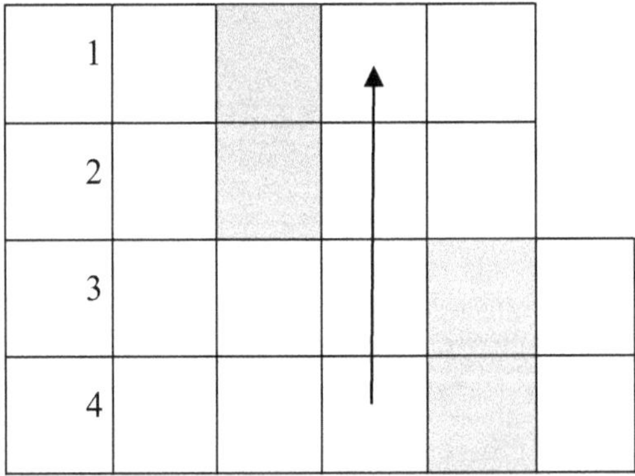

(8)This diagram represents multi-grade teaching; it also applies to three grade levels, only by adding one more grade level to each section.

The mixed two-session system is as follows:

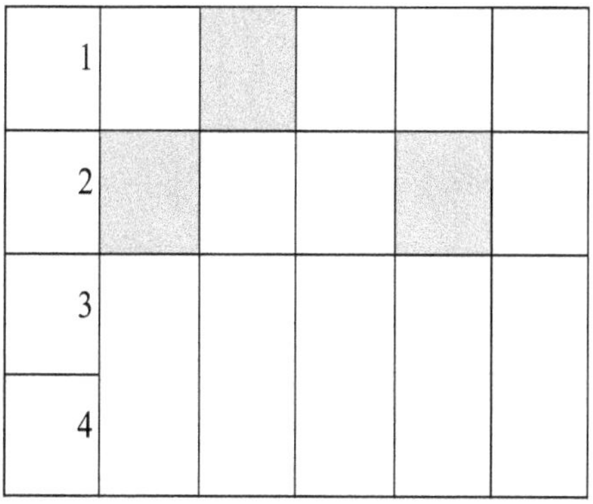

1

2

3

4

(9)This is where the two-session system is adopted for the first and second grades, while the combined-class teaching method is used for the third and fourth grades.

The two-session system for mutual implementation between primary education and mass education is as follows::

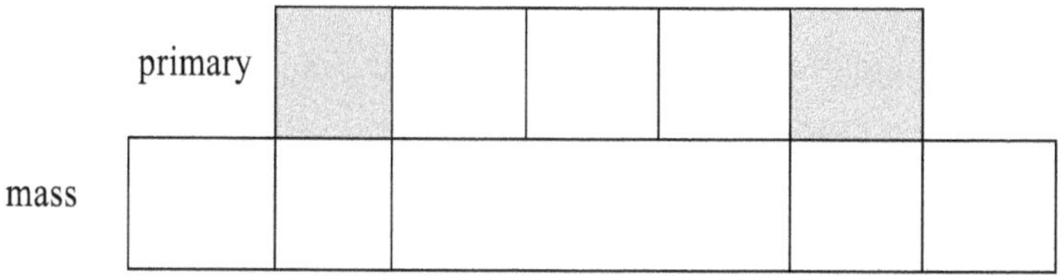

primary

mass

(10) The two-session system with Class One for primary school students and Class Two for mass education participants

primary

mass

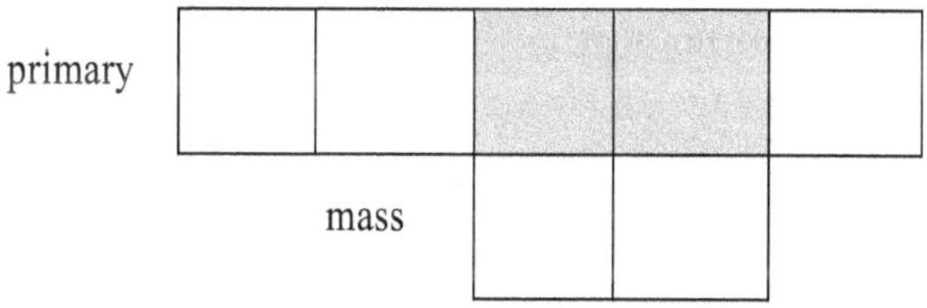

(11) The two-session system with one class for primary school students and one class for mass education participants

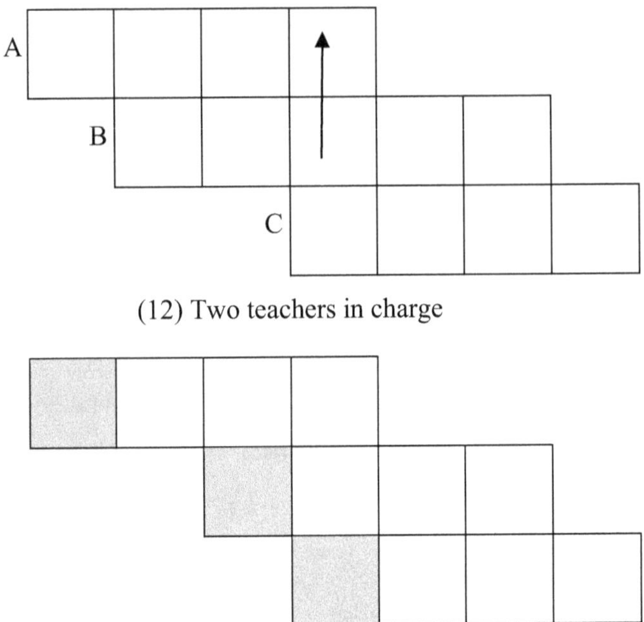

(12) Two teachers in charge

(13) Organization of Three Groups

Two teachers in charge of three groups is currently the most efficient way to implement the two-session system. Based on the examples listed above, other forms of organizational arrangements can be further derived.

At present, there are very few reference materials on the two-session system. If there are any occasionally, they are either too outdated or merely deal with abstract theories. The thirteen diagrams listed above may be of some help in practice. If your office deems them worthy of reference, please distribute and inform relevant parties accordingly. This is our reply.

Li Lianfang, Standing Committee Member and Director of the Henan Provincial Department of Education

August, the 22nd Year of the Republic of China (1933)

Published in *Kaifeng Experimental Education Monthly*, Vol. 1, No. 1, October 1933.

Opinions on the Chapter on National Education in the Draft Constitution

The Henan Provincial Government is deliberating on the draft constitution and conducting research by categories. I have been consulted for my opinions, and thus I would like to offer some insights based on my usual views on education, while also seeking feedback from education researchers across the country.

1. Article 36: "The main purposes of education shall be to cultivate noble character, enhance life skills, and foster healthy citizens."

Article 34 at the beginning of this chapter stipulates that "the Three Principles of the People shall be the fundamental principle of national education in the Republic of China." In practice, how this principle should be applied in education at all levels remains to be explored. If Article 36 can clearly indicate the direction, it could serve as a guide for implementing Article 34. However, the terms "noble," "life," and "healthy" in Article 36 lack clear scope and standards. In educational science, such terms may not seem vague because their meanings are analyzed and clarified in detailed discussions. Nevertheless, different educational theories often emphasize different aspects—personality, knowledge and skills, or responsibility—due to varying starting points or perspectives. In actual implementation, all three are usually addressed, but the prioritization of personality, knowledge and skills, or responsibility varies across theories, and only by adhering to a specific theory can its intended goals be achieved. If the constitutional provisions fail to convey a clear meaning here, the "main purposes" will become empty and rootless, mere superfluous words. Moreover, the main purposes stipulated in the constitution must outline a path for national education based on the country's historical traditions and global trends. Merely adopting general, abstract statements from educational science would make the provision meaningless.

2. Article 35: "All citizens of the Republic of China shall have equal opportunities to receive education."

Article 37: "All children of school age shall receive compulsory education, and all citizens who have not received compulsory education shall receive adult supplementary education." Article 43: "All public and private schools nationwide shall set up free tuition and scholarship quotas to encourage students with excellent conduct and academic performance who cannot afford to continue their studies." These three articles contradict each other. Article 37 mandates universal education, while Article 35 emphasizes equal opportunities for education. If education is a universal obligation, the concept of "opportunity" for education becomes irrelevant; conversely, if education is framed as an "opportunity," equality is impossible. Basic education is not yet universally accessible, and secondary and higher education do not admit outstanding children from all backgrounds. As a result, access to education is entirely constrained by individual circumstances and economic status. Poor children are fundamentally unable to afford education—can this be considered a "voluntary abandonment of opportunity"? The phrasing "opportunity" in Article 35 obscures the true meaning of equality and undermines the mandate of Article 37, effectively serving the interests of the powerful and wealthy, which contradicts the principle of equality in the Three Principles of the People. Furthermore, while Article 37 appears solemn on the surface, it fails to clarify who bears the responsibility for implementation, making it nothing more than an unfulfilled government policy. This is evident in reality: successive governments have issued explicit plans for phased implementation of compulsory education, yet education continues to decline. The root cause is that the law does not tie educational outcomes to official performance evaluations. Even so-called "enlightened governments" merely formulate a few plans and consider their duties fulfilled. Citizens do have an obligation to receive education, but the responsibility to ensure that citizens and their children can access and afford education lies with the government. Without stipulating the government's obligation to guarantee universal education, merely mandating that citizens "shall receive education" will amount to empty words. In advanced states, national education is universally accessible because governments invest substantial resources in its implementation, which is why their laws penalize parents who fail to send their children to school. In China, however, the number of people willing to receive education exceeds available school quotas, and many cannot afford education even if they wish to. This is not a problem individuals can solve; it depends entirely on the government's commitment and planning. If officials fail to plan or implement phased plans, or if non-competent agencies refuse to assist, they must be severely punished, with no leniency for other "achievements," and no other educational initiatives should hinder this effort. Only through such determined governance—expanding access while improving quality can the state have a hopeful future. The issue with these articles is precisely this oversight. As for free tuition and scholarships to assist students unable to continue their studies, even by Article 35's standards, this is contradictory. Since these quotas are arbitrarily limited by schools, even talented and virtuous poor students cannot all access education, while the wealthy face no such restrictions. Where is the equality of opportunity? Moreover, competition for these quotas turns schools into tools for manipulating students, and students resort to fraud or lobbying to secure spots—these harmful phenomena are plainly visible. Such measures are typical of bourgeois societies seeking to curry favor with the public; including them in the constitution of a republic based on the Three Principles of the People is particularly inappropriate.

3. Today, school education in China is on the verge of collapse.

The main cause is not merely that "education fails to meet practical needs," but rather the fundamental question of the school's role in the national system. In China's past, academies (shuyuan) and the imperial examination system (keju) coexisted but served different purposes: academies were places for scholarly discourse, not for obtaining official qualifications, thus attracting scholars genuinely dedicated to learning; the imperial examination selected talent without restricting candidates by their educational background, allowing any promising commoner to rise to prominence and encouraging lifelong pursuit of knowledge. While past systems had flaws and their methods may not suit today, the problem arose when China adopted Western-style schools: initially, schools replaced the imperial examination, merging scholarly discourse with the pursuit of fame, undermining academic ethics. Later, schools merely granted qualifications, while civil service examinations were held separately to select officials. For schools, graduation no longer guaranteed employment, yet qualifications remained the sole tool for seeking jobs; for examinations, content was largely based on school curricula, making it difficult for non-schooled individuals to participate, while the tested material often had no bearing on practical needs. This left students and educators increasingly disoriented, leading to the current unmanageable situation. Thus, today's education must address the following issues:

First, the fundamental issue of education: Whether in overall design or at each level, education should cultivate students' ability to apply knowledge, eliminate the tendency toward individualism, and orient them toward serving the state or society. Personal happiness cannot be achieved outside the state or society; otherwise, longer education would only greater harm to the state or society. This cannot be achieved through mere moral education, civic courses, or lectures on ideology, but requires clear regulations on the relationship between schooling, graduation, and the national and social systems.

Second, basic education: How can universal education be truly realized? How can vocational education and talent education ensure that all members of the state, unconstrained by economic factors, contribute to society? Though their implementation methods differ, both must be guided by a consistent ethos.

Third, education provision: Which types of education must be public, which can be private, which should be established by the central government, and which by local governments? These must be defined as immutable conditions in the overall educational framework.

Fourth, educational provision and talent selection: How can they complement each other while maintaining independence? Clear regulations are needed to break the current situation of superficial pretense and fragmentation.

If these three major issues are not properly resolved, all constitutional provisions will be irrelevant to reality and cannot form a national education system fitting for a republic based on the Three Principles of the People. It is earnestly hoped that the authorities formulating the constitution will pay attention to these matters.

Published in *Kaifeng Experimental Education Monthly*, Vol. 1, No. 6, March 1934.

Reply to the Education Department: Detailed Explanation on the Difficulties in Implementing the Two-Session System

We acknowledge receipt of your letter, which states that the principals of provincial primary schools have submitted reports on the implementation of the two-session system and requests our review, research, and reply.

After examining the original submissions, they appear to be general discussions on education in Kaifeng, with little research on the actual implementation of the two-session system. Before addressing the six alleged difficulties, we first clarify several overarching issues to avoid misunderstandings:

1. Regarding the "difficulties encountered since implementation" mentioned by schools, it remains unclear whether all schools have actually implemented the system, or only one or two schools have done so. Without information from your office on the number of classes implementing the system and their specific methods, we cannot conduct a practical study. We also question whether these difficulties are universally experienced by all schools.

2. The two-session system promoted by the Ministry cannot be conflated with the dual-track system proposed by our district. While the dual-track system incorporates features of the two-session system, it integrates organizational form with educational functions. Our district's proposal aims to break the rigid structure of textbook-centered teaching: as schools increase class numbers, they should redirect conventional equipment funds toward specialized facilities. This would gradually reduce the waste of exclusive classrooms per grade and enable the

establishment of specialized facilities without additional funding for extra classrooms. In contrast, the two-session system solely addresses expanding class numbers without significant budget increases. However, "not significantly increasing" funds means avoiding full budgetary increments per additional class, not restricting operations to the original budget of one class for two classes.

3. The application of the two-session system itself depends on context: half-day sessions should be adopted based on local needs, while full-day sessions involve broader issues of teaching and infrastructure. Enforcing the two-session system rigidly, without regard to context, makes practical success difficult.

With these clarifications, we address the schools' alleged difficulties. The third point, "insufficient original funding," is not purely a matter of adding two-session classes and thus requires no discussion. The remaining points, however, warrant disputes and are responded to below:

The first difficulty can be divided into three parts. The first part is "Insufficient school premises": This essentially means classrooms are only enough for each grade to have one general classroom. According to ministry regulations, lower grades have 1,140 minutes of weekly classes, averaging 3 hours and 10 minutes daily; upper grades have 1,530 minutes, averaging 4 hours and 15 minutes daily. Additionally, physical education, labor, and music classes are not held in general classrooms, while civics, moral training, hygiene, nature, and art classes are also not restricted to such spaces. Thus, lower grades actually use general classrooms for only 2 hours daily, and upper grades for 3 hours. Since each classroom can be used for 6–7 hours daily, any grade can share a classroom with another. The claim of "insufficient premises" is unfounded. The second part is "Without exclusive classrooms, students wander, disrupt order, lose belongings, grow distracted, and develop bad habits": This raises questions: (1) Is it necessary for each class to have an exclusive classroom, even when unused? (2) Is focus and habit correction entirely dependent on the constraint of an exclusive classroom? If the second were true, leaving classrooms idle (as in the first scenario) might be justified. However, good habits like orderliness and responsibility are cultivated through adapting to dynamic environments. Relying on exclusive spaces for prevention deviates from educational goals. Moreover, students have fixed classrooms for lessons and move elsewhere during breaks regardless of exclusivity. The claim that two-session students "wander" due to shared classrooms is inconsistent with reality. The last part is "Two-session classes borrow desks and chairs from higher grades, hindering physical development": This prompts further questions: Why borrow from higher grades instead of same-grade classes, assuming no grade is underpopulated? Schools rarely provide grade-appropriate furniture; most only differentiate between low, middle, and high grades. Singling out two-session classes for this issue while ignoring it for existing classes is unfair. Primary schools often receive 10 times more applications than available spots. Current classes already include students of widely varying ages, yet no concerns about stunted development have been raised. Objecting specifically to two-session classes is perplexing. In summary, the first point proves that any grade can share classrooms, rendering the latter two points irrelevant.

The Second Difficulty: It is claimed that "teachers in Jiangsu and Zhejiang primary schools teach 700–800 minutes weekly, while in our province they teach 1,300 minutes; the disparity in workload makes it impossible to increase their burden." While we sympathize with teachers' hardships, the claim is inaccurate. 700–800 minutes weekly averages only 2 hours daily—even university professors often teach more. If Jiangsu and Zhejiang teachers truly teach so few hours, they must be engaged in research with monthly publications, not just attending meetings or reading. As for the appropriate weekly hours for primary teachers or whether all teachers in our province teach 1,200 minutes, this involves administrative oversight, and our district declines to comment.

The third difficulty is omitted.

The Fourth Difficulty: It is alleged that "in two-session classes, each teacher is assigned nearly one subject." Given varying class hours per subject and differing numbers of classes across schools, no primary school could realistically implement a one-teacher-per-subject system—this has never been heard of in two-session teaching. While the dual-track system facilitates subject-specific teaching, this applies only to higher grades and is not a foundational principle. The claim that "either teachers must each take one subject, or existing subject teachers must take more two-session classes, and existing class teachers must switch to subject teaching" is unfounded. Adding classes naturally increases teaching loads, but schedules can be adjusted across classes; no rule mandates one teacher per class or requires class teachers to teach all language and arithmetic classes. Resistance stems from rigid adherence to current workloads and fixating on individual class disruptions rather than holistic planning.

The Fifth Difficulty: It is argued that "two-session classes are all lower grades, and difficulties will multiply when they advance to middle and upper grades." According to provincial regulations, primary schools add 1 teacher for every 4 lower-grade classes, 2 for 6 classes, and 3 for 10 classes; upper grades add 1 teacher for every 2 classes. If the two-session system works for lower grades, it should work equally for middle grades, and upper grades are even easier to manage. The claim of increasing difficulties contradicts facts. That said, additional teachers may be needed for existing classes, requiring proper administrative planning.

The Sixth Difficulty: It is claimed that "parents doubt the academic performance of two-session classes, and fewer students apply during admissions." The two-session system is an internal organizational matter, not a recruitment slogan. Whether half-day or full-day sessions are used depends on local needs; full-day sessions are no different from regular classes. Without evidence, these claims about parental doubts and declining enrollment are unsubstantiated. If such issues exist, they are unrelated to the two-session system itself.

The six difficulties raised lack merit and likely reflect unspoken concerns, which our district cannot speculate on. However, for a poverty-stricken state like China needing educational universalization, the two-session system is necessary. Even educationally advanced Japan has recently promoted it across Hyogo Prefecture via directives from three ministries—this deserves reflection.

In conclusion, we offer two final suggestions:

1. To enforce the ministry's order, short-term compulsory education and mass education must be integrated with the two-session system to maximize economic efficiency through holistic educational planning.

2. For future class expansions, equipment upgrades, and existing concurrent classes or special research funds, a consistent policy is needed: conventional facilities should not be wasted, and funds should be redirected to specialized equipment. Research funds must not be nominal. If new classes and empty projects continue to consume funds while two-session classes are starved of resources, implementation will be fatally hindered.

We respectfully submit these views for your consideration.

Sincerely,

Li Lianfang, Standing Committee Member

January 16, 1934 (23rd Year of the Republic of China)

Published in *Kaifeng Experimental Education Monthly*, Vol. 1, No. 6, March 1934.

Notes on *Yuwangtai and Fantta*[19]

Since the publication of the local teaching material Dragon Pavilion, it has been well-received by society, though there have been some discussions regarding what constitutes a "teaching material." From what I can gather, these discussions boil down to two points, which I shall explain as follows.

The First Point

It is said that the reference materials are not works that children can read. However, the editor's intention is to enable teachers to deeply understand the past and present of their environment, inspire children's activities, provide appropriate guidance accordingly, and fully supply materials that can inspire such activities. This allows teachers to formulate teaching outlines for each grade and select reading texts based on these materials. The goal is not to restrict children's real activities with fixed, subjective teaching materials—this is the approach that modern teaching should adopt at its outset, and it also represents a quest for the sources of culture in the learning process. For the part involving textual research, all sources are clearly indicated with annotations to facilitate further study.

---

19 *Yuwangtai and Fantta* is part of Li Lianfang's *Outline and Reference Materials for Primary School Teaching Activities*, published by the Teaching Materials Department of the Kaifeng Experimental Education District as supplementary materials to textbooks. These materials can be roughly divided into three categories. First, local teaching materials, such as *Yuwangtai and Fantta, Dragon Pavilion, Xiangtong Temple, Iron Pagoda and Huiji River, Yue Fei and Zhuxian Town*, and *Bao Zheng*; second, materials on commemorative days, historical events, or figures, such as *Children's Day Commemoration, National Day Commemoration, Commemoration of the September 18th National Humiliation, Battle of Fei River,* and *National Hero Shi Kefa;* third, materials on traditional Chinese festivals, such as New Year and Duanwu Festival. (See p. 360 of this book for the same note.)—Editor

The Second Point

It is argued that devoting so much effort to providing reference materials for a single teaching activity seems inefficient. However, one must recognize that the commonly used textbooks today, while formally interconnected as a system, are in reality collections of fragmented knowledge for each lesson. They are a variant of the ancient practice of compiling allusions in encyclopedias, which were once despised by scholars for their incoherence. Yet today, this format is almost regarded as the sole "scripture" for teaching, and error has become accepted as truth. How can such textbooks help children understand concrete life?

The materials provided here, for any single teaching activity, cover the entirety of the environment's past and present. When a teaching activity is completed, children will have gained a fairly deep understanding of the history and current state of their environment. Moreover, each activity can be advanced in stages—this is indeed the application of integrated curricula and large-unit design, forming essential reference materials.

If primary schools in Kaifeng adopt the booklets continuously compiled by our district as core unit topics, with each topic involving long-term activities that consolidate fragmented knowledge into large units, and if there is no rigid separation between teaching history, geography, nature, and language (but rather learning tailored to specific contexts), I can confidently assert that children will acquire knowledge and abilities far more authentic and rich than those gained through the old method of studying subjects and lessons in isolation. Furthermore, through direct observation and exploration, children will grasp the deeds of ancient sages more vividly than through mere biographical accounts.

In summary, the rigid format of textbooks and the fragmented learning of subjects are both harmful to primary education. Reformers, however, unknowingly perpetuate these flaws. It is imperative to change course. The editor adheres to this principle and sets forth these general remarks to seek the opinions of knowledgeable scholars.

Li Buqing (Lianfang)
Three days after the Duanwu Festival (Dragon Boat Festival), the 23rd Year of the Republic of China (1934)

Published in Li Lianfang et al., *Yuwangtai and Fantta*, compiled and printed by the Teaching Materials Department of the Kaifeng Experimental Education District, July 1934.

Basic Teaching Materials and Integrated Curriculum

Introduction

To study modern primary school curricula, one must break free from the rigidities of subject-based organization and the long-standing separation of instruction and moral education. Instead, curricula should adapt to real-life needs, establishing new standards within the context of children's developmental processes. Only then can curricula fulfill their function and meet the demands of the times. This article is formulated in accordance with this principle.

1) Building on Existing Preschool Education

John Dewey established an experimental school at the University of Chicago in his early years, admitting children aged 4 to 13. The entire curriculum centered on implementing the kindergarten principles discovered by Friedrich Froebel. Lewis Terman, in his essay Children's Intelligence, concluded from his test results that gifted kindergarteners could begin basic reading, while -graders struggling with reading should be given more opportunities for physical activity. Parker, in The Method of Teaching through Communication, provided detailed discussions on teaching equipment and curriculum design. In my view, preschool education offers three foundational elements for lower primary grades regarding teaching materials: First, nature study derived from direct contact with natural objects and phenomena; Second, knowledge of family and social life gained through interactions with human society; Third, literature, music, art, and other products of human wisdom. In terms of activities, expression is achieved through conversation, handicrafts, drawing, singing, role-playing, games, and more. These principles have proven effective in kindergartens. The lives of lower primary students differ little from those in kindergarten. While primary education gradually emphasizes organized, systematic learning, its foundation must align with preschool education to ensure unhindered experiential development. Expanding on this idea, two special chapters are included: Chapter One: Basic Design, defining the direction of curriculum organization; Chapter Two: Basic Teaching Materials, defining the direction for selecting curriculum content.

2) Cultivating Learning Attitudes

Attitudes form the foundation of human life; all learning activities are sources of attitude formation. Traditionally, moral education has been treated as separate from the curriculum. Even when included as subjects (e.g., ethics, civics, history), it focused solely on imparting knowledge in isolation. Educators often overlook how learning activities organize and apply knowledge, and how the acquisition of knowledge and skills influences behavior. Ancient education, though unaware of these relationships, embedded moral lessons throughout the curriculum. Societal norms were rooted in ancient teachings, so students, through constant recitation, inadvertently absorbed moral values while mastering basic skills. With the rise of practical subjects, this approach became obsolete, yet reforms remained superficial, clinging to traditional models. The separation of moral education and instruction has weakened education. Educational theorists emphasize holistic human life but often remain at the level of principles. Teaching research, focused on analyzing subjects, frequently neglects these overarching principles, favoring form over substance—a trend evident in various teaching methods. While Kilpatrick's concept of "incidental learning" offers a path, it remains theoretical and awaits practical application. Correcting habits is harder than cultivating them; thus, lower primary grades lay the critical foundation. Chapter Three: Basic Attitudes defines the norms for curriculum learning.

3). Mastery of Reading, Writing, and Arithmetic

Ancient curricula were almost entirely built around these foundational skills. Modern critics dismiss them as impractical, yet families and authorities still judge educational success largely by proficiency in these tools. In lower grades especially, independent learning is impossible without these tools. My proposed new curriculum does not reduce the time or standards for mastering these skills but differs from conventional views on what to learn and how to learn it. Chapter Four: Basic Tools defines the framework and application of these skills. This article focuses on basic teaching materials and integrated curricula, divided into the following sections:

1. Principles of Basic Teaching Materials

Teaching practice is built on teaching materials. The entire primary school curriculum forms the foundation of education. Academically, it is elementary education; personally, it is general education; socially, it is national education. Primary school materials embody these three meanings. Lower grades, as the foundation of primary education, require appropriate content to nurture positive learning habits and guide students toward new life paths. This section emphasizes this focus but also serves as an introduction to the entire primary curriculum, differing slightly from Basic Design, which centers exclusively on lower grades.

1.1 Broad Curriculum Content.

Primary school materials have expanded with societal progress. Recent efforts to integrate subjects, despite formal mergers, reflect the need to adapt to life's complexity. Two deeper implications of broad content: First, elements enhancing life—skills, habits, morality, and ideals—should be treated as integral to materials, transcending rigid boundaries in practice. Second, practical subjects like handicrafts and gardening should focus not on direct vocational training but on general educational value. These meanings stem from forming concrete experiences through each unit of material, rather than expanding scope through teaching methods alone.

1.2 Materials Suited to Central Integration

The idea of a "central teaching material" has a long history, traditionally centered on culture (e.g., history). Two decades ago, Chinese readers, with their comprehensive content, embodied this. The recognized value of handicrafts later made it a central material for lower grades. From a subject-based perspective, any subject could serve as a center for expanding knowledge. However, a single subject, no matter how interconnected its materials, cannot systematically integrate all disciplines. It may even distort concrete experiences due to subject boundaries. By breaking free from subject-based units, each teaching material should incorporate multiple disciplinary functions, determined by the learning context of the unit. It falls to teachers to ensure all essential content from various subjects is covered through careful planning.

1.3 Learning Rooted in Labor

Life education and work-based education, rooted in socialist thought, advocate integrating labor into learning. Modern education, shaped by the alliance of the leisure class and capitalist society, has produced both the impoverished and the idle—failures of poor education. Basic education should foster vocational interests, enable individuals to develop their abilities, and strengthen democratic values. This not only corrects educational inertia but also harmonizes cultural and practical education.

1.4 Starting with Environmental Materials

Object teaching and sensory training align with children's psychology, offering an effective path for lower grades. However, they often focus on isolated analysis of objects, failing to connect to developmental processes or social applications. Materials must be selected and organized to enhance life and form concrete experiences. Even activities based on intuition and senses should enable knowledge transfer or meaning expansion.

These principles define the guidelines for basic teaching materials. The following sections analyze their application.

2. The Issue of Subjects

2.1 Objectives of Official Curricula

Official curriculum standards include National Language, Society (including history, geography, and part of hygiene), Nature (including personal hygiene), Arithmetic, Work (expanded to include school affairs, housework, agriculture, commerce, etc.), Art (expanded to include visual arts), Physical Education, and Music.

Learning tasks are categorized by subject, arranged by grade, with weekly hours specified in the general curriculum guidelines.

Teaching methods emphasize integration. Social studies "should start with work education and integrate with ideology, nature, art, arithmetic, etc. through project-based learning" (Social Studies Teaching Guidelines, Point 1). Nature "should fully integrate with society, work, art, etc. through large-unit project-based learning" (Nature Teaching Guidelines, Point 9). Arithmetic "in the first and second grades may be taught through integration with other projects" (Arithmetic Teaching Guidelines, Point 1). Work "should fully integrate with society and nature; commercial valuation should connect with arithmetic" (Work Teaching Guidelines, Points 1 and 5). Music "should connect with national language, society, work, and physical education through project-based learning" (Music Teaching Guidelines, Point 5).

2.2 Subject-Based Curricula vs. Project-Based Learning

The official emphasis on project-based learning operates within a subject-based framework. However, isolating materials by subject hinders project implementation, raising critical questions. If centered on themes, how should units spanning multiple subjects be allocated to fixed subject hours? For example, a "small store" project blends art and work (for setup), nature, society, arithmetic, and language (for transactions)—activities impossible to split into isolated subjects. Even if separable, rigid timetables make coordination impractical. If centered on subjects, how can interdisciplinary content be contained within a single subject? Why maintain subject independence when content and value transcend it? Further, how to calculate hours for integrated units within fixed weekly subject quotas? A unit of material, containing elements of multiple subjects, connects not through arbitrary links between topics and subjects but through children's needs. What integrates children's activities is not subjects, but the materials they require. Some argue project-based learning should start with subjects, progress to subject clusters, and finally achieve full integration. However, "complete" vs. "incomplete" projects differ in wholeness, not structure. Those unfamiliar with project-based learning should avoid rushed implementation; those who understand it should reject a subject-based progression. Subject-based and integrated teaching are incompatible. Integrated teaching cannot truly be project-based. For prudence, educators should begin with broad unit planning, blending subject materials, and gradually refining practices. (Refer to my book

Discussion on Primary School Materials[20], published in *New Education* in 1923.) Without clarifying this, discussions of project-based learning are futile.

General Instructions for Primary School Curricula Issued by the Ministry: "Most experts argue that primary school subjects should not be excessive; those that can be merged should be merged as much as possible, and for those that cannot be easily merged, methods for connected teaching should be specified." It is true that subjects should not be overly numerous, but new things emerging with the times should also be learned as much as possible within feasible limits. However, just as no one today would advocate restoring the all-encompassing Chinese readers of the past, this should prompt us to reflect on curriculum design. The intention of the General Instructions regarding "connected teaching" seems to refer specifically to teaching materials in subjects that cannot be easily merged. A systematic examination reveals that the isolated materials of an independent subject can only form a limited number of concrete unit designs. This means that when individual unit materials are categorized under subjects, they are always in a state of connected teaching; even the merged subjects lose their independent function. If it is believed that most teachers are accustomed to traditional subject-based teaching and cannot adapt quickly, there is little more to say. But if educational reform truly requires a thorough restructuring of the curriculum, merely focusing on merging and connecting subjects may well lead us astray.

2.3 Teaching Materials for Integrated Curricula

While we oppose the allocation of teaching materials by separate subjects, the standard experiences accumulated through teaching and the condensed materials provided by disciplines, which have always been

---

20

presented in subjects, still hold reference value. Therefore, selecting necessary materials from various subjects and incorporating the essential knowledge and skills they offer to humanity is something that compilers of integrated curricula cannot ignore. However, in terms of the attributes and expressions of things, they are inherently multifaceted. From a logical classification perspective, the more detailed the analysis, the greater the contribution to academic research. But from the perspective of the overall relationships between things, their mutual functions cannot be analyzed; excessive fragmentation undermines their connections and, more importantly, diminishes beginners' interest.

For example, in the primary school subjects specified by the Ministry, such as National Language and Arithmetic, in essence, they must be attached to and expressed through materials from other subjects, and teaching in other subjects often relies on them to proceed—this will be discussed in a separate chapter. Subjects like Physical Education, with its basic exercises, do not need to be connected to other teaching materials to demonstrate their value. Music, while somewhat similar to a tool subject, still requires independent practice in areas such as listening, pronunciation, and musical notation; it also combines specifically with Physical Education as an independent game course. When music or sports activities arise from a specific unit task, they integrate with other subjects to form a project. For instance, if a game has the potential for an integrated project, various valuable teaching materials must be collected and selected. Intellectual games, which often involve calculation practice, will also be discussed in the section on basic tools.

The core materials of an integrated curriculum take Nature and Society as their foundation, with Work and Art as their applications. The two subjects of Nature and Society are particularly the sources of teaching materials. They are interdependent; learning them in isolation deviates from the essence of "education as life" and fails to foster a developmental process through concrete experiences. Their apparent separation lies in the origin or affiliation of individual things—namely, objects belong to Nature, and events belong to Society. Even when a learning unit aims to understand a single thing, it must examine the multifaceted relationships of that thing. These relationships, on one hand, pertain to the thing itself, and on the other hand, to the learning context: the former defines the necessary scope of understanding, while the latter is the focus of attention at that moment. Learning about Nature without considering its social connections renders such knowledge useless. For children, the study of flora and fauna is not about their general lives but about their significance to humanity; what is needed is not nature in the abstract, but nature as a space for human activity. From the perspective of Nature, all research is infused with social meaning. From the perspective of Society, emphasis is placed on current daily life, and historical customs and forms of ancient societies cannot be the center of study.

Thus, the substance of a teaching unit may draw from the interdependence of Nature and Society or aspects of either, while tools may involve elements of National Language, Arithmetic, Work, Art, Physical Education, Music, etc. Without the necessary tools, the learning process of a concrete unit cannot be completed. As for operational activities, teaching materials based on the interdependence of Nature and Society (or aspects of them) can be broken down into tasks related to housework, school affairs, agricultural, industrial, or commercial work, each forming specific problems. Art, largely similar to Work, includes painting, which, like National Language, must be learned in conjunction with Nature and Society. Therefore, all subjects are integrated into the materials of concrete units. Even if subjects sometimes exhibit unique functions due to the nature of the materials, they should not exist as independent entities, relying merely on "connected teaching" as a remedy.

3. Issues of Standards

3.1 The Essence of Standards

Discussing standards for teaching materials inevitably evokes the social context of educational functions. There is no doubt that future societies will increasingly move toward democratization. Democracy involves the continuous transformation of social organizations and forms of life; education, defined as a "life process of growth," is implemented in response to this principle. If we preset standards for our ideal society, it would only hinder the advancement of human activities. Needless to say, taking ancient or current societies as models cannot form a "standard society." Moreover, the very mention of "standards" imposes fixed norms on human behavior—a tool often used to control people in patriarchal, religious, feudal, or capitalist societies, which runs counter to the ethos of developing democracy. Since a "standard society" is unknowable, all we can discuss are abstract ideals. Thus, the concept of "standards" in teaching is fundamentally problematic.

Furthermore, regarding how to establish standards: China has traditionally formulated curricula by leaping from a few abstract principles directly to the allocation of teaching materials. These principles are purely subjective, with no rigorous research into how much material each principle requires or whether materials align with principles. This is true not only for textbooks published by commercial presses but also for the official curriculum standards. Recent discussions on curricula tend to favor scientific methods such as activity analysis, error analysis, vocational analysis, and content analysis. While applying scientific principles and techniques to curriculum design is reasonable, over-reliance on form or blind faith in methods—without grounding them in a broader educational philosophy—only makes methods appear more "scientific" on the surface while making teaching increasingly impractical. If the foundation is flawed, the principles themselves cannot be correct.

Does this mean standards should be abandoned entirely? No. Social growth and change arise from both existing strengths and flaws. Human learning, in particular, involves inheriting collective experiences to better address new problems and create opportunities for new goals. Although there is no universal measure for understanding things, the scope of learning—extending from direct experiences to achievable ideals—centers on what is most essential to life and most engaging to learners at a given stage; it is not boundless or arbitrary.

Our discussion here focuses on two aspects: shared goals and minimum requirements.

1) **Shared Goals.** In the past, curricula included "guiding principles" for each subject. Official curriculum standards now list objectives by subject. Regardless of whether these objectives are based on rigorous analysis or are overly vague, listing them by subject is fundamentally flawed. First, combining objectives across subjects cannot form the overall purpose of education. A quick review of aggregated subject objectives reveals gaps in fostering character. Second, materials derived from these objectives fail to fulfill their intended educational significance—a discrepancy evident when comparing listed learning tasks (excluding tool subjects) with their stated objectives in any subject. If objectives are merely meant to guide material selection and clarify meaning, without regard to their effectiveness, their division or integration becomes arbitrary. Why list them at all? One could directly evaluate materials without such superficial formalities. I do not oppose objectives outright, but a single objective often involves materials from multiple subjects, and

materials themselves often relate to multiple subjects. Even in subject-based teaching, objectives should be defined holistically. Listing them by subject is thus a fundamental error.

There are many discussions on the methods of formulating goals. To sum up, there are mainly three types:

First, the concentration of opinions. The compiler formulates goals for all courses respectively, breaks down each goal into several items, solicits opinions from experts and implementers, and then stipulates them; or formulates various inquiry forms, asks experts and implementers to put forward items, then collects and organizes them, and carefully reviews them. The former method focuses on goals. Now that the stereotypes of subjects have been broken, it generally follows the path of activity analysis. As far as the main body of categories is concerned, activities are naturally different. As far as the items to achieve the goals are concerned, they are mutually useful, but breaking down subjects still cannot avoid the disadvantages caused by the separation of subjects. Moreover, the analysis is mostly based on adult prejudices and cannot provide all materials for the curriculum, which can be generally seen from the goals listed by Cheng Xiangfan in “An Introduction to Primary School Curriculum”. Focusing on items, if the consulted persons doubt the goals, the recognized items will fundamentally lose their basis. The latter method, when put forward separately, will have many inconsistencies. If all are put forward as a whole, it is quite difficult for those who should respond; if they are fragmented, they are not systematic. For example, the subject - by - subject formulation by the Ministry of Education, the respondents are at most no more than six points, which is obvious from the facts. Moreover, only collecting opinions is purely subjective and is not allowed by scientific methods.

Second, classified investigation. The method is to collect facts, and what the facts show is only what items there are, not how to do what, so it cannot be regarded as a method to determine goals.

Third, the integration of subject content. This method takes the teaching experience of various subjects and the content of various textbooks, analyzes and lists them, checks them, and formulates them into integrated courses. This is naturally simple and easy to implement, but since integration is a reaction to separation into subjects, it is contradictory to still discuss life from past teaching.

2) Minimum Requirements. The officially prescribed curriculum standards include explicit regulations on minimum requirements, which appear comprehensive. However, doubts remain as to whether these requirements provide clear standards for teaching. First, subject-specific regulations often separate knowledge from skills, either disrupting the interconnectedness of teaching or encroaching on the effectiveness of other areas. Second, many provisions are overly vague, lacking measurable limits. Third, even the explicitly stated provisions are difficult to grasp.

Minimum requirements involve both qualitative and quantitative components. Since fixed teaching materials are unsuitable for new curricula, how should quality and quantity be determined? It should be understood that "standards" do not consist of lists of individual materials but rather reveal the goals that materials should serve. Once goals are established, the required quality becomes clear, without restricting educators to identical materials. With quality defined, priorities in quantity can be determined. However, only tool-based materials can be easily integrated to achieve clear limits. For integrated curricula, minimum requirements must transcend subject boundaries, adapt to new curriculum structures, and specify flexible areas.

3.2 Actional Units and Textbook Elements

1) Actional Units. The so-called unit in general teaching is a topic of a certain subject's teaching materials in a subject - based curriculum, while in an integrated curriculum, it is a design, that is, an implementation unit. Among the homework items stipulated by the ministry for various subjects, one item can be divided into several units, several items can be combined into one unit, a certain part of several items can be a unit, and one item is only a condition for many units to pay attention to. The outline of teaching activities in this city's experiment (see the "Special Issue on Primary School Textbook Experiment" of Henan Education Department) takes problems and matters as the outline, lists sub - items inside, and is more specific than the homework items, and the usage is actually the same example. The self - determined curriculum of other schools is more disorderly. Generally speaking, Chinese and society mostly have organized topics, and the rest are close to listed matters, which can be checked by randomly taking several primary school curriculums (recently, there are many primary school curriculums of Suzhou Middle School Experimental Primary School sold by various bookstores, which is one example). "Soviet Russian Primary School Curriculum" (Minzhi Bookstore, translated by Cui Zaiyang) lists the outlines; "On Designing and Organizing Primary School Curriculum" (The Commercial Press, translated by Zheng Zonghai) cites examples - both are close to laying down basic rules and are not regulations by school implementers. Those who advocate compiling the curriculum with scientific methods also have the so - called action unit, that is, under each goal, analyze into various activities or problems, such as the small notes listed under the goals in Cheng Xiangfan's "Outline of Primary School Curriculum". Because of this, the names are confused, and the content sometimes merges and separates. Discussants and compilers do not distinguish them very well, and implementers are prone to confusion and mistakes. Now, let's analyze clearly. What is listed in the homework items is generally the outline of teaching materials for various subjects, and sometimes the teaching form. How to form a unit is not considered. What is listed in the action unit is a separate matter of daily activities, and what kind of teaching materials are needed still needs to be sought. In short, the two only have analysis, no organization, and do not involve various relationships in terms of subordination. Although in separate listings, there may be those that have the scale of implementation units, they cannot be regarded as implementation units based on this. Especially the action unit, which belongs to the practical ability aspect, is easy to fall into the drawbacks mentioned earlier that are too numerous to mention; and it belongs to the general aspect, and is easy to be suspected of being ambiguous in meaning or too broad in application. The combination and separation of it and the implementation unit have more clues than the homework items. Among those who advocate compiling the curriculum with scientific methods, there is no shortage of propositions to analyze action units. When this is applied to practice, difficulties are immediately felt, and the procedures are cumbersome, and the results are not as expected. The details will be continued.

2) Textbook Elements. In the issue of subjects, when it comes to integrated courses, their general aspects have already been introduced. Now, let's further elaborate, dividing them into two types: raw materials and tools. Tools also have differences between essence and usage. For example, characters in Chinese, numbers and names in arithmetic, music notations and symbols are the essence. While grammar, syntax and copybooks in Chinese, integers, decimals and other numbers, calculation and counters in arithmetic, basic manufacturing methods and tool usage methods in industrial art, and basic techniques of games and sports in physical education are usages. The essence and usage of tools inherently have a connected nature. However, such as manufacturing methods and physical education techniques, their usage is not related to the essence, but to the activities of fingers or the body. All the examples mentioned here, regardless of how their forms change, their basic functions do not differ much, and there is a certain limit to be found. Therefore, it is easy to set standards. The method of examination: knowledge is formed through explanation, and skills are formed through use. In teaching, the two interact with each other. There are cases where skills are practiced after knowledge is understood, and there are also cases where knowledge is acquired through the process of use. The results may be that one can explain but not use skillfully, or one can use but not explain comprehensively. This depends on the learning situation and its methods. All along, school education has been completely built on tool learning. Even if the mechanical achievements are not significant, it takes the form of ordinary education, with a jumbled curriculum, leading to such results. If we only sort out from this superficial level, not only can we not complete the educational function, but also make all tools become drudgery. Even if education is for life, and life is not a growth process, such a teaching standard is only applicable in a class society.

Based on the above discussion, we should attach importance to the theory that the value of education does not lie in itself but in the needs of the time. The so-called needs of the time must be the social utility to cope with certain things, which is nothing more than using natural materials, accepting inherited experience, controlling the environment, and thus continuing to transform social organizations and life styles. Otherwise, learning is meaningless and not interesting. From this, we know that the tool standard is only a matter of one aspect of the curriculum content. Without a noumenon, tools become abstract and isolated. The noumenon is the raw material of teaching materials. From a spatial perspective, it is on the one hand the natural world and on the other hand the human world. From a temporal perspective, part of it is past memories and part is the current situation. To put it bluntly, it is only the interrelationship or one-sidedness of nature and society. Taking this as the basis for learning, on the one hand, it is the homework formed by combining subjects such as Chinese, arithmetic, work, art, physical education, music, etc. with the two (nature and society), and on the other hand, it is the truth that nature and society themselves should be understood. According to the former view, no matter what subject, if it leaves the materials or situations of nature and society, it loses its meaning. According to the latter view, the so-called understanding of the truth often lies in the homework formed by the combination of these subjects. However, the starting point of homework must be based on nature and society. Its matters must be matters of the school, family, agriculture, industry and commerce, etc., and problems composed of necessity, willingness, and possibility in children's lives. Its sources can be sought from the school garden, park, garden, vegetable garden, fields, woods, mountains, water, scenic spots, natural research rooms, museums, commodity exhibitions, and natural phenomena that change with time. Society can be sought from the body, among classmates, between neighbors, families, schools, factories, stores, hospitals, companies, ancient sites, temples, churches, villages, markets, public institutions, public construction, transportation institutions, charitable institutions, as well as books, pictures, utensils, newspapers, notices, and the living conditions of various professional circles, memorial days, festivals, etc. Although teaching materials are not specified here, there is a scope for selection. Even if the school facilities are inadequate, the environment provides materials that are not lacking for use in the lower grades, and implementation can be carried out according to local conditions. The standards of such teaching materials, in terms of quality, can be deduced from the above matters and sources, and in terms of quantity, they adapt to individuality and develop fully, with no minimum limit to speak of. Although their utility must be manifested through tools, their own significance still has their independent existence value. Therefore, the so - called common sense has become a mixed name of nature and society. In fact, such a naming and meaning, first, because of the transmission of books, regard this as the main component of knowledge, and second, because of the traditional emphasis on academic studies, must use written or oral tests as the judgment. It can be imagined that in subject - based teaching, nature and society are separated and independent from other subjects, becoming a kind of rote learning for memorization. Therefore, the common sense tests in lower grades, which do not elaborate local affairs, are quite difficult to be universal, and the implementation of teaching materials is even more obvious.

3.3 Social Needs and Children's Lives

1) Social Needs. The first thing to understand is the basic concept. The theory of life preparation takes adult life as the norm, making children strive for a future they know neither what it is nor why. On the one hand, it obliterates current voluntary activities; on the other hand, in terms of practical application, it cannot be connected and coherent. Thus, the theory of vocational training arose, which seems relatively closer to practical use. However, its needs still belong to adult society. Social situations are complex, and individual career choices cannot be predetermined in childhood. Especially with practicality as the goal, it tends to mechanical training and material enjoyment. Therefore, culture also becomes an important issue in education. In the past, the misunderstanding of culture often regarded it as purely inner cultivation or a spiritual product, leading to the division of manual labor and mental labor into two paths. The current separation of subjects is a phenomenon of the hodgepodge of culture and practicality. If we understand that the development of individual abilities is an important preparation for actual life, and that allowing abilities to develop according to the environment will naturally extend future needs from the present. We also know that the maintenance and promotion of society all rely on the cooperation and mutual assistance of individuals. Seeking practicality apart from the overall interests of society is not allowed in civilian education. Even things themselves have no existence value without social significance. Therefore, the ultimate goal of individual practicality is the creation of social culture. Culture and practicality do not oppose but complement each other.

From the above, social needs are rooted in human interdependence, which exists in communal life. In our society, where machinery and capital are underdeveloped, life is largely based on self-sustaining farming and handicrafts. Internally, many groups prioritize narrow interests; externally, the world pursues large-scale enterprises. Contradictions are evident everywhere. The social surveys and educational efforts required for implementing education in Europe and America differ greatly from our national context. For instance, while communal life in those societies can fully follow the path of division of labor and cooperation, ours must establish a foundation of independent self-reliance, then gradually develop the undertakings and spirit of division of labor and cooperation. Thus, the things and abilities needed in current society are not highly specialized; what is considered "ordinary" is broader, and the need for improvement is more urgent. Regardless, identifying these needs—what things and abilities are required—must be based on the functions of human interdependence. They should be investigated categorically according to local conditions, compiling relevant matters and problems before summarizing them into frameworks. Such surveys should be planned by local educational administrative agencies with the assistance of educational experts.

For lower-grade teaching materials, aside from local main products, children can imitate the actions of things they frequently encounter and interact with in daily life. Therefore, a detailed analysis of social needs will be omitted here.

1) **Children's Lives.** Doctrines like the "training theory," which focus solely on cultivating sensory abilities, are naturally to be rejected. However, the views advocated by naturalists—guiding children's activities at any time purely according to their interests—lack sufficient standards. The study of children's lives here is a crucial consideration in curriculum design, not the sole criterion for determining content. Yet defining "children's lives" is no easy task. Some argue that since children and adults live in the same society, their activities differ only in degree, not in the nature of their needs. Others equate children's lives to simplified versions of adult activities. If these views were unproblematic, adopting materials from traditional curricula would hardly contradict children's psychology. But why do such materials clash sharply with actual teaching practice? It is true that children's interests and actions are often stimulated by the interests and actions of adults in their environment, as evidenced by their imitation of adult activities in games and work. However, we must question whether this reflection of adult life stems from a genuine alignment of needs or merely temporary situational influences. Are these activities differentiated only by degree, or do they represent unique psychological expressions? A simple observation—children's preferences vary with age, and their curiosity and restlessness far surpass those of most adults—suffices to cast doubt on the above views.

However, although children's lives are not easy to fathom, according to the research results of modern scholars, there are already traces to follow. Let's take the discussions about lower grades and outline them. For example, it is said that small muscle movements, with a certain degree of control ability, can gradually progress from rough and heavy work to the level of controlling delicate and skillful equipment. Imagination develops from flowing and fantastical to more practical, and painting stories are an essential element to promote such activities. Imitative actions develop from the performance of relatively simple character actions to social practice in group life. Social interaction progresses from the family to friends and then to serving small groups. Personality, from being extremely fluid and easily suggestible, gradually comes to realize one's own abilities and desires to use them. For the materials and tools needed for this determination, curriculum compilers may select existing reading materials, toys, and handicraft teaching materials, etc., and have those with rich primary school experience evaluate them; or they may not list teaching materials, but only inquire about preferences regarding reading materials, toys, games, handicrafts, etc., investigate the answers of lower-grade children and teachers, and compile the results into spare teaching materials for lower grades. But this is also only possible for local educational administrative agencies or primary school unions to undertake with determination, and it is easier to succeed. The above two methods both have central value in curriculum compilation. According to the opinion of activity analysts, the teaching materials that best suit children among those with set goals are the most valuable, so the amount is specified, and this can be applied to higher grades. As for the teaching materials for lower grades, the so-called basic functions focus on inspiring wisdom and are not valued for direct application in society. There is no need for a certain limit on their quantity. Only by selecting teaching materials based on children's life needs and comparing them with the outline of social needs, and seeing which ones start from children's lives and can further achieve the function of a certain outline or item of social needs, can they be regarded as main teaching materials. Based on this, they should be arranged separately according to grades and seasons, and their content can still be expanded or contracted freely, so that implementers can refer to them at any time, which should be of great benefit.

2) Tentative Standards. Based on the above discussion, the standard significance and methods of basic teaching materials have been clarified. However, there still seems to be a need for curriculum compilation. For the convenience of implementers at present, the standards set by the ministry can be taken as a hypothesis first. But the ministry's regulations are all subject-based and not very suitable for integrated courses.

Combine all the homework items of the four subjects of society, nature, work, and art, as well as part of the homework items of arithmetic, classify them by category, and summarize them respectively. All the specific relationships of each kind of thing are connected, and it is easier to see the whole picture when organizing teaching materials. Although there may be omissions in the whole, taking this as a model, on the one hand, select the existing teaching materials of various subjects and gather them under a central purpose respectively; on the other hand, further adopt the investigation methods discussed above to add, delete and supplement; in the current curriculum compilation, it may have to be taken as the implementation standard.

4. Issues of Organization

4.1 Key Controversies in Curriculum Design

Before addressing this issue, we must clarify the various controversies surrounding curriculum design.

First, the debate between the logical and the psychological: Those who advocate the logical approach use scientific methods to collect appropriate teaching materials and arrange them systematically. The selection of materials in old - style curricula does not pay much attention to analysis and investigation. Even if they can make use of scientific methods, they only have more basis for choosing or rejecting materials based on social needs. If implemented in this way, from a social perspective, society is not static, so it seems inappropriate to take the current situation as the standard of life; second, the teaching materials from vocational analysis are difficult to adapt to the preparation for individual lives. From the perspective of children, only taking the process from easy to difficult and from simple to complex, thinking that this is the progress, there is no need to suppress what they can do, and it is even impossible to know whether they are willing or not. Those who advocate the psychological approach mostly focus on the content of actions, analyze the types of activities in children's periods, and take this as the basis for organizing teaching materials. This is indeed beneficial in correcting the rigid shortcomings of the past. However, teaching must have a purpose, and the role of the purpose in teaching materials lies not in the direction of the mind but in practical use.

Second, the dispute between fixed and self - selection: Those who advocate fixed [teaching materials] believe that primary schools should cultivate the common tendencies of citizens, and increase special teaching materials in response to local situations. However, common tendencies are not limited to using the same teaching materials; special teaching materials must correspond to the purpose of common tendencies. The meaning of this was already explained earlier when discussing common goals. It is not just about forcing learning, which completely loses motivation; it also leads to the mechanical style of producing personalities that are not suitable for the "casting mold". Those who advocate self - selection, in the design method already implemented in our country, roughly have two ways. One is to jointly propose topics at the beginning of the semester and decide on them. What is debatable here is whether the topics proposed in advance can maintain students' interest at that time. If we think carefully, this is almost the same as fixed teaching materials. Moreover, planning for the entire semester and predetermining it based on the reference opinions at one time is also quite inappropriate. When starting to learn a unit, it is decided by children's unanimous decision. Is the unanimous decision sought by the teacher a formal one or a real one? If it is real, if it is not based on the preparation scope or new problems arising in the homework, then the homework will inevitably be chaotic or scattered without a destination. If it is formal, relying purely on the teaching materials predicted by the teacher before class, then what is the point of a unanimous decision? (The above is the situation of general incomplete design teaching in our country.)

Third, the dispute between ultimate goals and current goals: Those who advocate ultimate goals have the drawbacks of both being logical and fixed. Those who advocate current goals focus on local teaching materials and they don't necessarily have full social value. Focusing on children's activities, it is easy to fall into the drawback of sensationalism. When the two advance together, it is easy to lose one while gaining the other. Based on the above discussion, a general conclusion can be drawn, that is, teaching materials are not limited to being fixed or consistent, but they cannot but be produced under the predetermined common goals. This common goal must have social utility. The teaching materials to achieve this goal start from children's current needs or interests and end in a logical plan. Also, the curriculum for each semester must, after the end of the previous semester, count the existing progress, refer to the curriculum standards of the next semester, estimate the necessary learning items, and plan them separately. This should be appropriate.

4.2 Criticizing Experimental Curricula

What has been said above is just a general overview. To further elaborate on the organization, we must comprehensively discuss the entire semester to fully understand the application of basic teaching materials. Now, let's first take several experimental curricula in our country, select some key points for criticism, which may make things clearer.

However, this curriculum seems to adopt subject - based design, which I fundamentally deny. Its organization of teaching materials is naturally not suitable for integrated curricula. Therefore, although I slightly feel that the essence and distribution of the aforementioned teaching materials are not entirely appropriate, I will set them aside and not discuss them. What is discussed here focuses on the formal organizational aspect, and this may also indicate the direction to avoid errors in curriculum compilation.

1) **Key Items Lack Flexibility in Integration, Adaptation, or Selection.** The project-based curriculum I advocate uses no fixed materials but requires holistic planning for complete units—a view shared by many practitioners of project-based learning in China. To resolve this challenge, curricula should outline core frameworks, each encompassing diverse materials. While teaching methods and sequences cannot be pre-determined, essential content must be covered (or revisited later if delayed). Within these frameworks, key items can form one or multiple projects, with adaptation and selection guided by real-time learning contexts. Importantly, frameworks must unite concrete topics, not separate subjects or fragments.

2)**Key Items Disrupt the Holistic Relationships of Things.** Social Studies curricula often suffer from scattered key items, but these experimental curricula err in the opposite direction: dividing content into "phenomena," "life," and "utilization," with subcategories under each. Superficially, this structure connects functions and relationships, and subcategories facilitate material selection. However, collecting materials (which benefits from analysis) differs from organizing materials (which requires preserving holistic, concrete relationships). Integrated units must also connect to other subjects—a feature that makes project-based learning embody "education as life." Traditional textbook-based teaching, which reduces experiential materials to fragmented text, is deeply flawed. Regrettably, many science and social studies textbooks still repeat this error, and experimental curricula should not follow suit.

3) **Arrangement by Grade Without Room for Flexibility.** The original curriculum, arranged by grade, has its own considerable progress. For example, in terms of key social topics, first-grade students study the life of families and neighborhoods, while second-grade students move on to personal and public needs; first-grade students spend one-third of their time on school-related topics. All these can be regarded as natural teaching materials and follow their natural sequence. With a few additional units, they form a complete two-grade curriculum. However, although each unit is convenient for sequential arrangement, apart from a few units arranged in a cycle, there is no clear standard for how the remaining units are allocated to each semester. Therefore, the curriculum of Suzhou Middle School Experimental Primary School, which arranges items by grade, cannot reflect the organization of specific units. The curriculum of Nanjing Middle School Experimental Primary School, although it has the organization of specific units, does not indicate the teaching objectives for each term. Thus, there is no basis for adding, deleting, or selecting content. Even if teachers arrange units and pay attention to the allocation of the progress of various subjects in their activity items, it will still become aimless education. As stated in the

preface of this curriculum, if the curriculum is the only tool to achieve educational goals, what basis will there be to demonstrate this?

Further examining the plan of its experimental process, it is divided into two aspects: dynamic longitude and dynamic latitude.

There are three components of dynamic longitude:

- Motivation – According to the preface, only one motivation is actually needed. For each unit, four hypothetical examples are provided as demonstrations.
- Dynamic waves – Enumerate the items of activities.
- Dynamic results – List four or three items.

Dynamic latitude is divided into five systems: general knowledge, language, arithmetic, art, and physical education. Each system's table includes two columns: key items and explanations. The key items are the activity items from the dynamic waves in the dynamic longitude, classified by system to show the progress of each subject. The explanations, depending on the nature of each item, either analyze or specify the content, while also outlining the general methods.

The preface further states that various materials require in-depth research in terms of methodology, and symbolic subjects (e.g., language, arithmetic) that need sufficient practice should be supplemented with additional activities.

Generally speaking, the curriculum design is quite comprehensive. However, a closer examination of the content reveals some questionable points.

First, regarding motivation: The experimenters already knew that only one motivation is needed, so why not record the facts of the preparations to induce a specific motivation beforehand and the actual implementation at that time? Instead, they resorted to hypothetical scenarios, following the same pattern as traditional lesson plans that prepare questions and indicate objectives—this is hardly sufficient as a demonstration.

Second, regarding dynamic results: Whether they are expected or achieved results, they must reflect the comprehensive functions learned from all items in the dynamic waves. If listed separately, they should be presented according to the steps or systems of the unit, rather than including indefinite items. For example, the first unit mentions "coming to school very early every day," and the second unit cites "being able to divide labor and cooperate." A further check of the curriculum's circular units shows that the 23rd unit's dynamic results include "familiarity with common knowledge of meetings," the 43rd unit's results state "enabling children to know common knowledge of meetings," and the 62nd unit repeats "enabling children to know common knowledge of meetings." If children were already familiar with this in the second semester of the first grade, but the first and second semesters of the second grade only aim to "make them know it," this would mean a regression.

Third, regarding dynamic latitude: This can be discussed in two parts. For systematically organized teaching materials, such as the language and arithmetic systems, each unit is accompanied by self-compiled Chinese textbooks, and arithmetic numbers and formulas are arranged in sequence to form a complete system. However, a closer look at the Chinese textbooks reveals that the texts are merely attached to the meaning of the unit, not derived from the application of activities or aligned with learning life. Compared to fixed readers, they do not significantly increase interest in learning; on the contrary, the constraints of the unit content may hinder the development of textual form and significance.

The arithmetic listed under the dynamic latitude of each unit, although numbers and formulas are arranged sequentially, the order of unit arrangement hardly aligns with the overall progress of arithmetic. It is necessary to supplement with additional practice time outside the units to complete the learning of arithmetic itself. Admittedly, the preface mentions that symbolic subjects requiring sufficient practice are supplemented with intensive activities. However, if project-based learning is adopted for the entire curriculum, it must be supplemented with additional units alongside major units, with symbolic practice being a key part of these supplements. Only such supplementary symbolic practice can occupy an independent position within the framework.

Those who study project-based learning often fail to grasp this key point. If they rigidly divide teaching methods according to subject forms, project-based learning will fall into the trap of the five-stage teaching method. Moreover, if the entire curriculum includes no practice units or small practice projects within major units, and no additional time is allocated, the learning outcomes of symbolic subjects will be poor. However, since the curriculum is organized using project-based learning, if symbolic practice is not integrated into the curriculum through projects, the curriculum is incomplete. For example, mastering multiplication tables cannot be achieved in a short time; if the curriculum only provides learning opportunities in one or two units, proficiency will certainly not be attained—this is an obvious flaw.

For teaching materials without a fixed system, such as music in the physical education system, lyrics are attached in the same way as Chinese texts, making it merely a tool for reading aloud. The general knowledge and art systems, unlike symbolic subjects, do not have a clear progressive sequence. The content listed under general knowledge is similar to a variant of language teaching; forcing it into a separate system undermines the unity of learning and disrupts the activity sequence. Art mostly consists of memory drawing and free drawing, which only indicates that each unit must include art activities for balance. In fact, what distinguishes project-based learning from fixed subject-based curricula is that each unit involves holistic activities. Although each unit may emphasize different aspects and not necessarily cover all subjects, there is no need to worry about monotony. If irrelevant learning content is added to the unit without a supplementary purpose, it becomes an unnecessary distraction.

There are two additional points open to discussion:

First, the learning items in the "dynamic waves" of each unit do not divide the process into smaller sub-units. Instead, they list a sequence of topics—usually more than 18 in number. Unless the entire semester's curriculum is organized around one or two major units, the activity process of each unit would never be this extensive. Naturally, several topics listed in each unit could be grouped into a few phases, but the topics themselves often take the form of heuristic questions.

Take a few units at random as examples:

Unit 1: "What is a school?" "How do children address each other?"

Unit 3: "What is the Cubs' Association?" "How to join the Cubs' Association?"

Unit 24: "Where was the Premier from?" "What disease did the Premier die of?"

Such questions cannot constitute activities within a single class period. If these items were assigned to different subject periods, they could be scattered piecemeal; but ignoring the learning process and merely assigning items to subjects based on their supposed affiliation would disrupt the natural flow of learning, defeating the purpose of project-based activities. Moreover, in project-based learning divided into subject periods, it is impossible to allocate appropriate class time without determining whether the nature of topics in each phase belongs to one or more subjects. To disregard the learning process entirely would reduce it to a form of traditional "connected teaching," bearing no resemblance to true project-based learning.

Second, each unit in this curriculum only records a total duration of 700 to over 1,200 minutes, with no breakdown to explain how this time is allocated. Total hours are composed of individual topic activities, whose duration depends on the volume of activities and learning contexts. Specifying the duration of each activity is essential for managing actual implementation, and aggregating these durations provides a reference for teaching standards. By failing to list individual activity times and only presenting total hours, the curriculum offers little value as a model.

Other issues with the curriculum need not be elaborated here. Through the critique of these two curricula, we may gain clarity on how to approach curriculum organization and make informed choices about its structure.

Excerpted from Li Lianfang: *On Integrated Curricula for Lower Primary Grades*, published by Zhonghua Book Company in September 1934. Abbreviated in this collection.

www.ingramcontent.com/pod-product-compliance
Lightning Source LLC
LaVergne TN
LVHW010625110826
845149LV00014B/2778

* 9 7 8 1 9 6 5 8 9 0 7 0 7 *